Work and Welfare in Europe

Series Editors: **Denis Bouget**, University of Nantes, France, **Sonja Drobnic**, University of Hamburg, Germany, **Ana M. Guillén**, University of Oviedo, Spain, **Jane Lewis**, London School of Economics and Political Science, UK and **Bruno Palier**, Sciences-po Paris, France

Titles include:

Birgit Pfau-Effinger and Tine Rostgaard
CARE, WORK AND WELFARE IN EUROPE

Martin Schröder
INTEGRATING VARIETIES OF CAPITALISM AND WELFARE STATE RESEARCH
A Unified Typology of Capitalisms

Rik van Berkel, Willibrord de Graaf and Tomáš Sirovátka
THE GOVERNANCE OF ACTIVE WELFARE STATES IN EUROPE

Work and Welfare in Europe
Series Standing Order ISBN 978–0–230–28026–7
(*outside North America only*)

You can receive future titles in this series as they are published by placing a standing order. Please contact your bookseller or, in case of difficulty, write to us at the address below with your name and address, the title of the series and the ISBN quoted above.

Customer Services Department, Macmillan Distribution Ltd, Houndmills, Basingstoke, Hampshire RG21 6XS, England

Health Care Systems in Europe under Austerity

Institutional Reforms and Performance

Edited by

Emmanuele Pavolini
Macerata University, Italy

and

Ana M. Guillén
University of Oviedo, Spain

First published 2013 by
PALGRAVE MACMILLAN

Palgrave Macmillan in the UK is an imprint of Macmillan Publishers Limited,
registered in England, company number 785998, of Houndmills, Basingstoke,
Hampshire RG21 6XS.

Palgrave Macmillan in the US is a division of St Martin's Press LLC,
175 Fifth Avenue, New York, NY 10010.

Palgrave Macmillan is the global academic imprint of the above companies
and has companies and representatives throughout the world.

Palgrave® and Macmillan® are registered trademarks in the United States,
the United Kingdom, Europe and other countries.

ISBN 978–0–230–36961–0

This book is printed on paper suitable for recycling and made from fully
managed and sustained forest sources. Logging, pulping and manufacturing
processes are expected to conform to the environmental regulations of the
country of origin.

A catalogue record for this book is available from the British Library.

A catalog record for this book is available from the Library of Congress.

Typeset by MPS Limited, Chennai, India.

To Caterina and Juan

Contents

List of Tables

List of Figures

Series Editors' Preface

Work and Welfare in Europe

Since the late 1970s, both labour markets and welfare regimes have been under intense economic pressure and have been challenged by profound changes in social and demographic structures, as well as in social norms. The work/welfare relationship has always been key to the modern state, but has undergone substantial change over recent decades. On the one hand, approaches to social provision have become more explicit in recognizing the importance of the relationship to employment, such that it is possible to suggest that social policies have become 'employment-led'. On the other hand, it is possible to argue that there is a profound 'disconnect' between labour markets and welfare systems, and that this partly explains the socio-economic problems that some countries are facing in terms of high unemployment and low activity rates in particular. Changes in labour markets, which have often tended to more flexibilization, often pose challenges to the protective goals of social policies; thus the financial and programmatic configurations of social policies are often held to have impeded job creation. These arguments over the nature and effects of the relationships between labour markets and welfare systems have been and are intense and need to be further analysed.

These relationships between labour markets and welfare systems constitute the backdrop for this series, which takes as its starting point the tensions that now characterize this centrally important relationship between 'work and welfare'. Among these tensions, one can mention the tension between the firms' demands for more labour market flexibility and citizens' need for economic security; the tensions between the increased participation in paid work and the importance of family life, the greater fluidity in family relationships, and the greater flexibility in the labour markets; the friction between quantity and quality of the jobs to be created, between job creation and maintaining or improving the quality of employment and finally the conflicts raised by the need to adapt (industrial) social protection systems to new labour market structures.

This book series has been created within RECWOWE, a European Network of excellence created within the 6th Framework Programme of the European Commission (FP6). The full title for the network's activities is 'Reconciling Work and Welfare in Europe'. Such a reconciliation is an important political objective for most EU member states. In order to meet it we need to improve our understanding of the relationship between work and welfare in very diverse national settings across member states. The RECWOWE series

publishes books that analyse work and welfare, and which pay special attention to the tensions that now characterize this relationship. Beyond the four
main tensions mentioned above, the series is open to any other forms of
analysis of the relationship between work and welfare. It is committed to
publishing work that focuses on the gender dimension of this relationship,
on the impact of the relationship on migrants, and, on its multi-level –
European, national and local institutional dimensions.

Denis Bouget, University of Nantes
Sonja Drobnic, University of Hamburg
Ana M. Guillén, University of Oviedo
Bruno Palier, Sciences-po Paris

Notes on Contributors

Paula Blomqvist is Associate Professor and Senior Lecturer at the Department of Government, Uppsala University, Sweden. Her research has focused mainly on the Swedish welfare state and its recent transformation, foremost in regard to privatization, consumerism and the changing relationship between local and central levels of governance. Her work has appeared in a variety of international journals, including *European Journal of Social Policy, Social Science and Medicine, Social Policy and Administration* and *Local Government Studies*.

Seán Boyle is Senior Research Fellow in Health and Social Care at the London School of Economics and Political Science. He researches and writes extensively on a range of policy and planning issues concerning the finance and provision of healthcare in the UK. In 2011 he published the Health System in Transition report on England, a comprehensive overview of the health and social care system in England.

Alban Davesne is a doctoral candidate at Sciences Po, where he studies the Europeanization of Health Policies and its comparative effects on health care systems in Sweden and in France. He published articles on cross-border health care and early projects of a European Health Community.

Eduardo González is Associate Professor of Management and Deputy Head of the Department of Business Administration at University of Oviedo (Spain). He has also coordinated the MBA programs during the last 10 years. His research interests include strategic management, efficiency and productivity analysis, and health economics.

Ana M. Guillén is Full Professor of Sociology and Head of Department at the University of Oviedo, Spain. She has written extensively on welfare state development, comparative social policy and Europeanization. She has acted as a consultant to the European Commission and several EU presidencies. She is also vice-president of the executive board of Research Committee 19 of the International Sociological Association and co-chair of ESPAnet-Spain.

Patrick Hassenteufel is Professor of Political Science at the University of Versailles Saint-Quentin-en-Yvelines and vice-dean of the Faculty of Law and Political Science. His main research field is comparative health policy; he also works more generally on the transformation of European Welfare States and on actor-centred policy analysis.

Monika Ewa Kaminska, PhD, works at the Collaborative Research Center 597 'Transformations of the State', University of Bremen. She has researched on post-communist transition, employment relations, social policies and healthcare reforms. She has recently published on healthcare issues in the *Journal of European Industrial Relations, Journal for Comparative Policy Analysis* and *Social Science and Medicine.*

Tanja Klenk is a research fellow at the Chair for Political Science, Administration and Organization at the University of Potsdam (Germany). Her research interests include comparative welfare reforms, the politics of welfare reforms, institutional and organizational changes in the governance and the administration of the welfare state. Her work has been published in *Administration & Society, Public Management Review* and *Comparative Governance and Politics.*

Ingalill Montanari is an affiliated researcher at the Swedish Institute for Social Research, Stockholm University and studies predominantly the development and possible convergence of social policies with a class and gender perspective.

Kenneth Nelson is Associate Professor of Sociology at the Swedish Institute for Social Research, Stockholm University. He has published widely in fields of comparative social policy, poverty and income distributions.

August Österle is Associate Professor at the Institute for Social Policy, Vienna University of Economics and Business, and Visiting Professor at the Corvinus University Budapest. His research interests include comparative welfare state research and health and long-term care policies.

Bruno Palier is CNRS Research Director at Sciences Po, Centre d'études européennes. He has a PhD in Political Science. He is studying welfare reforms in Europe. Between 2007 and 2011, he was the scientific coordinator of a European Network of excellence RECWOWE (Reconciling Work and Welfare). In Sciences Po, he is the director of a joint programme Sciences Po Northwestern University: 'Health Policy in Europe'.

Emmanuele Pavolini is Associate Professor of Economic Sociology at Macerata University, Italy. He researches and writes on comparative social policy and Southern European Welfare States. He has recently co-edited a book on long-term care reforms in Europe titled *Reforms in Long-Term Care Policies in Europe. Investigating Institutional Change and Social Impacts* (with Costanzo Ranci, 2012). He acts as a consultant to the European Commission and he is also member of the ESPANet board.

Juan Ventura is Full Professor of Management and Head of the Department of Business Administration at the University of Oviedo, Spain. He also coordinates the MBA program. His research interests include strategic management, health economics and leadership.

Giovanna Vicarelli is Full Professor of Economic Sociology and Organizational Sociology at the Politecnica delle Marche University, Italy.

She has been studying health care as well as health care professionals in Italy in a comparative perspective. She also co-ordinates an MBA program on Health Care Management.

Ulrika Winblad is Associate Professor at the Department of Public Health and Caring Sciences at Uppsala University in Sweden. Her research interest concerns health policy and public administration, foremost the marketization of health and elderly care. She has recently published in *Social Science & Medicine, Health Policy and Health Economics* and *Policy and Law*.

Introduction

Emmanuele Pavolini and Ana M. Guillén

European Health Care Systems (HCS) are very complex policy fields also in comparison with other institutions of the Welfare State. They have three peculiarities that, taken all together, make them unique: they are mostly based on services and not on transfers (as pensions for instance); they are at the same time a capital – and human- intensive sector, which requires a large amount of investments in technology, infrastructures, but also in high skilled professionals; they tend to offer, through various mechanisms, a universalistic-like coverage, with possible limited differentiation among users.

The present book develops a framework to analyse how well these European HCS function, connecting the answer to this question with the main HCS regulatory changes occurred in the last decades, concerning rescaling, privatization and managerialization.

The book proposes an integrated and multidisciplinary approach to the analysis of HCS. It adopts a perspective recently proposed also by Marmor and Wendt (2012). On one side, health economics has quite often focused either on micro-efficiency issues (comparative analysis of specific types of health care interventions) or on HCS performances, although frequently not sufficiently taking into account institutional dynamics and specificities.

On the other side, most of the political science, social policy and sociology literature on HCS have studied so far the reasons and the mechanisms explaining why different countries have chosen different institutional settings.[1] What it is interesting to notice is that the 'dependent variable' in most of these studies has been the HCS institutional structure (National Health Systems – NHS; Social Health Insurances – SHI, private markets, etc.), partially taking for granted that different institutional structures would have covered ('de-commodified') social rights in different ways and degrees. In the scientific literature, population coverage, access, provision and public health care expenditure have usually been the main indicators to measure HCS functioning.

Nowadays there are at least three good reasons to better define the 'dependent variable' (Clasen and Siegel, 2007) and to measure more in depth how well different HCS function and 'perform' in terms of economic efficiency but also of effectiveness, quality and equality. Once (almost) full population coverage has been reached in HCS in EU countries, there is the need to look for a more complex and sophisticated set of indicators to compare and to evaluate how effective HCS are in tackling health care issues. A more complex and sophisticated set of indicators is useful also to answer a quite relevant question: is HCS performance strongly influenced by the HCS regulatory framework (e.g. SHI vs. NHS) or are there other more relevant factors? Once an agreement is reached about which set of indicators on goals attainment and performance to use, it will be easier to evaluate the impact on the performance of HCS of the three main regulatory changes that were introduced (to different extents) in the last two decades in EU HCS, namely, rescaling, privatization and managerialization.

By rescaling, often meaning decentralization, we refer to the issue of the distribution of powers among actors in HCS at different territorial levels (national and local ones).

By privatization, in financing and delivery, we refer to the issue which deals both with the distribution of power between public and private actors and the distribution of health care expenditure between the State and the citizens, as well as different forms of 'hidden' privatization (Streeck and Thelen, 2005).

By managerialization, we refer to the distribution of power among professionals (first of all physicians), bureaucrats/managers and citizens/users in HCS.

The present book has focused on these three regulatory changes for two reasons. The distribution of powers and responsibilities between different layers of government, between public and private actors, and between professionals, managers and citizens all lay at the heart of any HCS. At the same time the vast majority of the policy reforms undertaken in the last two decades deal with one or more of these three regulatory issues. It seems that in European HCS, once almost full population coverage has been reached, the debate has concentrated on regulation: taking into account the contents and the aims of the main health care reforms over last two decades, we can conclude that at least eighty per cent of these reforms have dealt with either rescaling, privatization or managerialization.

There are already many interesting studies analysing the changes in these three regulatory dimensions.[2] What seems relatively less present in the literature is a comparative study adopting at the same time a unified approach, putting together all three regulatory changes; focusing on a relevant number of countries from different EU Welfare State 'regimes'/'families'; and connecting these different institutional settings to HCS functioning/performance. Overall the aim of our book is to analyse many different countries belonging to the various European Welfare 'regimes', focusing on the main regulatory dimensions of HCS reforms (privatization, rescaling and managerialization), which are usually studied separately, and connecting the regulatory issue to HCS functioning. In this book, the concept of HCS functioning concerns outputs and outcomes, but also the amount of resources spent for health care. With the first two concepts we refer to what is produced by health care systems (in terms of services, processes, etc.) as well as to goal attainments (in terms of health, health inequalities, etc.).

Altogether the literature on the functioning/performance of HCS is still quite limited. Even if there was a series of previous studies, the WHO *Report* from 2000 represents the first general attempt to develop a broad discussion about how to measure HCS performance from a theoretical and methodological point of view. The WHO report created a lively debate which was mostly characterized by the recognition of the importance of the task accomplished by the *Report*, but also, by a series of very strong critics. After the WHO 2000 Report and the relative debate, in most recent years, the main research developments in the field have included: researches focusing on single indicators (for example Tang et al., 2009 recently proposed a new method to measure health inequalities and HCS fairness); researches focusing on a different territorial level of analysis (shifting from comparison among national HCS in general to, for instance, comparison among hospitals in different countries) (e.g. the WHO produced reports on this issue); researches focusing on building a set of indicators (for example Mackenbach and McKee, 2013; Or et al., 2010). OECD can be considered the front-runner of the third type of research developments on HCS performance.[3]

This brief review shows how complex the task of HCS functioning measurement is and how relevant it is to propose a framework to study it. Moreover the recent literature, either on HCS functioning or on the three regulatory changes, tends to underestimate the relevance of connecting HCS functioning with these regulatory changes (rescaling, privatization and managerialization). From this point of view it becomes important trying to answer the question: what has been the impact of these types of changes on the level of HCS functioning?

We propose to frame HCS functioning and the relative reforms in terms of a 'quadrilemma' (Palier, 2011). HCS should theoretically combine together: an *economic objective* (to control costs and the increase in health expenditure); a *social objective* (to guarantee equality of access to healthcare for all), a *medical objective* (to guarantee the highest quality of care and the optimum condition of health for the population), and a *political objective* (to guarantee the responsiveness of the health system, and satisfaction, based on freedom and comfort of the patients and professionals).

The level of HCS functioning can be measured and studied starting from these goals, the trade-offs that arise among them (e.g. between patients' freedom of choice and equality or costs) and the impact of regulatory reforms on the four corners of the quadrilemma.

Deciding which European countries to analyse in order to understand reforms trajectories and HCS functioning is a complex task. There is an intense, and ongoing, debate on how to classify HCS. Traditionally the vast literature on HCS in Western Europe has put forward the presence of at least two different types of systems, NHS and SHI ones, characterized by different institutional, organizational and professionals patterns. Moreover, inside these two broad types, there are significant differences (for instance among Anglosaxon, 'Mediterranean' and Scandinavian NHS). The transformation (mostly towards insurance-based systems) of former Central-Eastern European countries after the collapse of socialist regimes must be also taken into account. More recent attempts (for a review of the debate, see Wendt et al., 2009 and Wendt, 2009) propose partially new classifications.

The book considers cases belonging to various contexts in order to understand the role played by different institutional-organizational settings in influencing the adoption of innovation or transformations (privatization, rescaling, managerialization) (Hassenteufel and Palier, 2007) and to compare the impact of different HCS types on functioning. The choice has been the following: Sweden, France, Austria, Germany, Poland, Spain, Italy and England.[4]

This set of countries is interesting because they belong to the main different European HCS, no matter what type of typology is adopted and their comparison can tell us something more about the relevance of different typologies in terms of more appropriate HCS classification. Moreover the eight countries of the study represent the vast majority of the EU population: 74 per cent of overall European Union population lives in them. Studying these countries means analysing the functioning and the reforms of HCS affecting three EU citizens out of four.

Four main hypotheses are formulated in this book with some caution, given the fact that there is no dense body of literature connecting health care functioning and policy reforms:

1. a relation between HCS 'regimes' (no matter how we define them) and functioning is to be expected;
2. different trade-offs in various HCS in terms of how to tackle the 'quadrilemma' goals should be expected;
3. financial resources matter! A good part of the political and scientific discussion about health care reforms and HCS functioning in Europe has focused more on changing regulation than also on the amount of resources dedicated to the system. Still, a more balanced approach should be taken into account, this meaning that it can be expected that increases in public expenditure will improve the functioning of the HCS substantially;
4. we need to take health care more seriously when studying welfare states trajectories of retrenchment! Our hypothesis is that, while other traditional

welfare state sectors (pensions and unemployment benefits) went often through a retrenchment phase, health care policies have quite more often mixed restructuring, recalibration and expansion.

The book is divided in two parts. In the first part the eight country case studies are presented. The structure of each country case study is similar. The first section of each chapter has been dedicated to describe the three main regulatory changes (rescaling, privatization, managerialization) in the country under study. The second section focuses on the politics of institutional change: why and how regulatory changes have taken place (if they really have) and what type of institutional change has taken place, if any. The third section of each chapter has been dedicated to the HCS functioning and the effects that regulatory changes had in terms of the 'quadrilemma' goals: evaluating the effects of reforms can be extremely complicated, especially when these reforms are quite controversial. Therefore single country chapters propose their interpretation of what happened trying to acknowledge the complexity of evaluation.

The book was developed and discussed among the group of researchers during the last three years. In 2010 the economic and financial crisis had started to bite HCS, but it was not clear then how long it would be lasting and how deep it would hit public health care systems. During the process of writing and discussing country chapters, it became increasingly evident that Austerity Plans were starting to play a relevant role also in many HCS reforms. Therefore a specific focus on the crisis and its effects on health care systems were developed in each chapter, even if in 2013 it is still not clear where some HCS are heading.

The second part of the book includes three comparative chapters, each focusing on the interplay among HCS reforms and their functioning.

Chapter 9 analyses comparatively the main reforms introduced since 2000s, framing them in a longer time span and taking into consideration the evolution of public expenditure in the field. Then, it considers which were the main drivers for change behind the reforms and who have been the main actors involved in the policy arena. The last section of the chapter focuses on the mechanisms of change and the main consequences of the reforms in terms of governance models.

Chapter 10 is dedicated to study how well HCS have functioned, connecting the answer to this question to the main policy changes occurred in the last decades in terms of rescaling, privatization and managerialization. In order to make what is discussed in Chapter 9 as consequential and comparable with the present one, the functioning of the different HCS is analysed in relation to the 'quadrilemma' goals, that is, economic, medical, social and political objectives.

Chapter 11 frames the eight countries comparative analysis in a broader context, looking at the relationship between health care and social citizenship rights and focusing on the issue of convergence and divergence among European HCS over time.

Finally, the book closes with a concluding chapter gathering the main results from the analysis and suggesting further directions for future research endeavours.

Notes

1. See for instance: Hacker (1998) and Immergut E. (1992).
2. In particular the international literature which deals with the issue of health care systems can be divided in three main branches: text books or readers introducing to the general theme of health care policy; books focusing on single cases or at the most in small number of countries comparison; books focusing on single issues (e.g. the role of professionals and the health care systems or the processes of decentralization).

   A good recent example of the first type of publication is the book by R. Blank and V. Burau (2010), which describes the main aspects of health care systems functioning, or Taylor G. and Hawley H. (2010).

   There are then many books mainly focusing on one single country (generally the US or the UK). Apart from them in recent years there are two publications that have a more general approach but they tend to remain centred around specific health care 'regimes' or 'families': Magnussen J., Vrangbæk K. and Saltman R. (eds) (2009) is focused on Nordic countries (Sweden, Iceland, Denmark and Norway); Rothgang H. et al. (2010) is a very interesting book and it makes the effort of analysing many countries (focusing on statistical data and overall information on single countries HCS institutional settings), and then focuses deeply on three HCS (Germany, the UK and the US).

   The third type of literature focuses on single regulatory issues. Kuhlmann and Saks (2008) and Kuhlmann (2006). Béland and Gran (2008) analyse the role of private actors and privatization processes in pensions and health care. Saltman R. et al. (eds) (2007) consider the issue of rescaling.
3. For example OECD (2012).
4. With the 'devolution' reforms taking place in the last two decades, it is increasingly difficult to study the NHS in the United Kingdom as a whole, given the fact that the Welsh and, especially, the Scottish NHS are developing in a somewhat different direction than the English one (Boyle, 2011). We have decided to focus on the latter. However internationally comparable data are often available at the UK level and, therefore, quite often the statistical information provided in the book is at this level.

Part I
Country Case Studies

1
Sweden: Continued Marketization within a Universalist System

Paula Blomqvist and Ulrika Winblad

Introduction

In this chapter we describe the regulatory changes that have taken place in the Swedish health care system during the 2000s. Three main reform trends are identified: privatization in the primary care sector, the strengthening of patient rights and re-centralization of regulatory power within the system. All these reforms have roots that go back to the 1990s, when patient choice and private alternatives were first introduced in the system and the central state began to try to find ways to take back some of the regulatory powers lost during its far-reaching decentralization in previous decades. All three reform trends were, however, reinforced during the 2000s. After 2006, when a centre-right government coalition took office, they were also given a more coherent and ideologically articulated frame, foremost in that values like private provision and patient rights were stressed.

Even if there are some transforming effects of the reforms introduced in the 2000s, we argue that these reforms have not fundamentally altered the system, but rather re-oriented and strengthened certain aspects of it. In this period, the Swedish health care system became more pluralistic in its provision of services and more accessible to patients, particularly in the primary care sector. The transparency of the system and the potential for quality monitoring on the part of the central government increased. At the same time, the hallmark of the system, its solidaristic, tax-based, financing structure, remains intact, as does the delivery structure of predominantly public provision of care services.[1] Moreover, even if some attempts have been made in the last decade to strengthen national supervision over the system, foremost with respect to performance and medical quality, it is still governed by the locally elected and largely autonomous county councils. Taking this into consideration, we believe that the reforms in the 2000s can be described mainly as second order in Peter Hall's terminology (Hall, 1993); in other words, that they concern means, rather than ends, and that their transformative effect is limited. Furthermore, the political goals which have underpinned recent reforms, such as improved access to care for patients, more innovation and private initiative on the provision side, and enhanced transparency in terms of its quality and performance are not new to the system. They have all been part of health policy discussions in Sweden for several decades. Given the incremental and partly disjointed character of the regulatory reforms undertaken in Swedish health care in the 2000s, we also argue that these policies should be understood as representing a gradual institutional change rather than disruption.

Regulatory reforms in the Swedish system in the 2000s

The Swedish health care system is financed by taxes and based on the logic of public planning. It is strongly decentralized, as both financing and provision of care rest with local bodies, the county councils. These are currently twenty-one in number[2] and governed by locally elected political assemblies. The county councils finance the provision of health services primarily through local income taxes, which make up about 80 per cent of the system's financing. The rest is state grants (17 per cent) and, to a smaller extent, user fees (3 per cent). The provision of health services has been a predominantly public responsibility in Sweden since the first state hospitals were founded by King Gustav Vasa in the 16th century. Since 1862, the main responsibility for operating hospitals has rested with the county councils. As a result of the still overwhelming domination of public providers in Swedish health care, medical staff are usually employed directly by the county councils. Until the 1960s, the provision of health services was subject to fairly detailed regulation by national health authorities such as the Ministry of Social Affairs and the National Board of Health and Social Services (*Socialstyrelsen*). After 1970, the system was gradually deregulated and decentralized, giving local policy makers substantial autonomy in organizing the provision of health services. In 1983, following the new Health and Medical Service Act, the county councils finally became fully responsible for both financing and production of health services, a change which led to the role of the central government being further reduced. At this time, the share of private providers in the system was very low, estimated at around 1–2 per cent.

During the 1990s, the Swedish health care system was gradually opened up to more competition from private providers. Following a legal change in 1992, the county councils were allowed to contract out the provision of care to private actors, including for-profit firms. This led to a period of intense organizational experimenting in the system, where some county councils developed their own quasi-market models for increasing competitive pressures and the share of private providers (Saltman and von Otter, 1995; Anell, 1996). Another central part of local reforms during the 1990s was the introduction of the principle of the right of the patient to choose health care providers. The first attempt to introduce patient choice within the system was the 1989 patient choice recommendation initiated by the central organization for the county councils, the Swedish Association for Local Governments and Regions (SALAR). Later, this right was legally formalized, but remained a distant goal in many county councils due to poor local implementation (Winblad, 2008).The political concern with patient choice during the 1990s should be seen in light of the relatively weak role of patients within the Swedish health care system and its alleged bureaucratic nature at the time, which led to public discontent. As the provision of health services was subject to detailed local planning by the county councils and offered to citizens on the basis of residency, there had been no possibility in the system for choosing one's care provider, even within the primary care sector. Typically, citizens were expected to seek care only at the public health centres and hospitals within their area of residence. During the 1980s, this led to a critical debate about the bureaucratic nature and lack of consumer friendliness of the system. An additional explanation for the emphasis on managerialist and market-orienting policies during the 1990s is the strong influence of new public management ideas in Sweden during this time, during both social democratic and right-wing governments (Blomqvist, 2002; 2004).

The managerialist reforms introduced during the 1990s, such as patient choice, purchaser–provider splits and the introduction of various forms of performance-related payments systems, led to the previous virtual public monopoly on care provision being abandoned in many county councils.[3] Since these reforms were largely experimental in character and initiated in some county counties only, the share of private provision as part of the total expenditure in the system was still relatively modest at the end of the decade, at only about 10 per cent (Blomqvist, 2004). The managerialist reforms during the 1990s can be said to have opened up the system to private providers and introduced more organizational diversity at the local level, while at the same time creating a higher level of cost awareness among the staff and more recognition of the rights of patients.

During the 2000s, the reformation of the system continued along similar tracks, albeit with a slightly different emphasis. Access to care, and, in particular, waiting times became a political concern for the central government along with the desire to increase the transparency of the system. After 2006, when the previous Social Democratic government was replaced with a centre-right governing coalition, there was a more strongly stated ideological drive towards increasing the share of private providers and making the system more consumerist in orientation. Three main reform trends can be identified during this decade. The first is the continued strengthening of *patient rights* through regulatory measures like choice, the legal right to information and co-determination, and the introduction of a so-called waiting-time guarantee in 2005. The second is *privatization of the primary care sector*, manifested in the introduction of so-called primary care choice systems in the county councils in 2010 (*Lagen of valfrihetssystem*). The third is the *re-centralization of regulatory powers* within the system as the central state has introduced various new measures to increase its capacity to supervise and direct the system.

The first reform trend, the strengthening of patients' rights, represents continuity in relation to the 1990s when patient empowerment was a political goal for both left- and right-wing governments. During the 2000s this goal was even more systematically pursued, with more emphasis on legal enforcement. In 2005, the then social-democratic government made an agreement with SALAR to introduce a so-called *waiting time guarantee* which stated that there should be a maximum waiting time of three months for treatment after a patient had been diagnosed. This was not the first attempt to shorten waiting times in the system in this manner, but this time the government provided substantive additional resources to the county councils. Even though compliance was formally voluntary, the reform was closely monitored by the government and new systems for collection of information regarding waiting times were set up. Also, SALAR helped the county councils to structure the implementation process, such as by arranging regular meetings where leading representatives from the county councils took part (Winblad et al., 2010). In 2010 the guarantee was legally enforced by the next (right-centre) government, which made it mandatory for the county councils to provide care for all patients within three months. If the clinics could not keep up with the guarantee, they were legally obliged to help patients seek care at another hospital at the expense of the home clinic. This created strong incentives for the clinics to shorten their waiting lists. Also, clinics that were able to honor the guarantee received an economic bonus (Winblad et al., 2010). Another reform carried out in the 2000s to strengthen the role of patients was the *Patient Choice Recommendation*, which was the result of an agreement between the central government and SALAR stating that patients should be provided with a free choice of care provider even across county council borders. The recommendation was met with strong resistance by some county councils, who feared the loss of budgetary control as patients would be allowed to seek care freely in other counties, but it was eventually endorsed by all (Fredriksson et al., 2012). Attempts to strengthen patient rights in the 2000s were also aided by amendments introduced in the Health and Medical Services Act in 1999 to legally enforce the rights of patients in the system. Examples of rights that were given legal status at this time include the right to full information regarding treatment alternatives, the right to co-determination in treatment decisions and – in cases of serious medical illness – the right to a second opinion by another care provider. These reforms, initiated to strengthen the role of patients within the system, can be seen as a continuing of the managerialist reforms of the 1990s, but with a stronger emphasis on the legal rights of patients.

A second reform trend that can be observed in the 2000s in Swedish health care is (continued) *privatization in the primary care sector* through the so-called primary care choice law enacted in 2009. The law, which came into force in 2010, stipulates that all county councils introduce a so-called choice model, whereby private care providers are free to establish themselves if they fulfill certain basic criteria and thereafter get reimbursed financially on the basis of how many listed patients they manage to attract. For patients, the choice models mean that they can choose freely where to 'enlist' among competing public and private GPs and health care centers, and that funds within the system will be distributed according to their choice, at no additional cost to themselves. In this manner, the primary care choice law also adds to the strengthening of consumer power within the system. In line with the Swedish tradition of localized decision-making in the health care system, the primary care choice law left it open for the county councils to design the specific features of the choice systems themselves, including what criteria must be fulfilled for private providers to establish themselves and how reimbursement formulas are constructed. Evaluations of developments in the county councils after 2010 have shown that the choice models have led to a 20 per cent increase in the share of private primary care providers in the country as a whole, albeit with great local variations (Swedish Competition Agency, 2010).

The central government's efforts to increase the share of private providers have so far been confined foremost to the primary care sector, even though the so-called stop law prohibiting sale of acute care hospitals introduced by the previous social democratic government in 2000 was overturned in 2007. Since then, there has been no further privatization within the hospital sector in Sweden (Anell, 2011), as there has been no apparent interest among the county councils to privatize hospitals. So far, only one acute care hospital in Sweden has been partially privatized as its operation was put out to tender (in Stockholm in 1999).

The third regulatory trend visible in the Swedish health system in the 2000s is *recentralization*. This trend is evident in a range of different political initiatives which have had the effect of centralizing regulatory control within the system, some of which were initiated in the late 1990s (Fredriksson, 2012 and Saltman, 2012). It should be noted that re-centralization here refers exclusively to regulatory powers, not the financial structure of the system or its institutions for providing care services, both of which remain locally governed. The post-war Swedish health care system has been characterized by a high degree of soft law or non-binding regulation. One part of this governance structure is the annual negotiations between the government and the county councils (represented by SALAR) on how to allocate the state grants, which are typically directed towards distinct areas which the government wants to prioritize. Such agreements about resource allocation and priority-setting are formally voluntary but have in practice usually been followed by the county councils. In recent years, however, the government has increasingly turned to binding legal regulation when governing the system. This inclination, evident foremost after 2006, reflects a desire to strengthen the role of the central state in relation to the county councils and has also been motivated by the documented geographical differences in health utilization and health outcomes across the country (Government Commission, 2012).

Another sign of the recentralization trend within the Swedish health care system is the increased focus on audit and quality monitoring within this sector. Since the middle of the 2000s, SALAR and the National Board of Health and Welfare produce yearly Open Comparisons (*Öppna jämförelser*), in which hundreds of quality indicators are presented for each county council. This provides a unique opportunity for the state to compare the quality within each part of the health care sector and puts pressure on the county councils to improve quality. In addition to this, the National Board of Health and Welfare produces national guidelines for several diagnosis groups (in collaboration with medical experts) in order to direct the distribution of resources at the local level and streamline the behaviour of the medical professionals (Fredriksson, 2012). A third sign of the increased recentralization within the system is reinforced regulatory control by national agencies. For instance, the National Board of Health and Welfare has begun focusing more explicitly on inspections of the health care units. Six regional inspection units have been set up during the 2000s. Having previously announced the inspections beforehand, surprise inspections are now more commonly used. Furthermore, two new national agencies have recently been created. In 2011, the Swedish Agency for Health Care Services Analysis (Myndigheten för Vårdanalys), and in 2013, the Health and Social Care Inspectorate (Inspektionen för vård och omsorg). The agencies were established by the government in order to monitor quality and strengthen the role of the patients within the system. Taken together, these re-centralizing reforms point to an enhanced regulatory role for the national government in the system in relation to the county councils.

How far-reaching are the changes in the Swedish health system in the last decade? Employing Peter Hall's three-level model, we would assert that most of the reforms described above concern policy *means*, rather than ends, and in that sense can be described as second-order changes. Even if there is a clear ideological component to some of the regulatory changes described above, we still see them foremost as means to strengthen certain aspects of the system rather than dismantling or fundamentally transforming it. The basic goals behind the reforms, such as strengthening the role of the patient, increasing the elements of pluralism and competition on the provision side and enhancing central governing power in relation to the county councils, are not new to the system but have been actively pursued by national political actors for decades. However, the means for realizing these goals, such as legal rights, free establishment on the part of private providers though choice systems and the use of binding regulation to enforce central government directives, represent novel policy tools in the system, which has been governed in previous decades foremost through soft regulation such as recommendations and voluntary agreements. It can be argued, moreover, that some of the goals behind the reforms in the 2000s reflect a stronger emphasis on certain political values, thereby possibly altering the hierarchy of goals somewhat in relation to earlier periods. For instance, it is clear that the 2006 centre-right government saw the opportunity of patients to choose private providers as a more central value than the previous social democratic government. In this sense, there might be an element of 'third order' change in some of the reforms during the 2000s as well. But as there has been no attempt to alter the basic structure of the system, either with regard to financing or provision – which is still predominantly public – or to question the basic values of solidarity, universalism and the strong element of public control within it, we still regard these reforms as limited in their transformative potential. Furthermore, it can also be noted that the political rhetoric surrounding the reforms has been non-confrontational in character, stressing the strengths of the existing system and underlining the intention of the centre-right government to preserve its basic structure and value foundations.

Why these reforms? Driving forces

The main driving force behind the regulatory changes in the Swedish health care system during the 2000s was central political agency in the form of government-initiated reforms. The motives behind the reforms appear to have been both ideological and pragmatic. Arguably the social democratic government in power during the first half of the decade had foremost a pragmatic agenda, aimed towards strengthening the legitimacy of the system by tackling the persistent problem of waiting times and increasing its efficiency through the strengthening of its competitive elements. The reduction of waiting times within the system has been a general political objective since the 1980s, but until the 2000s, largely without success. Previously, there has been a tendency to see waiting lines as a predominantly local problem, to be handled foremost by the county councils themselves. But as the issue became the topic of public debate during the 1980s and 1990s, the pressure on national governments to solve it increased.[4] The 2005 waiting-time guarantee was the first one with a more general character including all diagnoses. Attempts to deal with waiting times in the system have thus been motivated by public dissatisfaction with the system in this regard. Developments in the EU creating more opportunities to seeking care in other EU member states may have put additional pressure on the Swedish government, especially after the verdict of the European Court of Justice in 2003 in the British case of Watts, where the court made clear that 'undue' waiting time for treatment in the home country can serve as grounds for a patient to be entitled to seek care in another member state at the expense of the home country (Sindbjerg et al., 2009).

As noted above, a centre-right coalition government replaced the social democrats in 2006 and was re-elected again in 2010. The new governing coalition, led by a liberal party calling themselves the Moderates (*Moderaterna*), pursued reforms in the second half of the 2000s with a more distinct ideological content. This is evident not least in the case of private providers, where the largely pragmatic position of the social democrats during the 1990s and the first half of the 2000s had been to allow privatization in the county councils that wanted it, thus leaving this issue for the locally elected leaders to decide.[5] The post-2006 centre-right government has displayed a more ideologically charged pro-privatization agenda, stating that the share of private providers ought to increase in all parts of the country in order to make the system more flexible, efficient and patient-friendly (Government bills 2008/09:74 and 2008/09:29).[6] Hence, in contrast to the privatization reforms initiated at the local level during the 1990s, privatization in the 2000s has not been primarily motivated by cost savings or economic efficiency, but rather by ideological preference. The preferred mode of privatization through choice models, (also evident in other sectors such as elder and child care) where private and public care givers receive a fixed sum per listed patient, does not generate price competition and hence cannot be expected to be cost-reducing for the county councils. On the whole, cost concerns does not seem to be an important motive behind reforms in Swedish health care in the 2000s, not even after the international financial crisis in 2008–2009. This can be understood in light of the relatively quick recovery of the Swedish economy and stable employment levels throughout the period, which left the tax base of the county councils more or less intact. A second factor is the relatively strong financial situation of the county councils during the 2000s, which was a result of the substantive rationalizations in provision structure, foremost through hospital bed and staff reductions following the downturn of the Swedish economy in the early 1990s.

Instead, a main impetus behind the privatization and patients' rights reforms in the 2000s can be said to be an ideological belief in the dynamic effects of private entrepreneurship and consumer choice, both for quality development and patient responsiveness. The 2006 centre-right government has also been more ideologically explicit in its embracing of legal rights for patients as a means for patient empowerment. Against this backdrop, it can be argued that the shift in government in 2006 led to a more ideological health care policy agenda at the national level of the system and a general politicization of health care in Sweden.

Another driving force for both social democratic and centre-right governments during the 2000s has been to try to assert more central control over the system. This strive is visible during both the first and second half of the decade, but it has been enforced more strongly in the second half.

Where the previous social democratic government treaded more carefully to preserve the independence of the county councils, the 2006 centre-right government has been bolder in challenging this legacy by introducing binding legislation which forces the county councils to comply, for instance regarding the waiting-time guarantee and the primary care choice reform. Having had a more distinct political agenda this government had also strived for more control over the system than is provided by the 'soft' governing modes that had previously characterized it (Fredriksson et al., 2012).

Efforts to re-centralize regulatory powers within the system through legislation and national guidelines for medical treatment and priority-setting have also been motivated by a growing concern over the geographical variations in care quality and access to care that have been documented in recent years, both by social democratic and right-wing governments (SALAR and the National Board of Health and Social Welfare, 2008; 2011). Arguably, the general striving for increased transparency and improved monitoring of the system in recent years should also be seen in light of international trends in public management research, which have stressed the need for transparency, audit and performance measurement (Power, 1997; 2000). Reform initiatives at the local level during the 2000s have foremost been directed towards efforts to rationalize the provision of care and continue to search for new management models at the hospital and clinical levels. The general trend is towards increased specialization and concentration of care services to certain hospitals and continued experimentation with new managerial techniques such as Lean Health care and Total Quality Management (Kastberg and Berlin, 2011; Anell et al., 2012).

How have the reforms been introduced? The mechanisms of change

The regulatory reforms introduced in Sweden during the 2000s can be said to represent gradual institutional change. This is reflected, we argue, in the limited scope of the reforms themselves, the largely incremental manner in which they have been implemented and the high degree of continuity in relation to policies in the previous decades. Considering the origins of the changes, there is no doubt that most of them are the products of top-down steering, as they have been initiated by central governments. It should also be noted, moreover, that even if most reforms during the 2000s have been initiated from the central level, the county councils have taken active part in their implementation and sometimes also their design. This is true not least in the case of the primary care choice reform, where the county councils were given considerable discretion in designing local choice systems, and the national quality registers, which have been introduced through a process of cooperation between the county councils and the government's expert body, the National Board of Health and Social Welfare (NBHW).

The gradual nature of the reforms introduced in Swedish health care in the 2000s and their limited transformative potential should also be understood in relation to the managerial reforms in the 1990s, which in some ways constituted a more radical departure in relation to previous decades. The reforms in the 2000s can be said to have followed the policy path of gradual liberalization and marketization of the system that was initiated by a social democratic government in the late 1980s and speeded up by a centre-right government in the years 1991–1994. If anything, the liberalization pace during the 2000s has been slower than during the 1990s and more mixed up with other reform elements, such as re-centralization and the more systematic monitoring of quality developments.

The institutional changes introduced during the 2000s can also be said to be limited in scope because there was no broadly encompassing reform during this period, but rather a string of separate and somewhat disparate reforms. The primary care choice reform, legal adjustments to strengthen patient rights, national guidelines, the waiting-time guarantee and the introduction of the quality registers have all aimed at different aspects of the system, and each had fairly limited transformative potential in and of itself. The most comprehensive reform was the primary care choice reform, but even if this reform entailed a new method for distributing resources in the primary care sector and provided more opportunity for private entrepreneurship, it can still be regarded as limited in scope in that it concerned only a part of the system, the primary care sector. Moreover, it did not alter the financing structure of the system or the conditions for access as the system has retained its universalistic character. Furthermore, patient choice has been a central policy objective within the system since the early 1990s, even if the distribution of resources has not always been linked to the choices of patients in the systematic manner as in the new primary care choice system. For these reasons, the transformative impact of the reform should not be overstated, particularly in county councils which had a relatively large share of private providers in the primary care sector prior to its introduction.

The second reason for why we believe the institutional changes that have taken place in the Swedish system during the 2000s are best described as gradual in nature is that the reforms introduced have often proceeded in several steps. In this sense they have been *incremental*, rather than disruptive. One example of this is the primary care choice reform which was first introduced on a voluntary basis in 2007 before it was made mandatory for all county councils in 2010 (Blomqvist and Bergman, 2010). The choice systems introduced on voluntary basis (in three country councils) were evaluated and much debated – before the model was applied more generally. There were also some adjustments to the national legislation based on lessons learnt in the three voluntary cases. Another example of a step-wise reform is the waiting care guarantee, a reform which has been tried and adjusted since 1992, when the first waiting-time guarantee was introduced, followed by a second guarantee in 1997 and a third in 2005 before the most recent in 2010. A third example is the national guidelines for medical treatments, which were first introduced for a single diagnosis in 1996 (diabetes) and thereafter gradually expanded to cover more medical areas while at the same time becoming more detailed in their instructions to clinical practitioners.

A third argument in support of the gradual nature of change in the Swedish system in the last decade is that there has been a substantive element of continuity in relation to reforms during the 1990s, even with regard to reform measures initiated by political opponents. Therefore the reforms undertaken in the 2000s cannot be said to reflect a bold or disruptive reform agenda; on the contrary, they seem to signal a political will to change the system slowly and gradually and to maintain as far as possible a broad political consensus regarding the direction of change. The political ambition to preserve the tradition of a relatively consensual and inclusive policy-making process has also included the county councils, which have been given the opportunity to influence proposed reforms during the period and which retain substantial influence over the final design of reforms as these are implemented at the local level. This was evident not least in the most controversial reform introduced in the period, the primary care choice reform, where the county councils rejected the first government reform proposal which led to its withdrawal. The proposal was later introduced again with substantive moderations, foremost in that it gave the county councils considerable freedom to design local listing and reimbursement systems (Winblad et al., 2012) Another example is the patient choice recommendation in 2001, where the government allowed a long period of local implementation in order for the county councils to adjust to the expected effects of the reform with regard to new patterns of care consumption and travelling across county council lines to seek care. In this sense, the tradition of consensual policy-making and the usage of soft modes of governance in the system can be argued to have had a moderating effect on reforms introduced during the period.

The effects of the reforms on the performance of the system

We have identified in this chapter three main reform trends in Swedish health care during the 2000s: privatization in the primary care sector, the strengthening of patient rights and re-centralization of regulatory power. As for the impact of these reforms on the system's overall performance, the evidence is mixed. First, it is often hard to see any direct effect at all, given that there are so many factors aside from the regulation of the system (living standards of the population, socio-economic equality, technological developments, professionals training, etc.) that determine its overall performance. Second, some of the effects of the reforms undertaken in the 2000s may not be fully visible yet. It is also hard to differentiate between developments that have taken place during the 1990s and 2000s, as many of the reforms initiated in the later period originated or were prepared for in the previous decade. Third, to the extent that we can speculate about the effects of regulatory changes undertaken in the recent decade at all, we see some possible effects only in three out of six of the dimensions listed, namely, citizen satisfaction, social equality in access to care services and impact on the workforce in the system. Even in these areas, the impact seems marginal. Citizen satisfaction appears to have improved somewhat, which may be due to improved access through the waiting-time guarantee and primary care choice reform. Working conditions appear to have deteriorated somewhat, which may be related to re-centralization reforms such as the quality registers and Open Comparisons, which place higher administrative demands on the staff. It is also plausible that the increased competitive pressure and stronger financial incentives for productivity has led to higher demands on staff, for instance with regard to patient flows. Impact on social equality in access within the system is hard to assess, but some critics, at least, have argued that both the waiting-time guarantee and the primary care choice reform may undermine this goal as these reforms give an advantage to groups that are skilled in articulating their demands.

With regard to other performance dimensions, such as cost effects and organizational performance, we see no clear effects. Other, more basic regulatory features of the system, such as the ability to control budgets and plan the infrastructure by local authorities, appear much more important in this regard. The last indicator, the capacity of the system to generate improved health, also appears largely unaffected by the regulatory changes during the 2000s. Measured as quality indicators for various medical diagnoses, this capacity has been quite high in the Swedish system for several decades and seems more likely related foremost to other factors, such as general living standards of the Swedish population and the efficient dissemination of medical knowledge within the system.

Citizens' satisfaction and perceived quality over time

International comparisons show that patients' satisfaction with *quality* of care is very high in Sweden. In a European study respondents were asked to evaluate the overall quality of the health care in their country. Ninety per cent of the Swedish citizens were satisfied with Swedish health care. Only citizens in Finland, Belgium and Austria rated their health care higher (91, 97 and 95 per cent, respectively). On average, 70 per cent of citizens in the EU countries were satisfied with their care which is considerably lower compared to Sweden (Eurobarometer 2010). Another EU study validates the results: 90 per cent of Swedes think that the quality of hospital care is 'fairly' or 'very good' (Eurobarometer, 2007). When it comes to *access* to care, Swedish citizens have been less satisfied. A comparative study of five European countries conducted in 2007–2008 showed that Sweden performed significantly poorer than the other countries on this measure. For instance, one third of the citizens found it difficult to get access to hospital care. An even larger group of the population found it difficult to get access to a generalist, that is, primary health care. This was a significantly higher number than in the other studied countries (UK, France, Germany and Denmark) (Or et al., 2010). There are also indications that Swedes are somewhat less satisfied than patients in other comparable health care systems with patient *responsiveness*, an indicator which can be understood as measuring how patients experience the service level within the system (Swedish Agency for Healthcare Systems Analysis, 2012: 7).

Improved public satisfaction with the system was, as we could see above, one of the main goals behind the reforms undertaken in Swedish health care in the 2000s. While it is yet too early to evaluate such effects, it can be noted that several recent surveys point to a slight increase (a few percentage) with regard to the general level of satisfaction with the system on the part of the population after 2008 (Winblad et al., 2012). Given that both the waiting-time guarantee and the primary care choice reform did improve access to care for patients in the 2000s, it seems likely that the increase in satisfaction can be due at least in part to these reforms. As we have seen, the primary care choice reform led to a significant increase in the numbers of care providers in the primary care sector after 2010, especially in the bigger cities. Access to care also improved in other ways through the reform, for instance a higher share of citizens now reach primary care health centres within five minutes drive, and waiting times for appointments with GPs decreased significantly (Winblad et al., 2012). After the introduction of the general waiting-time guarantee, waiting times for specialist care in the system decreased significantly in most county councils as well. Evaluations by the National Board of Health and Social Welfare show that 9 out of 10 patients now wait less than three months for treatment, which is a significant improvement in comparison with the period prior to the guarantee (NBHW, 2011). However, there are as yet no studies in Sweden linking patient satisfaction to either the primary care choice reform or the waiting-time guarantee, why it is still too early to draw any firm conclusions regarding the relation between these reforms and the level of satisfaction with the system.

Social inequalities in access to care

Social inequality in access to care has generally not been perceived a big problem in the Swedish system, as it is based on the principle of equal access to care for all on the basis of citizenship. In addition, out-of-pocket payments for Swedish patients are generally low, compared to other

European countries. Even so, several studies have documented that there are persistent inequalities in health care utilization also in Sweden, a phenomena that can be related at least in part to differences in access to care or ability to articulate care needs, between different groups (Anell et al., 2012). In a recent study by the NBHW and the Swedish Institute for Public Health, it was shown that even though life expectancy continued to grow in Sweden during the 2000s due to improved survival of disease, differences between low-educated and high-educated groups increased in the same period (National Board of Health and Welfare and Swedish Institute of Public Health, 2012). The waiting times for care have also been significantly longer in some county councils than others, which can be seen as a form of geographic inequality.

As noted above, access to care in general can be said to have improved in Sweden in the 2000s as a result of the primary care choice reform and the waiting-time guarantee. There are some question marks, however, as to whether these reforms have affected the level of social equality of access negatively. One concern in this regard is whether the newly established primary health care centres, driven foremost by for-profit providers, will establish themselves foremost in more affluent areas. This scenario is made more likely by the fact that some county councils have chosen not to risk-adjust local reimbursement systems in the primary care sector on the basis of socio-economic status. So far, however, there is no conclusive evidence of this sort of geographical cream-skimming through establishment patterns, even if it is evident that most of the new primary care centres are located in the bigger cities. Since 2009, only two health care centres have been started in rural areas (National Competition Agency, 2010). As rural areas tend to have populations with lower levels of education on average, this signals that there is a risk that these groups, at least, will not benefit from improved access to care through the primary care choice reform. There are also some indications that the access of lower socio-economic groups has deteriorated after the introduction of the waiting-time guarantee, as this tends to direct resources to groups with minor health problems who are more likely to exercise their new right to speedy treatment. Such concerns have also been raised by Swedish doctors. In a national survey conducted in 2010, a majority of the orthopaedic doctors stated that they believed that the less-educated, elderly and severely ill tended to be down-prioritized in relation to well-educated patients who were more able to claim their rights to speedy care in adherence to the waiting-time guarantee (Winblad et al., 2012). This points to these reforms having a potentially negative impact on the social equality of access in the system. However, such effects may well be counteracted by the increased political efforts from the central government to reduce differences in the quality of care between the county councils through national quality registers and guidelines.

The impact on the workforce

There is a general lack of information regarding how working conditions in Swedish health care compare with those of other countries. There are, however, some indications that there has been a deterioration of working conditions in the health care sector in the last decade due to heavier workloads and increased stress. This appears to have affected all staff categories, even if the nurses' organizations have been most vocal about it in the public debate. A large survey of doctors comparing working conditions between 1992 and 2010 showed a significant deterioration. A majority of the doctors surveyed stated that they lacked support and feedback from their superiors. Many also felt that they have lost responsibilities and that they have too little time to update themselves with new knowledge in their professional field (Bejerot et al., 2011). The authors of the study concluded that the standardization of work processes had increased in the period, together with levels of monitoring and control, and that the doctors surveyed had to spend an increasing part of their working time on administrative tasks and documentation (ibid.). Another study found that more than half of the female physicians surveyed experienced a stressful work situation and that this share had increased over time. Interestingly, twice as many female doctors as male reported to be suffering from stress and poor working conditions (Parmsund et al., 2009). An important part of the explanation behind these reports of increased stress and deteriorating working conditions can be sought both in the rationalization and staff reductions carried out within the systems during the 1990s, when Sweden experienced an economic downturn, and many county councils implemented significant budget cuts in the health care sector. Even if the financial situation of the county councils improved significantly in the 2000s, many have continued to rationalize the provision of care by trimming staff levels. Furthermore, it cannot be ruled out that the regulatory reforms during the 2000s have added to the deteriorating working conditions of the staff in the health care sector, foremost through the introduction of various national quality registers and open comparisons which lead to increased administrative work at the clinical level in the form of data reporting and standardized work routines. The waiting-time guarantee and patient choice recommendation are other examples of reforms which place a higher administrative burden on the clinics, in addition to the increased pressure to admit and treat patients more quickly. Finally, there is also the increased cost pressure within the system, which comes both from the higher level of competition between care providers and the performance-based reimbursement systems, which tie financial rewards to the clinics more closely to performance and patient flows.

At the same time, the gradual privatization of provision within the system has also increased employment opportunities for medical staff within the Swedish health care system. There are also some indications of a higher level of satisfaction with working conditions among health care staff employed in the private sector. A study from three hospitals in Stockholm showed that staff at the privately operated hospitals perceived the working conditions to be better than those employed in public hospitals. The privately employed doctors felt that it was easier to influence working conditions and were also more satisfied with the leadership (Hellgren et al., 2006).

In sum, working conditions seem to have deteriorated somewhat in Swedish health care in recent years, at least with regard to work-related stress. Although it is hard to draw any firm conclusions about the origins of this development, it seems likely that it can at least in part be attributed to reforms in recent decades which have led to reductions in staffing levels and an increased administrative workload for doctors. A more positive impact of recent reform could be an improvement in working conditions for privately employed staff, even if their share is still relatively small compared to those who remain in public employment (over 90 per cent).

Economic performance

It is hard to see any direct effects of the regulatory reforms introduced in the Swedish health care during the 2000s on the overall economic performance of the system. Key economic performance indicators such as efficiency and cost containment show no clear signs of impact. This is not to say that such effects may not become visible in the future, for instance with regard to the continuing privatization of care provision within the system, which may well lead to increased costs, especially if patient access continues to be improved.

The overall impression of the economic performance of the Swedish system in 2013 is that it is relatively strong – with regard to both cost levels and the capacity for cost containment – and that this characteristic has not been affected in the last decade. The general efficiency of the system is testified to by the fact that it provides high-quality care while cost levels are average, as compared to other European countries. In 2010, Sweden devoted 9.6 per cent of its GDP to the health care sector. This is lower than France and Germany, but slightly higher than the UK, Norway and Finland. Health care costs as a percentage of GNP rose in Sweden from 8.3 in 1999 to 9.6 in 2010 (OECD health data, 2011), but this reflected an open promise on part of the national government to increase the expenditure on health care in the beginning of the 2000s, a decision which led to a substantive increase in state grants to the county councils after 2005. Many country counties chose to increase their spending levels during the 2000s as well, reflecting a general improvement in the Swedish economy during this period. Compared to other countries, the rate of cost increases during the 2000s were, however, been relatively modest (Anell et al., 2012; see also Figure 1.1). The deteriorating working conditions in the health care sector was recently confirmed by a report from the Swedish Work Environment Authority (*Arbetsmiljöverket*), which pointed to the role of bed shortages within hospitals as a source of staff stress (Swedish Work Environment Authority, 2012).

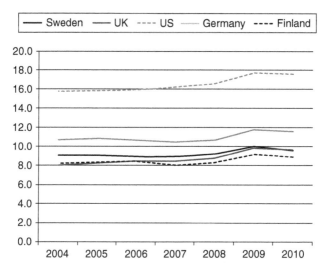

Figure 1.1 Health care costs as percentage of GNP (2004–2010)
Source: OECD health data (2011)

Looking into expenses at the county council level, these increased marginally in the 2000s. According to the Swedish Association of Local Authorities and Regions, the average level of increase during the period has been two per cent per year, a level of increase which corresponds well with the level of increase in demand which could be expected given demographic changes (SALAR, 2010). In 2010, the level of cost increase was suppressed again as an effect of the economic crisis in 2008/2009, a fact which testifies to the ability of the county councils to control spending levels and adjust them in response to changes in their external environment. Evaluations show, furthermore, that the primary care choice reform, in spite of having led to a significant increase in the number of care providers as well as number of visits to doctors after 2009, has so far not resulted in general cost increases within the county councils (Rehnberg et al., 2009; 2010).

The relatively high capacity for cost containment in the Swedish health care system can be explained mainly by the direct political governance of the system. Decisions on spending are made locally by the county councils. If costs are increasing, the county councils can reduce them by adjusting the budget for the following year. The system's capacity for cost containment has been demonstrated several times in the last decades. One example is the financial crisis in the beginning of the 1990s when the central government reduced state grants to the county councils and imposed a local tax freeze, which prohibited them from raising local taxes. The county councils responded by rationalization measures like cutting the number of hospital beds, reducing staffing levels and closing several smaller hospitals. In the beginning of the 2000s, when the financial situation improved, both the central government and the county councils increased health care spending levels again, only to return to a higher level of constraint when the new economic recession hit in 2008. This variation in spending levels in relation to economic conditions in the overall economy shows that the system is capable of adjusting spending levels when needed (even if the costs might be felt by both staff and patients, for instance in the form of increased waiting times) and that the interplay between the central and local levels of the system functions relatively well in this regard. Possibly, the primary care choice reform presents a certain challenge, in that it restricts the ability of the county councils to control the establishment of the health care centers. Still, the county councils are able to control the spending levels through the design of local payment systems.

Organizational performance

Organizational performance is another area where there are no obvious effects of the regulatory reforms carried out in the system in the 2000s. The structure and organization of the provision of care was reformed already in the 1990s in many county councils, which then undertook substantive rationalization measures in response to the economic crisis during this time (Anell, Glenngård & Merkur, 2012). Examples of such measures are hospital closings, a concentration of specialties to certain localities and reduction of hospital beds. The reduction of beds was carried out through several different measures such as reductions in the length of stay, investments in home-based care and a shift from in-patient to out-patient (day) surgery. As a result of these rationalizations within care provision, Sweden has today a substantially lower level of in-patient care than most other European countries. For instance, the number of hospital beds per capita is considerablly lower in Sweden than in Denmark (2.2 versus 3.1 per 1000 habitants) and Germany, where the corresponding level is 6.2 (Or et al., 2010). Some critics have argued that the bed reductions went too far, resulting in a severe shortage of beds in many hospitals in the country, particularly in the bigger cities (Swedish Medical Association, 2002). In part, these rationalizations have continued during the 2000s, albeit at slower pace. In some cases they have been met with open protests by staff and local citizens.

It should be noted, however, that even if the number of beds were significantly reduced in Sweden in the 1990s, the country still has an over-representation of specialized care as witnessed in the fact that the ratio between hospital doctors and GPs is still 3:1 in Sweden, which is higher than in several other comparable countries. The primary care choice reform does not yet appear to have affected this ratio more than very marginally, even if its full effect may not yet show.

In sum, most changes in the organizational structure of the Swedish system were introduced already in the 1990s, foremost in the form of local-level rationalizations in order to meet cost pressures. One effect of these was to shift resources from the system from in-patient care to out-patient care, a process which has continued in the 2000s through on-going restructuring efforts at the local level as well as new establishments of primary care providers, a measure that can be regarded as improving the organizational performance of the systems in the sense of increasing the number of visits per doctor in primary care (Anell, Glenngård & Merkur, 2012). Apart from this, however, there appears to be no clear effect of the reforms in the 2000s such as re-centralization and the strengthening of patient rights on the organizational performance of the system.

Capacity of the system to improve health

In international comparison, the Swedish system performs relatively well with regard to quality. Sweden is consistently ranked among the top countries when performance on basis medical quality indicators such as neo-natal mortality, life expectancy or survival in common forms of cancer, is compared (OECD health data, 2011). A study in which Sweden was compared with four other countries also showed that Sweden, together with France, rated the best on several different quality indicators. For instance, Sweden had the lowest neo-natal mortality rate (1.8 per cent per 1000 live births) and the highest five-year survival rate for breast cancer (Or et al., 2010).

What speaks against an impact on this performance of the regulatory reforms introduced during the 2000s is that there has been a gradual improvement on most health quality indicators for some time in Sweden, with no disruption or significant change in this decade. Statistics show that neonatal mortality has improved in Sweden since the end of the 1980s. In 1989 the mortality rate was 3.7 per 1000 live births. In 1999 the same number was 2.2 and, in 2008, 1.7 (OECD data, 2010). Following the same reasoning, life expectancy at 65 years has increased remarkably since 1989. In 1989 the life expectancy was 15.4, a figure that increased to 16.4 years in 1999 and to 18.2 in 2009. The survival in cancer after five years has also gradually improved in Sweden after the late 1999s. Taken together, quality indicators show steady improvement over time. Thus, it is dubious whether the reforms during the 2000s can explain these improvements. Whether the national guidelines and quality registers introduced in Sweden during this decade have had an effect on these quality measures is too early to determine, but this cannot be ruled out. The same pattern of gradual improvements can be seen in many other OECD countries during the same period; it therefore seems more plausible that these improvements in care quality are effects of developments in medical technology rather than organizational reforms.

Conclusions

In this chapter we have described the main regulatory reforms which have been carried out within the Swedish health care system during the 2000s. These reforms include the introduction of primary care patient choice systems on a nation-wide level, the strengthening of patient rights and the attempts to re-centralize some of the regulatory powers within the system. The first two of these reform trends can be said to have moved the system further down the path of gradual liberalization that was set in the 1990s. This is a form of liberalization, or market-conforming regulatory change, that so far has been confined to the provision of health services in the system (through its partial privatization) and the mode of consumption of care services, which can be said to have been oriented more towards individual rights and free choice of provider. The financing structure of the system, resting on local taxation and universal access on the basis of citizenship, has remained unchanged as it enjoys broad political support. It should also be noted that the privatization of provision, which has led to a slowly but steadily increasing share of private providers, has so far occurred mainly in the primary care and out-patient sectors. The third reform trend, re-centralization, implies that the central government has strengthened its control over the system in the last decade, both through its steering activities and its enhanced capacity to monitor outcomes, including medical quality. Taking the full scope of change during the 2000s into consideration, we argue that the reforms introduced amount to only second-order change in Peter Hall's terminology, as their transformative effect on the system as a whole appears limited and can be described as gradual in nature rather than radical or disruptive.

The main driving force behind the regulatory changes described in the chapter is political agency in the form of governmental initiatives. Governments during the period appear to have been driven both by ideological motifs and by pragmatic considerations. The main *ideologically* charged attempt to reform the system can be said to be the introduction of provider choice in the primary care sector in 2010 by a centre-right coalition government. This reform was presented as a way to ensure that private actors were given opportunity to establish themselves in all parts of the country and displayed a strong belief in private entrepreneurship as a means to vitalize the system and improve its care quality. The centre-of-right parties of the coalition government have also forcefully embraced the principle of 'choice' as a means to create a more dynamic and patient-centred system, in both health care and other areas (Blomqvist, 2013). What we would see as more *pragmatic* motives with regard to regulatory changes introduced during the period is foremost the desire to strengthen the legitimacy of the system by making services more accessible to citizens through reducing waiting lines and to monitor quality in order to diminish regional differences in treatment outcomes. These are objectives which have been embraced by both

Left- and Right-wing governments during the period. There has also been a long-standing political concern, by both right- and left-wing governments, to ensure that medical practice throughout the system is based on scientific evidence. During the 2000s, this goal was pursued through national guidelines for medical treatment and priority-setting issued by the National Board of Health and Social Welfare (NBHW). Economic considerations, such as cost reduction or efficiency enhancement, do not appear to have played a large role as motivation for the reforms introduced in the system in the 2000s; on the contrary, both central governments and county councils have tended to increase expenditure in the health care sector during this period, even if there has also been on-going rationalizations at the local and clinical levels.

To assess the impact of all these changes on the system's performance is a delicate task. In this chapter, we argue that we can discern possible effects (although limited) on three dimensions of performance: citizen satisfaction, working conditions for the staff and social equality in access. Citizen satisfaction appears to have improved somewhat, which may be due to the introduction of reforms like the waiting-time guarantee and the primary care choice reform, which both served to improve access to care. Working conditions appear to have deteriorated somewhat during the period, possibly as a consequence of transparency and quality monitoring reforms, which led to medical staff being more burdened with administrative work. Another factor behind this development may be the reduction of staff levels and hospital due to rationalization measures at the local level both in the 1990s and 2000s. The impact on social equality in access within the system – which can generally be said to be high, given the universalistic character of the system, – is hard to assess at this point, but some critics have argued that both the waiting-time guarantee and the primary care choice reform may undermine this value as these reforms are believed to give advantage to groups that are skilled in articulating their demands, such as the highly educated. Leftist critics of the primary care patient choice reform argued at the time of its introduction that it will lead to a tendency of new private providers to establish foremost in affluent areas, as these represent less medical and hence economic risk to these for-profit providers (Fredriksson et al., 2013). So far, this has mostly been evident in the tendency of private care providers to establish themselves foremost in urban regions.

With regard to other performance dimensions, such as economic effects, organizational performance and the ability of the system to improve the health of the population, we see no direct effects of the reforms in the 2000s as of yet, even if such effects cannot be ruled out in the future. When it comes to economic and organizational performance, more basic regulatory features of the system, such as the ability to control budgets and plan the infrastructure by local authorities, appear more important in this regard. As for the capacity of the system to improve population health, it also appears largely unaffected by the regulatory changes during the 2000s. Measured as quality indicators for various medical diagnoses, this capacity has been quite high and steadily growing in the Swedish system for several decades and hence seems more likely related to other factors, such as developments in medical technology, the general standard of living in the Swedish population and the active dissemination of scientific knowledge within the system through the NBHW. The last factor, dissemination of scientific knowledge, has been enhanced by recent reforms like the national quality registers and the introduction of national guidelines to medical professionals, but it seems too early to attribute any distinct quality improvements in the system to these measures even if it seems likely that they might well serve this purpose in the longer run. On the whole, we see the effects of the reforms introduced in the system in the 2000s as being most visible in how it is *governed*, rather than in its performance at this stage, a development which also entails a shift in the power balance between the different actors within the system, where the central government appears to have strengthened its role in relation to the local county councils. Even so, it is clear that the system also retains one of its main strengths, which is the flexibility provided by the cooperation, exchange of knowledge and shifting distribution of power and authority between its central and local levels.

Notes

1. Given that the primary care sector consumes about 20% of the system's total expenditure, a gradual increase in the share of private providers in this area will not more than marginally affect the total share of private provision, which in 2010 amounted to about 10–11 %.
2. More precisely, the Swedish health care system is run by 17 county councils and four regions (Västra Götaland, Skåne, Halland and Gotland).
3. There has never been a legal monopoly on public provision of health care in Sweden: private providers have been free to establish themselves wherever they wanted. However, to receive public funding they need a contract with the county council, which was rarely granted prior to 2010.
4. The first waiting-time guarantee was introduced by the centre-right governing coalition led by Carl Bildt in 1992, only to be followed by a second guarantee in 1997 by a social democratic government. In both cases, the guarantee covered only certain specified diagnoses, which led to undesired crowding-out effects.
5. The exception was emergency care hospitals, the sale of which was prohibited in 2000 through the so-called stop-law (*Stopplagen*).
6. As a result, it overturned the stop-law after being elected in 2006.

2
England: Health Reforms Have Improved the NHS

Seán Boyle

Introduction

Health services in England are largely free at the point of use. The National Health Service (NHS) provides preventive medicine, primary care and hospital services to all those 'ordinarily resident' in England. Over 12 per cent of the population is covered by private medical insurance, which mainly provides access to acute elective care in the private sector.

In this chapter, we provide an account of how the healthcare system has changed over the past 15 years. We observe a pattern of centralization, but with a shift to greater use of the private sector and the development of a more business-oriented approach. The new Conservative/Liberal Democrat coalition government is likely to emphasize this shift. Some observations on the impact of the global economic recession are also included.

We provide a discussion of the reasons for change – to improve quality, efficiency and equity, and highlight the political drivers behind change and discuss how policies were implemented, sometimes in the face of fierce opposition. We go on to provide an analysis of the impact of these changes – looking at economic performance, organizational performance, citizen satisfaction and quality; social inequalities in access to healthcare; the impact of changes on the healthcare workforce; and what has happened to the capacity of the system to improve health. Finally we conclude with a brief remark on the future direction of the NHS.

What has happened in the past 15 years

In this section, we consider the main changes that have taken place in the healthcare system since 1997. The focus is on changes that were introduced by a series of Labour governments from 1997 to 2010. A Conservative/ Liberal Democrat coalition government was elected in May 2010, and it secured the passage of the Health and Social Care Act 2012 on 27 March

2012 (TSO, 2012). The English healthcare system is thus currently in a state of flux, awaiting the outcome of what may be one of the most comprehensive changes to its structure since the introduction of the NHS in 1948.

Although the first decade of the 21st century was a period of change in the NHS, certain basic features remained. Thus far it is still largely dependent on tax funding; responsibility for ensuring access to healthcare rests with central government, and although the private sector role in provision has expanded, the public sector is still the main provider of care. Access to non-emergency hospital care remains under the control of GPs, and there is a clear distinction between purchasing or commissioning and provision, although the nature of both the providing and the purchasing organizations changed considerably and is about to change again. The 2012 Act heralds even greater changes.

The period of reform between 1997 and 2010 saw a mixture of strong central direction alongside the devolution of decision-making away from the centre. At the same time there was a massive expansion in public funding of the NHS: between 1996/97 and 2010/11, net government spending on the NHS in the UK increased from 5.4 per cent to 8.2 per cent of GDP, corresponding to an almost threefold increase in cash terms – from £42.8 billion to £121.3 billion (Harker, 2012).

In its first health White Paper, *The New NHS: Modern, Dependable*, the Labour Government had made it clear that it intended to reform the English NHS fundamentally (Department of Health, 1997). However, its focus initially was on regulation rather than major structural change. Thus, the National Institute for Clinical Excellence (NICE) was established in 1999 with a remit to ensure that treatment decisions were based on the best available clinical evidence. At first NICE directed its attention to the use of new drugs, publishing guidelines on their use and for which patient groups. NICE was soon to develop similar guidelines for other forms of treatment, and in 2005 its role was extended to publication of guidance on the promotion of good health and prevention of ill health (at this time its name was changed to the National Institute for Health and Clinical Excellence, although its acronym remained the same). Although the role of NICE could be characterized as one of restricting access to new drugs on the grounds of insufficient benefit to patients compared with cost, in fact between March 2001 and July 2010 only 39 of 370 technology appraisals resulted in outright refusal (NICE, 2010).

A second key regulatory organization was introduced, the Commission for Health Improvement (CHI), also in 1999. This was subsequently reinvented as the Commission for Healthcare Improvement in 2004 and as the Care Quality Commission (CQC) in 2009. The CQC is responsible for the licensing, monitoring and inspection of all healthcare providers: NHS, private-sector and voluntary-sector. It has enforcement powers to deal with individual providers and also undertakes national reviews of services where there may be concerns about quality and immediate investigations where serious issues arise.

In 1998 the Labour Government introduced a 'national performance assessment' as a way of monitoring service delivery against plans for improvement, using a set of indicators in six dimensions – health improvement, fair access, effective delivery of appropriate care, efficiency, patient and carer experience, and health outcomes of NHS care. These developed over time and were used by government as a way of holding the NHS to account for its use of public resources.

The NHS Plan

The publication of the NHS Plan in 2000 (Department of Health, 2000) signalled the clear intention of the Labour Government to bring about improvements in the NHS. Substantial new money was committed, and the Government set targets for how this extra money should be used. Thus there were to be over 100 new hospitals by 2010 with 7,000 extra beds in hospitals and intermediate care settings. GP premises would be improved and new IT systems introduced linking hospitals and GP surgeries. Substantial increases in staff were planned with 7,500 more consultants (hospital specialists), 2,000 more GPs, 20,000 more nurses and 6,500 extra therapists; 1,000 new medical school places were planned in order to facilitate the increase in number of doctors.

All of this was set within a structure of supreme central direction. The Labour Government was determined to ensure that the extra money was spent in a way that would result in the government's objectives being met. To achieve this, myriad targets were introduced to secure both staff and facilities as required but perhaps more importantly, to guarantee access to care and quality of care where that access was given. The most stringent set of waiting time targets ever contemplated were introduced, covering the overall waiting time from referral by GP to a specialist, to the start of elective treatment. Thus, in 2004, the Government announced an 18-week referral-to-treatment target for all conditions treated by a specialist, to be achieved by the end of 2008. This was an 'end to end' target covering all stages of the care pathway: similar targets had already been set for cancer in the NHS Cancer Plan. The 18-week target covered all delays, including delay related to waiting for diagnosis. The focus on these targets resulted in substantial improvements in performance. By February 2010, almost 98 per cent of non-admitted patients (those found after consultation and/ or investigation not to need treatment) were dealt with within 18 weeks, as were 92 per cent of admitted patients. By December 2009, the median wait for admitted patients was 7.7 weeks; the median wait for non-admitted patients was 4.2 weeks (Department of Health, 2010a).

Similarly, targets were introduced for patients attending an A&E department where waiting was to be limited to a maximum of four hours, and for patients using primary care to be able to see a primary care professional within 24 hours and a GP within 48 hours. These centrally monitored targets continued until the election of May 2010 when a Conservative/Liberal Democrat coalition government came to power promising to remove all unhelpful targets. Thus, the Secretary of State for Health, Andrew Lansley, abolished performance management of what he termed process targets for access to elective care and GP care saying,

> I want to free the NHS from bureaucracy and targets that have no clinical justification and move to an NHS which measures its performance on patient outcomes.
>
> (Press Release, Secretary of State for Health,
> Andrew Lansley, 22 June 2010)

His position stood in somewhat contradictory juxtapose to the accompanying statement that,

> Patients' rights under the NHS Constitution will continue, as will the accompanying legal requirements to ensure that providers are achieving the waiting time rights.
>
> (Department of Health, 2010b)

So rights, not targets, became the name of the game.

Devolution of decision-making

Even though there was this strong centralist tendency at work, the Labour Government, in the words of its NHS Plan, was intent on matching this with 'progressively less central control and progressively more devolution as standards improve and modernisation takes hold'. But how was this apparent contradiction resolved? The Government sought to empower providers in the NHS by creating a market in healthcare – starting with elective care, based on choices made by patients, where the government ensured the framework for those choices existed through the distribution of information about quality and a pricing structure that meant providers could compete for patients. In addition the NHS market was gradually opened up, mainly to the private sector, although some voluntary-sector providers also appeared.

A new framework evolved which has been characterized (Boyle, 2011) as emerging from four types of reform:

- Demand-side reforms, strengthening local commissioners of care and giving users choice and rights

- Supply-side reforms, reducing controls on providers and introducing new providers
- Transactional reforms, primarily financial reforms, that is, new payments systems but also new contractual arrangements
- System management reforms, expanding the role of independent regulators

Demand: commissioning care and patient choice

The Labour Government created new commissioning (purchasing) organizations, Primary Care Trusts (PCTs), which took over from the old district health authorities in commissioning care for geographically defined populations (in May 2010 there were 151 PCTs). These were cast as local organizations, although in practice there was little to distinguish them from their predecessors. Although they were expected to set their own strategic frameworks for commissioning services, this was always within the context of what had been set centrally and was closely monitored and assessed through annual measurement against standards and targets that were also set centrally on the whole.

More fundamental changes were introduced, allowing patients more choice over where they would be treated. In theory, patients were always free to choose a GP within the area in which they lived and were also free to be treated at any hospital in the country, provided their GP was willing to refer them. However, in practice the spectrum of choice has not been as great as this implies. In some areas it has been difficult to obtain a GP, and most patients relied on the GP's choice of hospital for referral, usually without any consultation as to their views.

Expanding patient choice became a key part of government policy under Labour. By January 2006, most patients being referred for planned care could in theory choose from at least four hospitals or clinics. Patients were also increasingly able to choose the date and time of their appointment using an electronic booking system called 'Choose and Book', which enabled GPs and other primary care professionals to book appointments for patients directly from their surgery. In May 2006, the list of choices available to patients was widened to include a national menu of NHS Foundation Trusts and Independent Sector Treatment Centres – known as the Extended Choice Network (Department of Health, 2007a). By April 2008, the patient's choice of hospital was extended to all NHS hospitals and many private-sector hospitals.

Supply: Less controls on providers and the introduction of new providers

Most NHS secondary care in the 1990s was provided by hospital, mental health or community NHS trusts, with a limited but not insignificant amount of use of private-sector providers. In 2003 the Labour Government introduced a new form of organization for hospital services known as NHS

Foundation Trusts (FTs). These had greater scope for raising funds for capital investment than NHS trusts, and they also enjoyed freedom from direct control by the Secretary of State for Health. Instead they became formally accountable to their local populations and, at the same time, they remained subject to national targets, their performance being closely scrutinized by their own regulator, Monitor, who could intervene if financial performance was poor.

The NHS had always made some use of private-sector providers. From 2002 onward, however, the Labour Government began to actively encourage the development of private-sector capacity. Initially claiming this would support achievement of the waiting time targets, the Government began a process of commissioning extra capacity for treatment of elective patients, and for diagnostics from private-sector suppliers in any part of the European Economic Area. As a result of this and subsequent rounds, a number of Independent Sector Treatment Centres (and similar facilities for diagnostics) were established to provide elective operations such as cataract removal, hip and knee joint replacement and heart surgery, in areas where waiting lists and waiting times had been long.

In 2004, the Government introduced legislation that opened the way for private companies to provide GP and related services. In addition, as part of a government-wide initiative to involve the voluntary and non-profit sector in the provision of public services, measures were taken to increase its role in healthcare. Despite an earlier commitment to open up the NHS to 'any willing providers', by late 2009 the Labour Government had backed off this apparent desire to introduce market forces into the NHS, effectively ruling out competitive tendering for services unless NHS performance was poor. However, with the new coalition government came a new set of opportunities for private-sector involvement, as we shall see.

Transactional reforms: New payment and contracting systems

Throughout the 1990s, purchasers contracted with hospitals for services typically using a block contract, which is a fixed payment for a whole service with perhaps some marginal pricing around the edges. From 2003/04 onward, a system known as Payment by Results was introduced, which operated at the level of individual procedures – much like activity-based systems that have developed in other countries. Prices were set in a national tariff determined by the Department of Health. Initially the tariff focused on elective care, but over time its scope was developed to include a greater proportion of hospital services. The tariff was initially set at the average cost of each treatment at NHS hospitals. However, the annual uplift of the tariff (the increase in prices) was kept below the expected rate of inflation so that providers would have an incentive to reduce costs. In addition, modifications were introduced to reward providers for improvements in quality and patient experience.

System management reforms: Expansion of the role of independent regulators

As mentioned earlier, at an early stage in its administration the Labour Government introduced independent regulation though NICE and the CQC as well as a formal system of performance management against a wide range of standards. The main components of a market in healthcare were in place by 2006, providing individuals the capacity to choose from a wider set of possible providers. It was therefore time to issue guidance on how services should be commissioned and providers should behave. A framework for contracting was introduced with the aim of promoting competition while not destroying the co-operative behaviour required to make care networks, such as those introduced for cancer care, work (Department of Health, 2008a). At the same time the Co-operation and Competition Panel was set up to advise on the implementation of the rules in particular cases, for example, when trusts wish to merge or wish to take over a primary care provider. The Panel made independent recommendations to the Department of Health, the regional Strategic Health Authorities (SHAs) and Monitor, on how cases should be resolved. However, the Department of Health was still the system manager. In particular, it determined the level and structure of the national tariff and other financial rules, for example, those determining the financial duties of NHS trusts, although Monitor was responsible for those relating to FTs.

New government, yet more structural reform

As indicated already, major changes are currently under way in the structure of the NHS as a result of a change in government in May 2010. One of the first actions of the new government was to publish a White Paper, *Equity and Excellence: Liberating the NHS* (Department of Health, 2010c), which set out the new Government's vision for the NHS.

After much controversy, protest and bitter political wrangling, the Health and Social Care Act 2012 was passed at the end of March 2012 (TSO, 2012). This introduced changes in five key areas:

- Commissioning care
- Provision – NHS and others
- Public health, local government and patient involvement
- Regulation – Monitor, CQC, NICE
- Duties of the Secretary of State for Health

Commissioning care

The Act set out a new structure for the NHS abolishing PCTs and SHAs from April 2013. Responsibility for local commissioning of healthcare rests with Clinical Commissioning Groups (CCGs) supported and overseen by NHS England that holds CCGs to account. CCGs are statutory corporate bodies mainly consisting of providers of primary medical services, that is, GP contract holders. NHS England is an executive non-departmental public body accountable to the Secretary of State for Health. Its main role is to ensure the NHS delivers better outcomes for patients within its available resources. It also commissions primary care as well as specialized, military, prison and some public health services. NHS England consists of two national offices, four regional offices and 27 local area offices. The Act places a number of duties on the NHSCB and CCGs including ensuring effectiveness, efficiency and quality; reducing inequalities; enabling choice; promoting patient involvement; and promoting the NHS Constitution.

Provision – NHS and others

The Act introduced changes to FTs, removing some restrictions and enabling new governance arrangements, increasing transparency in FT functions, signalling changes to the FT failure regime and enabling the abolition of the NHS trust model at some future date. Thus, all trusts are expected to become FTs although this will not happen by 2014, which was the initial target. Significant changes included that the maximum amount of income that FTs can derive from provision of care to private patients is increased from what was in most cases a relatively small proportion to 49 per cent of total income. However, an increase of more than 5 per cent requires majority approval by the FT's governors; moreover, each FT in its annual report must set out how its non-NHS income has benefited NHS services. FTs are now required to hold board meetings in public and to produce separate accounts for their NHS and privately funded activities. The Act set out arrangements for FTs undergoing organizational change in the event of mergers, acquisitions, separations and dissolutions, and established a new failure regime. Monitor continues to be responsible for oversight of FTs.

The Act specifically encourages the use of new providers through the 'Any Qualified Provider' policy (AQP). This extends patient choice of provider to new services, and from a range of providers – NHS, private-sector and voluntary-sector. Qualified providers must meet NHS service quality requirements, prices and normal contractual obligations. Since April 2012 commissioners have been required to apply AQP to a minimum of three new services. Thus it is intended that choice of provider will go beyond elective surgery to maternity care, care for long-term conditions, community healthcare, mental health and diagnostics. The details for what will happen in the event of failure of a non-NHS provider (that is if the business becomes unsustainable) are yet to be determined.

Public health, local government and patient involvement

Public health, which was part of the NHS, has become the responsibility of local government accountable to the Secretary of State for Health. The Act also introduced Health and Wellbeing Boards that from April 2013 have a duty to encourage integrated commissioning between health, social care and public health by bringing together representatives of those sectors. The Boards will also lead on joint strategic needs assessment, on developing a joint health and wellbeing strategy to inform local commissioning plans and on developing agreements to pool budgets. The Boards will consist of local government officers, representatives of each local CCG, a representative of local HealthWatch (see below) and as many local councillors as they choose. Boards will be accountable to the local authority's Overview and Scrutiny Committee.

The Act placed duties on the NHSCB, CCGs, Monitor and Health and Wellbeing Boards to involve patients, carers and the public. By October 2012, new patient and public bodies, known as local HealthWatch bodies, were commissioned by the local authority and held to account by the local authority's Overview and Scrutiny Committee. These HealthWatch bodies replaced the Local Involvement Networks established under the previous government and act as a point of contact for individuals, community groups and voluntary organizations when dealing with health and social care. They have a representative on the Health and Wellbeing Board. A national body, HealthWatch England, was launched in October 2012 as a statutory committee of the CQC, tasked to support local HealthWatch bodies. It represents people using health services at a national level and has a role in advising the CQC to review services where appropriate. All CCGs have a statutory duty to have regard to the joint strategic needs assessment and joint health and well-being strategy, and will be represented on the Health and Wellbeing Board.

Regulation – Monitor, CQC, NICE

The Act established a joint regulatory regime: the CQC continues in its role as primary arbiter of quality (clinical governance) while Monitor retains its key role in financial governance. In addition, Monitor is responsible for ensuring the working of the market in healthcare as established by the Act. The Act has also imposed a duty of cooperation on both regulators, and they remain accountable to Parliament.

The CQC continues to register and regulate health and adult social care providers to assure quality of care and inspects as appropriate to ensure standards are met. But from April 2013 there has been a joint licensing regime of providers of NHS care. Monitor runs a system of licensing of providers of NHS services, setting and enforcing requirements so as to ensure continued provision of NHS services. It publishes a register of such licence holders. Monitor is also concerned with the prevention of anti-competitive behaviour which is against the interests of patients. However, Monitor is not permitted to set or modify licence conditions purely for the purpose of promoting competition or to encourage the growth of the private sector over existing NHS providers. Likewise it cannot discourage competition nor encourage the growth of NHS providers. Monitor, working with NHS England, is also responsible for regulation of prices for NHS services through a national tariff, and refers disputes for adjudication to the Competition Commission.

NICE became a non-departmental public body with its role extended to include social care. It is now known as the National Institute for Health and Care Excellence (although its acronym remains NICE).

The duties of the Secretary of State for Health

There are changes to the responsibilities of the Secretary of State reflecting the fact that the functions of commissioning services and provision of services are no longer delegated by the Secretary of State but are directly conferred on the organizations responsible for performing them. The Secretary of State's role is to ensure that these functions are carried out effectively. Thus, the Secretary of State for Health is no longer responsible under the Act for the provision of services. However the Act states that the Secretary of State has a duty to promote a comprehensive health service and is accountable to Parliament for the health service. The Secretary of State is held accountable for the system through a new duty to keep under review the effective exercise of functions by the national-level bodies – NHS England, Monitor and the CQC – and to report annually on the performance of the health service. The Secretary of State also has direct responsibility (with local authorities) to protect and improve public health.

The Secretary of State must publish and present to Parliament a document to be known as 'the mandate' before the start of each financial year. This must set out what the Government expects from NHS England for that period, comprising a series of objectives relating to the current financial year and such subsequent financial years as the Secretary of State considers appropriate. In this way NHS England has a single annual set of objectives and requirements, allowing it to develop effective medium- and long-term planning assumptions.

The impact of the recession on NHS finances

The world is in the grip of a global recession. Tax revenues had increased steadily over the previous ten years, but the UK saw a fall in tax revenue (in cash terms) from £547 billion in 2007/08 to £513 billion in 2009/10. Revenue increased to £551 billion in 2010/11 and is forecast to increase to £624 billion by 2013/14. Government spending in real terms (at 2011/12 prices) increased from £644 billion in 2007/08 to £706 billion in 2009/10 (due in the main to increased debt charges and spend on social security as the recession began to bite). Government expenditure is forecast to fall back to £687 billion by 2013/14 (Institute of Fiscal Studies, 2012a; 2012b).

The result has been a sharp fall in the rate of increase in public funding for the NHS and this has had an impact on the delivery of NHS services. NHS spending in real terms (at 2010/11 prices) increased from £92.4 billion in 2007/08 to £102.5 billion in 2009/10, but in 2010/11 it fell back to £102 billion, and it was forecast to increase to just £103.7 billion by 2014/15 (Harker, 2012).

At the same time the Department of Health requires all NHS bodies to make substantial efficiency savings, thus:

> To meet the rising costs of healthcare and increasing demand on its services, the NHS will release up to £20 billion of annual efficiency savings over the next four years, all of which will be reinvested.
>
> (Department of Health, 2010d)

A two-year public sector pay freeze was in place for 2011/12 and 2012/13, to be followed by a further cap on public sector pay of 1 per cent per year for the next two years. This represents a substantial decrease in real income for the NHS workforce. But it has also provided an opportunity to reduce expenditure as pay is a large proportion of overall NHS costs.

The Audit Commission noted,

> The total efficiency savings as reported by PCTs, NHS trusts and FTs in 2010/11 is £4.3 billion... . Some of the savings were non-recurrent. Most of the NHS trust and PCT savings have been made through clinical productivity and efficiency, pay and workforce savings.
>
> (Audit Commission, 2011)

Overall, PCTs, NHS trusts and SHAs in 2010/11 reported a surplus of £1.5 billion, about 1.5 per cent of NHS resources (Audit Commission, 2011). The NHS Chief Executive in his annual report claimed the NHS has made further efficiency savings of £5.8 billion in 2011/12. In addition, there was a surplus of almost £1.6 billion (Nicholson, 2012).

So actual NHS expenditure has come in at less than initially planned. These surpluses can be explained partly by the fact that the budgets of PCTs were top-sliced by 2 per cent to cover non-recurrent expenditures in 2011/12; there was a similar requirement in 2012/13. In addition, there have been year-on-year reductions in NHS tariffs of 1.5 per cent, and of course the pay freeze. The NHS is certainly feeling the squeeze.

Summary

The changes that took place under successive Labour governments reflected their natural centralizing tendencies but were combined with a desire to set the various actors in the healthcare system free to choose among competing demands on resources to meet a range of healthcare needs. There was certainly some movement toward increased use of the private sector for provision although responsibility for paying most healthcare costs remained firmly with the government. There is no doubt that the system became more business-like with an increased emphasis on management, on financial probity and on costs; at the same time efforts to rein in the power of the medical profession met with little success and although the rhetoric of consumer/patient choice was writ large, the reality on the ground was somewhat different.

The changes that will take effect under the Conservative/Liberal Democrat Government may follow a similar pattern although the overall result looks like being one of more decentralization, more privatization and a more business-like approach resulting in a transfer of power to those managing the system, or perhaps we should say business.

Why have changes happened?

The Labour Government came to power in 1997 with a commitment to improve the delivery of NHS care, to be achieved through an increased focus on quality. Prior to 1997 there had been 18 years of continuous Conservative government. This had seen a shift in the overall focus of the NHS from one of local administration of a range of health services to a more managerial approach introduced as part of the enactment of the Griffiths Report (Griffiths, 1983). This was followed in the 1990s by a fundamental change in the structure of the NHS with the implementation of the NHS and Community Care Act 1990, separating for the first time the commissioning and delivery of healthcare services, thereby introducing the 'internal market'. The NHS became a system based on a series of contracts between purchasers and providers of NHS healthcare. The intention was to increase efficiency through competition between providers (Oliver, 2005).

But the new Labour Government was confronted with an NHS where the quality of care remained poor, especially in terms of easy-to-measure items such as waiting times, where there seemed to be widespread inefficiencies in delivery, where too much care was delivered in old buildings with a lack of modern facilities and equipment, and where there were wide disparities in access to care and its quality across the country. It is this that the Labour Government set out to remedy in 1997. It became clear more money was a prerequisite: considerably higher levels of expenditure were required if the NHS in England was to match the performance of other high-spending countries in Europe and the rest of the world. Over much of the period of Conservative rule, NHS expenditure had increased in real terms at less than the historical average rate – since 1950/51 there was an average annual increase in NHS expenditure in the UK of 3.8 per cent (Harker, 2012).

One crucial driver of change was the desire to improve the quality of care. A key Labour election pledge in opposition was to deal with the issue of access to elective care: there were long waiting lists with over one million people waiting for treatment by March 1997 and with people waiting anything up to two years. Various past initiatives had failed – mainly because of lack of resourcing. At the same time there was evidence that the quality of healthcare was not good, with various critical reports published prior to 1997 by the Audit Commission, the National Audit Office, the Clinical Standards Advisory Groups and others. But these tended to be one-off reports. There was little in the way of regular publication of information on the quality of healthcare provided by the NHS and how this varied across the country. Moreover where there was information it was not usually open to examination by the public at large.

Efficiency has always been a consistent concern for the NHS and was a driving force behind the reforms introduced by the Conservatives during their 18 years in charge. Labour's first health White Paper suggested this would be no less an important consideration, urging the promotion of,

> ...efficiency through a more rigorous approach to performance and by cutting bureaucracy so that every pound in the NHS is spent to maximise the care for patients.
>
> (Department of Health, 1997)

Often this was equated with a shift in care from 'expensive' acute hospitals to care in primary and community settings – a change in the balance of use of resources – although a convincing case was rarely made for how this would produce efficiency savings. Nevertheless improved efficiency was a second key driver of change.

A third driver of change was the recognition that the NHS was still not a genuinely national service delivered in a fair and equitable way throughout England. There were considerable variations in both quantity and quality of care between different parts of the country, between urban and rural areas, and between different groups of population. This was nowhere more obvious than in health outcomes and their determinants with vast differences in, for example, life expectancy between different parts of the country and between different socio-economic classes. For many people this was the issue that the NHS had been created to address and so far it had singularly failed to do so.

This then was the context in which the Labour Government set about changing the NHS. As discussed earlier, a new government came to power in 2010 with if anything a more radical set of proposals for overhauling the structure of the NHS. The rationale behind the changes – at least as stated in the Government's White Paper (Department of Health, 2010c) – was strangely familiar: to improve outcomes, to allow patients more choice, to increase the autonomy of healthcare providers and to cut bureaucracy in the NHS. We await the results of these changes which only began to be implemented in April 2013.

How have changes taken place?

Over the last 60 years or so, the impetus for the introduction of major structural change to the NHS has been largely political. Other stakeholders – clinicians, healthcare trade unions, patients, the public, healthcare businesses, financiers – while perhaps partially influencing the direction of change, and at times resisting strongly the proposals of politicians, were never the key driver. Moreover it has tended to be the central government, not local, that has brought about the major shifts observed. That is not to say that certain changes to individual elements of the way healthcare was delivered were not primarily driven by other groups; for example, clinical input into the development of systems of stroke care, the input of financiers and business into the development of the Private Finance Initiative.

The Labour Government that came to power in 1997 was committed to improve the delivery of NHS care. Labour's manifesto, *New Labour because Britain deserves better* (Labour Party, 1997), promised that Labour in government would,

> safeguard the basic principles of the NHS .... but will not return to the top-down management of the 1970s. So we will keep the planning and provision of healthcare separate, but put planning on a longer-term, decentralised and more co-operative basis. The key is to root out unnecessary administrative cost, and to spend money on the right things - frontline care.

Labour promised 'integrated care, based on partnership and driven by performance', rejecting both the 'command and control system' of the 1970s and the market system of the 1990s. A number of pledges on the NHS were made including: reducing the number of people on NHS waiting lists by 100,000; ending the internal market; ensuring people did not wait for cancer surgery; introducing quality targets for hospitals; and increasing expenditure in real terms every year with a promise that the money would be spent on patients not bureaucracy. In addition Labour promised a new drive to promote public health.

In its first two years in power, the Labour Government set about producing the changes that had been promised. With a substantial majority in Parliament, and the support of many of the professional bodies, this should not have been a difficult task. As remarked upon already, new regulatory organizations aimed at improving quality, NICE and CHI, were established in 1999. In addition, national service frameworks were introduced to:

- Set national standards and define service models for a specific service or care group
- Put in place programmes to support implementation
- Establish performance measures against which progress within an agreed timescale would be measured

New waiting time targets were set for people with suspected cancers. In 1999 the Labour Government introduced targets – to be achieved by 2010 – for mortality from coronary heart disease and stroke, cancer, mental illness and accidents. Local health authorities were required to produce plans to reduce inequalities in health; the NHS Plan in 2000 announced the government's intention to set a national target for reducing the gap in infant and early childhood mortality and morbidity between socio-economic groups and to target inequalities later in life.

But none of this provided a quick fix that would achieve the Labour Government's key goals: improvements to quality, efficiency, equity and the devolution of decisions to local bodies while retaining overall strategic oversight. The promise to increase real expenditure was almost meaningless given that real expenditure on the NHS had only fallen twice in the previous 25 years. It was soon evident that what was required was a major boost to spending on the NHS, and this is what was promised in a memorable pledge (delivered on a Sunday morning TV programme) by the Prime Minister, Tony Blair, in January 2000, that there would be increases in real expenditure of 5 per cent per annum over the following 5 years which would bring UK spend up to the EU average (Guardian, 17 January 2000).

But if there was going to be such a large increase in expenditure then the Government wanted to be sure that this money would not be wasted: this is reflected in the production of the NHS Plan later in 2000. As discussed earlier, the period between 2000 and 2007 was one that combined increased central control with the establishment of a framework for delivery that allowed increasing autonomy to providers of healthcare. The result was some improvement – as we discuss later – but whether there was one driving force behind this improvement, or several, is not clear.

If we consider improved access, the increase in NHS expenditure was probably crucial. It allowed a substantial increase in the number of operations and diagnostic tests performed (Harrison and Appleby, 2009). Between 1998/9 and 2008/09, the total number of elective procedures in hospitals went from 5.4 million to 7 million with growth in some procedures much greater: cataracts 73 per cent, hip replacement 47 per cent and PTCAs 227 per cent (Information Centre, 2010). From 1998/99 to 2009/10, the number of MRI scans quadrupled from just over 0.5 million to almost 2 million and CT scans almost trebled from 1.25 million to 3.72 million (Department of Health, 2010d). But, active performance management by the Department of Health combined with targets was also important. It ensured that every senior NHS manager or clinician was aware that the targets had to be met, and they were.

The targets for GP access were also supported by an increase in resources. The number of GPs, particularly in areas that were under-doctored, was increased substantially. By 2009, 50 new GP-led health centres were open, and there were 65 new practices in areas that previously did not have enough doctors. In addition, financial incentives were offered to GPs to open for longer hours. By July 2009 more than 77 per cent of practices had agreed to open longer at evenings or weekends compared to 38 per cent the year before (Department of Health, 2008c; 2009). Ease of access was also promoted through a programme of walk-in centres in high streets or at transport hubs for those, particularly those in work, who might find conventional opening hours inconvenient.

Quality on the other hand was a trickier issue. Labour had set some of the foundations for improvement through more visible regulation. Previously NHS organizations were required to adopt processes that would ensure financial probity, but now the concept of clinical governance came to the fore – with the expectation that NHS managers would also be responsible for the quality of services delivered. The Government also set out to improve the quality of care provided by the individual professional. The scandals arising at the Bristol Royal Infirmary (Bristol Royal Infirmary Inquiry, 2001) and the behaviour of individual clinicians such as Harold Shipman (Smith, 2004) led to the White Paper, *Trust, Assurance, and Safety* (Department of Health, 2007b), which made a large number of recommendations designed to reduce the chances of such events recurring. Some were implemented quickly, for example, the re-structuring of the General Medical Council (GMC); others were slow, for example, the proposal that all health professionals should be subject to a process of revalidation was not implemented by the GMC until December 2012.

As government policy developed, quality remained at its core, and many of the targets that were established in this period reflected this. Nevertheless, for all the rhetoric about quality, safety issues remained. Thus, for example, it was claimed Stafford general hospital had excessive mortality levels – up to 400 extra deaths – between 2005 and 2009 (The Mid-Staffordshire NHS Foundation Trust Inquiry, 2010). When Darzi carried out his review of the NHS for government, he found '…unacceptable and unexplained variations in the clinical quality of care in every NHS region' (Department of Health, 2008b).

Labour also introduced a raft of polices designed to ensure an NHS that was more responsive to the needs of patients, and to use resources more appropriately and in a more efficient manner. These are often referred to as the introduction of choice and competition although in fact neither of these was new to the NHS. What was perhaps new was the increased emphasis given to both by Labour policies, plus the apparent freedom given to provider organizations to pursue what appeared to be market strategies. But the overall aim remained to provide quality care to patients in an efficient way. This was never going to be an easy task. Once again there were some improvements – as we discuss later – but it is impossible to attribute these to one factor above another.

These 'market-orientated' changes did not go unopposed. There was debate within the Labour party itself, and opposition from professional bodies, trade unions and commentators who saw these as the thin end of a privatization wedge (Kmietowicz, 2003, Unison, 2003; 2007).

But this was as nothing compared to the furore stirred by the Health and Social Care Act 2012, introduced by the Conservative / Liberal Democrat Government, that finally passed into legislation in March 2012. Part of the problem was that most people do not seem to have expected another round of radical changes to the NHS. As McLellan et al. (2012) noted,

> The Coalition Agreement ... focused on clinical leadership and patient and public empowerment ... was generally well received by those now at daggers drawn with the reforms. But through a combination of poor political judgment and reluctance to engage with criticism, a set of (mostly) reasonable objectives morphed into an old fashioned top down reorganisation. This was the very thing the agreement had pledged to avoid. It also resulted in a bloated and opaque piece of legislation, the goals of which could have largely been achieved by other, more effective, means.

Some professional groups opposed the changes almost from the outset. By the time of the Bill's final passage through Parliament, there was little support for it among the public and probably less among health professionals. Even political colleagues of the Secretary of State for Health, Andrew Lansley, may have wished it away. Nevertheless the Government's majority in Parliament saw the Bill pass, and we now wait as the consequences unfold.

The impact on the performance of the healthcare system

In this section we consider the impact of the Labour Government's reforms on the performance of the healthcare system considering six key dimensions:

- Economic performance
- Organizational performance

- Citizen satisfaction and perceived quality
- Social inequalities in access to healthcare
- Impact on the healthcare workforce
- Capacity of the system directly to improve health

It is too early to pass judgment on the reforms of the current government.

Economic performance

First, taking economic performance, we consider how efficient the system has been in managing expenditure, looking at productivity as our measure. However, measuring overall increases in productivity in the NHS is no easy matter given the lack of prices for most services produced. Prior to 2004, a simple measure of health output was used which reflected movements in 16 different activities or services (including inpatients, day cases, outpatients, GP consultations, and prescriptions) with the aggregate index being a simple weighting based on how much was spent on each activity – a cost-weighted activity index. However, this was not comprehensive and each individual series was at a high level of aggregation. There has been a concerted attempt across government to improve the measurement of public sector productivity, resulting in considerable changes to measurement as well as attempts to include measures of quality in addition to simple output.

According to recent official measures, which include an element for quality improvements in output, NHS output in the United Kingdom[1] increased rapidly between 1997 and 2008, at over 4.5 per cent per annum, but less rapidly than the increase in inputs used to produce it, which increased by almost 4.75 per cent per annum. The result, as Figure 2.1 shows, is that NHS productivity as a whole fell over this period by an average of over 0.2 per cent per annum. Productivity fell sharply in 2002 and 2003 with the only significant increase happening in 2006. Productivity declined again in 2007 and 2008 and remains 2.7 percentage points below its level in 1997 – see Figure 2.1 (Phelps et al., 2010).

This fall in productivity is primarily due to a central failure to control costs, particularly pay costs. Input costs rose by over 25 per cent in four years alone, between 2001 and 2005.

Peñaloza et al. (2010) suggest that quality adjustments accounted for an average of 0.6 percentage points growth a year in output between 1995 and 2008 (0.66 between 2002 and 2009). Without this adjustment the decline in productivity would have been even greater. These adjustments relate mainly to improvements in acute hospital care: short-term survival rates, health gain following treatment in hospital, and impact on health gain as a result of changes in waiting times for health treatment. There are also some small gains associated with improved outcomes in primary care and the results of patient experience surveys.

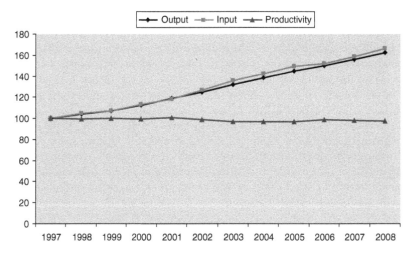

Figure 2.1 Changes in NHS productivity in the United Kingdom (1997–2008)
Source: Phelps et al. (2010).

More recent research by Bojke et al. (2012) suggests NHS productivity in England has been more or less constant over the seven years between 2003/4 and 2009/10, increasing by an average of just 0.1 per cent per year. Inputs have increased in this period: the number of staff by 18 per cent, buildings and equipment by 24 per cent and all other inputs, such as clinical supplies and energy costs, by 76 per cent. But there has been a corresponding increase in both the quantity and quality of output. Growth in activity and changes in quality have matched the growth in inputs, implying that the NHS is operating more or less at a point of constant returns to scale.

Organizational performance

In this section we consider how well the system used the extra resources that were made available during this period in terms of allocation of resources between different sectors – for example, was there a movement of care out of hospital into the community – and how technically efficient production was. By 2010 the Government had succeeded in making major improvements to the hospital capital stock and also in increasing the workforce. However, the attempt to shift resources away from hospitals to community-based services appears to have had only limited success with the exception of mental health where the balance was successfully changed from inpatient to community care.

Allocation of resources

The Government made various attempts to change the way resources were used but the evidence for any change in direction being more efficient, for example, from hospital to community settings is quite limited. A number of policies were introduced that were designed to promote easier access, some of which resulted in shifts in the balance of care between sectors. However, the changes in allocations that have taken place at best reflect a series of unrelated initiatives rather than a single plan to bring about a different set of allocations to those prevailing in 1997. Moreover, despite these government efforts, historical distributions of resources have tended to dominate.

In addition, often it is unclear or unknown what the 'true' purpose of government policy has been. For example, the shift of care from acute to community settings has long been a policy of successive governments. This may result in improvements in allocative efficiency if the delivery of care in the community is seen to be an improvement and therefore more valuable; but it may also be viewed as a more technically efficient way of delivering the same service, that is, if community provision is known to be cheaper.

Technical efficiency

Although the Government succeeded in reducing some of the input costs of healthcare delivery, for example, cost per drug item, it failed to do so overall, primarily because of its failure to control pay costs and to use its staff, particularly medical staff, more effectively. Thus, as we note later, there were substantial increases in wages and salaries so that a large proportion of the increase in financial resources was consumed by higher input costs. Similarly, the investment in hospital facilities through PFI has resulted in increased capital input costs.

There have been changes in the way that services are delivered – for example, increased day case rates, but many of these are simply following a well-established trend. The average daily number of available acute hospital beds fell in England from 121,170 in 1989/90 to 100,621 in 2009/10. At the same time, there was an increase in activity shown by an increase in hospitalization per head of population, that is, hospital utilization rates. Hospitals have coped with increased activity within a reduced bed stock through three factors: increased occupancy of existing beds; reduced stays in hospital, that is, lengths of stay; and an increase in the number of patients who do not need an overnight stay, that is, are treated as day cases. Thus there was an increase in the number of day case procedures performed so that 73 per cent of elective procedures were day cases in 2008/09, combined with a falling length of stay for patients admitted (in 2008/09 the length of stay for emergency patients was 3.3 days and that for elective inpatients was 3.0 days) and an increase in the acute bed occupancy rate from 79 per cent in 1996/97 to 86 per cent in 2008/09 in English NHS hospitals (Boyle, 2011).

Citizen satisfaction and perceived quality

The Labour Government aimed to secure year-on-year improvements in patient satisfaction as measured by independently audited surveys. This was achieved in the period between 2000 and 2010; although satisfaction fell dramatically in 2011.

Satisfaction with the NHS has been measured as part of official government surveys for many years, as well as one-off surveys from time to time. The Labour Government decided that there should be regular surveys of public and patient satisfaction with the NHS in general, and with particular services, so as to assess how well the NHS was doing overall. Thus, since 2004 there has been a centrally run programme of patient surveys covering a range of areas including hospital services, maternity services, ambulance services, local health services (GPs and dentists) and mental health services. Surveys on the experiences of people using healthcare services commissioned by the NHS were coordinated by the CQC.

In a review of NHS performance, the King's Fund reported that overall satisfaction with the NHS, based on data from the British Social Attitudes Survey, increased between 1997 and 2007 from 35 per cent to 51 per cent (Thorlby and Maybin, 2010). Using more recent data from the same survey, Appleby (2011) has shown satisfaction continued to increase to 59 per cent in 2008 and 64 per cent in 2009. He also showed that satisfaction with individual parts of the NHS had increased. Between 1999 and 2009, satisfaction with outpatient care increased from 56 per cent to 68 per cent, with A&E care from 53 per cent to 59 per cent, and with GP care from 76 per cent to 80 per cent, although satisfaction with dental care fell from 53 per cent to 48 per cent, and inpatient care was more or less unchanged at 57 per cent. The 2010 survey showed overall satisfaction reached 70 per cent, its highest level ever. Research by Boyle et al. (2010) suggested patients were also broadly satisfied with services provided by their GPs.

Table 2.1 shows that in 2009, 92 per cent of people who had been inpatients in NHS hospitals in England believed the quality of care they had received was good, very good or excellent: this proportion has hardly changed since 2002. In fact, there has been an increase in the proportion of people that rate their care as excellent, from 38 per cent to 44 per cent.

Table 2.1 How acute hospital inpatients in England rated quality of care (2002–2009)

	2002	2005	2006	2007	2008	2009
Excellent	38%	40%	41%	42%	43%	44%
Very good	36%	37%	36%	35%	35%	35%
Good	17%	15%	15%	14%	14%	13%
Fair	7%	6%	6%	6%	5%	5%
Poor	2%	2%	2%	2%	2%	2%

Note: Based on surveys of acute hospital inpatients in the above years.
Source: Care Quality Commission (2010).

Since 2009 the NHS has been collecting patient-reported outcome measures (PROMs) for four hospital procedures: hip replacement, knee replacement, hernia repair and varicose vein surgery. Although these may give some indication of the patient's perception of quality, they have not been collected for long enough to be used as an indicator of change.

Social inequalities in access to healthcare

Income inequality as measured by the Gini coefficient on a 0–100 scale increased in the UK between 1994/95 and 2009/10, from 37 to 40 (Department for Work and Pensions, 2011). In this section we consider how well the system avoids differences among citizens in access to healthcare on the basis of their income, gender, race or where they live, for example, rural or urban areas, or more economically developed areas or poorer areas.

First we consider measures of life expectancy before going on to consider access. The Labour Government announced two national health inequality targets in 2001:

- For children under one year: By 2010 to reduce by at least 10 per cent the gap in infant mortality between manual groups and the population as a whole
- for health authorities: By 2010 to reduce by at least 10 per cent the gap between the fifth of areas with the lowest life expectancy at birth and the population as a whole (Department of Health, 2001)

However, it looks like these inequality targets have been missed as the relative gap in both male and female life expectancy widened from the baseline year (1995–97), by 2 per cent and 11 per cent, respectively. Similarly, the gap in infant mortality is wider than that recorded at the 1997–99 baseline year.

There are significant differences in life expectancy at birth across the social classes. Although there have been improvements in life expectancy across all social classes since 1972, the gain in life expectancy at birth between 1972–76 and 2002–05 for the professional class exceeded that of the unskilled by 1.9 years for men and 2.2 years for women. Also for women, taking the more recent period between 1987–91 and 2002–05, the gap, by social class, in life expectancy gained, was 2.5 years whereas for men the position is reversed with the gain in life expectancy for the unskilled just exceeding that of the professional class.

Access

The budget mechanism used by the Department of Health to allocate funds to local areas is based on an approach known as 'weighted capitation'. This has been developed over a period of over 35 years. The original aim, to address geographical inequities in hospital supply and better match resources to local needs, has since been refined and extended to two objectives: to provide equal access to healthcare for people at equal risk and to contribute to the reduction of health inequalities. A health inequalities factor was included in the allocation formula in 2008.

Although government policy over this period was also concerned with improving outcomes for people from lower socio-economic groups there has been little effective policy directed specifically at ensuring the fair use of resources across such groups, that is, equity of access – and the same applies to other classifications, for example, by ethnicity, age, gender. A review of the literature looking specifically at differences by socio-economic group in use of services in Great Britain found that 'The utilisation of GP services is broadly equitable, but that of specialist services relative to need tends to favour the better off' (Dixon et al., 2007).

The NHS has remained an equitable system as far as financing is concerned, and a commitment to ensuring the equalization of financial resources relative to needs in each part of the country continues. However, the availability of services in different parts of the country continues to be highly variable in ways that could not be justified in terms of variations in the need for care. Moreover, there is little or no evidence that equity in terms of other societal classifications has improved over this period.

Impact on the healthcare workforce

The Government in the NHS Plan promised increases in the number of doctors, nurses and other professionals, and this was achieved during the period to 2008. The terms and conditions (including pay) of medical and nursing staff was largely determined by their respective pay review bodies; moreover pay rises were required to attract people, particularly nurses, into the NHS. The combination of higher staff numbers and higher pay meant that a significant proportion of the increase in NHS resources after 2000 was absorbed by pay costs. Wanless et al. (2007) estimated that 43 per cent of the £43.2 billion cash increase in NHS resources between 2002/03 and 2007/08 was absorbed by higher input costs.

The Government attempted to increase staff productivity by renegotiating their contracts. The consultant contract was renegotiated in the hope that it would lead to better use of consultant time. The GP contract was also renegotiated with the aim of creating a closer link between workload and remuneration. However, the new agreements have been almost entirely ineffective in terms of reducing the cost of the medical inputs to hospital and community care (NAO, 2007).

For around 1.1 million other staff, the pay system was reformed with the aim of making it easier to introduce more efficient and effective working methods worth, it was estimated at the time, a year-on-year increase in productivity of some 1.1 per cent to 1.5 per cent. However, as with medical staff, the National Audit Office (NAO, 2009) has found no evidence of any such gains.

So, in conclusion, during most of this period there was no deterioration in working conditions for healthcare staff in terms of working hours, contracts or workloads, and most enjoyed substantial increases in pay. However, it is ironic that the global economic crisis may succeed in producing cost savings where government policy had found this all but impossible. Thus, although there has been no detailed analysis so far of the impact of the public sector pay freeze on NHS labour costs, it seems likely that a four-year period of low or almost zero wage growth, coupled with a zealous approach to cost-cutting, will substantially reduce costs and may also lead to worse working conditions for NHS staff.

Capacity of the system directly to improve health

We now consider the impact of the healthcare system on the health of the population. First we look briefly at life expectancy, although acknowledging that it is related to many factors beyond the performance of the health-care system. There have been improvements in both male and female life expectancy as Table 2.2 shows. Looking at average annual improvement in life expectancy in the 10 years up to 2001, and in the six years up to 2007, Table 2.2 shows an increase between these two periods in the annual rate of improvement for both men and women. However, looking at healthy life expectancy, the rate of improvement for women has remained static whereas for males, there has been considerable annual improvement – at 0.32 years per annum.

Mortality amenable to healthcare

Although overall improvements in life expectancy cannot be associated only with the healthcare system, there is reasonable evidence that some causes of death are likely to be amenable to medical intervention – for example, breast cancer, pneumonia, abdominal hernia (Nolte and McKee, 2011),

Table 2.2 Average annual change in life expectancy and healthy life expectancy at birth, England (1991–2007)

	1991–2001	2001–2007
	Years	Years
Life expectancy at birth, females	0.17	0.22
Life expectancy at birth, males	0.26	0.28
Healthy life expectancy at birth, females	0.12	0.12
Healthy life expectancy at birth, males	0.08	0.32

Source: Boyle (2011).

and these have formed the basis of several studies that have taken a list of such causes (mortality amenable to healthcare) and produced comparisons between countries and over time.

International comparisons show that the United Kingdom performs badly on this indicator, ranking 15th out of 16 countries in 2006/07 (Nolte and McKee, 2011). However, as Figure 2.2 shows, there has been substantial improvement since 1997/98, a 36.5 per cent fall in amenable mortality rate, but from a very poor starting point. Other countries have also seen substantial improvement over the same period.

Wheller et al. (2007) found that the amenable mortality rate in England and Wales fell substantially for males, by 46 per cent, and females, by 41 per cent, between 1993 and 2005; over the same period, unavoidable mortality fell by just 9 per cent for males and 5 per cent for females. It is tempting to conclude that this is due to health system improvements. However, as Kamarudeen (2010) points out there is no study that 'explicitly used a healthcare activity or quality variable in their analyses ... (and so) ... it is rather difficult to draw definitive conclusions about the relationship between amenable mortality and the healthcare system'.

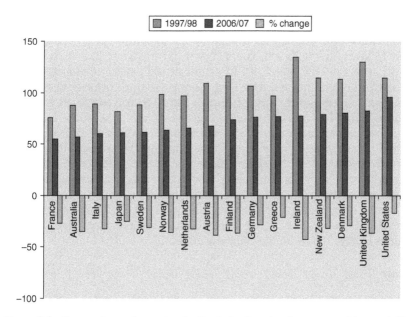

Figure 2.2 Comparison of age-standardized death rates from amenable mortality per 100,000 population, people aged 0–74 years, selected countries (1997/98 and 2006/07)

Note: countries are ordered by performance in 2006/07.
Source: Nolte and McKee (2011).

Table 2.3   Infant and perinatal mortality, England (1976–2008)

	1976	1981	1991	2001	2005	2008
Infant mortality rate	14.2	10.9	7.3	5.4	5.0	4.7
Perinatal mortality rate	17.6	11.7	8.0	8.0	8.0	7.6

Note: Infant mortality is defined as deaths under one year per 1,000 live births; perinatal mortality is defined as stillbirths and deaths under one week per 1,000 live births and stillbirths. In October 1992 the legal definition of a stillbirth was changed from a baby born dead after 28 completed weeks of gestation or more, to one born dead after 24 weeks, and so data prior to this are not strictly comparable with those after.
Source: ONS (2009).

Infant mortality rates

As in other parts of Europe, the most dramatic decreases in infant and perinatal mortality rates in England occurred between 1976 and 2001. Between 2001 and 2008, as Table 2.3 shows, infant mortality fell rather less quickly, from 5.4 per 1,000 live births to 4.7. There was also a fall in perinatal mortality over the same period from 8.0 to 7.6 deaths per 1,000 live births.

Conclusion

There have been substantial changes in the structure of the NHS over the last 15 years, involving a plethora of Acts of Parliament. The latest of these was passed on 27 March 2012. It is difficult to predict the outcome of the restructuring that has resulted. If opponents are to be believed then this is the first step toward the dismantling of the NHS with wholesale privatization of provision and the eventual morphing of CCGs into German- or Dutch-style health insurance or sickness funds, or US-style health maintenance organizations. Proponents on the other hand emphasize the removal of the dead hand of the state with increased choice for consumers from among a wide range of competing providers of care, resulting in increased efficiency and quality, and cuts in bureaucracy.

On the other hand, the NHS has a curious way of confounding politicians and commentators alike. Plus ça change, plus c'est la même chose (The more things change the more they stay the same).

Note

1. The pattern of productivity change in the United Kingdom mainly reflects changes in England (Peñaloza et al., 2010).

3
Spain: Quo Vadis? From Cost Containment to Structural Reforms

Juan Ventura and Eduardo González

Introduction

The aim of this chapter is to critically describe the evolution of the Spanish National Health System (NHS) in the last 25 years and its current situation. We will also revise the main reforms which are currently under debate. During these years, even with its ups and downs, the NHS has become a cornerstone of the Spanish welfare state. Mostly financed through taxes and with the predominance of public provision, the system has been able to incorporate the latest medical advances, offering quality health services almost universally. At the same time, in an *ad hoc* and rather hasty manner, the system has gone through a decentralization process that started with the devolution of health competences to the so-called historical regions, and was finally extended in 2002 to the 17 Spanish Autonomous Communities (ACs).

In our description, we clearly distinguish three stages in the recent evolution of the NHS: 1) A first development stage from 1986 to 2002, 2) a second stage from 2002 to 2009, in which the system is completely decentralized, raising cohesion and equity concerns across ACs and, also, a considerable increase in health expenditure, and 3) finally, a third stage that starts in 2010 in response to the effects of the economic and financial crisis, which in Spain requires radical measures to cut expenditure and poses threats to the sustainability of the NHS.

In order to understand the facts, we follow Peterson's (1997) model of the social learning process, which distinguishes between substantive learning, based on scientific evidence, and situational learning, based on political convenience. The model helps in understanding the complexities of the current NHS model, which includes 17 regional political actors and a central government making decisions in a context in which the rules of the game are ill-defined and, therefore, lack credibility. The chapter concludes with some considerations about the main structural reforms that, in our view, need to be addressed in the road map of the future NHS.

What has happened?

We can distinguish three different historical stages in the development of the modern Spanish NHS. The first stage starts in 1986 with the enactment of the *Ley General de Sanidad* (LGS)[1] and extends until 2002, when the devolution process of health competences to the ACs is finally completed. The second stage goes from 2002 to 2009. During this period, each of the 17 ACs has managed its regional health system autonomously, within legally established limits. This process has contributed to the fragmentation of the NHS, giving rise to heterogeneous organizational models and outcomes and raising concerns about the lack of coordination between the ACs and potential problems of equity in access across territories. The third and final stage starts in 2010, when the authorities become fully aware of the threats that the economic crisis poses to the sustainability of the NHS. This stage (re)opens the debate about the reforms that need to be made in order to assure the future solvency of the system. This section briefly reviews the main features of each stage.

First stage (1986–2002): the development of the NHS

During this first period, the NHS was able to finance, organize, manage and deliver quality health services to almost the whole Spanish population. This impressive achievement was accomplished within a political context characterized by the development and consolidation of a greatly decentralized nation (almost federal) and the incorporation of Spain to the European Union (EU). During this stage, the NHS consolidated as a cornerstone of the Spanish welfare state, an essential element that contributes to social cohesion and equity. The most notable milestones of this period are the following:

- Extending health coverage to almost all the Spanish population. Universal coverage is the ultimate goal of the system.
- Free delivery of health services (which are financed through taxes), with the exception of medicines that have a 40 per cent co-payment. Pensioners are excluded from any form of co-payment.
- Deep reform of primary care with the introduction of primary care teams (PCTs). In addition to delivering health services, PCTs serve as gatekeepers to specialized health services.
- Extending the benefits of the NHS granting access to new technologies and medicines.
- Predominance of public provision with direct management of health centres.
- Civil servant status for human resources.
- Continuous process of devolution of health competences to the ACs. This process started back in 1981 with Cataluña and was subsequently

extended to Andalucía (1984), País Vasco and Comunidad Valenciana (1988), Navarra and Galicia (1990) and Canarias (1994). The remaining ACs were managed by a central organization called INSALUD Gestión Directa until the devolution process was completed in 2002.

The evolution of the NHS during this first stage is therefore asymmetrical, creating a dual system. The ACs with health competences, which represent 60 per cent of the Spanish population, autonomously manage and organize their regional health services. In the remaining ACs, the health services are still centrally governed by INSALUD GD. In 1991, the Abril Report[2] analysed in detail the performance of this dual system. This report detected relevant problems within the NHS that contributed to the continuous growth in health expenditure, suggesting a series of reforms in order to control expenditure and improve efficiency in the use of resources (Ventura, 1992). If we observe this with a historical perspective, the Abril Report anticipated, more than 20 years ago, the main issues that are included in the current proposals to reform the NHS today. These include promoting consciousness of cost in both the demand and supply sides in order to adjust the aspirations of the population to the actual economic possibilities of the country.

The Abril Report advocated a clear delimitation of the core services that should be freely and universally covered by the public NHS (supply side control). As for the demand side, the Report suggested introducing co-payments for some services and the delivery of token bills to explicitly state the costs of provision to both patients and medical staff. These steps were considered useful in controlling the permanent excess of demand suffered by the NHS, which contributed to waste and to increases in the waiting lists. The reforms were deemed essential to solve the permanent financial deficit of the system.

The report also included recommendations to improve the efficiency in the use of resources. The most relevant step in this regard was the separation between finance (public) and provision (public or private). Legal reforms were required in order to make possible the transformation of some hospitals and health centres into state-owned enterprises with financial and managerial autonomy. A second suggestion was to replace civil servant contracts with (more flexible) regular labour contracts, while maintaining acquired rights. Finally, the report recommended developing internal markets for health provision in the line of the recommendations that the white paper *Working for Patients* proposed in 1989 for the UK (Department of Health, 1989). The main idea underlying this recommendation is that competition between health centres would certainly increase efficiency.

Despite the political debate on the convenience of putting those recommendations into practice, the actual reforms undertaken by INSALUD GD and the ACs with health competences within the 10 years after the publication of the Abril Report were only marginal. Some ACs selectively introduced new formulas that allowed for a variety of health providers, including public foundations, state-owned firms, consortiums, for-profit private firms under concession and even private–public joint ventures (Martin, 2003). But the bulk of the NHS remained unaltered during this period.

Second stage (2002–2009): regional decentralization

The second stage is characterized by the generalization of the decentralized model between the central government and the ACs. The functions of the central government are restricted to warranting equity across the territory. This is done by delimiting the common core benefits that are included in the services portfolio. The central government also retains the pharmaceutical policy and some auditing functions. In turn, the regional health authorities are autonomous to organize and manage the provision of health services within their respective territories. The decentralization process implies the advance in the financial autonomy of the ACs. In order to finance their new competences, financial resources are transferred from the central government to the ACs. But these funds are not tied to particular expenditure concepts such as health or education. Instead, the funds, which are theoretically transferred to finance the new health competences, merge into the global budget of the AC, which then has to establish the expenditure priorities.

The *Ley de Cohesión y Calidad del Sistema Nacional de Salud*[3] was enacted in 2003 to regulate the relationship between the Spanish Central Government and the 17 ACs with regard to the health system. The coordination is based on the new *Consejo Interterritorial del Sistema Nacional de Salud* (CISNS),[4] composed of the 17 regional Ministers of Health and chaired by the National Minister (Figure 3.1). There are six cooperation dimensions: benefits, pharmacy, human resources, research, information systems and quality. Therefore, the NHS starts this stage with an organizational architecture which has been completely decentralized and with the CISNS as the only coordinating body. Unfortunately, the CISNS is severely limited by the difficulties of reaching consensus in a highly polarized political context with continuous friction between the ACs governed by the conservative party (PP) and the Central Government of the social-democrat party (PSOE).

An indicator of the difficulties in reaching consensus within the CISNS is that the first relevant development of the *Ley de Cohesión y Calidad* had to wait until 2006. The *Real Decreto 1030/2006* establishes a new services portfolio delimiting the basic coverage and benefits of the system. The Act also establishes the requirement of using cost-effectiveness analysis and technology evaluation to update the portfolio in the future. A Quality Plan for the NHS is also designed for the period 2006–2010 to improve clinical practices and information systems. The plan advances to the development of electronic clinical records and the introduction of a unified health card to receive care in all the ACs. Furthermore, the *Ley 29/2006*[5] introduces measures to rationalize the use of medicines and to control pharmaceutical prescription.

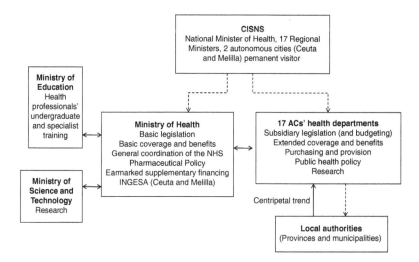

Figure 3.1 Organizational structure of the Spanish health care system
Source: Adapted from García et al. (2010).

Recent history evidences the difficulties to reach consensus within the CISNS and, still worse, to put agreements into practice. For instance, the unified health card is not yet available six years after its introduction was agreed. Furthermore, provided that the basic services portfolio is respected, each AC autonomously determines the full benefits portfolio that will be supplied within its territory, which creates important differences across ACs.[6] In the same vein, the evaluation of new technologies and drugs is not coordinated. Some ACs have their own evaluation agencies (País Vasco, Madrid, Cataluña, Galicia, Andalucía and Canarias), which add to the national agency (Instituto de Salud Carlos III).

During this period, the organization of the NHS does not depart significantly from the structure that characterized the previous stage. The ACs with health competences before 2002 maintain their management formulas, while the ACs that received the competences in 2002 have adopted the INSALUD GD model, with marginal innovations. However, the ACs have indeed exercised their new autonomy to satisfy the different regional stakeholders in a never-ending race to match the advancements of the nearby ACs. This, of course, has resulted in important increases in public health expenditure. Such behaviour unavoidably leads to financial deficit. However, those are days of economic growth and prosperity (up to 2007) and the ACs are playing the game of not falling behind in the process of expanding services, benefits, facilities, labour conditions, and so on. When the financial situation becomes unsustainable, the ACs turn to the Central Spanish Government for a bailout.[7] Central Government clears the financial deficits of the ACs, making the (irresponsible) strategy of the ACs right. It has to be noted that the devolution of health competences implies transferring a service, which accounts for around 35 per cent of the ACs' budgets, with an inflationary trend. Health services are very sensitive to public opinion and, therefore, to the political electoral market.

If we compare the evolution of public expenditure in health and GDP (both per capita) during this stage, the gap between both variables is self-revealing (see Figure 3.2). There is an immediate jump in expenditure just after the devolution of competences in 2002. The gap grows dramatically in 2008, as GDP levels off as a result of the economic crisis while public expenditure on health keeps growing. The situation in 2009 seems critical, with Spain entering recession and expenditure on health still growing, although at a lower rate.

Part of the growth in public expenditure on health can be explained by the increases in personnel and salaries. Both variables rose above 20 per cent during the period (Puig-Junoy, 2011). The general improvement in labour conditions is explained by the behaviour of some ACs trying to match other ACs with better labour conditions. Pharmaceutical expenditure is also responsible for these increasing trends. Per capita expenditure in medicines increased by 25 per cent during the period.[8] Even worse, growth in hospital pharmaceutical expenditure rocketed to 55 per cent between 2006 and 2010. Part of this increase may have been caused by the progressive ageing of the Spanish population.[9] The number of hospital beds has remained stable, although now there are more small hospitals, which perhaps are below the efficient scale.

In sum, at the end of this stage Spain has sunk into a huge financial and economic crisis with an urgent obligation to control public deficit (which

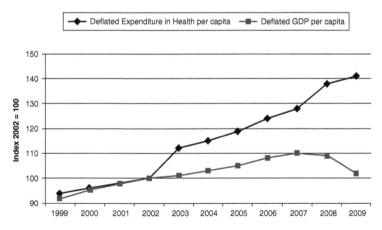

Figure 3.2   Evolution of expenditure on health and GDP per capita (1999–2009)
Source: Puig-Junoy (2011).

is also imposed by agreements with the EU). In this context, the authorities and public opinion have become aware of the dangers that threaten the sustainability of the NHS as we know it. But until 2009, the ACs did not introduce any relevant measures to confront the solvency problems they will suffer in the near future. We can say that Regional Authorities behaved as if the *tsunami* wave that the economic crisis launched in 2008 would stop at Central Government and will not threaten the ACs' shores. Electoral concerns may also explain the inaction.

Third stage (2010–2012): crisis reforms and sustainability of the NHS

The third stage starts in 2010, as the authorities (both national and regional) become fully aware of the deep consequences of the economic crisis and the urgency to reduce public deficit and debt. Serious concerns are raised about the sustainability of the NHS if reforms to preserve it are not urgently implemented.

Within this dismal context, at the beginning of 2010, the CISNS reaches a new agreement to control the growth in health expenditure. These measures are the first steps in the adjustment of the NHS to the delicate economic circumstances.[10] Some of them have proved effective. The *Real Decreto 4/2010* aims to rationalize pharmaceutical public expenditure and achieved a reduction of 2.36 per cent during 2010, which has been followed by a stronger reduction of 8.8 per cent in 2011.[11] In May 2010, President Zapatero announced the content of a new *Real Decreto 8/2010* with a large number of extraordinary measures with the objective of reducing public deficit from 11.2 per cent to 6 per cent in 2011. These measures included an average reduction of 5 per cent in the salaries of civil servants, the freezing of retirement pensions, the elimination of birth incentives and a new adjustment to pharmaceutical expenditure.

Historically, the Spanish NHS has faced the challenge of satisfying a growing demand for services, incorporating the best technological and pharmaceutical advances, but without any effective control on the demand or supply sides. This situation has led to recurrent solvency problems which are solved by punctual bailouts from Central Spanish Government whenever the situation reaches some critical point. It has also provoked significant delays in payment to suppliers and the hiding of actual expenditure figures. The economic crisis has done nothing but bring the old structural problems of the NHS, highlighted in 1991 by the Abril Report, to the surface.

The recession in the Spanish economy has intensified with a contraction of real GDP of –0.1 per cent in 2010 and a small recovery of 0.7 per cent, in 2011. Prospects for 2012 are even worse with a contraction of –0.3 per cent in the first trimester. The new conservative Government, elected in November 2011, has had to face a real deficit of 8.51 per cent, a figure higher than the 6 per cent expected and greatly influenced by the hidden deficits of the ACs.

In addition, the situation with the Spanish economy is more delicate as a consequence of the crisis in some important commercial banks which has extended to the whole Spanish financial system. These facts have deepened the loss of trust that international markets already had in the Spanish economy, which has made the situation financially unsustainable. The result is that interest rates for the Spanish national debt rose above 6 per cent.[12] There was a real threat that the situation may end in a financial rescue by the EU, with the consequences that this would have implied.[13]

Of course, the NHS has not been immune to the measures to control expenditure. The *Real Decreto-Ley 16/2012* has introduced two important measures unthinkable just a couple of years ago: 1) Extending pharmaceutical co-payment to pensioners and, 2) Ending the, *de facto*, universal coverage of the NHS. The right to have access to health care that was previously related to just being resident in Spain or having Spanish citizenship is now associated with being insured by the Social Security or a private insurer. This implies excluding uninsured immigrants and casts doubts about the status of the young unemployed above 26 that have not entered the Social Security system (López et al., 2012).

At a regional level, each of the 17 ACs (now mostly governed by the same conservative party in the National Government[14]) will have to face the challenge of controlling their deficits to be below 1.5 per cent in 2012. Given that health expenditure represents about 35 per cent (on average) of their budgets, and the importance of health and social services for an ageing population, preserving the system requires increasing efficiency and the introduction of effective controls on expenditure. The fundamental difference that emerges in 2012 is that, for the first time, the possibility of sanctions and interventions from Central Government to the ACs which fail to fulfil the deficit ceilings becomes credible.

The period 2010–2012, has been characterized by budget restrictions and cuts in the NHS, which can be quantified as €140 per capita or, in other words, an average reduction of 10.4 per cent (Federación de Asociaciones para la Defensa de la Sanidad Pública-FADSP, 2012). The cut was more pronounced in some ACs such as Comunidad Valenciana, Cataluña, Murcia, Navarra and Castilla la Mancha. These ACs implemented a restrictive policy that has closed operating rooms, beds and human resources, increasing waiting lists and creating tensions between professionals and users of the system. As for the near future, many voices are claiming there is a need to introduce important reforms to establish priorities in the allocation of health resources to warrant the sustainability of the NHS. The solutions will not imply indiscriminately cutting expenditure, but to rationally divest by following priorities based on cost-effectiveness evidence (Bernal et al., 2011).

To sum up, there is uncertainty about the sustainability of the system and its ability to adjust to the new context with its almost federal structure. The implementation of individual solutions by each of the 17 ACs may create

Table 3.1 Spain: the three stages – a summary table

	Stage 1	Stage 2	Stage 3
Rescaling/ centralization	• Dual Model: INSALUD + some ACs	• Decentralized model: 17 ACs + CISNS	• Ongoing debate about rescaling several functions
Delivery of health services	• Free delivery of health services (cornerstone of the NHS) • Pharmaceutical co-payment (except for pensioners) • Private health care (marginal)	• Free delivery of health services (cornerstone of the NHS) • Pharmaceutical co-payment (except for pensioners) • Private health care (marginal)	• Free delivery of health services (co-payment under discussion) • Pharmaceutical co-payment (including pensioners) • Private health care (potential increase)
Managerialization	• New models of management under public provision • No real separation between finance and provision	• Increasing managerialization in some ACs (Cataluña, Comunidad Valenciana, Madrid)	• Ongoing debate about new models of management • Concerns about good governance of the system
Coverage	• Expanding, with universal coverage as a goal of the NHS	• Quasi-universal coverage as an achievement of the NHS	• Restricted to those insured by Social Security and beneficiaries (excludes irregular immigrants)
Basket of services	• Expansion	• Expansion without coordination between ACs Health Bubble	• Contraction • Ongoing debate between cutting or reforming health services
Financing	• Insufficient	• Not earmarked (and not credible) • Central Government bail out ACs	• New rules of the game (crisis) • Budget credibility

equity problems across the Spanish territory. If the former stage in the game was not to fall behind in the race to add new services and match the leading ACs, the current stage has started a race not to fall behind in the rescaling of the system in order to be financially sustainable. But this new game requires different abilities from the health authorities. They must find the way to cut or divest up to the required point, while still preserving the core features of our NHS. In order to do so, they will need to reach stable consensus within the CISNS.

Why it has happened?

Peterson's (1997) *social learning* model can help us understand the evolution of the Spanish NHS as described in the previous section. The model describes the sequence of events between policy reforms, highlighting the role of social learning as an explanatory factor.

At a conceptual level, we can distinguish between two broad types of social learning processes, which exert a joint influence on the evolution of the health system. Firstly, *substantive learning* is based on cumulative experience, observation and thorough analysis of facts and results. In other words, it is based on cumulative technical and scientific knowledge. Secondly, *situational learning* explores the potential reforms that are actually feasible from a political viewpoint, and is based on the perception of norms, cultural values, vote counts and opinion surveys of the moment. Substantive learning influences situational learning but it is not its only driver. Some reforms that are sensible from an analytical perspective can be unacceptable from a situational viewpoint.

The main actors that take part in the social learning process are experts, organized interests and politicians. Experts analyse the features of existing policies and elaborate on reports that contain recommendations about superior alternatives. Organized interests try to manipulate policy-making to their advantage. Eventually they also elaborate on reports showing scientific support for their claims (disguising particular interests by having the appearance of substantive knowledge). Finally, politicians hold the formal authority to initiate political reforms on behalf of their constituencies. In doing so, they make use of substantive learning, but the periodic evaluations of their constituencies make them emphasize situational social learning; this is, looking for what is 'doable' within the social context and can attract a majority of votes.

Another important feature of the model is the scope of the reforms that emerge from social learning processes. Two broad categories may be distinguished: major reforms and routine reforms. Social learning processes can produce routine reforms as a response to new information emerging from substantive learning which applies to some limited area. In contrast, major reforms require intense processes of social learning in which all the actors are active.

Let us apply this framework to describe the way in which ACs organize and manage their regional health services and the type of organizational learning that occurred during this period. Even though the reforms have been mostly routine, the dominant type of social learning has been situational and based on political calculus. In contrast, there is a huge body of reports and recommendations elaborated on by experts, which date back to the Abril Report in 1991 and which advocate for profound reforms in order to guarantee the sustainability of the system. Unfortunately, such substantive recommendations have been systematically ignored by political authorities.

The most common organizational structure in the regional health services is the following. The Regional Ministry of Health is the top decision making body, being responsible for establishing health policy, health regulation and planning. The next level, the Regional Health Service, is responsible for the provision of health services. The third level is composed of health centres and hospitals.

The dominant resource allocation system is functional. Resources are allocated on the basis of the different functions to be performed[15]: primary care (about 16 per cent), specialized care (about 54 per cent), pharmacy (19.8 per cent) and public and preventive health (1.4 per cent). Health services are provided through direct management, i.e. through a network of public hospitals and primary care centres, which do not have legal status and, as such, do not have their own assets or cash. Therefore, management is highly conditioned by the need to comply with legal requirements and regulations, ensuring that everything is done within the bounds of law. Unfortunately, the focus on legal compliance sometimes goes against the flexibility that is needed in order to achieve efficiency in the use of resources. Furthermore, human resources are civil servants and this particular status makes it very difficult to introduce effective incentives.

In 1992, the INSALUD GD established the so-called program-contracts to regulate the relationship between the health authorities (finance) and the health centres (provision). The program-contract simulates a negotiation between the parties to establish the activity that is expected to be performed (with certain quality indicators) to which a prospective budget is assigned. The problem is that program-contracts are just legal fiction with serious credibility issues. Deviations have been common and no consequences are clearly derived from them (Ventura et al., 2004). However, different studies have found efficiency improvements since the introduction of program-contracts, which are attributed to the spreading of information (González et al., 1996; Ventura et al., 2004). But problems of comparability across ACs since the end of the devolution process in 2002 have prevented the emergence of new evidence on the efficiency in health provision.

Besides the dominant model, and in a selective manner, different ACs have experimented with new organizational formulas. These include providing a legal status to some hospitals or creating new health centres as public foundations, state-owned firms or consortiums. These experiments maintain governmental control but escape some of the limitations of bureaucratic legal controls. Galicia, Cataluña, Madrid and Andalucía have been the most active ACs regarding the introduction of these new formulas. Other ACs (especially Comunidad Valenciana) have expanded the formula of private provision which is publicly financed through capitation schemes. Currently about 20 per cent of the population of Comunidad Valenciana is covered under this type of concession.

Cataluña has also been innovative with the creation of health care entities called EBAs (*Entidades de base asociativas*).[16] These are legal, private entities constituted by professionals which deliver primary health care to a population under a capitation reimbursement system. EBAs may also have a budget to purchase specialized attention for their population. They were introduced in Cataluña and have been extended, albeit timidly, to other ACs.

Summarizing, the great majority of the NHS has followed the dominant model of direct management with public provision, with some marginal experimentation by separating financing (public) and provision (private) under capitation payment. The ACs that received the health competencies in 2002 have stuck to the INSALUD GD model. Politicians are well aware of the importance of the NHS for (voting) citizens and they refrain from undertaking major reforms (situational learning). Therefore, the majority of the experiments undertaken in those ACs can be considered to be routine reforms, such as improvements in the design of program-contracts or in information systems. Not taking political risks and escaping forward by continuously improving the benefits in the services portfolio without undertaking major reforms has been the dominant trend.[17]

How it has taken place

The Spanish Constitution of 1978 states that the Spanish State is organized territorially into municipalities, provinces and ACs that may be constituted. During the Spanish transition to democracy in the 70s, certain ACs (Cataluña, Galicia and País Vasco) were recognized as historical territories[18] and obtained wide competences. Since then, through a complex political process, the rest of the ACs receive similar competences to those initially granted to the historic regions. This process has included numerous negotiations, consensus and confrontations, related to the transfer of competences from Central Government to the ACs, with Cataluña and País Vasco acting as the forefront in demanding new competences.

With regard to health competences, the devolution of competences to the ACs started in 1981 with Cataluña, followed by Andalucía in 1984. Gradually new ACs received the health competences and in 2002, the NHS was in fact a dual system in which two thirds of the population was covered by transferred health services, while the rest were governed by INSALUD GD in a centralized way.

Year 2002 is the turning point in the recent evolution of the NHS. Before 2002, INSALUD GD had developed new management formulas since 1992 that experimented with a degree of separation between finance and provision, based on program-contracts. It had also developed clinic information systems such as the CMDB (Conjunto Mínimo de Datos Básicos). It had introduced improvements in quality control and had enough information to make comparisons between health centres. At the end of 1997, INSALUD GD published a Strategic Plan that included an ambitious reform to modify the organizational design of the system. Of course this proposal generated intense debate, at both the situational (political) and substantive (learning) levels, including in this case the cumulative evidence of Spain and other developed countries, especially the reforms undertaken in the UK. The main idea was to transform health centres into Public Health Foundations, with legal status and labour contracts. This was believed to be an advancement in the separation of functions (finance-provision) and in the efficiency of management.

When everything was ready in 2001 to start the process, the Government of the Conservative Party (Partido Popular) decided (unexpectedly) to abandon this reform and, instead it transferred the health competences to all the remaining ACs. After a brief but intense negotiation (imposition) process, the competences were happily received by the Regional Authorities eager to control a larger budget with more competences and personnel. Something similar to the usual *Empire Building* problem in large corporations, by which department managers always want their departments to grow. The ACs were made responsible for granting access of the population to the health services in a framework of increasing fiscal co-responsibility. Curiously enough, once the health competences were received, the managerial model implemented by these ACs can be deemed as a clear continuation of the inherited model, that had been considered outdated by INSALUD GD. Therefore, the great majority of these ACs just got on with the inheritance, introducing only minor changes, perhaps to avoid any criticism from the citizenship on a very delicate issue such as health care (situational learning).

In this context, the relevant stakeholders[19] seemed to reach a tacit consensus to run forward with the significant growth in public expenditure generated from improvements in the benefits basket and improvements in labour conditions, including remuneration, of civil servants. When regional deficits arise, there is a rational expectation that Central Government will come to the rescue (which actually was the case). During this process, which corresponds to the second stage described (2002–2010), the main stakeholders of the system (politicians, health care professionals and users) seem to be satisfying their expectations. Regional Authorities (politicians) found a way to increase votes by increasing the benefits basket. Health professionals were happy to gain access to technological and scientific advancements.

Professional associations also fulfilled an active role in defending the interests of professionals by defending the prevalence of medical criteria over financial concerns. Health care managers are appointed by the Regional Authorities and are accountable to the authority that appointed them.[20] We can talk about health administration that respects bureaucratic rules and guidelines which emerged from the political bodies, but there is scant real health management. Finally, the population is happy with the improvements in the benefits basket, partially offset with some concerns about the length of waiting lists.

This unreal equilibrium crumbled in 2010 (third stage), when the *tsunami* generated after the earthquake of the Spanish financial and economic crisis finally reached the shores of the ACs. Now they were forced to control the impacts of the satisfaction of each stakeholder with the regional budgets (something that should not be news, but was). Regional Authorities had to reduce some benefits in order to accomplish the deficit target which was, for the first time, credible. Credibility comes from the enforcement by the EU authorities of the targets imposed on the Spanish Central Government. Health professionals have seen how their labour conditions worsen. Health managers are forced to manage efficiently in order to meet a limited budget, reducing X-inefficiencies.[21] Finally, citizens will pay higher taxes and receive lower benefits.

Impact on the performance of the health care system

As we have already mentioned, public health expenditure in Spain has increased significantly during the last decade, from €32,672 million in 2000 to €70,340 million in 2009. This is equivalent to a steady annual raise of 8.9 per cent each year. In contrast, the cost of living only increased at an average annual rate of 3 per cent. Part of the increase in public health expenditure is attributable to the rise in the Spanish population during the decade, which was notably driven by immigration. The population rose from barely 40 million in 2000 to nearly 47 million in 2010. But, even if we consider the population effect, the increase in public expenditure is still considerable. The real (deflated to year 2000) expenditure in the public health system per capita rose from €806 in 2000 to €1,148 in 2009. This figure still implies an average annual increase of 4 per cent. On the other side, private expenditure on health per capita only rose at a moderate annual rate of 2.6 per cent. The final overall result is that the share of health expenditure (both private and public) within the Spanish GDP has rocketed from 7 per cent to 9 per cent in just 10 years.

As illustrated before, the devolution of health competences to the ACs in 2002 fostered the desire of Regional Authorities to dedicate more resources to their regional health services. This process was accompanied with a financing system that transferred financial resources on the basis of the

Table 3.2 Facts and figures about Spanish ACs

	Population 2011	GDP per capita € 2010	Public Deficit/ GDP % 2011	Public Debt/ GDP % 2011	Public Expenditure in Health per capita € 2011	Only Public Coverage %	Satisfaction with Health System %
Andalucia	8424102	17011	3.2	9.5	1175	90.8	71.47
Aragón	1346293	24034	2.9	10.3	1442	86.9	80.39
Asturias	1081487	21374	3.6	8.8	1478	86.1	83.43
Baleares	1113114	23923	4	16.8	1088	74.1	78.81
Canarias	2126769	19413	1.8	8.2	1243	92.8	54.86
Cantabria	593121	22891	4	9.7	1270	92.7	75.55
Castilla-La Mancha	2115334	16977	7.3	18.3	1441	92.4	75.59
Castilla-León	2558463	22388	2.3	8.8	1386	88.8	79.27
Cataluña	7539618	26251	3.7	19.7	1251	74.9	71.75
Com. Valenciana	5117190	19945	3.7	19.9	1114	88.5	72.37
Extremadura	1109367	16407	4.6	11	1506	97.3	71.59
Galicia	2795422	19901	1.6	12.4	1331	91.1	77.5
Madrid	6489680	29338	1.1	7.9	1158	75.3	72.61
Murcia	1470069	18588	4.3	10	1445	91.6	77.09
Navarra	642051	28963	1.9	11.1	1548	94.4	87.88
País Vasco	2184606	30623	2.6	7.9	1641	79.5	84.38
Rioja	322955	24366	2	11.8	1404	92.0	81.63

Sources: Instituto Nacional de Estadística (INE), Banco de España and Ministerio de Sanidad, Servicios Sociales e Igualdad.

population in 1999, adjusted by age. The system proved inefficient, since real expenditure has notably exceeded the regional budgets, with a gap that is estimated at 23 per cent in 2009 (Umpierre and Utrilla, 2012). While the ACs have responsibility for their deficits (there is no separate transfer of finance for health but a global transfer for the ACs' budgets), some empirical estimations of the regional health care cost functions point to deficiencies in the 2001 finance system. Most notably, it severely underweights the effect of ageing on health expenditure (De la Fuente and Gundín, 2009). The Spanish population has also increased dramatically during this decade and population trends regarding headcount and ageing are not symmetrical across ACs. This soon made obsolete a system that was initially based on already outdated data.[22] As a consequence, the Spanish Central Government has punctually transferred additional funds to eliminate regional deficits, but in doing so the government then raised doubts about the credibility of the regional financing system. The ACs' financing system was finally reformed in 2009 in an attempt to control these deficits and to create a new scenario of budget stability. In the case of health care, a more complex system of age adjustment was put into practice.

Table 3.2 shows some statistics that show the differences across Spanish ACs. First of all, ACs vary greatly in population from the 8.5 million of Andalucía (the biggest) to the 0.3 million of La Rioja (the smallest). There are also notable variations in GDP per capita that distinguish the rich ACs (Navarra, País Vasco, Madrid, Cataluña) from the poor ones (Andalucía, Castilla-La Mancha, Extremadura). In 2011, public expenditure on health per capita ranged from €1,088 in Baleares to €1,641 in País Vasco. While some of this gap may be due to ageing and other health expenditure drivers, some is also due to the different benefits offered by the ACs. Public debt and public deficit figures also vary greatly across ACs. While all the ACs will have to make efforts to reduce these figures, the situation is especially problematic in Castilla-La Mancha, Cataluña and Comunidad Valenciana. Not surprisingly, these ACs have been the first to implement severe cuts in the third stage. We also see differences in the percentage of population that is exclusively under public coverage.[23] Baleares, Cataluña, Madrid and País Vasco are the ACs with a greater presence of private insurance, while public insurance is nearly the unique coverage in Extremadura. The table also shows the percentage of people who are, in general terms, satisfied with the NHS, which is over 70 per cent in all ACs except in Canarias.[24] As expected, there is a positive strong correlation (0.53) between public expenditure in health per capita and this satisfaction index.

With respect to the performance of the Spanish NHS, despite a shared perception of misuse of resources, the comparison with other developed countries reflects that the system spends less per capita and obtains remarkable health outcomes. In the famous report of the World Health Organization on the efficiency of health systems in 1999, Spain ranked 6th in a list of 191 countries WHO (2001). More recently, using data of 2004, González et al. (2010) found similar evidence, with Spain ranking again 6th within the group of high income countries. With barely €2,000 per capita (€1,500 public and €500 private), Spain achieves good outcomes regarding disability adjusted life expectancy or infant mortality, and offers (almost) universal access to a health system that includes costly technology. Some analysts point out that this situation is only possible because of the low comparative wages of the medical staff in Spain (García, 2011). The health system is labour-intensive. Even though medical remuneration in Spain is lower than in other OECD countries, it represents 45 per cent of total expenditure on health and there has been an increasing trend in recent years. Between 2005 and 2009, after the devolution of competences to the ACs, this share increased by 7 per cent.

With regard to specialized health care, while hospitalization cases have increased about 10 per cent during the decade, the total number of hospital beds dropped a moderate 1.2 per cent. This has been possible because the occupation ratios remained steady at about 80 per cent during the whole decade, while the average in-patient stay dropped from 7.8 days in 2000 to just about 7.2 in 2010. These figures point to a rationalization of hospitalization criteria. However, the percentage of public expenditure attributable to hospital care increased from 45.5 per cent to 51 per cent from 2005 to 2009. Efforts have also been made to reducing waiting lists, one of the endemic problems of the NHS. For instance, the average delay for non-urgent surgery dropped from 83 days in 2005 to 65 days in 2010. However, delays for specialist visits remained stable at around 54 days on average.

Primary care plays a key gatekeeping role in the NHS. The number of primary care centres and professionals increased significantly during the period considered. The population assigned per professional was 1,498 in 2010 for general practitioners, almost 100 less than six years before. We see similar figures for nurses. In contrast, the ratio for paediatricians levelled off at around 1,030 during the entire period, which has generated episodes of a scarcity of professionals. The number of health care centres also rose slightly from 12,901 in 2004 to 13,133 in 2010. Therefore, an effort has been made to reinforce the role of primary care within the system.

The perception of the NHS is very positive, as we showed in Table 3.2. Despite some concerns about an ever-increasing expenditure and perceived inefficiencies, most Spanish people positively appreciate the quality and universal coverage of the system. The historical data of the *Barómetro Sanitario 2010* shows a clear positive pattern (Figure 3.3). The percentage of people who are satisfied with the system has notably increased since 1995; it

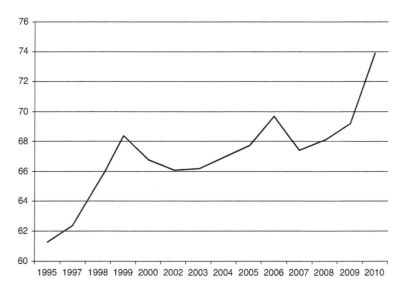

Figure 3.3 Percentage of people who are highly satisfied with the health system (1995–2010)

Source: Health Observatory (various years).

has remained steady at around 68 per cent during most of the 2000 decade and peaked in recent years to almost 74 per cent. In contrast, the percentage that regards the system as being so bad that it needs to be entirely reformed has dropped from around 10 per cent in the 1990s to barely 3 per cent in 2010. When asked to rate the public health system, from 1 to 10, the average goes from 5.94 in 2002 to 6.57 in 2010. From these figures, we can conclude that the users of the system are highly satisfied. This is consistent with the model of the decade in which all stakeholders of the health system have found their expectations satisfied, at the cost of significantly increasing health expenditure.

What about inequality? Table 3.2 reported important differences in public expenditure in health per capita across ACs. However, while some studies have reported the existence of socio-economic inequalities in access to health care services on the basis of income (Rodríguez and Urbanos, 2008), these differences have not increased during the last decade (Palencia et al., 2013). For the same level of need, low income citizens make a more intensive use of primary care and emergencies, while high income users are more likely to use specialized services (Urbanos, 2001). Health inequalities in Spain are moderate and lower than those reported in other developed countries (González and Barber, 2006).

The data on perceived equity even point to moderate increases of equity in access to health care during the last decade. Figure 3.4 shows the percentage of respondents that perceive there is equity in access, regardless of the AC of residence, rural-urban status of residence, age, socio-economic condition, gender, etc. (Barómetro Sanitario, 2010). While there is considerable variation among these potential sources of inequality, the general trend from 2002 to 2010 is moderately upwards. Therefore, perceived equity has also improved during the decade. However, the data also point to territorial differences in access as being the most severely perceived by the population, since less than 50 per cent of respondents believe there is equal access regardless of the AC of residence or the urban/rural status. In fact, territorial issues are perceived as causing larger inequalities than the legal/illegal status of residents. This finding is consistent with the big differences in expenditure in health per capita across ACs, as shown in Table 3.2. These gaps, however, cannot be considered as an indicator of territorial inequity, since they are also driven by other causes, some of which (prices, ageing, etc.) are not related to equity concerns (Cantarero, 2010). On the positive side, variables such as age, gender or socio-economic condition are not perceived as causing important problems of inequality in access to health care.

With regard to variations in performance, several studies report important differences across hospitals in several procedures such as, for instance, caesarian-section rates (García et al., 2010). Territorial variation is also found to be very important in the utilization rates of emergency services. In a recent study, the AC factor explained 29 per cent variance in emergency visits and,

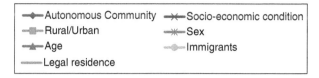

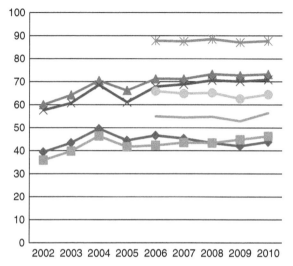

Figure 3.4 Percentage of people who believe there is equity in access for different groups (2002–2010)

which is more worrying, 82 per cent variance in admissions (Peiró et al., 2010). Therefore, effective inequity concerns are justified when the variability in medical protocols and procedures is so important between ACs.

The Spanish NHS presents good health outcomes. Table 3.3 summarizes the evolution during the last decade of some health indicators of the Spanish population, regarding life expectancy, age-adjusted mortality rates, infant mortality rates and infant vaccination percentages. The evolution of these variables is certainly positive. Life expectancy has increased by 2 per cent between 2002 and 2007. Disability adjusted life expectancy (DALE) also increased by 2.7 per cent. The increase in healthy life expectancy (HALE) was more moderate at about 0.4 per cent. If we analyse age-adjusted mortality rates related to different diseases, the evolution is extremely positive for all of them, except for Alzheimer's, which increased to 43 per cent. It is difficult to evaluate the share of responsibility of the health system within these figures. Prevention policies may be responsible for a significant part of it, for instance those related to smoking or alcohol consumption which have been moderately successful. Infant mortality rates have also notably improved between 2000 and 2007, which is indicative of the good health of the system.

Table 3.3   Performance of the Spanish health system (indicators)

	2002	2007	Var 2002/2007
Life Expectancy at Birth	79.4	81.1	2.12%
Disability-Adjusted Life Expectancy (DALE)	70.7	72.6	2.69%
Healthy Life Expectancy (HALE)	55.1	55.3	0.36%

	2000	2007	Var 2000/2007
Age-Adjusted Mortality Rates (per 100000)			
Total Mortality Rate	611.5	534.0	−12.67%
Circulatory System Disease	198.4	157.8	−20.47%
Ischemic Heart Attack	65.4	50.4	−22.86%
Cerebrovascular Disease	56.0	40.8	−27.04%
Malignant Tumour	170.3	157.1	−7.78%
Breast Cancer	20.5	18.4	−10.52%
Colorectal Cancer	15.2	15.1	−0.51%
COPD (Chronic Obstructive Pulmonary Disease)	25.5	19.5	−23.44%
CLD (Chronic Liver Disease)	10.8	9.0	−16.47%
Diabetes Mellitus	14.4	12.7	−11.89%
Alzheimer's	7.8	11.1	42.82%
Traffic Accidents	14.0	8.2	−41.61%
Suicide	7.3	6.1	−15.98%
Pneumonia and Influenza	12.7	10.6	−16.52%
AIDS	4.0	2.7	−32.68%
Smoking	193.3	154.7	−19.99%
Alcohol	56.4	45.1	−20.16%
Infant mortality (per 1,000)	4.4	3.5	−20.94%
Neonatal Mortality (per 1,000)	2.8	2.3	−18.76%
DTP Vaccination (% children under 12 months)	95.0	96.4	1.47%
MMR Vaccination (% children under 12 months)	95.0	97.2	2.32%

Concluding remarks

The review of results in the last section shows that the problem of the Spanish NHS is not with the quality (outcomes) of the system, but with its future financial sustainability. We end this chapter with a review of the reforms that are being proposed now by different experts in order to warrant the sustainability of the NHS, preserving its core features which are so positively appreciated by the population.

A) Supply control (selective financing)

The NHS must undertake serious steps to control the technologies and medicines that are incorporated in the services portfolio on the basis of cost-effectiveness criteria. For this purpose, it will be necessary to create a central agency that can inform in a binding manner to the Central and Regional Authorities, in the line of the British NICE (*National Institute for Health and Clinical Excellence*). This will make a remarkable departure from the actual model, in which all types of benefits can be financed if politically convenient. Selective financing with the implication of experts (not politicians) is an efficiency requirement to preserve the core features of the Spanish NHS (Bernal et al., 2011).

B) Demand control (co-payment)

There is an increasing body of experts clamouring for extending co-payments as a tool to discourage the inappropriate use of the system. Of course, co-payments should be carefully designed and should include limits to prevent taxing the most ill (Rodríguez and Puig-Junoy, 2012). When services are completely free, there is the tendency to abuse the system. Some figures speak for themselves: in 2006 a Spanish citizen visited a physician more than eight times a year, which is 40 per cent more than the average in the UE-15 (OECD, 2011); it is also considered that between 30 per cent and 80 per cent of 'emergencies' are not actually urgent; pharmaceutical expenditure per capita is 40 per cent higher than in countries such as Portugal, the UK, Belgium or Denmark; and 70 per cent of pharmaceutical prescriptions was concentrated on the 20 per cent of the population which was free from any co-payment (i.e. pensioners). These facts also point to the urgency of reforming the current medicines co-payment structure (Rodríguez and Puig-Junoy, 2012). Consequently, even though it has a significant political cost, the Spanish Government has very recently reformed the pharmaceutical co-payment system. The reform includes pensioners who will have to co-pay 10 per cent of medicines from July 2012, with the lower rents paying a maximum of €8 a month. Some on very low pensions and long-term unemployed will be exempt from co-payment.[25]

C) Redefine the priorities of the NHS

The Spanish NHS is excessively biased towards patient treatment and does not pay enough attention to prevention and public health. Spain is the second EU country in numbers of smokers and the fourth in overweight.[26] The increasing ageing of the population and the prevalence of chronic diseases also calls for a new definition of priorities, which implies providing more resources to these types of services. Specialized care also dominates over primary care and both levels lack desirable coordination.

D) Foster transparency at all levels

The existence of an NHS composed of 17 regional health systems with full autonomy to organize and manage their health services provides an extraordinary opportunity for substantive social learning based on benchmarking. Unfortunately, such learning has not occurred due, in part, to the lack of disaggregated and transparent information. The lack of transparency has been a result of the decentralization process. A consensus is needed to provide the means of knowing the results of each health centre or hospital. This will eliminate significant barriers to substantive social learning and debate.

E)   Improving governance

The organizational structure of the NHS has not been effective in providing desirable coordination and cooperation between health services and Central Spanish government. If we want an NHS that is more than a collection of 17 microsystems, there is an urgent need to redesign its organizational architecture. Some experts point to the need to recover some health competences by the central authorities and to achieve consensus within the CISNS (Repullo and Freire, 2008).

Decentralization can have certain advantages, such as a better use of local knowledge (regarding the differing needs or preferences of the population), but it also incorporates severe drawbacks that need to be accounted for. For instance, some (very specialized) health services require having a big risk group to be incorporated in the system (rare illnesses, for instance). Bargaining power with suppliers (tools and medicines) can also be improved by mixing larger volumes. Integrating these and other functions with the necessary cooperation between services could save time and money. There is also a need to transfer knowledge from one part of the system to another without regional barriers.

Other interesting aspect that could be significantly improved is the system through which the top managers of the public health centres are selected. This is currently done following the political logics of political parties. As a result, sometimes there is a worrying lack of professionalism in these important positions. Freire and Repullo (2011) advocate for a competitive administrative selection system, which can promote professional excellence in the access to managerial positions within the NHS.

Introducing effective practices in the management of human resources is another important pending matter. Again, coordination between ACs is needed in order to avoid disparity in labour conditions that fragment the health labour market and push salaries upwards. The introduction of effective incentives based on performance is also essential. But Regional Authorities are reluctant to transfer decision making power to central authorities or evaluation agencies that then limit their discretional power. Once and for all, authorities must weight substantive learning over situational learning and initiate major reforms even if they imply losing autonomy.

To sum up, the consequences of the economic crisis in Spain offer a unique opportunity to establish a solid basis to preserve the Spanish welfare state on principles of transparency and responsibility. This task requires the courage of citizens, professionals and politicians. It is time to discuss how to preserve what is socially most valuable and discard ineffective practices and structures.

Notes

1. Health Care General Act.
2. The full title of the report was 'Informe y recomendaciones de la Comisión de Análisis y Evaluación del Sistema Nacional de Salud', but since Fernando Abril was the Chair of the commission that produced the report, it is widely known as the Abril Report.
3. NHS Cohesion and Quality Act.
4. Inter-territorial Council of the NHS.
5. Guarantees and Rational use of Medicine and Health Products Act.
6. For instance, each AC has different vaccination calendars.
7. In 2005, the Central Spanish Government injected some €1.7 billion to finance the ACs' deficits.
8. The number of prescriptions per capita increased by 30 per cent, but the average real price of medicines dropped by 11 per cent due to several measures introduced by the Central Spanish Government.
9. During the period, the population over 65 increased by one million persons, a circumstance that has had a significant impact on per capita expenditure on health.
10. The measures included the following: regulation of maximum waiting lists, unified vaccination calendar, promotion of e-health and e-health records, refinements in human resource planning, reinforcement of technological evaluation for new services, creation of a national system of health indicators and measures to control pharmaceutical expenditure.
11. The decreasing trend has continued during the first months of 2012.
12. A risk premium over the German bond above 500 points.
13. In fact, the rescue has already taken place with regard to the banking system, with a fund of up to €100,000 million. Therefore, the Spanish financial system has now, *de facto*, been intervened in by the EU. The situation is so difficult that the EU had to revise the deficit objectives for Spain in July 2012 to 6.3 per cent in 2012, 4.5 per cent in 2013 and 2.8 per cent in 2014. The agreement has included new efforts for the Spanish population that include measures such as tax rises (mainly via VAT) and further reductions in the salaries of civil servants.
14. With Cataluña, País Vasco, Andalucía and Asturias as notable exceptions.
15. Ministerio de Sanidad y Política Social (2009).
16. Association-based entities.
17. The broader reforms undertaken in other ACs that depart from the dominant direct management model have received criticism and debate between the different actors in the social learning process. The debate is polarized between those that defend the traditional public provision model and those who consider that it is possible and convenient to separate financing and provision. There is, however, little evidence on comparing both systems, because the authorities that experiment with new formulas do not want them to be perceived as a failure even if they are. In a context of opacity, there are doubts about the credibility of risk transfer to the insurance companies that manage health provision under capitation reimbursement systems.
18. With all the competences as regulated in Art. 149 of the Spanish Constitution. The other ACs were regulated by Art. 148 with fewer competences.
19. While the role of health users' associations in Spain has been marginal, some associations of patients with certain pathologies such as cancer or mental illness have gained some influence.

20. Another important actor is the pharmaceutical industry, which can exert a significant influence on the consumption of medicines with their marketing techniques, which include frequent visits to prescribers. They also exert considerable bargaining power vis-à-vis the health authorities through the industry association *Farmaindustria*. In fact, a good deal of the reforms undertaken since 2010 have tried to reduce pharmaceutical expenditure, a competence that is still centralized by the Spanish Government.

21. Leibenstein (1966) coined the term X-inefficiency to refer to the slack that generates in organizations that do not suffer external pressures to make an efficient use of resources, such as monopolies. Managers of these firms will take it easy as there is no threat to firm survival or profits, because there is no competition in the marketplace. This type of inefficiency describes perfectly the slack that accumulates in public bureaucracies when they do not face external (credible) pressures to behave efficiently.

22. The system was established in 2002 using population data from 1999.

23. The rest is covered by private insurance or, more frequently, a mix of both public and private insurance.

24. The figure indicates the percentage of people who say that 'the system works rather well' or 'the system works well, but requires some changes'. The other options are 'the system needs fundamental changes, although some things work' and 'the system is so bad that it should be entirely reformed'.

25. Real Decreto Ley, 16/2012.

26. Even though this figure has dropped significantly during the last decade, in 2009 26.2 per cent of Spanish adults were still daily smokers. Overweight is also a significant public health concern, since it is present in 50 per cent of the population.

4
Italy: A Strange NHS with Its Paradoxes

Emmanuele Pavolini and Giovanna Vicarelli

Introduction

In the last 20 years the Italian National Health Care System (NHS) has experienced a significant process of transformation. The NHS was introduced in 1978 substituting a previous Social Health Care Insurance model (Vicarelli, 2011). While the 1980s represented a decade when governments tried to implement the new institutional design for health care, the 1990s were already a time of discernible change: at the beginning of the decade, for a series of reasons that will be explained later in this chapter, attempts were made to dismiss the NHS and shift to a more private-like system. These attempts failed but important transformations took place nevertheless (Vicarelli, 2011).

NHS reforms had to follow a difficult path between cost containment given the huge public debt of the Italian State and innovation, which though often costly, was required by an increasing exigent and aging population (and electorate).

In order to solve the dilemma of containing costs and trying to keep pace with social demand, the institutional changes in the NHS reform took different directions, three of which are of particular interest: rescaling, privatization and managerialization. Two reforms were passed in the 1990s, one at the beginning of the decade (1992–93), the other at the end (1999), setting the main aims and goals of innovation in relation to the three directions. The last decade saw neither a general NHS reform nor attempts made in this direction but only smaller and more focused regulatory changes which are having a noteworthy impact on the overall functioning of the NHS today.

As in many other European countries, rescaling largely meant a shift of power and responsibilities from the national level to sub-national (regional) governments. Following the regionalization reforms of the 1990s a good part of the regulatory public power in health care was shifted from the national State to Regions: the former essentially maintained two tasks (a substantial part of financing and setting 'homogeneous standards of health care provision' over the country), the latter received all other tasks (from planning to managing health care provision). As a consequence, health care became one of the most important policy fields for the Regions, given the fact that at least 60–70 per cent of Regional spending in each Region is allocated to its provision (Pavolini, 2011).

In the same years and chiefly through the same laws, a strong attempt was made to modernize NHS administration following for the most part, a New Public Management approach: the local health care authorities (USLs – *Unità sanitarie locali*) created by the 1978 reform were transformed into health care agencies (ASLs – *Aziende sanitarie locali*) and Hospital Trusts (AOs – *Aziende ospedaliere*). Politicians appointed by local governments were substituted by managers (called 'General Directors' – *Direttori generali*) heading the agencies and trusts. These managers have fixed-term contracts and are appointed directly by the Regional Government. The managerialization approach not only shaped the NHS top decision making process in a new way, but also the day-to-day running of hospitals and other health care facilities: a whole new set of instruments (primarily, but not solely, referring to budgeting, costs controls, etc.) was introduced, trying to foster a shift from a traditional bureaucratic approach to a more post-Weberian one (Vicarelli et al., 2009).

In connection with managerialization, the 1990s also witnessed the introduction of competition and a broader use of private providers within the NHS. This paved the way for using 'quasi-markets' and replacing an increasing number of public provision with provision contracted-out to the private sector. In the 1992–93 reforms, 'managed competition' was considered one of the main tools in making the Italian NHS more efficient. However, in the 1999 reform, 'managed competition' among different providers was partially replaced, at least in national legislation, by 'managed cooperation', thus proposing a view of public and private providers as single component parts of a complex and integrated care network.

In comparison with the 1990s, the last decade was quite different. Apart from the Constitutional Reform of 2001 (introducing a more federalist-like institutional design of the Italian State) which could be seen as the last act in line with the wave of changes sweeping through the previous decade, no major reforms were passed by Parliament. Nonetheless, significant transformations occurred in the Italian NHS. These took a more 'hidden' form and yet brought, and continue to bring, profound changes to how the health care system works (Hacker, 2004).

The first decade of the new century: what's new for the Italian NHS?

As often happens with complex policies, health care in Italy also underwent a series of processes in the last decade which were related both to medium-long term dynamics and to more recent ones.

Privatization

From the unification of Italy (1860) to the creation of the NHS (1978), the basic problem of Italian governments was to limit the inclusion of health care among the direct tasks of government and public administration. Governments avoided the issue of instituting a universalistic Health Care System (Vicarelli, 1997). This decision, whilst preventing direct State intervention, entrusted it to private providers and religious organizations. This difficult path towards health care 'statalization' continued up until the second half of the 1970s when the creation of the NHS began a new phase. This phase was no longer based on private over public predominance, but rather of public over private, albeit under various forms. The years 1992–93 marked a turning point for Italian politics and also for the NHS: during the political scandals (the so-called dirty hands affairs) that wiped away a good part of the traditional post-war party system and the financial crisis that hit Italy severely, two bills were passed by Parliament (No. 502 and No. 517) aimed at completely reorganizing the NHS. In the discussions preceding and following the adoption of the bills, two different coalitions and conceptions of the NHS emerged (Vicarelli, 2005): one more liberal, steering towards the partial privatization of the NHS, thus relying on families, communities and market forces to foster health care provision; the other more social-democratic, with the goal of strengthening the NHS, whilst also adopting tighter financial control. In the last decade these two conceptions of the NHS were advocated respectively by the main centre-right and centre-left political coalitions. As a matter of fact both coalitions, once in power, tried to implement their vision of the NHS but with limited results. Centre-Left governments between 1996 and 2000 (and for a short term between 2006 and 2007) focused on improving the NHS, and hence passed a bill (n° 229) in 1999. Centre-right governments tried between 2001 and 2006, and after 2007 to foster a process of (partial) privatization and increased competition.

When discussing 'privatization', we might refer to two different phenomena: the privatization of expenditure (State financing is reduced or does not increase at the same pace as private expenditure); the privatization of provision (the State maintains its level of expenditure but it increasingly contracts out the delivery of health care services to private providers). Comparing the data in Figure 4.1 and Table 4.1, it notably seems that the second type of privatization took place, whereas the privatization of expenditure was more prevalent in the 1990s than in the last decade.

When analysing how the role of private expenditure changed over time in relation to total health care expenditure, a single straightforward pattern cannot be clearly identified. Figure 4.1 shows what occurred in the period 1990–2010, comparing the Italian situation with that of other Western European countries (EU-15). The incidence of private health expenditure in Italy in the period 1990–2010 followed a bell curve path. In the first part of the 1990s there was a dramatic increase in the share of health expenditure

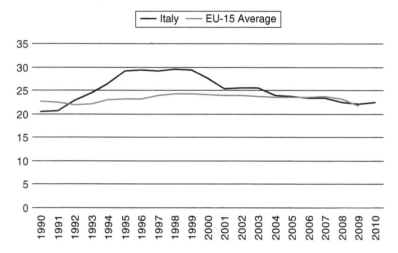

Figure 4.1   Incidence of private expenditure on total health care expenditure
Source: OECD (2013).

Table 4.1   Private in-patient hospital beds as a percentage of all beds (1990; 2000; 2010)

	1990	*2000*	*2010*
Austria	23.5	25.3	29.1
France	35.2	34.4	37.5
Germany[a]	49.1	59.7	69.2
Poland	n.g.	n.g.	24.4
Spain	32.1	33.3	32.6
Sweden	7.6	n.g.	n.g.
United Kingdom	3.1	n.g.	n.g.
Italy	23.5	30.4	31.6

[a]Data for Germany refers to 1991
Source: OECD Health database and WHO Health for All database (2013); for Germany Statistisches Bundesamt (2010).

paid by households: from 20.5 in 1990 to 29.4 per cent in 1996. In the second part of the same decade, the process settled and remained relatively stable. In those years Italy was a clear outlier among the EU-15 states. At the beginning of the last decade the situation changed and the gap between Italy and EU-15 narrowed down and no difference was visible by 2004 onwards.

If a clear and explicit trend towards expenditure privatization did not take place, some scholars argue that it took two other forms: reduction in the access to care and the partial transformation in the composition of private expenditure. CEIS (2010) shows that a certain number of Italians are giving up part of health care because either they cannot pay for it or they risk impoverishment: in this case statistics would not show a rise in private expenditure, even in the presence of less public financing, simply because it would not occur. Although the CEIS interpretation seems plausible, the data available is not sufficiently clear to give us a conclusive answer on this issue. For instance, the Eurostat EU-Silc data on the percentage of individuals who had to forgo some health care treatments in the previous year suggest that Italy has a high percentage of people who find themselves in such a condition (around 7 per cent). This percentage, however, has remained stable over last decade. So it is possible that a 'hidden' privatization of expenditure has taken place, but it is difficult to define the phenomena in more precise terms. Moreover, in 2000 'Integrative Health Care Funds' were introduced in order to strengthen the 'second pillar' of the Italian health care system.

If an increase in the privatization of expenditure took place mainly in the 1990s, then perhaps it assumed a more 'hidden' form whilst a more straightforward process could be detected in terms of privatization of health care provision. At the beginning of the 1990s around 23 per cent of total hospital beds in Italy were private. Two decades later they reached around 32 per cent. Again, also in this case, the increase happened mainly in the 1990s. If we compare Italy with other countries, we can notice the following (Table 4.1): after Germany, it is the country where there was the highest increase in private provision (at least according to the data available); this level of private provision is in line with the one in some other HCS (Spain, France and Austria), lower than in Germany, and quite higher (as far as data suggests) than in the Anglo-Saxon and Scandinavian NHS.

Decentralization

In the same decade the NHS was introduced (the 1970s), Regions started acquiring institutional recognition that included health care issues. However, until the mid-1990s their role in the NHS was limited. They were more 'policy takers' (mainly concerned with the implementation of centrally set policies) than 'policy makers' (France, 2008). Only in the 1990s, their role changed thanks to the marked process of strong political devolution, a process definable as 'health care federalism'. Since then, two different phases of NHS regionalization can be traced.

The first phase of devolution started in 1992 with two bills, No. 502 and No. 517. The end came in 2001, when devolution was recognized at the constitutional level by an amendment to Art. 117 of the Italian Constitution going well beyond the health care sector. It marked a further shift in the balance of power between State and Regions in favour of the latter. During the 1990s, the process of regionalization changed the way health policy was made: France and Taroni argue that 'policy is (since then) made less in Parliament and in the central ministries and more through negotiations between the national government and the regions' (2005: 184). Therefore, inside a relatively loose national institutional setting, Regions were able to develop their own Regional Health Care Systems (RHS) with different choices in terms of provision organization. One of the striking features of this regionalization in the 1990s and the first part of last decade was the existing asymmetry between health care spending by Regions and revenue raising responsibilities. Due to a nationally centralized taxation system dating back to the 1970s, the NHS was mostly financed by the central State. In comparison to other European countries, the process of devolution in Italy during the 1990s implied neither a tighter central control/steering nor the devolution of revenue raising responsibilities. The result was a policy of deliberate under-financing from central government, and an increase in financial deficits, especially in those Regions with less cost control capacities (Pavolini, 2011).

The second phase of NHS Regionalization started at the beginning of the last decade and gained momentum in the latter half: central governments (regardless of political orientation) attempted to find better ways of controlling regional health expenditure, thus imposing tougher budget constraints. More specifically, the second part of the last decade saw the introduction of a new tool, the *Piano di rientro dal deficit* (Plan to cut health care deficits). The 'Piano di rientro' was an agreement between central government and single regional governments who had accumulated health care deficits. The national government agreed to cover part of the debt in exchange for a sustainable 'industrial' plan by regional governments to reorganize their health care system. This was to prevent future deficits (through cuts in hospitalization rates, hiring freezes of new health care staff, tighter control of pharmaceutical expenditure). In order to avoid possible opportunistic behaviour from regional governments with high deficits, these sub-national governments had to automatically introduce increases in their regional taxation system so as to cover a good part of the deficit produced, as well as new or higher forms of co-payments for health care services and goods (drugs).

The following governments continued to adopt the same approach. Given the fact that out of 21 RHS, seven had significant deficits, these Regions in particular experienced more of a 'return' of Central Government in running their health care: 'the "seven regions in difficulty" are in such dire financial straits that they have been prepared to accept severe limitations of their freedom of action. This exercise of central spending power represents a dramatic break with the period pre-2001 when state financing was granted virtually unconditionally' (France, 2008: 18).

Therefore nowadays, in comparison to the 1990s, Central Government, using financing power as leverage, is regaining a more central role within the NHS and the RHS. This however applies mainly to the Regions who have deficits whilst the remaining Regions still enjoy a high degree of freedom (Pavolini and Vicarelli, 2012).

Managerialization

From the second part of the 1990s onwards, two different phases are detectable in the regulation and the role of 'General Directors' and generally in relation to the introduction of other New Public Management tools. The two phases are the following: the second part of the 1990s; the last decade.

The second part of the 1990s saw the early stage of managerialization which took place with the transferral of power to Regions. In 1995, DRGs were introduced and they were extended over time to the whole hospital system in order to better monitor and reimburse health care expenditure. Thanks to the DRGs hospital care financing shifted from an ex-post and historic form of financing (the State reimbursed hospitals on the basis of average expenditure from the previous years) to a more precise model of financing where the reimbursement closely followed the types of care effectively provided. Moreover, in the definition of the reimbursement ratio of each DRG, the National and Regional governments could better steer the behaviours of professionals, specifically doctors (e.g. incentivizing more day hospital care than traditional long stays in hospitals for similar kinds of diseases). From a regulatory point of view, it was and continues to be the national Ministry of Health which defines the lists of services and provision with the relative tariffs covered by the NHS.

Apart from DRGs the other main innovation of this first stage was the introduction of top managers in the running of health care and hospital authorities. In the 1990s, Regions acquiring new managerial and direct provision powers were not fully capable of controlling such a complex 'machine' as health care: on average ASLs and AOs had thousands of workers and needed substantial investments in technology, equipments and facilities. Therefore in these first years, the 'General Directors' and all the rest of their new managerial staff enjoyed a relatively high level of autonomy in running health care facilities and decision making. Initial steps, especially in Central-Northern Italy (see below) were taken in order to control costs, in a situation where the real costs of regional and local NHS were not particularly clear (Vicarelli, 2009).

The second phase was characterized by a power shift: Regions started to reduce the autonomy of General Directors and to use them more as 'middle-level' managers (as implementers rather than strictly independent decision-makers). Health care management in this phase became more region-centred with very few significant players (the President of the Region, the Councillor in charge of health care, the Regional General director for health care) (Pavolini, 2011).

In relation to the tools for steering the system, the use of DGRs became more sophisticated as they were employed, together with planning and monitoring activities, to better control local provision as well as limit expenditure. For example, many Regions began introducing 'production and expenditure caps' to health care providers (privately contracted-out and public hospitals) in relation, not only to overall expenditure, but also to the provision of each single type of care (for example Regions put caps on the amount of caesarean births that could be delivered in an AO or ASL in a given year).

Moreover, apart from DRGs, national and regional regulation also developed in other directions: one of the most important directions was an increasingly complex and articulated system for the 'accreditation' of health care services and facilities in order to better control their performance.

The NHS and austerity

In more recent years, changes might strongly affect the functioning of the Italian NHS. The economic and financial crisis did not have a short term impact on the public health care system. Until 2010 no relevant changes (cuts) were put in place, even if Italy maintained a relatively lower level of public expenditure: the public per capita expenditure in 2009 was equal to 3,137$ (PPT) in Italy, and almost 4,000$ in the EU15 (OECD, 2012). Due to the huge public debt (around 120 per cent of the national GDP) and the persisting crisis, 2011 was the first year which saw the Government intervene decisively in the NHS in terms of co-payments and public expenditure.

The 2011 'Finance Law', the main national law regulating the amount of resources given yearly to the public sector, might be a very important turning point for the Italian NHS: for the years 2013–2014, it introduced an amount of expenditure cuts equal to around 8 billion Euros (the overall NHS financing from the State in 2012 was around 106 billion Euros). Among the measures that the Law introduced there were: the substantial hiring freeze of new health care workers in the NHS; from 2014 there are new 'nationally-set' co-payments on pharmaceutical goods and health care services, for an amount equalling 2 billion Euros.

Why it happened

Different trends could be noticed in relation to the introduction of decentralization, managerialization and different forms of privatization. In most cases, however, clear straight-forward trajectories cannot be observed in these three fields: privatization of expenditure and in part decentralization followed a bell-curve path; managerialization meant more autonomy for health care managers in the 1990s, but this autonomy was then reduced in more recent years by regional governments; privatization of provision took place mostly in the 1990s, decreasing in more recent years.

If the 1990s were a time of significant changes, the last decade seems to have started to reverse or to stop some of these trends. Why has this happened? In order to answer this question, we have to take into consideration three types of factors: economic, political and institutional ones.

Economic factors: cost containment and fear of skyrocketing growth in public health care expenditure

As everywhere else in the Western world, public health care in Italy has shown one of fastest expenditure increases in the last decades. This has been due to a mix of factors ranging from a raise in needs coverage, to a wider use of costly technology and a change in care needs (from simply acute care to chronic care, with patients needing assistance for longer periods of time) (Blank and Burau, 2010).

In the Italian case two additional economic features were important: the ongoing huge Italian public debt (on average equal to 110 per cent of the national GDP in the last two decades) and chronic deficits in running the health care system: in every year of the last two decades, the NHS had a deficit ranging from 2 to 7 per cent.

Privatization (both in terms of provision, with the introduction of quasi-markets, and expenditure, with higher co-payments), decentralization and managerialization were all seen as tools to foster a more efficient way of running health care (given the fact that decision makers and users would have been closer to each other), as well as a possible mechanism of shifting the blame for possible cuts from national governments to other actors (private providers, managers and local governments).

Political factors: the rise of independentist movements and the crisis of political parties

A second order of factors is related to how the political landscape in Italy changed over the last two decades. Two phenomena in particular played and still play a major role: the 'earthquake' that shook parties in the first part of the 1990s with the disappearance of those that had enjoyed great importance in the previous decades; the rise of new parties, some of them gaining influence and advocating more Federalism or even Secessionism.

The crisis of the Soviet Union at the end of the 1980s was also a crisis for the biggest Communist party in Western Europe: the PCI (*Partito Comunista Italiano*) had gained more than 30 per cent of the total votes in general elections. At the beginning of the 1990s the party dissolved and its members started to create new parties (some were neo-communist, the majority of others social-democratic). Still to this day, the whole left-wing faction remains unsettled in its divisions. Centre and Centre-Right parties were strongly hit by corruption scandals in the first part of the 1990s and they too disappeared.

A huge wave of political discontent and disillusionment swept across the electorate (and still to some extent today). One of the parties that profited the most from this situation is the 'Northern League': at the start of the 1990s and even more so during the last decade, the Northern League became a key player in Italian politics. Not only did it become indispensable to Centre-Right coalitions in order to win general elections, but the Northern

League was also able to put the issue of federalism (if not independence) for the richer Italian Northern regions at the centre of political discussions.

These political changes had an impact on health care. The issues of decentralization, privatization and managerialization were discussed and implemented not only in relation to economic pressure but also political pressure. Lack of trust in and distaste for political parties meant that: managerialization was seen as a tool for public institution to regain legitimacy (giving power to experts); privatization as a way to introduce more market mechanisms in a health care system strictly controlled by the State (and political parties); whereas decentralization became, not a technical issue (is there a more effective and efficient way to deliver public goods?) but a deeply rooted political one (what type of State do we want? Can Northern Italian citizens accept to be controlled by Rome?).

Institutional factors: the interplay among the three reforms

Apart from more traditional institutions usually considered in policy analysis (in this case for instance, the presence of an NHS instead of a Social Health Insurance), a factor that has explained some of the tendencies in the last two decades, is the interplay among the three reforms: specifically decentralization and the decentralized governments' capacity to run the NHS have strongly affected the way privatization and managerialization have worked. This has happened for a series of reasons, related to territorial differences in terms of: previous institutional settings (for example some regions had traditionally high level of private provision before the reforms of last 20 years); the distribution of social capital and public administration capacity, as indicated by Putnam et al. (1990), with a clear North–South divide; economic development levels (Southern Italian regions have an average GDP per-capita quite lower, around 16,000 Euros, than the one of Centre-Northern regions, around 29,000 Euros).

Privatization in terms of provision did not occur at the same pace in the regionalized NHS. In particular, regions with higher private provision generally increased the provision, whereas the regions with lower levels maintained or even reduced this presence (Pavolini and Vicarelli, 2009).

How it happened

Actors and coalitions

In comparison with other European countries, over the last two decades in Italy it is impossible to identify a clear reforming coalition that pushed through innovations (of any kind). Instead, what can be discerned, are different and often fragmented alliances that for certain respects were able to come together, albeit only for limited periods of time.

A first actor, possibly going unnoticed in the policy arena as happened instead in a country like France (see Chapter 5), were national level top-bureaucrats. They were absent from the debate, following a traditional Italian weakness in terms of independence and capacity to influence the drafting of new policies by bureaucracy (Capano and Gualmini, 2010).

Political parties and regional governments played a central role. If in the 1990s there were clear-cut divisions between the Centre-Left parties and governments (keen on maintaining the NHS and reinforcing its public status) and the Conservatives (aiming at privatizing the NHS or, at least, to reduce the public role in health care), the last decade was a time of convergence in Parliament towards a model that did not deny the importance of the NHS, focusing less on a general discussion of its public status and more on cost-containment strategies.

Regional actors came into play, especially in the last decade, with an increasing role given their powers in managing the NHS. Indeed, during the 2000s major reforms in the NHS did not occur in comparison with the previous decade. This is mainly related to the fact that Regional governments substantially had the right to use their discretion when implementing National regulations to issues such as privatization of provision and some forms of managerialization.

General trade unions played a limited ('veto players') role, focusing mainly on defending NHS workers rights. They were only partially successful in this attempt. This was also due to the fact that with regionalization, a good part of the decisions were transferred to the local level. Trade unions in different territories varied in their capacity to interact and influence policy.

Moreover, traditionally in relation to the health care sector there was a strong fragmentation of (private) providers and workers' representative bodies, which made it even more difficult for these actors to collectively influence public policy. The most that could often be achieved were, and are, 'particularistic' agreements, unrelated to general issues of the NHS organization, and requests coming from specific groups.

This interpretation holds even more true for one of the traditionally most powerful groups in health care: doctors. The fact that there was and still is a strong fragmentation in this professional group (between GPs and hospital doctors, among different trade unions representing the same professional group) has made them relatively 'weak veto players', scarcely able to influence the managerialization and privatization process (perceived by them as a 'loss' of autonomy and power in the NHS).

Among the 'losers' we can add citizens, patients and their associations: using Hirschman categorization (1970), if citizens had a little 'voice' in the 1980s and early 1990s, their possibility of influencing policies faded away in the last two decades and today citizens tend to adopt more 'exit' strategies (moving from a region to another in search for better care or shifting to the private health care market) (Pavolini, 2011).

Forms of change

The analytical toolkit, developed by Streeck and Thelen (2005) and by others (Hacker, 2004) to study institutional change, is quite useful in order to frame what happened in Italy in the past two decades, especially because different trajectories and processes seem at work at various times (see Table 4.2).

The 1990s were a time when there were clear attempts to adopt a 'breakdown and replacement' strategy: specifically the reforms of the first part of the decade, as well as the Constitutional ones at the end of it, tried to significantly reshape the NHS. Decentralization became one of the main cornerstones of the new NHS, replacing a previous system more controlled by the National Centre: the Constitutional reform of 2001 defined at an even higher legal level the new institutional design. Managerialization was also a big breakthrough for the NHS organization: in health authorities politicians and traditional bureaucrats (with backgrounds in legal studies) were increasingly replaced by experts, often from economic backgrounds.

In terms of privatization, an initial major attempt at a 'breakdown and replacement' strategy came into force at the beginning of the 1990s: some

Table 4.2 Shapes and trajectories of institutional change in the Italian NHS in the last two decades

	The 1990s	The last decade	Overall result after two decades
Rescaling	Breakdown and replacement: decentralization – from a Unitary NHS to a Regionalized NHS	Gradual transformation: Hidden partial re-centralization	Some changes but also a 'survival and return' situation
Managerialization	Breakdown and replacement: from many politicians to single managers	Gradual transformation: Hidden return of politics over management	Some changes but also a 'survival and return' situation
Privatization: expenditure	Gradual transformation: strong increase in private expenditure	Gradual transformation: new increase in public spending	Some changes but also a 'survival and return' situation
Privatization: provision	Breakdown and replacement: the introduction of quasi-markets	A polarization and diversification process: Regional NHS went different ways	Some changes but also a 'survival and return' situation

reform proposals wanted to discharge the NHS and substantially privatize health care. These attempts failed but some of the ideas behind 'hard' privatization were integrated nonetheless in the reforms passed in 1992–93: quasi-markets were substantially introduced and, even if not formally stated as a 'policy goal', substantial cuts to public health care expenditure were made.

In comparison with the 1990s, the past decade witnessed almost totally different trajectories: using Streeck and Thelen (2005) terminology, it was a time of 'gradual transformation', when first and second order policy instruments were changed (Hall, 1993), having a strong (and silent) impact on the overall institutional architecture, deeply transforming it without explicitly declaring to do so.

In terms of rescaling, the second part of the last decade witnessed a new (hidden) form of recentralization of powers: the 'Piani di rientro' was a strong and effective tool through which National Governments could impose decisions to Regions with deficits (the closure of hospitals, the hiring freeze of new professionals, different drugs policies etc.).

Managers in the NHS have not seen any formal change in their status nor have new models of governance been introduced for local health care authorities. However, year after year, Regional top administrators (Presidents, Health Councillors, heads of the Health Care departments etc.) have gained an increasing amount of power over 'General Directors', who in many cases have tended to become more policy implementers than policy innovators and middle-managers *à la* Drucker (2010). Privatization of expenditure witnessed a drastic reduction in the last decade and followed a bell-curve shape even if there might be some suggestion of a 'hidden' privatization. Assessing what happened in the privatization of provision is more complicated: due to the simultaneous process of decentralization, different Regions chose different approaches. As briefly discussed earlier, certain Regions adopted the quasi-market model (e.g. Lombardy as the first front-runner), but many others simply dismissed the idea and mostly kept their system in public hands (e.g. Tuscany) (Pavolini and Vicarelli, 2009). Therefore the regional landscape looked quite fragmented and polarized with a relatively limited number of Regions giving more room to private providers and many others mostly maintaining a public-planning and delivery system.

If we try to put together the trends in the 1990s and those in more recent decade, it is difficult to detect a single linear trajectory depicting institutional change, as a consequence of partial (hidden) countertrends in the last few years. Therefore changes have taken place but their final result (at least until 2013) is closer to a 'survival and return' situation than a real 'breakdown and replacement' or a 'gradual transformation': 'survival and return' indicates that formal disruptive institutional change has resulted in a return to the previous model. Italy has a decentralized NHS, where in more recent years the National government has started to play an increasing and robust role. The quasi-markets are relatively present in some regions but in many others there are no signs of them. Managers are still present and formally powerful, but their role has increasingly weakened over time. Furthermore, private expenditure has almost fallen back to the levels of the early 1990s.

It makes sense to ask why different institutional change models were at work in different decades. The answer is complex. The 1990s were a time when a political earthquake shook both parties and politicians. It was also a time of high public deficit, slow economic growth, at least in the first half, with Italy trying to get into the (forthcoming) Euro-zone. Regionalist/ independentist parties grew. All these factors created a 'window of opportunity' for policy change: political parties at the national level tried to legitimize themselves showing that they were bringing health care closer to citizens (decentralization), also substituting the State with the market and bureaucrats with managers (managerialization and privatization of provision). Once the earthquake was apparently over, political parties again started asking for room to manoeuvre in health care (with respect to managerialization). It also started becoming more evident that decentralization and privatization were not necessarily the most effective solutions. For instance privatization of provision did not prove to be more efficient than almost totally public delivery systems (Pavolini and Vicarelli, 2009). Decentralization brought in more difficulties of controlling expenditure, given the implementation of a regionalized and fragmented policy-making structure (Mosca, 2006). For those interested in reversing or changing the trajectories of the previous decade, new 'windows of opportunity' to 'breakdown and replacement strategies' could not be seen on the horizon. If political legitimation was not as low as in the 1990s, any formal attempt by political parties 'to put their hands' on local NHS management (by getting rid of *direttori generali* and replacing them with boards headed by politicians) would have been too dangerous in terms of reactions in public opinion. A similar case applies to decentralization: with a party such as the Northern League, that was able to hegemonize the discussion around State institutional design, it would have been impossible to directly criticize this form of rescaling on strictly technical reasons, because the discussion would have immediately become a political discussion about the 'rights' of Northern Italians to be more 'free'. Therefore the whole strategy developed in the last decade was a 'silent' attempt to change the NHS regulation without directly stating so.

The impact on NHS functioning

In order to analyse how well the Italian NHS has functioned and the role of the three regulatory changes (rescaling, managerialization, privatization) we can start by giving a general overview, comparing the Italian case with the other biggest (in terms of population) four health care systems in Western Europe (Spain, France, UK and Germany), hereby defined as EU-4.

The Italian NHS is in line with (or sometimes even better than) other Western European healthcare systems (Table 4.3). Italy shows better performance rates than the other EU-4 in terms of bed occupancy rates, relatively low level of child mortality and relatively high survival rates after serious cardio-circulatory diseases. Italy shows a similar functioning in terms of prevention.

These favourable results were obtained using fewer resources (measured by the lower incidence of health care public expenditure on GDP) compared to the other countries and without significant differences in terms of private expenditure. However, there are also other indicators that highlight lower performance in the Italian NHS. Health and social care integration is more limited, especially in the case of the elderly. There are important differences in access to services based on income (and social class). There are also huge

Table 4.3 Functioning of the Italian NHS in a comparative perspective (years 2007–2009; mostly 2009)

Dimensions	Indicators	Italy	EU-4
Human, financial and technological resources	No. magnetic resonance units for each 1 million inhabitants	21.6	7.9
	Public health care expenditure as a percentage of GDP	7.4	8.3
	Private health care expenditure as percentage of total health care exp.	22.5	22.3
Prevention	Percentage of women undergoing mammography, age 50–69 years	68.0	62.2
	Pertussis vaccination, children	96.2	96.3
Hospital Efficiency	Average length of stay: acute care, days	6.7	6.5
	Acute care occupancy rate (percentage of available beds)	79.5	78.1
Integrated social care and health care	No. of residential facilities beds for frail elderly per 1,000 elderly	17.4	31.6
Citizens satisfaction	Percentage of people unsatisfied with their health care systems	46.0	30.6
Results	Infant mortality rates	3.7	3.8
	Mortality rate for heart attack after 30 days of hospitalization	4.0	6.2
Equity and inequality	Percentage of individuals with an unmet medical need due to excessive cost	3.6	0.7
	Percentage of individuals with an unmet medical need due to excessive cost in the lowest quintile of income	7.2	2.1

Source: Authors' elaboration from OECD (2012) and Eurobarometer (2010).

differences in terms of user satisfaction (approximately a 15 per cent gap): these differences are also related to problems of long waiting lists that were not sufficiently dealt with by policies during the last two decades (Fattore et al., 2013).

Furthermore, the gap between Italy and the other four EU countries decreased (Pavolini and Vicarelli, 2012).

In conclusion, the cost-containment of public resources in the Italian NHS in the last two decades has neither led to an ongoing increase in private spending (this phenomena took place only in the 1990s) nor has there been a decrease in quality and performance, if compared with other EU countries. A set of problems appears relevant in the Italian case. Let us now consider what happened in light of the three phenomena discussed so far.

Decentralization and functioning

If decentralization was expected to serve as a tool for public retrenchment, it failed, except perhaps during the mid 1990s. As also stated by other studies, the reduction of financial public resources to sub-national Governments did not affect citizens' well-being at the national level (Piacenza and Turati, 2010).

Nonetheless, an increasingly decentralized NHS highlighted some of the main limits of the Italian NHS: its territorial dualism with the richer (in terms of GDP per-capita) Centre-Northern Regions performing far better than the poorer Southern ones.

A document from the Ministry of Health is very helpful in providing a concise picture of this situation (Ministero della Salute, 2011). The Ministry started evaluating regional health care systems using a complex and comprehensive set of indicators referring to their functioning in terms of prevention (for example the percentage of women regularly undergoing mammography screening), ambulatory and territorial health care (for example the diffusion of hospice beds in relation to the total number of people who died from cancer), and hospital care (for example hospitalization rate). Through a weighted comparative methodology each region's functioning was evaluated. The result for 2009 was that out of 17 regional health care systems studied, eight were considered good performers, three partially good performers (which means they had problems with just some dimensions of provision) and six showed poor performance. It must be noted that situations of critical performance were found only in Lazio and in southern regions, whereas situations of good performance only in north-central regions.

Other studies (Mapelli, 2007; Pavolini and Vicarelli, 2012; Pavolini, 2011) also confirm the presence of two different types of RHS: the systems in the Centre-North of Italy with a relatively medium to high level of performance; the Southern healthcare systems with a relatively medium to low level of performance.

To measure the different performance of these two clusters of regional healthcare systems, Pavolini and Vicarelli (2012) used a set of indicators. Table 4.4 confirm significant gaps between Centre-North and Southern healthcare systems. Not a single indicator shows the Southern situation to be better than that of Central-Northern Italy.

Moreover, this divide has increased in the last two decades while the process of NHS decentralization was being implemented. Apart from infant mortality rate, all the other indicators used in Table 4.4 show a widening gap between the two areas of the country (Pavolini and Vicarelli, 2012).

These findings are also supported by other studies. Marinacci et al. (2010) show that social health inequalities in Italy are closely linked to territory: among other (more traditional) social factors related to education and social class, living in the South increases the chances of having health problems. Van Doorslaer and Masseria (2004), studying income-related inequality in the use of medical care, found that the degree of inequity, in favour of wealthy people, in seeing a doctor is high in Italy: regional (Centre-North versus South) differences mainly account for this.

This territorial divide in the performance of healthcare finds no parallel in other Western European healthcare systems. Table 4.5 shows the differences within Italy and across the four other countries already mentioned, using two indicators: citizens' satisfaction with their local healthcare services;

Table 4.4 Performance of Central–Northern and Southern regional healthcare systems (2008)

	Centre-North (1)	South (2)	Gap (1–2)
Healthcare deficit as a percentage of total public healthcare expenditure	–.1	5.2	–5.3
Pre-op average hospital length of stay (days)	1.8	2.1	–0.3
Hospitalization rate	106.5	134.2	–27.7
Percentage of women 50+ years old receiving mammography (2005)	64.8	41.2	23.6
Percentage of elderly in nursing homes or receiving home integrated care	8.0	3.4	4.6
Ratio Percentage of high educated women to of low educated ones receiving mammography (2005)	2.2	3.3	–1.1
Infant mortality rate	3.2	4.4	–1.2
Percentage of people very satisfied with their local health care system	45.3	22.2	23.1

Source: Istat (2012).

Table 4.5   Territorial divide in performance of the Italian NHS in comparative perspective, 2006–2008

	% citizens satisfied with their healthcare system (Urban Audit) (2008)		% citizens reporting unmet medical need due to excessive cost (EU-Silc) (2006)	
	EU-4	Italy	EU-3**	Italy
Richer Regions (A)*	83,0	71,5	2,0	1,1
Poorer Regions (B)*	84,5	40,6	2,0	5,6
Gap (A-B)	−1,5	30,9	0,0	4,5

* Richer and poorer regions in each country are defined respectively as showing at least 90% of the national GDP per-capita (A) or being below this threshold line (B).
** UK missing.
Sources: Eurostat: Urban Audit (2010); EU-Silc (2008).

and people reporting an unmet medical need in the previous year due to problems with their healthcare systems. The results clearly highlight a gap between richer and poorer regions in Italy which is highly disadvantageous for poorer regions, while little, if any difference, is found in the other countries.

Privatization and functioning

The role of private provision and its impact on health care functioning has often been characterized, in Italy as well as in other countries, by ideological rhetoric regarding either the goodness of private provision, competition and freedom of choice in health care as a value in itself, or the opposing view of how wrong it is to have 'private (self-)interests' in the public sphere. Although the debate is quite heated, there is limited empirical research on this issue. Vicarelli and Pavolini (2009) tried to test whether different levels of privatization provision had an impact on the overall institutional performance of Italian public health care systems. As briefly described before, the characteristic of the Italian situation is a regionalized system where there is a strong heterogeneity in terms of private provision: therefore the possible existence of a correlation between RHS performance and the level of private provision can be analysed. A complex index of health care and economic performance[1] was built, using as a proxy in the latter case, the level of RHS budget deficit, expressed as a percentage of total RHCS expenditure in the years 2004–2005. No particular correlation was found: it seems that a good part of the debate on the role of private provision in the NHS is ideological (with 'fans' and 'foes' of private provision), whereas a more pragmatic approach would be needed. The main result of the analysis indicate that the 'the government capacity to control private provision'[2] by RHCS is the key variable in explaining what might be the outcomes of private provision inside an NHS.[3] In terms of RHS performance it did not seem relevant whether there was a high or low level of private provision in a single region, or whether Region had adopted a quasi-market model: what seems more relevant is the capacity of regional governments to introduce effective tools to manage and to control private providers. Where there are 'strong' RHS in terms of steering ability, partnerships can produce innovation and a diversification of the supply system. Where the RHS are 'weak' in controlling provision, the risk of poor economic performance rises. An empirical research conducted by Mapelli (2007) showed similar results.

Managerialization and functioning

Cost-containment has always been prominent in Italian health care policy, as in many other countries. In the 1990s, public finances came under tremendous pressure due to the enormous public debt accumulated in the late 1970s and 1980s and the need to comply with the EU stability pact. In the 1990s, when the main managerial reforms came into effect, public health care expenditure was in line with the EU-15, but in the following years Italy started spending less per-capita and in terms of GDP percentage. As already shown, this decrease in public funding only led to a strong increase in private funding during the 1990s. Consequently, the slowing down of public expenditure was not transferred to the private sector and to households, especially in the last decade. This was because the majority of the regional governments made efficient use of the limited financial resources given by Central Government for health care management. Even if resources given to Regional governments increased at a considerably slower pace than in the rest of Europe, over the last 20 years, only a limited number of Regions (most notably five out of twenty-one) generated financial deficits in running their health care systems. Specific analysis of the causes of healthcare deficits in these Regions show that these deficits were not related to underfinancing by the government, but rather to problems in the way the health care delivery system was organized – for instance, an oversized hospital sector, a large number of accredited private providers, weak community-based and outpatient services, and inability to control the costs of goods and services (Tediosi et al., 2009).

So far managerialization has been quite successful in at least maintaining a decent NHS performance, within a context of scarcer but increasingly efficiently used resources.

Professionals and the NHS

If in the last two decades changes affected NHS users in various ways, an element which is often overlooked in the analysis of HCS is the role and the impact of changes on professionals. Using OECD data (2012), in Italy at the end of last decade 7.3 per cent of the civil labour force worked in health and social care. Although this percentage increased over time (it was around 6.2 per cent in 2000), it remains smaller than in many other countries: Germany and the UK show percentages around 12–13 per cent, whereas the Scandinavian countries score at least 15 per cent. A specificity of the Italian NHS is the fact that it is centred on doctors: in Italy there are almost 250 thousand professionally active physicians (equal to a density of 3.5 per 1.000 inhabitants). This percentage is one of the highest among the countries of this study. If doctors are quite well spread, nurses and midwifes are relatively less present: they show a density equal to 6.6, whereas in all the other countries in this study the percentage is quite higher, apart from Poland and Spain.

Another characteristic of the system is the 'aging' of the professional population, in particular of physicians: at the end of last decade almost 40 per cent of them was aged 55 or older. A similar percentage is found only in Germany and France, both countries with SHI. None of the NHS countries reach percentages analogous to those in Italy (around 13 per cent in the UK, 32 per cent in Sweden and 22 per cent in Spain). A high number of doctors is matched by lower average incomes: the yearly remuneration of Italian salaried specialists was equal to approximately 92 thousand (PPP in $) at the end of last decade, whereas the amount received in many other countries is higher (for example 124 thousand in the UK). The increase in salaries has also been quite limited: during the last decade it improved by around 10 per cent, whereas practically in all other countries where data was available the increase was quite more consistent.

Therefore doctors still play an important role in the NHS but their condition, as well as the one of other professional groups in the NHS, is becoming more problematic: on one hand, managers and managerial activities are putting them under increasing pressure (Vicarelli et al., 2009) and are lowering their autonomy; on the other hand, cost containment policies are considerably blocking more opportunities for hiring new professionals (this phenomena explains the aging of the professional population, at least in relation to doctors) and therefore more pressure and workload is burdened onto aging doctors (Vicarelli, 2011). Moreover, as already explained, in the last two decades health care professionals in general, including doctors, were unable to influence policy transformations: they were only able to play on the 'defensive', trying to limit the impact of the reforms on their working conditions.

Conclusions: the Italian paradox

The Italian NHS changed quite significantly in the last two decades. The three phenomena studied in this chapter all affected the way the NHS system worked. Decentralization brought deep transformations, as did managerialization and different forms of privatization. Nowadays the NHS works better than 20 years ago: this is of course related to technological improvements not studied in this book, but also to changes in regulation. If this brief reconstruction holds true, there are some elements that deserve more attention.

Firstly, the last 20 years did not show a linear and continuous pattern. Many trends registered in the 1990s were partially reversed in the last decade. Quite often this change took place in a 'hidden' rather than in an explicitly declared form.

Secondly, the transformations did not have similar impacts on all actors. A clear and increasing territorial contrast can be identified: in Italy there is not only one NHS but two (the Southern and the Northern), with very significant differences in performance.

As a whole, the Italian NHS illustrates a paradox: it appears to be less costly than other HCS, it often obtains a similar level of functioning, yet individuals are less satisfied with it. How is this possible? Future research will have to find suitable answers to this question: how can Italy have a system which performs well whilst spending less, yet is unable to satisfy its citizens?

Moreover, austerity measures that have come into force in more recent years will tell us in the near future how this 'strange' NHS (generally well functioning with limited economic resources but with strong territorial divides) will eventually change again and in which direction. There is a strong need for a NHS 'recalibration', pushing forwards to better respond to needs (especially the ones related to chronic illnesses) and further strengthening the functioning of primary care (Vicarelli, 2012). The recent austerity plans risk putting this possible 'recalibration' at stake, given the level of severe cuts in a NHS that is already showing lower public expenditure than many other Central and Northern European health care systems.

Notes

1. The index was built, using principal component analysis (PCA), on the basis of a series of variables on the NHS functioning at the regional level: human, financial and technological resources, prevention, hospital efficiency, integrated social care and health care, citizens' satisfaction, results, equity and inequality. The variables are mostly the ones described in Table 4.4.
2. The index for government capacity of RHCS to control and regulate private provision has been built using as a proxy, the development of 'accreditation' systems (the ways, requirements and actions that RHCS ask from private providers that want to become part of the regional NHS provision system).
3. The correlation between the different performance indices and the private providers role in the RHS (expressed in terms of incidence of private discharges among the total public discharges) has been controlled for the following variables: political (political orientation of regional governments and their stability over time); socio-cultural (civicness); economic (level of economic regional development); socio-demographic (complexity of health services demand); governance (for more details see Vicarelli and Pavolini, 2009).

5
France: Squaring the Health Spending Circle?

Bruno Palier and Alban Davesne

Introduction

As in most Western European countries, the financing of the French health care system became a critical issue following the 1970s economic downturn. However, contrary to some other countries, it has never subsequently ceased to monopolize the social agenda. The combination of slow economic growth, extended access to universal medical care and the improvement of health technologies contributed to continuously increase both the total health expenditure and the share of public resources devoted to health care. The French sickness insurance funds have thus been in deficit from 1969 to 1979, in 1981, 1986 and continuously since 1990. Short-term measures by and large failed to tackle the growing deficit of the *Sécurité sociale* funds,[1] despite no less than 18 saving plans between 1975 and 1995. The traditional way of curbing social security deficits was to impose low prices on health care services and pharmaceuticals ('frozen tariffs'), to find new resources devoted to sickness insurance (such as the flat social ear-marked tax created in 1990, which now covers 35 per cent of health care resources) and to increase co-payments by patients. Altogether, these three financial instruments have been unable to cut the deficit at its roots. The institutional characteristics of the French sickness insurance system have made it indeed very difficult to control health care expenditure and a consensus emerged among policy-makers in the late 1980s on the need for a broader reform agenda addressing the structural and organizational determinants of persistent deficits.

From the onset, the French health care system has been a synthesis of state control and autonomous regulation. This dual institutional arrangement encompasses a wide range of hindrance for change and provides many actors with veto possibilities. The financing, regulation and provision of health care sector are indeed traditionally dealt separately by various actors (social partners, the State and private doctors), making the health care system difficult to govern as a whole (Palier, 2005). The sickness insurance system provides a generous universal coverage of health-related risks.

The Sickness funds reimburse health care expenses to patients on an *ex post* basis, which means that they exert little control over the supply and consumption of health care services (Palier, 2010: 74–7). They have long been autonomously managed by social partners, rendering state control over expenditure extremely difficult. Moreover, medical freedom of doctors and free choice for patients is a key feature of the French health care system. This ensures a good responsiveness to most health care needs but it comes at a high financial cost for sickness insurance funds and creates territorial inequalities. Finally, the supply of health care is fragmented between public (65 per cent of hospital beds – DREES, 2012: 81) and private actors: 35 per cent of hospital beds are run by private or non-for-profit hospitals and clinics, and the ambulatory health care is almost entirely private ('liberal').

By retracing the main trends of French health care reforms from the mid-1990s to 2012, this chapter shows how learning processes and the emergence of a reformist coalition contributed to bring about institutional and organizational change within the health system. Confronted with uncontrollable *Sécurité sociale* deficits, the government has been trying to curb health expenditure by setting an annual national spending limit by law. The aims of regulatory changes have then been to enable health authorities to make health actors comply with them – while avoiding politicians to face the occasional outburst of health professionals and other stakeholders. We argue that the implementation of incremental regulatory changes in terms of rescaling, managerialization and creeping privatization follows a specific trajectory which is framed by lessons learned from past failures and by the power struggle between sickness insurance officials, government officials, trade unions and employers associations, and medical professions. Since the mid-1990s the government has been reinforcing the control and regulatory capabilities of the state over the financing and the planning of the health care system and increasing the cost-efficiency of health care through managerial reforms. Next to the financial measure and the more structural reorganization of the system, a third type of change is leading to a privatization of access to health care. We will investigate how far-reaching these three institutional changes are in terms of their distributional implications for health actors. To address this question, this chapter will analyse the institutional and political context in which recent regulatory reforms took place, explain the major trends that can be found throughout these regulatory changes and will eventually discuss their implications for the overall performance of the system.

The political and institutional context of regulatory reforms

Controlling the tariffs reimbursed by the mandatory sickness insurance system had long been identified as an efficient regulatory tool by *Sécurité sociale* and government officials prior to the 1980s. This however could not stop the increase of health expenditure. During the 1980s, a programmatic coalition advocating for structural reforms emerged among high level civil servants specialized in social protection – the 'elite of welfare' – and constructed a shared diagnosis about the need for increased state control and more efficient modes of management in the provision of health care (Hassenteufel et al., 2010). These actors were mainly ministry officials in charge of *Sécurité sociale* supervision (*Direction de la Sécurité sociale*), members of the French national audit office (*Cour des comptes*) and Social security officials (especially the employee sickness insurance fund – *Caisse nationale de l'assurance maladie des travailleurs salariés*, CNAMTS). They have been supported, among others, by a centre-left Union (*Confédération française démocratique du travail*) who also promoted a far-reaching reform of the health care system. In the hospital sector, this coalition was led by ministry officials in charge of inpatient care (*Direction de l'hospitalisation et de l'organisation des soins*). By promoting a better medical use of health care resources (*'maîtrise médicalisée'*) and advocating for structural reforms as a prerequisite for curbing the sickness insurance funds deficit, this reformist coalition distanced itself both from the purely financial approach of the ministry of finances and from the liberal-corporatist positions of medical doctors. New deficit heights in the early 1990s and lessons from past policy failures created a favourable political context for those 'change agents' (Mahoney and Thelen, 2010: 22) to advocate for structural reforms.

Hospital fixed budget: early financial success and long-term side-effects

The hospital sector was hit first in the early 1980s by the 'fiscal imperative' of structural reforms (Freeman, 2000: 70). The ministry of health's strong hold on the public hospital sector made a financing reform less difficult than in ambulatory care. The socialist minister of social affairs Pierre Bérégovoy substituted the old *per diem* funding system by a prospective global budget, which allowed adjusting *a priori* the budget allocated by the *Sécurité sociale* to public hospitals. This important reform was implemented in 1983 for main hospitals and in 1984 for smaller public hospitals. It forced hospitals to lower their expenses. The share of public hospitals in the total health expenditure decreased from 41 per cent in 1980 to 34 per cent in 2000 (Tabuteau, 2006: 275) and the average duration of a stay in French hospitals (5.7) is now among the lowest in all OECD countries (OECD, 2012). Setting global budget for hospitals has been an effective instrument in cutting hospital expenditure overall, but it created disincentives to improve hospital governance and did not bridge inequalities between hospitals. This system 'froze' the 1983 hospital governance and distribution, despite some regional adjustments in the 1990s (Vincent, 2005: 51). Thus, various actors demanded new structural reforms in order to make public hospitals more efficient and responsive to evolving constraints and needs.

Ambulatory budget cap: failed implementation

Controlling the supply of ambulatory care in a sickness insurance system has proved to be a much more complicated task, especially so in France where the principles of the *médecine libérale* laid down in the 1927 charter of medical professions (freedom for patients to choose doctors, freedom of prescription for doctors, fee-for-service payment) are considered by a large majority of medical doctors as sacred and inalienable (Hassenteufel, 2009). During the 1980s, the ministry of social affairs tried to apply a budget cap (*Enveloppe globale*) to ambulatory care, but its implementation was left to conventional negotiations between the national sickness fund and medical unions, and the latter refused to implement cost-containment measures that could harm their medical freedom (Pierru, 2011: 418). Meanwhile, rising health expenditure prompted the government to turn to more assertive means to implement cost-containment measures. In 1991, the left wing government led by Michel Rocard introduced the objective of reducing the health care supply based on medical needs and a medical evaluation of therapeutics (*Maîtrise médicalisée des dépenses*). The government therefore released medical guidelines on best therapeutic practices (*Références médicales opposables*) which were first included in the 1993 convention between the sickness fund and medical unions. But no thorough sanction mechanism came to support the implementation of these guidelines (Palier, 2010: 101).

A first major shift occurred in November 1995, when right wing Prime Minister Alain Juppé proposed a structural reform of the whole Social insurance system, including a dramatic restructuring of the financing and organization of the health care system. An effective implementation of medical conventions in the ambulatory sector was the cornerstone of this reform. The first objective of the Juppé plan was to enforce the health budget cap in the ambulatory sector. A constitutional revision adopted in February 1996 allowed the Parliament to determine every year the resources devoted to the *Sécurité sociale* funds (Social Security finance bill – *Loi de financement de la Sécurité sociale*) and to set a budget cap for sickness insurance expenditure for the next year (national health spending objectives – *Objectif national des dépenses de l'assurance maladie*, ONDAM). Sickness insurance funds then negotiated conventions with health practitioners on the basis of these objectives set by the Parliament. The sickness insurance funds and the medical professionals remained in charge of negotiating the conventions, but an ordinance released in April 1996 allowed the government to set the national health spending objectives itself in case social partners were unable to come up with an agreement within 65 days (abandoned by the 2004 'Douste-Blazy' reform). In order to get liberal practitioners to comply with the national spending objectives, the Juppé plan introduced potential financial sanctions against practitioners who would disregard the spending objectives (sanctions were to be imposed by the social partners and then by the state according to the 1999 *loi de financement de la Sécurité sociale* – Palier,

2010: 102). This reform was clearly in contradiction with the principles of liberal medicine, its funding based on a fee-for-service and its professional self-regulation. The implementation of constraining budget caps for ambulatory care triggered a massive strike of medical students (*internes*) during the spring of 1997, while medical unions led a successful juridical battle against penalties. The sanction mechanism was severely watered down in 2000 by a ruling of the Council of state (*Conseil d'État*) which denied the government the right to force health professionals to pay a fine to sickness insurance funds. The reform was thus left incomplete. Neither the annual objectives voted by the Parliament nor the negotiated conventions signed by sickness insurance funds and social partners have been respected until very recently. Moreover, doctors' discontent about the Juppé plan led subsequent right wing government to endorse their claims to charge higher fees. Statutory tariffs increased, while extra fees have spread dramatically (+40 per cent since 1996 – Aballea et al., 2007: 9). Fifteen per cent of general practitioners (GPs) and 38 per cent of specialists charge patients according to the 'Secteur 2' extra-billing system.[2] Only for specialist care, the amount of extra-billing rose from €763 million to €1.578 billion between 1990 and 2004 (Aballea et al., 2007: 11). Instead of curbing health expenditures, the failed 1996 reform and its aftermath thus fed the inflationary circle of ambulatory care.

The creation of an annual health budget cap in the mid-1990s has been a milestone for cost-containment reforms in France. But the politics of health care reform that unfolded were both contrasted and paradoxical. Firstly, they were contrasted because the situation of the hospital and ambulatory sectors was very different. The global budget reform contributed to lower hospital expenditure but created numerous organizational problems. The provision of ambulatory care, however, has been shielded from constraining cost-containment measures. Secondly, the mid-1990s reforms were paradoxical. On the one hand, the ONDAM provided more legitimacy to support regulatory reforms (Palier, 2010a: 87) and opened for a new sequence in health politics where the 'reformist coalition' led by high civil servants learned from past failures and was eventually able to implement structural reforms. Yet, on the other hand political elites have also learned from past turmoil and have been refusing for the last decade to implement reforms that would alienate the medical power. These two conflicting trends shape the main regulatory reforms that have been implemented since 1996.

Major trends in French health care reforms (1996–2012): rescaling, managerialization and privatization

Since 1996, traditional cost-containment measures have been complemented by organizational reforms aiming at fostering a better regulation of health care supply (cost-efficiency), through *étatisation* (increased state control) and managerialization (introduction of 'new public management' strategies) (Hassenteufel and Palier, 2007). Although these trends seem somehow antagonistic, they follow a same rationale according to which performance-oriented state supervision over health care provision should bring about a more rational use of financial resources to both hospital and ambulatory sectors. The third trend, 'creeping privatization', stands out as a cumulative change rather than a new clear-cut organizational reform. It derives from the oldest and the most persistent trend in French health care politics: whenever organizational reforms are stranded or insufficient, patients end up paying for the residual cost-containment efforts.

Rescaling health care regulation: the reinforced state supervision over Sécurité sociale and health care regulation

Complementing the inception of an annual parliamentary vote on the *Sécurité sociale* budget in 1996, the reforms of the last decade significantly increased the authority of the state not only on health care rules, but also on health care provision through controlling sickness insurance funds and the regulation of health care supply. In this respect, the major novelties of the reforms are the centralization of sickness fund steering and the successive agency creations.

Breaking the 'inflationist consensus': increased state supervision over sickness insurance funds

The power balance between the state and the social partners (employees and employers representatives) has first been altered by the Juppé Plan and the subsequent constitutional revision which introduced the annual Parliament vote on the national health spending objective. With this annual vote, the collective bargaining between the sickness fund and medical unions has first been put under tighter supervision by the state (the state taking over when social partners were not able to reach an agreement), before the state progressively crowded out the social partners' traditional role within the health care system. The legitimacy and ability of social partners to manage the sickness funds has indeed been weakened with the creation of the national Union of sickness funds in 2004 (*Union nationale des caisses d'assurance maladie*, UNCAM). This institution is in charge of harmonizing and coordinating health policies between the national sickness insurance and other funds. The director of the UNCAM is appointed by the Prime Minister, which is a clear sign of *étatisation* and politicization of sickness insurance funds regulation. His two most important tasks are to determine reimbursement rates and to lead conventional negotiations with the medical professionals, thus marginalizing the administrative board of the funds chaired by social partners. High profile jobs within the sickness insurance funds have shifted from social partners to civil servants, both at national and at local levels. The institutional model behind this change is clearly one of state agency (Hassenteufel and Palier, 2007).

Territorial hospital regulation and coordination of health care services

While the 1983 global budget reform provided hospital with steady sickness insurance funds transfers instead of *per diem* and uneven local resources (real estate, donations, among others) this systematic financing system (bed per inhabitants) did not provide health authorities with any regulatory tool able to bridge the territorial inequalities and financial waste created by the unregulated hospital constructions of the early 1960s (Coldefy and Lucas-Gabrielli, 2008). Having failed to restructure and rationalize hospital care from the top in the 1970s (*Carte sanitaire*), the ministry of health attempted to coordinate the supply of regional public and private inpatient care through regional objectives (*Schémas régionaux d'organisation sanitaire*) agreed upon by local stakeholders.[3] This new instrument was intended to contribute to cost-containment policies by allowing to curb the supply of hospital beds (and indeed, the global number of beds decreased by 10 per cent between 1998 and 2008 – DREES, 2010b, 57) and to encourage a more efficient territorial provision of inpatient care by assessing and anticipating the evolution of regional health care needs (for example, the shift from surgery beds to elderly and long term care facilities). The purpose of this regional planning system was pretty much to implement national strategies (Delas, 2011), but this weak top–down approach was often thwarted by local administrations who often stand for small hospitals as a part of their local economic and social life. In order to make the planning of hospital care more efficient, the government decided in 1996 to set up regional hospital agencies (*Agence régionale de l'hospitalisation*, ARH) in charge of controlling the financial soundness of public and private hospitals and to monitor the planning of health care supply.[4] Although the creation of regional agencies seemed to reinforce local actors, it has rather intensified the supervision of the state closer to local health care politics.

The regional health agencies (*Agence Régionale de Santé*, ARS) created in 2010 further embody the commitment of the ministry of health to strengthening its steering capabilities on the supply of health care within and across the regions.[5] The dispersion of regional authorities between regional sickness funds, hospital agencies and public health promoters was seen by ministry officials as a hinder for a more coordinated and coherent health system. Seven public instances (including regional levels of sickness insurance funds) responsible for organizing and financing health care at the regional level have been merged into one regional health agency. Regional agencies can thus, among many competencies, foster the creation of local hospital communities (*Communautés hospitalières de territoire*) in order to improve the coordination between outpatient and inpatient care.[6] Although it is too soon to determine the organizational outcomes of this rescaling process, one must point out that regional health agencies directors have been given significant regulatory instruments to coordinate and monitor the health strategy of their region. The fact that ARS directors are appointed by the ministry of health (and that some of these directors are very high profile, either former minister of health, or former directors of the national sickness insurance fund) is fully in line so far with the general trend of French health care rescaling: they are expected to channel more efficiently the cost-efficiency and rationalizing efforts of the ministry of health. Rather than the devolution one might have expected (that is more power to local governments), the territorial restructuring of hospital regulation led to an *étatisation* of inpatient care planning through the concentration of important regulatory powers in the hand of regional health agencies. This structural change, although still recent, is most likely to be of major importance in terms of policy outcomes, as it allows a more coercive implementation of the cost-containment strategies and efficiency-oriented management techniques promoted by the ministry of health.

Uneven developments towards a 'state-led managed care health policy'

The development of management techniques in the health care sector is closely linked to the above-mentioned rescaling reforms. In many respects, *étatisation* and territorial restructuring have been instrumental in the implementation of new managerial policies. The changes of the last decade converge towards a model of state-led managed care health policy,[7] with 'medico-economic efficiency' as a new buzz-word. Much like rescaling, managerialization has been most thoroughly implemented in the hospital sector and is only emerging in the ambulatory care – despite recent headways.

Hospital care: a new state-led managerialism

Despite its relative satisfactory budgetary results, the global budget in the public hospital sector was criticized because it tended to discourage innovative management and shielded under-achieving public hospital, while private clinics (which account for the third of all acute beds and two third of surgery beds) continued to be financed on a fee-for-service basis, much like ambulatory care. Policy-makers and leading experts advocated for an activity based payment system (*Tarification à l'activité*, T2A), inspired by the American diagnosis related group system (DRG) and similar to what already existed in other European countries. This financing system combines an administrated pricing system and a competitive internal market where the income of each hospital is linked directly to the number and case-mix of patients treated as defined in terms of homogeneous patient groups (*Groupe homogène de malades*) (Or, 2010a). Hospitals were thus expected to be more transparent in their management, to improve cost-efficiency and to be more responsive to the needs of the local population in terms of access and quality of care.

This managerialization process began in the early 1990s with the experimentation of a medical information system (*Programme de médicalisation des systèmes d'information*), assessing the activity of hospitals based on the diagnosis related group method, which paved the way for a shift to an activity-based financing system. The institutionalization of this standard-ized data system was a 'rocky path' (Steffen, 2010: 377) and took more than a decade to be completed. In 2003, a national reform called '*plan hôpital 2007*' brought public hospitals one step closer to full-fledged activity-based pricing. The aim of this plan was to foster competition between hospitals by creating a level playing field for public and private hospitals. Such T2A pricing system applies to private clinics since 2004, while public hospitals implemented it in 2008 for the most common specialties (medicine, surgery, gynaecology-obstetrics and odontology). Besides activity-based financing, public hospitals have been granted a specific budget for 'public interest missions' such as teaching and research activities (*Missions d'intérêt général et d'aide à la contractualisation*). They make up for 11 per cent of the income of public hospitals[8] but this amount is still considered by many experts and stakeholders a poor compensation for the vital but non-profitable services that fall on public hospitals. The socialist government elected in 2012 is committed to better incorporate the variety of public missions into the system and to pursue a more gradual and differentiated approach regarding public hospitals.

The most controversial aspect of the 2008 reform was the explicit goal to achieve a total convergence of public and private tariffs in 2012, which re-ignited traditional tensions between public and private hospitals. The latter claimed that economic risks should be rewarded, pointing out that only public hospitals are safe from bankruptcy, while public actors stood up against what they saw as a detrimental tariff convergence, both in absolute and relative terms. Indeed, unified *Sécurité sociale* tariffs were expected to be aligned on the less generous pricing system applying to private hospitals, which would increase the profitability gap between the health services pro-vided by public hospital and clinics. In 2011, the government virtually gave up this measure by postponing to 2018 the deadline for achieving the pub-lic–private convergence and the new left-wing President François Hollande clearly rejected it, calling it unfair for public hospitals.[9]

At a more general level, questions have been raised about the relevance of such centralized volume-price control system when it comes to meet the annual ONDAM spending ceiling. There are concerns that they could create incentives for hospitals to increase their activity (or to report more expensive activities, a manipulation referred to as 'upcoding') in order to make up for their loss and thereby go back to feeding the inflationary cir-cle of old time's hospital financing. Zeynep Or notes that both public and private hospitals indeed appear to have reacted to the implementation of T2A tariffs by increasing their activity in 2005 (Or, 2008). Introducing a diagnosis-based pricing system has been a deep organizational change. It will thus understandably take some more years to assess fully its effects. A key element in the success of this reform will certainly be the role devoted to the state and regional agencies, and their ability to keep this pricing system both coherent with global objectives (cost-containment, quality and equity) and well-suited to local health needs (responsiveness).

A further important change concerning public hospitals is the emergence of managerial imperatives in the daily activities of all hospitals, as directors are expected to keep the finances of their hospital balanced in a context of an increasingly constraining regulatory framework and more competitive environment. The above mentioned rescaling and managerialization changes have indirectly impacted the internal organization of hospitals by altering their environment. While hospitals used to operate in a vacuum, their managers and medical staffs now have to behave more as strategic actors, aware of local competition and more responsive to the structure of regional and national opportunities (need to compete for financial grants, incentives to participate to local hospital communities and so on) (Delas, 2011). But national reforms have also directly altered hospital governance over the last decade by promoting a business-like entrepreneurial model of hospital management. The leadership of hospital directors (public servants) has been reinforced by the 2009 reform, following Nicolas Sarkozy's motto: '*Un patron et un seul à l'hôpital, le directeur*'.[10] Much like private enterprises, hospitals now also have both a board of directors (*Directoire*) and a supervisory board (*Conseil de surveillance*). While local politicians used to sit in the directors' board before the 2009 reform, the latter shifted power to the managers and takes strategic decisions away from the newly created supervisory board chaired by the Mayor. At the same time, the 1996, 2005 and 2009 reforms sought to bring health professionals closer to economic and administrative decisions. The management of hospital services is devolved to medical units (*Pôles d'activités*), each managed by a doctor who sits at the board of directors. When taking important decisions, the director of hospitals also consults a medical advisory committee (*Commission médicale d'établissement*). Since doctors and directors have often being at odds on cost-containment measures, recent reforms have obviously tried to appease the medical staff and to involve chief doctors in the drafting and implementation of the 'hospital project' (*Projet d'établissement*) that each director must elaborate in order to make his or her hospital more competitive and innovative, and thereby to secure its funding. Medical units are thus compelled to become full-fledged stakeholders of the development of their organization and of broader territorial health care networks. Moreover, financially struggling hospital are closely monitored by the ARS and could receive extra credits only after long negotiations and at the price of internal restructuration and painful organizational adjustments (for example, closing services).

An important aspect of managerialism is the introduction of quality standards and evaluation of health services. The 1996 reform promoted and generalized the evaluation of therapies in the health care system with the creation of a national agency for accreditation and evaluation (*Agence nationale d'accréditation et d'évaluation de la santé*), incorporated in the high authority on health (*Haute Autorité de Santé*) created in 2004. This agency releases 'medical references' for ambulatory care (containing therapeutic norms and norms for prescription) and opinions on the efficiency of drugs which could lead to de-reimbursement measures.

Regional hospital agencies, and later regional health agencies, have been given monitoring and sanction competences. They provide hospitals with variable budgets, based on the evaluation of their performance and they have the right to close inefficient hospitals after an accreditation enquiry. Local hospital mergers and unit restructuring are encouraged to make the coordinated care system more efficient and less redundant in term of specializations. ARS negotiate a multi-years activity programme with hospital (*Contrat pluriannuel d'objectifs et de moyens*), which must stay above a turnout threshold.[11] For instance, local surgery units which are not able to perform more than 1500 procedures annually are shut down, for financial reasons but also because such small units do not perform a sufficient volume of surgeries to keep up with the best quality and safety standards. Following the Vallancien report in 2006,[12] the government was planning on closing 54 of such surgery units but local politicians opposed it strongly and the publication of the application decree was postponed *sine die* in August 2010. This could also lead to a paradoxical situation where small hospitals tend report more activity in order to remain above the threshold. At a macro level, this contributes to an increase of the ONDAM which could be sanctioned by an authoritative reduction of *Sécurité sociale* tariffs for each patient group (Delas, 2011).

Ambulatory care: a slow but significant move towards rationalization

So far, managerialism has gone the furthest in the hospital sector where the state is stronger. Despite a recent multiplication of initiatives, managerial control of the liberal ambulatory sector by the state and the sickness funds remains limited. Since the attempted reforms of the mid-1990s, the main concern of the right wing governments (in power from 2002 to 2012) has been mostly to appease the tensions which upset liberal health professionals.

The state has only limited possibilities to control the supply of the liberal ambulatory care and thereby avoid induced over-consumption of medical care. One of the ways to achieve this is to allow only a limited number of students to start a medical career. A *numerus clausus* regulation was introduced in 1971 and contributed to limit the global supply of ambulatory care (although France is still above the OECD average with 3.3 GPs per 1000 inhabitants – OECD, 2012). One of the advert consequences of doctors' freedom of instalment is that, despite this high number, the geographical and disciplinary distribution of health professionals is rather uneven. In the past years, there has been growing concerns about the lack of general practitioners in certain rural areas and unattractive regions (less than 80 GP per 100000 inhabitants in average), whereas Paris and the Côte-d'Azur are over-medicalized (more than 100).[13] Massive demonstrations by medical students contributed to water down the 2009 Bachelot reform which first aimed to impose a stronger regulation of ambulatory care provision. Instead, a voluntary contract system has been set up, providing medical students with a grant for their studies in exchange with a commitment to serve for a given period in an under-medicalized area (*Contrat d'engagement de service public*). The 2011 convention signed by the UNCAM and the medical unions also introduced a program which rewards doctors who establish their practice in rural or poorer regions (*Option Santé solidarité territoriale*).[14] But these are only incentives, and no public control of doctors' instalment has been implemented yet.

Policy-makers met much less resistance when restricting patients' mobility within the health system than when they tried to confront private health care providers' professional autonomy. Some patients are suspected to take advantage of the free choice of providers notably by requesting several examinations for a same condition. This behaviour is often referred to in the public discourse as 'medical nomadism'. A convention signed in 1997 by the national sickness fund (CNAMTS) and a medical Union (MG France) encouraged patients to choose a general practitioner as their preferred or treating doctor (*médecin traitant*) to be entrusted with the monitoring of their medical records and to act as a gatekeeper into the health care system. The 2004 reform went one step further and the law is now providing that all patients older than 16 years old must register to a practitioner whom they must consult before seeing other general practitioners (GP) and specialists if they want to get full re-imbursement by sickness insurance funds.[15] The aim of this reform is to set up a more coherent treatment pathway for patients in which the treating doctor acts as a gatekeeper, thus saving health care resources by avoiding redundant consultations. The treating doctor, who is most of the time a general practitioner, is also trusted to bring medical benefits to patients through a better follow up of their treatments. This measure has been successfully implemented: according to the CNAMTS, 85 per cent of the insured persons have reported their gatekeeper to the national sickness insurance funds. In order to enforce this new system, the government introduced in 2007 a 50 per cent co-payment fee for patients who would disregard the 'coordinated medical pathway' (*Parcours de soins coordonné*) and did not refer to their treating GP before requiring further medical care (this co-payment has been increased to 70 per cent since January 2011). The implementation of such new practices represents a restriction on the freedom of choice, which constitutes a cornerstone of the French liberal medicine, but it was fashioned in a way that it would benefit general practitioners. Potential sanctions are once again directed on patients (increased co-payment) and not on health professionals who even benefit from this new regulation. Indeed, GPs reinforce their central position in the primary care system and specialists are allowed to apply higher charges if patients are not referred by their GP.

The ministry of health also launched in 2004 a system of medical files in order to provide an individual database (*Dossier médical personnel*, DMP) on patient's history which could be used by practitioners throughout the health system. Despite the repeated public statements made by the minister of health on the benefits of such a device, both for limiting global health consumption and improving patients' health, the implementation of the DMP system was delayed[16] and when it was launched in April 2011, it was only facultative. Although two million online medical files were expected by the end of the year 2011, only 260000 files were created by late December 2012 (Cour des comptes, 2013: 208). The delays could be explained by the important financial investments needed, the technical and ethical difficulties inherent to such a database, but also by the hostility of many general practitioners towards any device which would affect their professional autonomy.

Fee-for-service funding is, together with free choice of patients and free establishment of health providers, an anchor of the French liberal ambulatory sector. Yet, this mode of funding has a strong inflationist bias. Following British pay for performance (P4P) experiments, the sickness fund (CNAM) experimented on a voluntary basis a new contract aiming to make ambulatory care more cost-effective and leading doctors to focus more on prevention (*Contrat d'amélioration des pratiques individuelles*, CAPI). Sixteen thousand practitioners (38 per cent of eligible doctors) had already signed a CAPI contract in April 2011, despite the hostility of leading medical unions. This unexpected success led the UNCAM to extend this scheme and include it in the general medical convention signed in July 2011.[17] After intense negotiations, stakeholders agreed on objectives and indicators, 60 per cent of them dealing with disease screening and preventive actions (number of elderly vaccinated against the flu, breast cancer screening). The remaining indicators reward cost-efficiency (organization of the office, use of electronic medical records, ratio of generic drugs prescribed). The convention offers a bonus funding amounting up to €11.4 per patient for practitioners who would reach all these health-status and efficiency indicators.[18] Although it is premature to draw any conclusion on its implementation and effects, this innovation shows at least that the liberal sector of French health care system is progressively opening up to new modes of financing which combine cost-containment and disease prevention. A more integrated and prevention-oriented ambulatory sector is expected to curb health care consumption in the longer run, but in the shorter term this convention will add up to health care expenditure, as medical unions ruled out individual sanction mechanism and obtained the convention to be solely based on financial incentives. GPs complying with the P4P scheme could receive up to €9100 bonus every year, although the director of the sickness insurance fund announced that the objectives will not be reached easily and that he expected the average bonus to be rather around €4500.[19]

Creeping privatization through 'responsibilization' of patients

The issue of privatization is very sensitive in the fragmented hospital sector, as public and private hospitals and clinics compete for the supply of care. With this respect, it must be pointed out that gross statistics on the ownership of hospitals or the share of health spending do not show any sign of privatization. The public–private mix of inpatient care supply seems to be fairly stable (DGOS, 2010). However, we pointed out that managerial changes might affect the type of health care that each sector will specialize in, with private organizations focusing even more on highly profitable services.

A much more significant – and better documented – change of the French health system is the creeping privatization of health risks, as co-payment measures gradually shift the burden of health expenditure to voluntary private insurances and patients. The reduction of collective risk coverage has indeed been a key cost-containment policy instrument since the late 1970s. Besides the above-mentioned institutional changes, and in the waiting for their financial effects, cost-sharing measures are still being implemented to cope in the short term with unsolved financing problems. When facing financial hardships, reduced reimbursement rates (*Tickets modérateurs*) have been trusted by governments to reduce the financial burden on sickness insurance funds and to promote a better use of health care services by patients. Beyond the savings directly related to the reduced reimbursement, state and national sickness fund officials expected on the long run patients to refrain from excessively consuming health care services (hence the rhetoric of 'responsibilization'). In 2011, the legal reimbursement rate of ambulatory care amounted to 70 per cent of the standard *Sécurité sociale* tariff for doctors' consultation, and 30 per cent outside the coordinated pathway. However, the effects of co-payments on the demand for health service have been partly compensated by the rise of facultative private sickness insurances (*mutuelles*) as substitutes for *Sécurité sociale* schemes. That is why governments progressively introduced non-reimbursement deductibles which cannot be covered by any voluntary insurance scheme.

The 2004 and 2008 Social security financing plans introduced a general co-payment called medical fees (*franchises médicales*). It amounts to one Euro on each consultation (created in 2004). Since 2008, a €0.5 fee is applying to drugs, paramedical and medical acts and thus concerning almost all health expenses. A two Euros fee even applies to health transportation.[20] The cumulated amount of these fees cannot exceed €50 per person and per year, but this new co-payment measure nevertheless triggered many protests. For patient organizations, *franchises médicales* have indeed become a symbol of an increasingly unequal health system that puts a growing financial burden on patients, and especially low income ones. The government announced that the savings brought by the new medical fees are worth about €850 million per year, but the national audit office covers less than half of the annual cost of the 2005 and 2007 consultation tariff increases granted to medical doctors (which cost €2.2 billion – Cour des comptes, 2008: 102).

While most doctors apply the standard *Sécurité sociale* tariff, the introduction of the so-called second sector (*Secteur 2*) in 1980 created a *de facto* co-payment for patients whose doctor applies free tariffs. They are still reimbursed on the basis of *Sécurité sociale* tariffs (€15.10 for a GP) regardless the actual price of the consultation. As Richard Freeman puts it, '*the expansion of sector 2 provision in France by definition brings with it extra billing*' (Freeman, 2000: 72). The cost of extra-billing has doubled since 1990 and covers in 2012 almost the half of all out-of-pocket expenditure (€2.3 billion over €5.7 billion).[21] This issue has been raised by the new left wing government as one of its first priorities in 2012. The minister of social affairs Marisol Touraine asked the sickness insurance and medical unions to come up with a voluntary agreement limiting extra-billing in 2013 under the close supervision of the government which announced that it could legislate if negotiation fails.

The government also introduced co-payment for hospital care (*forfait hospitalier*) in January 1983, which has been regularly augmented since (20 Francs per day in 1983, 50 in 1991 and 70 in 1995). The government decided in 2004 to apply an annual one Euro increase to the hospital fee in order to save each year €0.3 billion. Hospital out-of-pocket payments jumped from €13 per day of hospitalization in 2004 to €18 in 2010. Patients pay in average 20 per cent of hospital costs, but co-payments remain lower than those applying to drugs and ambulatory care.

The average reimbursement for drugs is about 75 per cent (Cour des comptes, 2011: 115). This figure has been stable for the last decade and is slightly better than in 1995, despite the de-reimbursement of inefficient drugs. Since 1999, an expert Committee (*Commission de transparence du médicament*) is in charge of advising the minister of health to determine the rate of reimbursement for medicines.[22] These reimbursement rates been severely lowered in 2004 and now vary from 100 per cent, 65 per cent, 35 per cent and 15 per cent according to the medical efficiency of the drugs (*Service médical rendu*). In April 2003 the minister in charge of health decided to cut the reimbursement rate from 65 to 35 per cent for 617 medicines (blue label: *Service médical modéré*). In March 2006, 152 medicinal products have even been removed from the reimbursement list altogether. Finally, 191 medicines whose medical usefulness is limited are now only reimbursed up to 15 per cent since April 2010 (orange label: *Service médical faible ou insuffisant*). The sickness fund signed in July 2004 with two pharmacist unions (UNPF and USPO) an agreement fostering the use of generic medicines in order to curb health expenditure (in average, they are 30 per cent cheaper than the original drugs). Whenever possible, pharmacists are encouraged to substitute drugs by their generic equivalent. Over 800 medicines are thus reimbursed to patients on the basis of the lower price of generic substitutes (*Tarif forfaitaire de responsabilité*).

The consequences of the reforms on the health care system's outcomes

A new health system is progressively unfolding. Cumulative structural changes occurred in the last decade, allowing the state to better control the organization of health care services. This *étatisation* led to an introduction of managerial methods in hospital care, and to a lesser extend to ambulatory care. Together with creeping privatization, these organizational changes have had important consequences on the sanitary, economic and social performances of the French health care system. Could these cost-efficiency measures combine improved health results and sustainable economic performance? As new financial turmoil has hit European countries since 2008, a critical question is also to assess whether those structural changes will render the French health care system more or less financially robust and socially inclusive through hard times to come.

Health status and capacity of the system to directly improve health

The French population's general health status remains above the average of developed states. For instance, France was third out of all OECD countries with the lowest mortality rates from strokes in 2009 (OECD, 2011: 29). The infant mortality rate in France is of 3.9 deaths per 1000 births, below the OECD average of 4.4 deaths (2011: 37). Female age-standardized mortality index from all cancers is also much lower than the OECD average (111 against 124 per 100000 women), although the performance for males is slightly higher (211 compared to the OECD average 208 – OECD, 2011: 31). The death rate after a stroke is much lower in France than in the average of OECD countries (19 per 100000 women and 50 per 100000 men, compared to 60 and 117 – OECD, 2011: 29). Overall, most figures demonstrate continued good performances of the French health care system in terms of health quality. These performances do not correspond however to the high level of financial investment in health. France is amongst the four main spenders on health, whereas its health results are not even amongst the top four countries (rather within the best first third). The French health system is lagging behind Nordic countries in terms of public health and preventive care, because of the curative bias of its ambulatory sector and the lack of coordination between health providers. We pointed out that both issues have been addressed in the past years, but the outcomes of these changes remain to be seen.

Economic performance

Thirty years of cost-containment reforms could only slow down the rise of health expenditure, but not stop it, and the reforms of the last decade still have not shown decisive results in this respect. Overall health spending grew from 7.0 per cent of the GDP in 1980 to 10.9 in 2003, then stabilized from 2004 to 2008 and went back on the rise in 2009 and 2010, reaching respectively 11.7 per cent and 11.6 per cent of the GDP (Table 5.1). The total health expenditure in France was $3974 per capita in 2010, which is more than the $3268 average of OECD countries. France is still the first European country for pharmaceutical consumption per inhabitant and second among OECD countries for antibiotics consumption (OECD, 2012).

In other areas, however, organizational changes have started to pay off. The total of outpatient care consumption has stabilized around 23000 since 2003 (although it was only 18000 in 1995 – IRDES, 2012). The use of hospital care has also been rationalized, as the average duration of inpatient care has diminished between 1997 and 2008, in all specialties except respiratory and infectious diseases. The number of beds in public hospitals dropped from 392644 in 1981 to 277910 in 2008 (DREES, 2010a: 203) and the turnover rate for acute bed is stable since 2000, averaging 74.4 per cent in 2009 (close to the OECD average, 76.1 per cent – OECD, 2011: 85). Although at a different pace across sectors (as shown in details in Table 5.3), the overall trend since the mid-2000s is one of stabilization of the gross health consumption. As a result, health spending per inhabitant has increased in a slower pace than in similar countries. It went up by 2.2 per cent per year in average between 2000 and 2009, compared to 4.0 per cent for all OECD countries (OECD, 2011: 149). Looking only at public spending covered by the sickness insurance, it is worth noting that the pace of expenditure growth stabilized below 3 per cent since 2010, and for the first time since 1997 ONDAM spending objectives set by the Parliament have been respected in 2010 and 2011 (Table 5.2). The deficit of the sickness insurance funds is still a problem, although it dramatically went down from –13.6 billion to –4.4 billion between 2004 and 2008. This trend was broken in 2009, with a 10.6 billion deficit, which stabilized in the past years (–11.6 in 2010, –8.6 in 2011 and –6.8 in 2012, the latter figure being only an estimation).[23]

The 2008 financial crisis seems to be an obvious explanation for the deficit escalation in 2009, but the national audit office asserts that most of the sickness insurance funds' debt in recent years is overwhelmingly due to structural factors rather than to the economic crisis (Cour des comptes, 2011: 80). In such difficult economic context, the previous government put a strong political emphasis on cost-containment and took several emergency austerity measures. According to the European hospital and healthcare federation (HOPE), those measures have had a limited impact on the health care system and chiefly consisted in accelerating or reinforcing the implementation of reforms previously launched, such as the financing system based on DRGs, which was expected to produce savings of around €150 million in 2011, or the pooling of hospitals purchases though territorial reorganization which was expected to save €145 million.[24]

The implementation of managed competition and new hospital financing schemes seem to have worsened the financial situation of hospitals and thereby made them more vulnerable to the financial crisis. In order to cope

Table 5.1 National health expenditures (% of GDP) (1970–2010)

1970	1975	1980	1985	1990	1995	2000	2001	2002	2003	2004	2005	2006	2007	2008	2009	2010
5.4	6.4	7.0	8.0	8.4	10.4	10.1	10.2	10.6	10.9	11.0	11.2	11.1	11.1	11.0	11.7	11.6

Source: OECD Health Data, 2012.

Table 5.2 National health spending objectives – expected and actual annual variations (1997–2012)

	1997	1998	1999	2000	2001	2002	2003	2004	2005	2006	2007	2008	2009	2010	2011	2012
ONDAM	+1.7%	+2.4%	+1.0%	+2.9%	+2.6%	+4.0%	+5.3%	+4.0%	+3.2%	+2.5%	+2.6%	+2.8%	+3.3%	+3%	+2.9%	+2.5%
Real variation	+1.5%	+4.0	+2.6%	+5.6%	+5.6%	+7.2%	+6.4%	+4.9%	+4%	+3.1	+4.2%	+3.3%	+3.5%	+3%	+2.9%	2.5%
Difference	–0.2	+1.6	+1.6	+2.7	+3.0	+3.2	+1.1	+0.9	+0.8	+0.6	+1.6	+0.5	+0.2	0.0	0.0	0.0

Sources: Commission des comptes de la Sécurité sociale, Cour des comptes, 2013 (ONDAM 2012 was lowered to 2.5 per cent by the Fillon Government as part of a commitment to drastically limit the *Sécurité sociale* deficit before the 2012 elections. The newly elected socialist President François Hollande announced a +2.7 per cent ONDAM for 2013).

Table 5.3 Evolution of the consumption of health services and products between 1995 and 2010 (billions of current Euros)

	1995	2000	2005	2008	2009	2010
Hospital care	47.6	52.7	67.6	76.2	79.1	81.2
Ambulatory care	26.8	31.2	40.9	42.1	43.2	44.0
Medicines	18.5	23.6	31.5	33.4	34.1	34.4
Transportation of patient	1.5	1.9	2.8	3.4	3.6	3.8
Other medical goods	3.7	5.7	8.4	10.7	11.0	11.6
Consumption of health services and products	98.0	115.1	151.2	165.7	171.0	175.0

Source: DREES, 2010a (base 2000 until 2005; base 2005 since).

with increased competition and following public incentives to reorganize to supply of care, public hospitals have heavily invested in modern buildings and new medical equipment. Investment of public hospitals jumped from 3.7 to €6.4 billion between 2003 and 2010 (Bocquet et al., 2012). Public hospitals recorded in 2010 an overall deficit of €220 million, but the situation is slightly less dire than in 2007, when deficit peaked at €485 million.[25] Public hospitals extensively resorted to the bond market with some success, but concerns rose when credit rating agencies downgraded French hospitals in July 2012.[26] Despite a declining trend in profitability, private clinics seem to be better off, as only 28 per cent of them were in deficit in 2010. This could be explained by earlier restructuring of their activity towards more profitable care, regrouping in bigger facilities, and delocalization to more attractive areas (Delas, 2011). The private sectors underwent the most dramatic changes in the last decade. Between 2003 and 2008, the number of private clinics decreased by 8.1 per cent, compared to only 1.4 per cent in the public sector. Among the 1146 hospitals that have been restructured over this period, 51 per cent belong to the private sector, 14 per cent to the non-profit sector and 34 per cent were public. The type of change diverged even more: 85 per cent of hospital closures affected private hospitals and 10 per cent non-profit, while conversion of activity and fusion has been the favoured type of restructuration for public hospitals (Bocquet et al., 2012).

Patient and health professional satisfaction

The French population remains attached to its health care system and remains satisfied by the services provided. In 1999, 65 per cent of the French declared to be satisfied with the provision of health care (Blendon et al., 2001: 16). This figure grew to 77 per cent in 2010 and ranges above the EU average 64 (Eurobarometer, 2010: 140). 42 per cent responded that it stayed the same over the last five years and the same number responded that it worsened. Only 11 per cent have the feeling that it got better, very much in line with EU average (Eurobarometer, 2010: 143). According to a study made in 2011 by the Cercle-Santé-Société, 59 per cent considered the organization of their health system 'good' or 'excellent'; 41 per cent judged was 'average' or 'bad'.[27] Yet, these results are mitigated when the issue is investigated closer. While the French still announce an overall satisfaction with their health care system, the answer is not so clear-cut if the questions asked are more detailed. For instance, according to a 2009 TNS-Sofres poll, 56 per cent of interviewees state that they are not satisfied by delays to get an appointment with a specialized doctor outside hospitals, and 51 per cent feel that this situation deteriorated over the past ten years.[28]

A similar dissatisfaction may be found dealing with public hospitals, which have been plagued by chronic staff shortages and have been disorganized by the implementation of the general law limiting working time in 2001 (35 hours a week). A sanitary crisis caused by a heat wave during the summer of 2003 once again put this issue on the public agenda. This period of high tension has however deeper roots in structural managerial problems, which reflect in the polls regarding the satisfaction of the hospital professionals. Between 1998 and 2003, the number of people working in hospitals feeling that they do not have enough time to accomplish their work rose from 32 per cent to 41 per cent. Those who feel that 'they always have to rush' rose from 19 per cent to 23 per cent. And those who say that their 'work rhythm is imposed by production norms or deadlines to meet in one hour at the most' grew from 24 per cent to 48 per cent over the same period of time (Le Lan and Baubeau, 2004: 7). In 2011, the former minister of health Xavier Bertrand set up an enquiry mission on public hospitals, in order to investigate on the tensions generated by the implementation of the 2009 reform. The findings of the missions, released in January 2012, show that many actors in public hospitals need a pause in reforms, feeling that time and human resources spent on implementing changes could better be devoted to health services. The pace of reforms additionally provoked a feeling of uncertainty and instability for actors in public hospitals.[29] In the ambulatory sector, the dissatisfaction of rural and suburban general practitioners has reached the political agenda, as it jeopardizes the renewal of medical coverage in many regions and questions the very model of liberal practice (in 2010, 903 doctors left their job to become employed, substitute or hospital doctors – Le Breton-Lerouvillois, 2011). Medical students seem even less reluctant than their forerunners to give up some autonomy and freedom in exchange for the convenience of medical centres or hospitals: only one out of ten new doctors became a *médecin liberal* in 2011.

Access to public health care: social and territorial inequalities

The rise of social inequalities in the access to health care services shows in the growing percentage of people declaring that they had to renounce care due to financial reasons. Twelve per cent of the whole population faced this situation in 2002 and this figure rose to 15.4 per cent in 2008. Among the most precarious people, they were above 40 per cent to postpone treatments because of financial difficulties (Després et al., 2011: 2–4). The Jospin government instituted in 1999 a specific additional means-tested health scheme (*Couverture médicale universelle*, CMU), targeting people lawfully living in France and whose specific employment status did not offer any insurance scheme (more than two million people benefited from a basic CMU coverage in 2011[30]). The CMU scheme was also extended to people who cannot afford any complementary insurance, thus suffering the most from increasing co-payments (*Couverture Maladie Universelle Complémentaire*, CMUC). They were 15 per cent of the population without any complementary sickness insurance by the end of the 1990s (Destais, 2003: 132). 4.4 million people benefited from the CMUC program in 2011.[31] However, it is estimated that the access to health care is often denied by a significant number of practitioners to the beneficiaries of the CMU scheme, 41 per cent of specialists and 39 per cent of dentists in 2006.[32]

These extensions of universal health protection did not entirely compensate the adverse social impacts of co-payments in terms of health inequalities. So far, acute and long-term care have remained well covered by the compulsory sickness insurance, but co-payments measures contribute to a 'silent privatization' (Hassenteufel, 2001: 88) that firstly hit the most deprived, particularly – but not only – for smaller risks. Overall, 60 per cent of health care expenses are devoted to the full coverage of heavy and long-term conditions by the sickness insurance funds (16 per cent of the population) and this share increases steadily. The basic sickness insurance coverage of primary and ambulatory care declined in the past decade to an average reimbursement rate of about 55 per cent (Tabuteau, 2010: 47).

In addition to social inequalities, territorial inequalities have become a major issue. The density of doctors (GPs and specialists) is about 417 for 100000 inhabitants in Provence-Alpes-Côtes-d'Azur region, whereas the Picardie region has only 256 doctors for 100000 inhabitants.[33] Despite hospital planning, the supply of inpatient care is uneven. For instance, the Limousin region has 4.3 hospital beds for 1000 inhabitants whereas the bordering Poitou-Charentes region has only an average of 3.2 per 1000 inhabitants (DREES, 2010a: 124). The median travel duration to access hospital care is between 20 and 26 minutes for short-term hospital care (and only 17 minutes for maternity care). This figure is fairly stable across regions, but one can notice significant inequalities between smaller territorial divisions (*départements*), mainly due to geography, different levels of urbanization and unequal density of health care supply. For instance, the national longest median travel duration (43 minutes) in Alpes-de-Haute-Provence drops to a national lowest in neighbouring Alpes-Maritimes (nine minutes). One can assume, although data is still lacking, that recent closures and concentrations of small hospitals may increase such territorial imbalances (DREES, 2010b: 16).

Conclusion

After decades of failed attempts at curbing health care expenses, political and administrative actors have in the last decade carried on significant and – surprisingly enough – rather coherent structural and organizational reforms of the French health system. Led by a reformist coalition which promoted State-led managerialism as a way out of the inflationist consensus between medical unions and sickness funds, these reforms build on learning from past failures and a compromise with doctors. The first change is the redistribution of competencies among public actors (between the state and sickness insurance fund and between the state and hospitals), leading to a greater *étatisation* of health care regulation. This structural change has paved the way for a second stream of reforms at the organizational level: managerialization. First applied to hospitals, the diffusion of managerial methods has recently hit the ambulatory sector, with the new performance-related funding of private practitioners. The implementation of these changes in the coming years will determine whether they are only a mean to push medical costs down, or if it is also a mean to drive quality in health care, coordinate health care and public health and promote cost-efficient preventive measures. Meanwhile, inequalities in health and access to health care are worsened by the creeping privatization of health risks through patient responsibilization which has been consistently used in the last 30 years of health care reforms as a fallback option when other cost-containment measures are insufficient, very much in line with a traditional implicit choice in French health care politics: freedom and responsiveness of the health care system still prevail over the principle of equal access of citizens to health care.

Notes

1. In France the whole social insurance system, including mandatory sickness insurances, is called *Sécurité sociale*, and people generally designate the sole mandatory sickness insurances with the same terms, hence we will sometimes use this notion to name the compulsory sickness insurance system.
2. In the ambulatory sector, doctors can choose either to follow strictly the tariff set by the *Sécurité sociale*, or to charge higher fees (*dépassement d'honoraires*). Patients are reimbursed by the public schemes on the base of *Sécurité sociale* fees, but they can have a complementary private sickness insurance (a *mutuelle*) that would cover the extra-billing.
3. Loi n° 91-748 du 31 juillet 1991 portant réforme hospitalière, JORF n°179 du 2 août 1991, p. 10255.
4. Ordonnance n° 96-346 relative à la réforme de l'hospitalisation publique et privée, JORF n°98 du 25 avril 1996, p. 6324.
5. ARS started to operate in July 2010. They are in charge of driving the regional hospital planning (former attribution of the ARH), of the coordination between public and private health institutions, and to determine the funding of health providers.

6. Pr Guy Vallancien, 'Réflexions et propositions sur la gouvernance hospitalière et le poste de président du directoire', rapport à l'attention de Madame Roseline Bachelot-Narquin, Ministre de la santé, de la jeunesse, des sports et de la vie associative, juillet 2008.
7. Term used by Victor Rodwin and Claude Le Pen to define the recent reforms, by which they mean 'the coordination and finance of medical practice to control spending and promote effective treatment' (Rodwin, 2011).
8. Assemblée Nationale, 'Rapport en conclusion des travaux de la mission d'évaluation et de contrôle des lois de financement de la Sécurité sociale sur le fonctionnement de l'hôpital', Commission des affaires sociales, n°2556, 26 mai 2010, p. 17.
9. 'Hollande promet la fin de la convergence tarifaire public-privé avant juin 2013', *Le Quotidien du Médecin*, 4 avril 2012.
10. '*A one and only boss in the hospital: the director*', speech, 18 September 2008; Loi n° 2009-879 du 21 juillet 2009 portant réforme de l'hôpital et relative aux patients, à la santé et aux territoires, JORF n°0167 du 22 juillet 2009, p. 12184.
11. Circulaire n° DGOS/PF3/2012/09 du 10 janvier 2012 relative au guide d'élaboration des contrats pluriannuels d'objectifs et de moyens (CPOM).
12. Pr Guy Vallancien, 'L'évaluation de la sécurité, de la qualité et de la continuité des soins chirurgicaux en France', rapport à l'attention de Monsieur Xavier Bertrand Ministre de la Santé et des Solidarités, avril 2006.
13. Observatoire National de la Démographie des Professions de Santé, 'Rapport 2006–2007', 2008, p.16.
14. Assemblée Nationale, 'Rapport d'information de M. Jean-Luc Préel en conclusion des travaux d'une mission d'évaluation et de contrôle des lois de financement de la Sécurité sociale sur la prévention sanitaire', Commission des affaires sociales, n°4334, 8 février 2012.
15. Loi n°2004-810 du 13 août 2004 relative à l'assurance maladie, JORF n°190 du 17 août 2004, p. 14598.
16. Assemblée Nationale, 'Rapport d'information de M. Jean-Pierre Door sur le dossier médical personnel', Commission des affaires culturelles, familiales et sociales, n°659, 29 janvier 2008.
17. Assemblée Nationale, 8 février 2012, *op. cit.*
18. Arrêté du Ministre du travail, de l'emploi et de la santé du 22 septembre 2011 portant approbation de la convention nationale des médecins généralistes et spécialistes signée le 26 juillet 2011.
19. 'Après le CAPI, le P4P: jusqu'à 9 100 euros de bonus sur objectifs', *Le Quotidien du Médecin*, 25 juillet 2011.
20. Loi n° 2007-1786 du 19 décembre 2007 de financement de la Sécurité sociale pour 2008, JORF n°0296 du 21 décembre 2007, p. 20603.
21. 'Tarifs médicaux : enquête sur les dépassements d'honoraires', *Le Monde*, 10 juillet 2012.
22. Décret n° 99-915 du 27 octobre 1999 relatif aux médicaments remboursables et modifiant le code de la Sécurité sociale, JORF n°253 du 30 octobre 1999, p. 16289.
23. Loi n° 2011-1906 du 21 décembre 2011 de financement de la Sécurité sociale pour 2012, JORF n°0296 du 22 décembre 2011, p. 21682.
24. HOPE, 'The Crisis, Hospitals and Healthcare', April 2011, pp. 67–8.
25. In 2010, the 30 per cent of hospitals in deficit, mainly big hospitals, have lost a total of €600 million, which means that the 70 per cent others were in surplus and earned a total of €380 million (Bocquet et al., 2012).

26. 'Le gouvernement est prêt à mobiliser les fonds du grand emprunt pour les hôpitaux', *Les Echos*, 30 juillet 2012.

27. CHAM, 'Les soins de santé en Europe et aux Etats-Unis', Baromètre Cercle Santé Société – Europ Assistance, septembre 2011.

28. TNS Sofres, 'Etude pour l'Observatoire sociétal de la santé et de la qualité des soins en France', novembre 2009.

29. Francis Fellinger, Frédéric Boiron et al., 'Rapport de la mission Hôpital Public', juin 2011 – janvier 2012.

30. Fonds CMU, 'Références. Lettre du fonds de financement CMU', n°48, juillet 2012.

31. Fonds CMU, 'Rapport d'évaluation de la Loi CMU', novembre 2011, p. 28.

32. Conférence nationale de santé, 'Résoudre les refus de soins. Rapport annuel sur le respect des droits des usagers du système de santé adopté en séance plénière de la Conférence nationale de santé le 10 juin 2010', septembre 2010.

33. Sénat, 'Rapport d'information de M. Jean-Marc Juilhard sur la démographie médicale', Commission des Affaires sociales, n°14, 3 octobre 2007.

6
Germany: Mixing Rescaling, Privatization and Managerialism

Patrick Hassenteufel and Tanja Klenk

Introduction

Since the early 1990s, European public health care systems have experienced dynamic transformation processes. Health care systems have come under the pressure of strong financial constraints, indicating the end of the 'golden age' of welfare state policy. Thus, the most important issue at hand is cost control. Various tools have been employed in order to contain rising costs. The broad range of different reform measures can be categorized into three major reform types, namely privatization, managerialization and rescaling, for example the reshaping of the distribution of decision-making authority.

Germany constitutes no exception in this transformation process. In fact, the German health care system has been subject to continual reform efforts and is still subject of a fierce debate. The following case study assesses the impact of the regulatory changes on the German health care system, once considered as the ideal type of a conservative-corporatist welfare state. In this introduction we explain what is meant by rescaling, privatizing and managerializing public health care systems as each of the three reforms trends is a fuzzy concept, which has been understood and defined in manifold ways. Then we describe *how* privatizing, managerializing, and rescaling have altered the German health care system in outpatient and inpatient care. In the following section we deliver assumptions *why* change has taken place. Our final part outlines some possible impacts of these reforms on the performance of the health care systems.

Rescaling

Who has the power and responsibility to decide on the delivery, the financing and the planning of health services? Over the past decades this question has been answered in Europe in manifold ways. Processes of de- and recentralization in European public health care systems can be described as subsequent 'reform waves' (Saltman, 2008). In the post-war period it has been part of the 'received wisdom' that a good health policy is characterized by decentralized decision-making authority (Saltman et al., 2007; Saltman, 2008: 104). With the turn of century, however, this commonly shared belief has been challenged and key functions of health care systems have been centralized. This process was driven, as the chapter below will show, from budgetary, legitimacy, as well as from power issues.

Decentralization and centralization are best understood when considered as the endpoints of a continuum. Slightly altering Vrangbaek's definition (2007: 45) we define rescaling as the transfer of formal responsibility and power to make decisions regarding the management, production, distribution and/or financing of health services either from a higher to a lower level of government or administration, or reverse.

Privatization

As in the case of 'decentralization' there are considerable differences in the meanings attributed to the term 'privatization'. Early studies on privatization have depicted privatization as a question of who *owns* assets and have defined privatizing as the sale of public assets. Newer studies on privatization, however, have replaced the narrow understanding of privatization with a wide definition that encapsulates a broad range of different practices. Shifting the balance of the public–private mix towards more private action can encompass different instruments such as *formal* privatization, where the public authority remains the most important or complete owner of the service, but the supply is taken care of in private structures and legal frameworks, or *material* privatization, in which case the majority or even entire ownership is transferred from public authorities to private institutions. *Functional* privatization, a third instrument, allows public entities to receive assistance from private actors such as the provision of diagnostic or therapeutic equipment, the construction of a new building or even the management of the whole hospital. Finally, a fourth type of privatization can be differentiated, namely the privatization of social risks. A risk shift from the whole society/insurance risk pool to the sole individual takes place when, for instance, user fees are introduced (Leisering, 2011).

Managerialism

Managerialism can – to put it simply – be defined as the pursuit of maximum output with minimal input. Managerialism is rooted in economic values: efficiency, cost-effectiveness, competition, entrepreneurship and progress are the central norms (Maier et al., 2009; Rüb, 2004; Edwards, 1998).

One of the main arguments against managerialized public institutions is the threat of depolitization and its negative impacts on democratic accountability. As managerialization goes hand in hand with decentralization and an increased importance of private actors – here the linkage to the other two reform trends becomes obvious – it may undermine or at least impede political control. Moreover, the New Public Management's faith on scientific management and evidence-based management can on the other side of the coin be considered as a profound mistrust in professional self-governance. It undermines, as we will see in the case of hospitals, the professional autonomy of physicians and questions traditional power relations. Finally, with its emphasis on results and outcomes managerialism threatens other components of welfare governance such as participation, member orientation or voluntarism. New managerialism can be used by central actors in order to strengthen control over previous autonomous or semi-autonomous actors. It is also possible to consider new managerial actors as an emerging group which play a growing role not only in the implementation of governance reforms but also in the elaboration of reform proposals.

Reorganizing the German health care system – relief from the Bismarckian legacy?

Until recently, Germany has been considered to be the ideal type of a conservative-corporatist social insurance state (Gerlinger and Schmucker, 2009; Bandelow, 2009; Hinrichs, 2010). The health system is characterized by a purchaser–provider split. The statutory health insurance funds, which are in the centre of the health care system, insure the main part of the population. Only self-employed, civil servants and employees with an income above a certain ceiling are allowed to opt out and choose private health coverage. The governance of the funds is marked by both a strong element of self-regulation and the idea of social partnership. The health insurance funds are organized as statutory corporations under public law: they design their own statutes, and the agency head is appointed by a board consisting of representatives of the employers and the insured. The board members are – as a general rule – elected by the insured and the employers, respectively. The revenue of the statutory health insurance funds stems mainly from payroll contributions. For a long time the insured and the employers have shouldered equal contribution shares until in 2004 regulatory changes implemented with the Health Insurance Modernization Act have broken with this general rule (see below).

With regard to health care provision, there is a strong division between inpatient and outpatient care. In the outpatient sector the *Kassenärztliche Vereinigungen*, the mandatory associations of statutory health insurance physicians, are the most important actor and negotiate with the (associations of the) health insurance funds in 'joint self-governance' *(gemeinsame Selbstverwaltung)*. In the inpatient sector self-governing committees are known, too. As the states *(Länder)* are not only heavily involved in hospital financing, but take part in negotiations between purchasers and providers too, the idea of self-governance is in the inpatient sector less pronounced, though.

Despite its fragmented governance structure and the high number of self-governing bodies, German health care policy has always been highly regulated by the central government. The policy autonomy of the self-governing bodies remains low: due to the objective of maintaining equal living conditions embodied in the German constitution, decisions on entitlements and benefit levels of the health insurance funds are for instance made by the federal government. And – as we will see – in the background of cost control efforts the competences of the health insurance funds got restricted even more.

The German health care governance reform trend has started in the early 1990s with the introduction and intensification of competition between sickness funds. The continuity from the Health Care Structure Act in 1992 to the Law to improve health care provision of 2011 is obvious. The other main reforms of 1997 (Health Insurance Reorganization Act), 2004 (Health Insurance Modernization Act) and 2007 (Competition strengthening Act) also tackle the issue of competition. Therefore our first question is how far the competition reforms, which mainly concern outpatient care, have led to rescaling, privatization and managerialization of the German health insurance system. Then we will analyse the same dimensions for inpatient care.

Health insurance funds and outpatient care: the multiple dimensions of competition

The 1992 Health Care Structure Act (*Gesundheitsstrukturreformgesetz-GSG*) was intended to progressively introduce competition among public health insurance funds – the *Krankenkassen* or 'sickness funds' – by giving statutory insured individuals a free choice among them. As services were not allowed to differ beyond legislatively defined limits, competition for members was based on the level of the contribution rate in order to fulfill the main goal of the reform: the stabilization of this level (which differed a lot between funds before the reform). At a first glance competition leads to decentralization and privatization, but the present health insurance landscape can be more accurately characterized by managerialism and centralization.

Competition and decentralization

Before the 1992 reform the statutory health insurance system was already highly decentralized. More than 1200 sickness funds were mainly organized at the local level and enjoyed great autonomy for fixing the level of their contribution rates and for the negotiations with the statutory health insurance physicians organizations (*Kassenärztliche Vereinigungen*). This is why in 1992 decentralization was neither an issue nor a goal of the reform. This situation changed with the 2004 Health Insurance Modernization Act (*GKV-Modernisierungsgesetz*) which enabled sickness funds to differentiate the range of services available to their enrollees by selective contracting with networks of local providers and by developing prevention or disease management programmes.[1] The 2007 law reinforced the possibilities given to sickness funds to conclude special agreements with individual doctors or groups of doctors (that means not with the *Kassenärztliche Vereinigungen*) especially concerning integrated care. At the end of 2008 about 6400 contracts in the field of integrated care were signed (BQS, 2009: 67). The main outcome of these new contracting possibilities is the growing territorial differentiation of outpatient care depending on different developments of governance patterns and actor constellations within the German *Länder* (Bandelow, 2009: 59). Even if collective agreements with the statutory health insurance physicians still regulate an overwhelming proportion of outpatient care, the trend towards the erosion of uniform arrangements is obvious (Gerlinger and Schmucker, 2009: 8).

Competition and privatization

The link between competition and privatization is not as obvious as it seems to be at a first glance. The first reason is that private insurance companies, which insure nowadays around 10 per cent of the German population, are not included in the new competition framework in health care. Competition was introduced between statutory sickness funds but not between them and private insurance companies. Only people earning more than ca. 4000 € monthly, civil servants and self-employed people can choose a private insurance instead of a public sickness fund. Even more, the control and regulation of private health insurance has been increased with the obligation to implement elements of solidarity and consumer protection. The creation of a basic tariff in 2007, the limitation of premium costs, new rules for cancellation, transferability of old-age provision and the restriction to the freedom of concluding new contracts can be seen as a demarketization process in the private health insurance sector (Böckmann, 2009).

The second reason is that privatization has several meanings and dimensions as we explained before. No material or formal privatization has occurred, but a privatization of risk with the growth of user fees can be noticed. This trend began with the 1988 Health Care Reform Act, which introduced patients' co-payments for pharmaceuticals, hospital inpatient stays, physical therapy and spa cures. It was pursued in 1997 (but the main measures were withdrawn shortly after the change of government in 1998). The privatization of sickness risk coverage has again been more visible since 2004. The Modernization Act of 2004 increased the level of co-payment and created a fee of 10 € per trimester and per pathology for certain visits to specialists (if not following a family doctor's consultation).[2] Moreover, a voluntary private health insurance is now supposed to cover teeth prostheses, and some benefits are not covered anymore like thermal cure, drugs without prescriptions, sterilizations, medical transports, dental prosthesis and glasses. However, individual health expenses were limited to 2 per cent of annual revenue (1 per cent in the case of chronic sickness). The latest step towards privatization of health risks is directly linked to competition: the 2007 Act allowed sickness funds with financial difficulties to ask their members an extra 'health-premium' (*Gesundheitsprämie*). This possibility was extended with the 2010 Health Insurance Financing Act (*GKV Finanzierungsgesetz*) which withdraw the limitation of the level of these extra 'health-premiums'.

Competition and managerialization

Germany, contrary to Anglo-Saxon countries, did not open up to NPM ideas before the early 1990s (Wollmann, 1999; Mattei, 2009). With regard to NPM reforms, Germany was a latecomer – partly because of the German reunification, partly because many of the NPM ideas were already at place in the traditional German welfare governance. A purchaser–provider split, decentralized governance or a sound welfare mix were known from the very beginning of health policy in Germany. In the wake of the introduction of competition in the health insurance system, however, a shift to a managerial system could be observed. Health insurance funds developed from passive 'payers' to active 'players' (Bode, 2006), meaning that they made much effort to increase their competitiveness and improve the market position of the fund. The changed organizational strategy became obvious, amongst others, in the funds' relationship to its members, now considered as 'customers'. Adopting management practices from private business firms such as marketing and sales approaches, health insurance funds not only tried to win new members but to target especially 'good risks', namely young, healthy members with a higher income. Special advantage offers such as packages with complementary insurance, reductions on contributions for enrollee's participation in health-improving activities, refunding of contributions in case of non-consumption were designed to address young members in order to improve the risk-structure of the fund in the long run. While trying to reorganize their funds according to the principles of private business management, the CEOs of the funds considered the participation of the lay members in the advisory board as disruptive to their new strategy and thus tried to reduce their influence on every-day management. As the government made no attempt to reform the self-administration model by strengthening the rights of the stakeholder board, the idea of self-administration as a countervailing power to the principles of private business management became step by step meaningless for the organizational identity of the funds.

Competition and centralization

Competition between statutory sickness funds was not only thought as a tool to stabilize the contribution level but also as a way to reduce the discrepancy between the contribution rates of the different funds. Those two goals led to a growing centralization of the health insurance system.

First price competition incited funds to close down offices, to slim down their administrative staff or to merge with competitors in order to reduce their costs. Between 1993 and 2012, the number of health insurance funds has dramatically diminished from more than 1200 to 146. Second the 1992 Act also introduced compensation rules between sickness funds – the *Risikostrukturausgleich* – aimed to reduce differences in the expenditures of the funds due to differences in the risk-mix of the funds. The *Risikostrukturausgleich* can be considered as an element of solidarity within the system of statutory health insurance which counterbalances mechanisms of competition between the funds. The last step was, in 2007, the creation of the Health Fund (*Gesundheitsfonds*), directly linked to the federal state. Payroll contribution rates are since the implementation of the 2007 Act set in a centralized way, with a unified payroll contribution rate for every sickness fund. Thus, sickness funds lost one of their main rights, which is transferred to the federal state.[3] The Health Fund collects the contributions and taxes financing the statutory health insurance and redistributes them to the different sickness funds following the new compensation rules of the *Risikostrukturausgleich* (taking in account not only age and gender as in the past but also morbidity criteria and the income of insured persons).

Other aspects of the reforms increased the power of federal authorities. The traditional self-administration of German health care by sickness funds and doctors' unions has progressively been eroded by the growth of state control starting in 1992 (Structural Reform Act). With this reform, the state exerts stronger control over negotiations among sickness funds and unions, as well as over the functioning of these institutions. The health ministry can intervene directly if the actors of the self-administrated system do not implement the budget caps for medical activity and prescriptions.

A further aspect of this trend is the establishment in 2004 of the *Institut für Qualität und Wirtschaftlichkeit im Gesundheitswesen* (Institute for quality and economic efficiency in health care) with wide-ranging powers to evaluate the benefit and quality of diagnosis and treatment methods. It expanded the weight of scientific expertise, but its autonomy is limited by the fact that it is allowed to assess diagnosis and treatment methods only at the request of the Federal Health Ministry or the Federal Joint Committee (*Gemeinsamer Bundesauschuss-GBA-*), the most important self-administration body in the health care system. Created from the merging of numerous national committees, the GBA is responsible for the implementation of the legislation concerning ambulatory care. Its authority has been expanded to all sectors of the statutory health insurance system in 2004 and it acquired a multitude of new powers. But it is forced to fulfill its responsibilities in a more restrictive frame of action set by the Federal Ministry of Health which reduced its autonomy by professionalizing its members with the 2007 Reform. It also gave the Ministry, as the supervising authority, the right to request additional statements and information when scrutinizing directives (Gerlinger and Schmucker, 2009: 9–10). The creation of the Federal Joint Committee in 2004 and of a Federal Sickness Funds Organization – a new umbrella association for all sickness funds – in 2007 enables more control from the Health Ministry (Bandelow, 2009: 49).

The pattern is clear: competition and the creation of new federal institutions led to a growing centralization of the regulation of the German health insurance system. This trend is less obvious in the hospital sector.

The new governance of the inpatient sector

The inpatient sector experiences major challenges and is subject to an intensive reform discussion, too. Technical development and demographic change lead to an increasing demand for inpatient care. The growing demand for cost-intensive inpatient care, however, meets the increasing claims of public authorities to restrain spending.

Contrary to the outpatient sector, taxes play an important role in hospital funding. The Hospital Financing Act of 1972 introduced a dual financing system: while health insurance funds pay for operating costs and care provision, the investment costs are financed out of taxes from state and federal level. The state governments *(Länder)* are also responsible to set up hospital plans. Only the hospitals approved in the hospital plan are eligible for the 'two pillar funding system' and receive tax-based subsidies from the *Länder* and revenues from the health insurance funds. Ownership, however, does not matter in this respect. Quite to the contrary, in line with the leitmotif of 'subsidiarity', the Hospital Funding Act of 1972 is committed to sustain a sound welfare mix. The principle of subsidiary, though, was above all designed to maintain the tradition of 'free' welfare associations, non-governmental and non-profit organizations delivering social services. Private for-profit hospitals, although being in theory eligible for the two-pillar-hospital system, played until recently only a negligible role in the German hospital industry.

The control of the constantly rising costs has been in the centre of hospital policy since the early 1980s. The first major structural reform, however, was not implemented before 1993. With the Health Structure reform (1992) hospital remuneration through health insurance funds has been restructured: the cost coverage principle was abolished and replaced by legally fixed budgets. While these early reforms had had only incremental character, the introduction of a flat-rate payment system, which was introduced in several steps in the early 2000s, can be considered as a major structural reform.

The states' governments, too, strived to curb spiraling costs. Despite intensive reform discussions, the states were not able to agree on comprehensive regulatory reforms to reorganize the system of hospital investment. Instead, the states pursue pure cost containment policies. The financial means for hospital investment decreased steadily throughout the past decade, bringing about a severe investment backlog.[4]

Towards centralization?

Since almost two decades, there is an ongoing debate about how to cope with the shortcomings of the dual financing system and about how to put hospital funding on a sound financial base. One idea is to replace the dual funding system by a monistic system with the statutory health insurance as the only payer. This reform plan, however, is highly contested: the states and communities fear losing their influence on hospital governance. Up to date, the *Länder* were successful in keeping their competences for planning and funding. Most recently, they demonstrated their veto power in the *Bundesrat* (the second chamber representing the *Länder*) during the law-making procedure of the Hospital Financing Reform Act of 2009 (Böhm, 2009).

Nonetheless, there is a creeping centralization of hospital governance to observe. The introduction of the flat-rate payment system is a shift of the responsibility for the remuneration of hospitals to the national level since the definition of the diagnosis-related groups is made at the federal level and is supposed to be the same for all German hospitals (Böhm, 2009). Like the Federal Joint Committee for the outpatient sector the German Hospital Federation (the umbrella organization for hospitals) has growing responsibilities and defines jointly with the association of statutory health insurance funds the national fee schedules for stationary treatments (Gerlinger, 2010: 128–9). In the background of the growing pressure exerted by the flat-rate payment system on planning and the desire of the health ministry to switch to a monistic funding system, the question is how long the states can maintain their competences for planning and funding (Gerlinger, 2008).

Towards a privatized hospital industry

Unlike centralization, the trend towards privatization is much more obvious. Both the introduction of DRGs and the shrinking resources for hospital investment have fostered considerable changes of the welfare mix in the hospital industry. In order to cope with increasing financial pressure, cities and local communities, which are for the most part the owners of public hospitals in Germany, have welcomed market solutions. A prominent reform strategy is to use private law to re-organize public services. The legal form of a hospital is changed, but public authorities remain nonetheless the majority shareholders. The share of public hospitals run under private law has risen significantly: in 2010, 58.4 per cent of all public hospitals operated under private law (Statistisches Bundesamt Deutschland, 2010; Table 6.1). Formal privatization gives hospitals their own legal personality and as a result a greater autonomy in day-to-day operations.

Moreover, new forms of public–private partnerships have evolved. Some private hospitals such as the Sana Kliniken GmbH have specialized in this kind of business. They offer public owners 'encompassing services for all non-medical tasks in a hospital' (http://www.sana.de/wir-ueber-uns/unser-unternehmen.

Table 6.1 Legal forms of German public hospitals (2002–2010)

Year	Public law without own legal form	Public law without organizational autonomy	Private law
2002	22.4	54.9	24.7
2003	15.1	54.1	30.8
2004	15.6	47.6	36.8
2005	18.6	37.2	44.2
2006	18.1	30.7	51.2
2007	20.1	23.8	56.1
2008	21.7	20.6	57.7
2009	22.8	18.1	59.1
2010	18.8	22.7	58.4

Source: Statistisches Bundesamt (2010).

html) and run public hospitals on the base of a management contract. Unfortunately, empirical data to assess the range of functional privatization and its impact on health care performance lack entirely and research is needed (Mosebach, 2009).

Both formal and functional privatization allow for 'de-administration', for example the replacement of bureaucratic organizational structures with a more commercial management. Thus, managerialism and entrepreneurial leadership occurs not only in private for-profit hospitals, but also in (functionally and formally privatized) public hospitals, as we will see in the following section in more detail.

The most pronounced type of privatization we can observe in the inpatient sector, however, is the disposal of the entire public hospitals to a private owner. While in 1991 only about 15 per cent of all hospitals were private for-profit hospitals, their share has meanwhile more than doubled: 32.9 per cent of all hospitals operated on a private for-profit basis in the year 2010 (Figure 6.1).

Interestingly, the financial crisis of 2008 ameliorated the financial situation of the hospital industry – at least for a short time. To work against a potential recession, the German government launched several recession-busting measures in 2009, amongst others a municipality-based infrastructure programme (Konjunkturprogramm II (StabSiG); Deutscher Bundestag 2009). Nationwide €1.3 billion additional benefits were assigned for the hospital industry. The economic recovery programme helped especially community hospitals to fight against financial distress. As a result, the number of communities considering the disposal of their hospital as a last resort shrunk. The mitigating effects of the economic recovery programme, however, were only short-lived: first, the transfusion of money was non-recurring; second, hospitals were only allowed to use the additional money for infrastructure measures such as sustainable energy solutions. The

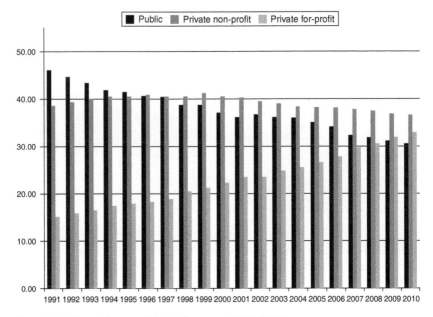

Figure 6.1   Hospital ownership in Germany (1991–2010)
Source: Statistisches Bundesamt (2010).

recession-busting measures were not designed to overcome the 'investment backlog' generally. In the long run, the pace of the privatization process has only been decelerated by the economic recovery programme – in no case has it been stopped. A reversal of the privatization trend with a respective revival of public ownership in the German hospital industry is *not* observable.

Managerialization of hospital governance

The managerialization of organizational hospital governance has been pressed ahead in particular with the introduction of DRGs. The reorganization goes far beyond the introduction of new hospital reimbursement practices. While hospital reimbursement under the 'old' cost compensation-model was a comparatively simple procedure – a fixed price has to be multiplied with the duration of stay – reimbursement on the basis of DRGs requires a developed information system documenting detailed information on diagnosis, treatments, duration of stays, etc. From the perspective of the hospitals the invention of DRGs not only meant a tightening of cost pressure, but also a considerable increase in administrative complexity, as the following examples show.

- *Process and logistic-management:* In the aftermath of the introduction of DRGs process and logistic management have become a crucial aspect of hospital governance. In order to respond to cost pressure and efficiency demands hospitals reorganize their internal work flow and their relationships to external suppliers. Standardizing – for instance by organizing care along pre-defined 'care paths' – and centralizing – for instance by establishing centralized purchasing – are considered as best practice.

- *'Admission'-management:* Process and logistic management includes also the management of the flow of patients. The introduction of DRGs can be regarded as a shift from a supply-driven to demand-driven remuneration of the hospital sector. Influencing demand has therefore become important for hospitals, especially for the bottomline oriented amongst them. The introduction of DRGs came along with the evolution of a new management task, for example admission management. In order to secure a steady flow of patients, hospitals try to establish close relationships to important gate keepers such as emergency doctors and – even more important – office-based practitioners of the outpatient sector who make out over 50 per cent of the hospital referrals. Different instruments are applied: besides the above mentioned and by recent health care reforms fostered integrated care arrangements, hospitals offer professional development or even (illegal) financial incentives to secure the steady flow of patients into their operating theatres. While in other countries – especially in the US health care system – such 'patient feeder systems' (Lindorff, 1992: 26) are known for long time and have been steadily perfected, admission management in Germany is a new and still underdeveloped management field. Against the background of augmented competition, however, it is expected that hospitals will establish respective divisions and increase their efforts (Behar and Wichels, 2009). Overcoming the borders between the inpatient and outpatient sector is for sure a necessary precondition for any improvement of health care provision in Germany. Close business relationships between office-based doctors and hospitals, however, create also new moral tensions for physicians and involve the danger of monopolized health care structures, as the US case shows impressively (Churchill, 1999).
- *Quality-Management:* The introduction of DRGs, thirdly, has altered the requests for quality management. Quality management in hospitals has already become obligatory with the health care reform 1988. This reform, however, proved to be with no effects. As a next reform step, the health care reform 2000 introduced external and comparative quality assessments which are conducted by a newly established agency for quality assurance. Finally, the Cases Fee Act 2002 (Fallpauschalen-Gesetz, FPG) introduced biannual standardized quality reports which the hospitals have to place since 2005 at the disposal of the health insurance funds (§ 137, 3 SGB V). The associations of the health insurances funds in turn are expected to publish theses reports completely and unmodified and to make the results of the reports available for the general public

(Tiemann et al., 2010: 61ff). The standardized quality reports should provide information for both medicines and patients and enable them to compare hospitals and to consider quality aspects in the planning of hospital stays. The effectiveness of the current quality management concept, however, is critically discussed. Empirical studies have shown that the expressiveness of the quality reports is very limited (Lütticke and Schellschmidt, 2005): The reports are too complex and are overloaded with technical terms. The German hospital quality reports are readable only for those patients who dispose of above-average communicative skills (Friedemann et al., 2009).

To sum it up: privatization and NPM ideas have reshaped hospital governance. To cope with increased cost pressure, public owners have opened to different types of privatization. Furthermore, hospitals have changed (or are on the way to change) their management routines and planning processes fundamentally, as these short glimpses on recent reorganization processes have shown. In terms of health performance, the impact of managerialization remains still unclear and empirical research is needed. In terms of power distribution, however, it is obvious that the reforms had severe impacts on the role of the employees whose working conditions have deteriorated tremendously, especially those of the medical and non-medical staff. Concerning the professionals, the administrative reforms not only question their claim to leadership. Moreover, under the pressure of the new administrative tasks the professionals have become themselves managers, spending more and more time on documentation and controlling duties at the expense of the time they could concentrate on the treatment of patients. Hospitals try increasingly to counteract this negative impact of the DRGs system with the introduction of new jobs: 'Medical controllers' and the 'DRG assistants' shall relieve the professionals from their administrative burdens. This further differentiation of the medical profession, however, is only at its early stages.

Explaining change: from economic to political factors

Most scholars stress the impact of economic dimensions in the reform process of the German health system. As we already noticed since the end of the 1970s cost containment is the main issue in German health care policies because health care expenditures increased much faster than the economy grew. As for pension or unemployment insurance, the first main response to this trend has been to increase the social contributions paid to health insurance funds. During the 1980s, increasing the level of health insurance contributions appeared to become an economic dead end because it threatens the competitiveness of German products and the location of economic activity in Germany due to growing personal costs. Therefore the main motive for reforms was to relieve employers from the financial burden of social insurance contributions. The cost of the German reunification process accelerated the pressure on reforms in the early 1990s and explains the adoption of the Structural Act in 1992. Like in most of the OECD health systems financial constraints have led to the desire to improve both equity and efficiency of health care delivery (Cacace et al., 2008). It helps to explain the transnational diffusion of policy tools like market mechanisms, new public management principles, quality evaluation and new financing systems (especially DRG's in the hospital sector).

But looking only at economic factors of health care reform is misleading because they are not able to explain the difference of contents in the transformation of European health care systems: these policy instruments have been adapted to specific national contexts. This translation process, in the sense used by Campbell (2004), was done by policy actors sharing not only interests but also reform programmes. In the German case it is possible to identify a 'programmatic coalition' (Hassenteufel et al., 2010) believing that the improvement of the efficiency and equity of the health care system relies not only on economic tools but also on a greater autonomy of the state towards corporatist interests (especially doctors but also the social partners managing the sickness funds) seen as the main obstacle to structural reforms. This programmatic coalition is composed of two main categories of actors: political actors (the Minister of health,[5] the state secretaries for health, the health policy spokespersons of the leading political parties, the health ministers of some *Länder*, members of the parliamentary health commission) as well as the so-called political civil servants (*politische Beamte*) at the top of the federal health administration, appointed at the discretion of the Health Minister.[6] There is a great continuity in the reform process since the structural reform of 1992, prepared at the end of the 1980s by a parliamentary commission for the structural reform of the health insurance system composed of parliamentarians and experts (the *Enquete Kommission Strukturreform der gesetzlichen Krankenversicherung*). This commission can be considered as the matrix of the reform ideas. In it, we find the actors who subsequently play an important role, like Franz Knieps, member of the staff of this commission and then head of the Health Insurance Department of the Health Ministry from 2003 to 2009; Klaus Kirschner, head of the commission and then of the health commission in the Bundestag; and Horst Seehofer, member of the commission and then minister of health from 1992 to 1998. This programmatic coalition had a clear reform programme, combining competition among sickness funds and regulation by the state. Progress towards these goals was slowed in the 1990s because of German unification, which reinforced the established institutional pattern of the heath insurance system, but returned to the top of the health agenda after 2000.

The two most important reforms of the last twenty years, in 1992 and in 2003, were negotiated by the two main political parties (SPD and

CDU-CSU). The 2007 Competition Strengthening Act was prepared and decided by a bipartite commission in charge of elaborating a new reform project, composed of 16 political actors coming from the Parliaments and the *Länder* belonging to the two parties of the governmental coalition. It is also important to note that members of the German parliamentary social and health commissions have won substantial autonomy from interest groups (Trampusch, 2005). The autonomy of this programmatic (and rather political) coalition is limited by the fact that they are not involved directly in the implementation process (where self-administration still plays a great role). Doctors are excluded from the decision process since 1992, however. Finally, expertise was institutionalized through the creation in the mid-1980s of the Expert Committee for the evaluation of the health system (*'Sachverständigenrat zur Begutachtung der Entwicklung des Gesundheitswesen'*), which has a role in agenda setting and the framing of the policy debate on health care, and sometimes prepares policy decisions (Brede, 2006: 441).

The impact of reforms on the performance of the German health care system

In this last part we try to give some evidence on the impact of the reforms. The most obvious concerns the economic performance.

Economic performance of the German health care system

In Germany, health care costs have continued to rise. In 2009 – the newest data available – the expenditure for health care accounted for approx. €278,3 billion. Germany spent €3.400 Euro per person on health and devoted 11.6 per cent of its GDB for health. The major part – 77 per cent – stems from public sources, in particular social contributions paid by the employees for statutory health insurance coverage; another 9 per cent of the overall expenditure is covered by private insurances and 13 per cent derive from out-of-pocket payments, either direct or as co-payments. The latter has increased by 1.5 per cent in the period from 2000–2009. This increase, although appearing quite small at a first glance, is remarkable inasmuch the majority of OECD countries has reduced out-of-pocket payments in the same period. Only Slovenia, Portugal, the Czech and the Slovak Republic have experienced a same or even higher rise in out-of-pocket payments (OECD, 2011: 147 ff.).

In all three dimensions – overall expenditure, expenditure per capita and expenditure in relation to GDP – Germany is above the OECD average; spending per person is in Germany even one third higher than the OECD average. Compared with its neighbouring countries Austria, France, Belgium or Denmark, however, health expenditure in Germany is not peculiar. Together with the Nordic countries and the core Bismarckian group, namely Austria, Belgium, Luxembourg and France, Germany is among the OCED-top group in terms of health spending.

Two developments, however, are worth mentioning: first, in the 2000s health care costs have risen in Germany with a slower pace than in the years before. Second, the growth of health spending in Germany was one of the lowest in all OECD countries. Although strict casual relationships should be drawn cautiously, one could see the decelerated pace of the rising health expenditure as a first result of the cost containment policies of the last years. This trend, however, is not steady and highly dependent from the overall economic development, as a short look on the years 2008 and 2009 – the years following the worldwide financial crisis – reveals: in these years, the growth rate of health expenditure in relation to GDP was significantly higher than the years before.

In Germany, as in all conservative welfare states, labor market problems result in immediate financial straits for the social insurance system. As the social insurance funds are financed via payroll defined contributions, their capital decreases when the unemployment rate increases. To put it differently: just in the moment when there is an increased need for welfare programmes due to economic downturn, the financial resources of the health insurance funds dwindle away.

To countervail the impact of the financial crisis on the health insurance system, the black-red 'big' coalition, which formed government at that time, made use of the newly introduced health fund ('Gesundheitsfonds') and implemented a two-step recovery programme. First, the health insurance rate was lowered from 15.5 per cent to 14.9 per cent to allow citizens to stimulate the market and to follow an 'individualized Keynesian investment program'. Second, the government increased the amount of tax-based public subsidies assigned for the health insurance funds: In 2009, more than €3 billion of additional benefits were invested to compensate the loss of revenue of the funds (Pfeiffer, 2009; StabSiG, article 13 and 14).[7]

Compared to the neighbouring countries, however, Germany is comparatively less affected by the economic crisis. In the time this article has been written there was a highly controversial public debate on how to deal with the *surpluses* of the statutory health insurance funds. It is estimated that the statutory health insurance funds can cover health expenditures in 2011 and 2012 easily with expected rise of health expenditure already considered. The working capital of the statutory health insurance funds accounts for approx. €4.4 billion.

Organizational performance

In terms of organizational performance the changes in the payment methods, cost caps and the intrusion of for-profit provider undoubtedly show their effects: the number of hospital beds has decreased remarkably since 2000, the year of the introduction of DRGs. Nonetheless Germany is with 9.2 beds per 1,000 inhabitants (in 2009), still not only clearly above the OECD average of 4.9 beds per 1,000 inhabitants, but with Japan, Russia, Korea, and

Austria also among the top five-group of the OECD-countries in this respect (OECD, 2011: 85). Overcapacity in the inpatient sector is often considered to be an indicator for inefficiency in the health care sector. A low number of hospital beds per capita, however, may also lead to high waiting times. Thus, a better indicator for the efficiency of the hospital sector is to set the number of beds in relation to the average length of stay in hospitals and the hospital occupancy rate (Geissler et al., 2010: 26–7). For the German case, however, these indicators suggest possibilities for rationalization, too. In fact, the average length of hospital stays has decreased over the past years – but not so much as in other countries and it is with 9.7 days still above OECD average. The occupancy rate of acute care beds, in turn, is only slightly above OCED average. But whereas Italy, Austria and Spain have managed to increase the occupancy rate, this figure has developed negatively in Germany.

Moreover, efforts made in terms of de-hospitalization such as the promotion of integrated care and ambulatory surgery have up to date displayed only minor effects: the number of cases in hospitals is still rising and outweighs the reduction in the number of beds. Next to improvements in the interplay between the inpatient and the outpatient sector, coordination within the ambulatory sector, particularly between general practitioners and specialists, is still a critical issue. The German health care system allows for easy access to specialists. Patients make intensive use of these opportunities: nearly half of all patients (47 per cent) are under treatment by at least four doctors simultaneously (Koch et al., 2010: 431) and requesting a second opinion from a specialist is a widespread habit. The possibility for health insurance funds to offer their insured gate-keeper programmes in exchange for a reduced contribution rate has not showed the intended outcome: first, the number of insured taking part in these programmes is still very low; second, when it comes to the number of consultations with doctors there are only insignificant differences between insured participating in gate-keeper programmes and those who do not (Krause, 2010).

Citizens' satisfaction and perceived quality

Long waiting times or difficult access to specialists, aspects which lead to dissatisfaction in a lot of other European countries, are not a critical issue in Germany (at least not in densely populated areas). Dissatisfaction rather results first from insufficient communication between the doctors and the patient, second from the already mentioned lacking coordination between the different sectors of health care provision. Several studies revealed that the patient–doctor relationship in Germany needs improvement in terms of shared decision making (Koch et al., 2010; Bestmann and Verheyen, 2010; Sawicki, 2005): patients are not satisfied with their involvement in the doctor's decision-making process. 36 per cent complain the aims and priorities of treatment plans have neither been discussed with them nor even been mentioned (Koch et al., 2010: 431). Moreover, they feel poorly informed when it comes to the possible risks and side-effects of the prescribed drugs (Bestmann and Verheyen, 2010: 20).

The above described easy access to specialists is a source of both satisfaction and dissatisfaction. On the one hand the possibility to consult (several) specialists is highly appreciated and frequently used; on the other hand patients complain to waste their time due to the poor organization of the German health care system. As there is no system of information sharing between different health care providers, doctors often are not aware of the medical history of their patients and thus came to differing conclusions concerning the necessary treatment, leaving the patient with the final decision alone. Organizational reforms to improve coordination in the German health care system have improved neither the organizational performance of the system (see above) nor patient satisfaction (Lüngen and Siegel, 2011). These programmes, however, are still comparatively new and effects might reveal only in the long run.

Yet, the current insufficient performance of the German health care system in terms of patient satisfaction comes clearly to light when compared with other Western health care systems. In 2008, only a share of 24 per cent thought that on the whole the health care system in Germany works pretty well and only 34 per cent considered the quality of medical care in Germany as very good or even excellent (Koch et al., 2010: 430). In New Zealand, to the contrary, 66 per cent regarded the quality of their health care system as excellent. Quite surprising, even in the US, the country which is well-known for its expensive and nonetheless poorly performing health system, a majority – 55 per cent – considered the quality of the system as excellent.

However, while interpreting these data one should bear in mind the methodological problems of measuring patient satisfaction, namely national differences in reporting styles. Empirical studies have shown first that patients in Germany have higher expectations than patients in other countries; second Germans tend to assess their health status more critically than other nations (Koch et al., 2010: 433). Thus, the reported results surely give important hints for the problems of the German health care system. Nonetheless, they have to be considered as statements of *perceived* performance which might differ from more objective assessments.

Social inequalities in the access to public healthcare

The German health insurance system guarantees the access to health care to every citizen, especially since the 2007 Act which strengthened the right to keep a public insurance or to go back to it. Already one year after the implementation of the reform the number of people without health insurance decreased from 200,000 to 100,000. But this quasi-universal access to health care does not mean the absence of inequalities. The main inequality is territorial[8] as the recent (and long) discussion concerning the Health care provision structure Act (*GKV-Versorgungsstrukturgesetz*), which was passed at the end of 2011, shows. The lack of doctors in rural areas, especially in the eastern part of Germany, has become a main issue in health policy debates. In 2010, 27 planning areas (*Planungsbereiche*) were lacking GPs, all located in the eastern *Länder*: 12 areas in Sachsen-Anhalt, 10 in Mecklenburg-Vorpommern and 5 in Brandenburg. And 4 areas are lacking pediatricians (KBV, 2011: 68). Two other evolutions explain the growing concern about access to GP. On the one side the number of GP is decreasing (1.3 per cent decrease in 2010); on the other side GPs are becoming elder: the average age is 52 years (it was 47 years in 1993) and 16 per cent of them are over 60 years old.

Impact on the workforce working in the sector

Even if data is lacking for this aspect, it is possible to pinpoint the growing dissatisfaction of doctors concerning their working conditions. In 2006 doctors' unions organized four national days of protest not only because of the financial constraints (capped budgets) but also because of the growth of bureaucratic activity for doctors (another consequence of health care reforms) evaluated between 1/5 and 2 hours every working day. At the same time conflicts also occurred in the hospital sector. During this conflict the hospital doctors' trade-union, the *Marburger Bund* (2006), underlined the differences of income between German hospital doctors and hospital doctors in other western countries and the growing number of German doctors working in another country (especially the United States, the UK, Switzerland and Austria): 2400 doctors left Germany in 2007 (as compared to 1400 in 2001). Not only doctors' organizations stress the loss of attraction of the medical profession and of satisfaction in their job: 43 per cent of doctors interviewed for the MLP Health Report 2008[9] answered that they had already seriously thought of leaving the profession, and 50 per cent of them would discourage students to become doctors. And the last *Marburger Bund*'s inquiry among its members[10] (2010) pointed out that the average working time length of doctors in hospital is 55 hours a week (and one third of them is working more than 60 hours a week).

Capacity of the system to directly improve health: putting input in relation to output

Like in the other chapters of this book we choose three indicators from the latest OECD data (OECD, 2011) that can be linked to the impact of the health care system on health. The first one is infant mortality. The German rate in 2009 (3,5 deaths per 1000 live births) is below the OECD average (4.4) but thirteen OECD countries are performing better than Germany. The German average annual rate of decline since 1970 (4.7 per cent) is close to the OECD average (4.5 per cent). The second indicator is the survival rate to cancer. The breast-cancer five-year survival rate between 2004 and 2009 in Germany (83.3 per cent) is close to the sixteen OECD countries average (83.5 per cent) and increased from 74.5 per cent between 1997 and 2002. The same remarks can be made for the five-year relative survival rate to colorectal cancer: the German rate for the 2004–2009 period (58.9 per cent for men, 62 per cent for women) is also close to the OECD average (59.5 per cent for men, 61.7 per cent for women). The third indicator which gives an indication of the health improvement of the system is the in-hospital mortality following a cardio-circulatory accident. Here Germany is less performing: the German age-sex standardized mortality rate following acute myocardial infarction, based on hospital admission (6.8 per cent in 2009), is one of the highest among OECD countries and above the average (5.4 per cent). The performance is better for the age-sex standardized in-hospital case fatality rate within 30 days after admission for ischemic stroke: the German rate in 2009 (4.0 per cent) is far below the average for OECD countries (5.2 per cent).

To sum it up the health improvement performance of the German health care system is not particularly high, especially if you compare it to the high level of health care expenditures. This is confirmed by a recent multidimensional analysis of health care system performance which compares the components of resources (human, material, technological and financial) mobilized, services produced and health outcomes (level of health and longevity, reduction of risks for illness and disease, and health care equity) in 27 OECD countries (Tchouaket et al., 2012). Germany is characterized (with 9 other countries) with a 'limited performance profile'. It has an average level of absolute performance (high level of resource mobilization, average health outcomes and average production) but a below-the-average relative performance (lower level of efficiency and lower productivity). Germany is therefore classified among the countries that mobilize more resources and invest proportionally more in the health care system to achieve its level of health outcomes, which is not among the highest in the world.

Conclusions

On the whole, the German health care sector has undergone major regulatory changes. Each of the three key regulatory reform trends in health policy – rescaling, privatization and managerialization – has affected the governance of the system, altering thereby this welfare state, that once has been the ideal type of a conservative-corporatist welfare state, into 'something uncertain else' (Lamping and Rüb, 2001). As a result of simultaneous centralization, privatization and upholding old structures, features of different systems currently coexist side by side. Therefore 'the emerging regulatory model can be characterized as state-domesticated competitive corporatism' (Gerlinger, 2010: 136).

The paper has shown *how* and *why* the German health care system has changed: we stressed the role of a programmatic coalition of political and administrative actors in the policy decision process since the early 1990s. We also gave some information about the impact of these regulatory reforms. The economic performance, due to rather successful cost-containment policies, seems better than the organizational and health improvement performance. It helps to explain why the world and European financial crisis did not have a big impact on the economic regulation of the German health care system. The most recent significant measure taken to tackle this issue was the rise of the level of the social insurance contributions in 2010. Germany experienced neither deficits of its health insurance system nor drastic austerity measures (like a decrease of reimbursement rates) since 2007.

Last, we stressed the growing issue of territorial inequalities which has led to a new rescaling movement with the Health care provision structure Act 2011 that increased the autonomy of the *länder* and regional doctor's unions in order to tackle the issue of emerging 'medical deserts' in rural areas. After a long trend of centralization and growing State control, since the 2009 election (which brought a new governmental coalition and a liberal health minister after eight years of social-democrat ministry) a new period of greater autonomy for local and non-state actors could be in progress.

Notes

1. The Health Insurance Reorganization Act in 1997 and the 'Reform 2000' already introduced the possibility of pilot projects and of new contracts options for sickness funds in order to improve the cooperation between primary care and inpatient services. But the results were rather limited and disappointing (Bandelow, 2009: 48).
2. Interestingly, the fee of 10 € has been abolished only a few years later. One aim of the private co-payment was to regulate the number of doctor visits, especially with regard to the consultancy of medical specialist. While the fee of 10 € was to low to produce control effects, it created considerable additional administrative burden for doctors and health insurance funds. As a result, the conservative-liberal coalition und chancellor Merkel disestablished the fee quietly in 2012.
3. More precisely to the insurance office depending from the Health Ministry, which manages the Health Fund.
4. In 2008, all public subsidies according to § 9 KHG (financial means for investment according to the *Krankenhausfinanzierungsgesetz* (Hospital Financing Act) amounted to €2.69 billion; this means a steady decline by −34,48 per cent throughout at last decade (reference year 1998, see DKG, 2009).
5. Three factors give the health minister a central role: the *Ressortprinzip* (autonomy for each ministerial administration), the creation of a Ministry of Health separate from the Ministry for Social Affairs since 1991 and the longevity of two ministers: Horst Seehofer, Health Minister for health from 1992 to 1998 and Ulla Schmidt, Health Minister from 2001 to 2009. All the important reforms during this period were adopted under their ministerial mandate.
6. Their careers are less purely administrative: a growing number of the political civil servants in the health sector come from the staff of political parties or from the sickness funds.
7. The tax-based subsidies for the health fund were increased as follows: in 2009 from €4 to €7,2 billion, in 2010 from €5,5 to €11,8 billion in 2011 from €7 to €13,3 billion, and in 2012 from €8,5 to €14 billion (Pfeiffer, 2009: 51).
8. The only OECD data for social inequalities concerning Germany is the horizontal inequity index for probability of a doctor visit. In 2009 Germany was among the lowest among OECD countries.
9. www.mlp-gesundheitsreport.de
10. 12,000 of 80,000 members answered.

7
Austria: A Health Care System between Continuity and Gradual Changes

August Österle

Introduction

Rescaling, privatization and managerialization have been on the agenda in many European health care systems over the past two decades. The objective of this chapter is to study the importance of respective debates and changes in Austrian health care reform efforts, focusing in particular on the developments in the most recent decade since the year 2000. It will explore the character of reform plans and of changes that have taken place in that period and discuss these with a view to rescaling, privatization and managerialization. It will analyse the drivers and mechanisms behind reform activities as well as the impacts on the performance of the health care system. As will be shown, Austria did not experience any paradigmatic change or any fundamental abrupt reform over the past 10 years. Changes have been incremental rather than transformative. In fact, major principles of the social health insurance system that were established in the 1880s are still valid in this country. Social health insurance is mandatory insurance; health insurance funds act as self-administered organizations and insurance funding is based on income-related contributions shared by employers and employees. The extension of coverage towards the entire population is a major long-term effort incorporating a characteristic of the national health system model. Also, and this differs from other social health insurance systems, funding of the Austrian health care system has for long been characterized by a substantial proportion of tax funding. While performance indicators confirm a high level of quality, affordability and accessibility of the system, structural deficits in the organization and governance of the system are widely recognized. Together with budgetary constraints and the issue of cost-containment, these structural issues have repeatedly been put forward in the past decade, and again more intensely in the 2012 debates about budgetary consolidation.

After the introduction, this chapter starts with an overview of the major changes to the Austrian health care system since the year 2000. The section attempts to identify the major trends in terms of rescaling, privatization and managerialization. The next section studies the main drivers and pressures behind reform efforts, before the mechanisms of reform (and of non-reform) are examined in more detail. This then leads to an assessment of the impact of changes, considering major performance indicators including efficiency, organizational performance, citizens' satisfaction, inequalities in access to health care, workforce variables and health indicators. In the final section, the results are brought together in a brief concluding discussion.

Health care reforms since the year 2000

Austria is a democratic republic with a federal structure. From a welfare state perspective, Austria is described as a conservative corporatist welfare state with the social insurance principle characterizing major branches of social policy (for example Obinger and Tálos, 2010; Österle and Heitzmann, 2009). In the comparative analysis of political systems, Austria has traditionally been described as a consociational democracy (Lijphart, 1977) with strong consensus orientation among political parties and social partners. According to the constitution, health care is shared federal (framework legislation) and provincial (enabling legislation and implementation) responsibility (Trukeschitz et al., 2013). Different from other federal systems, however, provinces do not have the power to tax. Rather, a system of fiscal equalization – agreed upon for periods of between four and six years – applies for the allocation of funds. Linked to the split of competences, state-provinces treaties are a common approach to deal with problems arising from this split and to agree on reform plans. Given the aforementioned funding regime, the duration of the state-provinces treaty is usually linked to the duration of the agreements on fiscal equalization. Provinces, apart from their regulatory role, also play an important role as providers of health care through hospitals, which are organized in quasi-public holding organizations at the provincial level. Additionally, private non-profit hospitals play a major role in coverage of the general population, while private for-profit hospitals are limited to those using private insurance or paying out-of-pocket. Administration of social health insurance is currently with 19 insurance funds organized along territorial criteria (9 funds, one fund for each province), employment background (4 funds) or membership to companies (6 occupational health insurance funds), covering about 98 per cent of the population. The Main Association of Austrian Social Security Institutions (*Hauptverband der Österreichischen Sozialversicherungsträger*) is the umbrella organization of all social insurance branches. Corresponding to the corporatist tradition, professional bodies and statutory associations are important players in the Austrian health care system. It is, for example, the Chamber of Physicians that is negotiating with health insurance funds on reimbursement. Private insurance, except for a small group of the self-employed, is supplementary.

Social health insurance was established in 1888 and became effective from August 1889. Mandatory insurance, social insurance funds as para-fiscal organizations with independent administration (*Selbstverwaltung*) and health insurance contributions shared between employers and employees characterize the system up to date. The first decades in the 20th century have been characterized by extensions in material and personal scope (Tálos, 1981; BMAS and Hauptverband, 1989). After the Second World War, social insurance principles have been re-established with previously fragmented legal sources now brought together in the General Social Security Act (*ASVG, Allgemeines Sozialversicherungsgesetz*) introduced in 1955. An extension of social health insurance to the self-employed only took place in 1965 (farmers) and 1966 (self-employed). In 1970, coverage has reached 91 per cent of the population. The period after 1970 has brought about further extensions, including personal coverage (by, for example, extending the definition of dependants in the early 1980s) and the extension of material coverage including preventive services (for example in 1973) and medical home nursing care, medical rehabilitation and clinical psychology (in 1991). Also, in 1993, a new long-term care system was introduced. Different from the German reform, following the social insurance model, the Austrian long-term care system is tax-funded. Extensions in personal health care coverage went along with extensions in the package of services covered and also meant a further increase in health expenditure. The latter development has started to influence debates and policies from the 1980s. From the mid-1990s, health care reforms increasingly emphasized budgetary control, cost-containment and efficiency orientation. Major reforms in the second half of the 1990s include the introduction of a DRG-oriented hospital financing scheme (in 1997), further developments of the Hospitals and Major Equipment Plan, some revisions to the long-term care system, but also increases in co-payments or the introduction of new co-payment schemes. The latter includes, for example, a new patient charge for the outpatient sector and a co-payment for spa and rehabilitation services (Hofmarcher and Rack, 2001; Österle, 2006).

Changes since the year 2000 can be divided into adjustments of specific parameters with an immediate effect, including changes in contribution rates or co-payments, and more structurally oriented reforms with expected mid and longer term effects. The first bundle of changes to the Austrian health care system aims at a direct impact on health care costs or at harmonizing standards for different social health insurance funds. These include regular changes, such as the adjustment of co-payments or the assessment base for social insurance contributions to inflation, but also changes going beyond simple price adjustment. For example, from 2006, the previous co-payment for doctoral visits (€3.63 covering doctor visits for a quarter of a year) was replaced by an annual health e-card fee of €10. In 2001, a new outpatient clinics fee was introduced with the aim to limit access to hospital infrastructure. This, however, was soon abolished again in 2003 after some heated debates in the media and administrative resistance. Another major area of cost-containment was the pharmaceutical sector. In 2003, a new regulation for stricter price control was introduced. Changes in social health insurance contributions were partly driven by budgetary considerations, but also by a long-term aim to standardize social health insurance contributions across different health insurance funds. This aim was finally reached in 2008, with a harmonized contribution rate of 7.65 per cent. A different mode still applies for pensioners, who only had to pay the employee share of the contributions (3.75 per cent) until 2003. Since then, the contribution rate has increased in several steps to 5.10 per cent in 2012.

A second bundle of reform efforts deals with more structural issues of the governance of the health care system. As mentioned earlier, state-provinces treaties are a common way to agree on reform plans in areas where competences are split between the federal and the provincial levels. And this approach is also applied in health care as a way to find agreement on major reform directions. The 2005 health care reform was laid down in such a state-provinces treaty covering the 2005–2008 time span. The major content of this agreement is structural reforms. First, it introduced the so-called reform pool activity. According to the reform pool agenda, 1 per cent (for 2006) and 2 per cent (for 2007 and 2008) of total funding for the inpatient and outpatient sector should be used for programmes facilitating the integration between the two sectors and furthering a shift of services from the inpatient sector to the outpatient sector. The implementation of reform pool projects, however, was slow and – in terms of financial volume – far below the intended level.

The 2005 reform agenda also attempted a structural reform aimed at improved coordination and cooperation between the federal level, provincial levels and social health insurance funds. In a first step, new institutions have been established on the federal and on the provincial levels: the Federal Health Agency and the Federal Health Commission as its executive body, and, on the provincial level, Provincial Health Funds and its executive body, the Health Platforms. All major stakeholders in the health sector are represented in the Federal Health Commission and the Provincial Health Platforms. These include representatives of the federal government, the social insurance funds, provinces, cities and local communities, the legal entities operating hospitals that are funded from the provincial funds, patients' ombudsmen and the Austrian Chamber of Physicians. While federal responsibility is mainly with the development of guidelines (including planning of provision and funding, quality assurance or the aforementioned reform pool projects), provincial levels are responsible for implementation and monitoring.

A further major element of the 2005 reform agenda is the introduction of the Austrian Structural Plan (*ÖSG, Österreichischer Strukturplan Gesundheit*), following the earlier Hospitals and Major Equipment Plan. The aim of the Austrian Structural Plan is to develop a tool for integrated health care planning covering not only the inpatient sector and major technological equipment (as with the earlier planning process), but also the outpatient sector, rehabilitation and long-term care. For the latter three sectors, the initial task is to determine the status quo of resource infrastructure. Further changes with the 2005 reform agenda include the Quality Act 2005, which attempts to develop a more coherent quality strategy, including regular quality reporting and the establishment of the Federal Institute for Quality in the Health Sector (*BIQG, Bundesinstitut für Qualität im Gesundheitswesen*). This institution becomes responsible for the development of quality standards and recommendations and their regular monitoring, with a potential longer term perspective to develop into a role similar to that of NICE in the UK.

The 2008–2013 state-provinces treaty confirms and follows up on the reform plans of the 2005–2008 agenda. Not least, it is a reaction to critique that implementation of some of the measures has been slow and weak. The steering bodies on federal and provincial levels are confirmed. Further developments in the Austrian Structural Plan shall also focus on the outpatient sector, with the overall perspective to ensure the principles of accessibility, quality and efficiency. Opportunities for funding from the reform pool are extended, with a particular focus on disease management programmes and pilot projects attempting to overcome the structural deficiencies in funding and steering health care provision. Another reform plan referred to in the 2008–2013 agreement is the introduction of an electronic patient documentation.

The recent economic crisis and the related increase in public debt have fuelled attempts to intensify more substantial structural reforms in the health care sector. According to the austerity programme published in February 2012, the health care sector is expected to contribute €1.372 billion (that is 5.7 per cent of total public health expenditure in 2010) for the 2012–2016 period. At that stage, apart from the figure, no details have been published on the ways to achieve the cost-containment objective. In June 2012, a paper accorded by representatives of the federal government, the regional governments and the social insurance institutions presented some basic principles for the reform. Accordingly, the parties involved agree to develop a system of objectives referring to provision, funding, quality, structures and processes in health care. Contracts between the actors should strengthen common responsibility in health care funding, enforced not least through an upper limit for health care expenditure. In terms of the institutional setting, the reform agenda envisages the establishment of commissions on federal and provincial levels, planning and coordinating a system of health objectives. Regular monitoring linked with enforcing measures should help to achieve the objectives. This is expected to lead to a cost-containment effect of €3.43 billion until 2016. Major criticism was put forward by the Chamber of Physicians, referring to cost-containment policies putting the quality of health care at risk and referring to growing bureaucratic burdens. Despite the critique of doctors and their threat to call out a strike, all other major actors supported the reform ideas. This led to a proposal for a respective law on health reform that was sent out for review early 2013. It is expected that the law will pass the parliament in spring 2013, and could then come into effect from January 2014. While the agreement is widely regarded as an important step for health care policies, there is still some scepticism to what extent the reform ideas will materialize when the details and practicalities of the reform have to be accorded between federal level, provincial levels and social insurance funds in the course of 2013.

Taken together, reform debates and changes to the health care system since the year 2000 attempted to (a) deal with increasingly tight budgetary constraints and to (b) develop new governance structures that should allow a more efficient steering of the system. Rescaling, privatization and managerialization were (partly hidden) elements of the debates behind reform efforts, but to very different extents. And, Austria did not see a major abrupt transformation in any of these areas.

Competences split between federal and provincial levels as well as social insurance funds and a lack of integration in the funding and provision of inpatient and outpatient care and the resulting complexity and weakness in the steering power are seen as major sources of inefficiency. Rescaling, more specifically the role of federal and provincial actors, has therefore for long been at the centre of health care debates in this country. While many experts and the federal level call for stronger central control and steering, provinces attempt to maintain and strengthen the role of decentral actors. In terms of reforms towards rescaling, the establishment of new federal and provincial agencies and the respective executive bodies changed the institutional context, clarified federal and provincial roles, but did not change the general split between federal and provincial competences. It strengthened the role of the federal level in terms of developing guidelines, and it strengthened the role of provinces in the implementation. But sanctions in case of non-compliance with federal guidelines remain limited and have so far not been executed.

Privatization, but also managerialization, in financing and provision is much less articulated than rescaling. With regard to managerialization, several changes attempt to strengthen the managerial approach in health care. Examples include the introduction of the DRG-related hospital financing system in 1997 or the establishment of new institutional actors with the 2005 reform. Aiming at cost-containment, the 2005 and the 2008 reform agenda, but also the 2012 debates towards a new reform effort, emphasize the objective to extend the performance orientation in health care funding from the inpatient sector to the outpatient sector and to improve the coordination

Pressures and drivers of health care reform

The main issues in health care reform debates in Austria since the year 2000 were (a) an increasing recognition of structural shortcomings and (b) budgetary pressures and cost-containment considerations. With regard to budgetary pressures, from the 1990s, increasing costs have regularly been addressed as 'cost explosion', even if relative increases – in international comparison – remained on relatively moderate levels after the mid 1990s. This was also the case in the debates around the current economic crisis. In the media, but also in political debates, the sharp increase in health expenditure as proportion of GDP from 2008 to 2009 (growing from 10.5 per cent to 11.2 per cent; see Table 7.1) has often been referred to as cost explosion. This statement ignores the fact that total health care costs (as well as public health care costs) did not exceed average growth rates of the past 10 years. Rather, it was the recession that led to a decrease in GDP and, as a consequence, to a relative sharp increase in health expenditure measured as proportion of GDP. But, this debate has fuelled another attempt to start more substantial structural reforms in the health care sector.

In addition to increasing health care costs, reform debates refer to general public deficits and resulting limitations for future public expenditure. This was the case in the 1990s when the Maastricht criteria required a limitation of annual and cumulated public debt, later more moderately with the stability and growth pact of the European Union, and in particular with the public deficits increasing as a consequence of the financial crisis in recent years. Early 2012, these debates and pressures from the EU, from international financial institutions and rating agencies led to an austerity programme with a volume of €26.5 billion until 2016, including €19 billion of expenditure cuts and €7.5 billion in tax increases. The health care sector is expected to contribute €1.372 billion in that period (that is 5.7 per cent of total public health expenditure in 2010). However, while expenditure cuts are specified for some areas (such as pension policies and public employment), the austerity programme only fixed the volume for health care. In 2012, a memorandum of understanding on health reform was reached in June 2012, indicating a cost-containment effect of €3.43 billion until 2016. Based on this memorandum of understanding, a proposal for health reform was sent out for review in early 2013.

A second element of budgetary pressures arises more specifically from inside the health care system. In 2007 and 2008, deficits accumulated across health insurance funds resulted in a broader debate about health care financing and warnings that the system might collapse. This resulted in an agreement to reach a balanced budget until 2014. Since then, social insurance funds have been rather successful and it is expected that social insurance funds will reach the aforementioned aim by 2013 already. However, as outlined above, a substantial part of public funding in the Austrian health care system is from tax funding, mostly from provinces and to a smaller extent from local communities. While the social health insurance system is fully funding – and hence has control over – the outpatient sector, the inpatient sector is funded from social health insurance and from provinces and local communities. While social health insurance funding already has a budgetary cap, provinces not only have to contribute the share agreed upon in the Provincial Health Fund, but also have to cover any remaining deficit of the publicly owned hospitals.

Structural shortcomings are the second major driver of recent health care reform debates since the year 2000. The sources of these structural problems are mostly seen in the split of competences in the health care sector between the federal level, the provincial level and the social health insurance funds, different funding modes for the outpatient sector (funded by social health insurance) and the inpatient sector (with different modes of combining social health insurance funding and tax funding on the provincial level), and in related limitations in steering the system. A large bed density in Austria (see Table 7.1) as compared to the OECD average, the duplication of hospital infrastructure and enormous political barriers in closing down hospitals or hospital departments, large increases in inpatient sector health expenditure, a relatively low level of day clinic treatments, and a lack of coordination and integration between the inpatient sector and the outpatient sector are discussed as the main inefficiencies arising from these structural deficiencies.

While calls for cost-containment and structural problems have been driving health care reform efforts for more than a decade, other factors have been taken up in the debates, but without having a strong continuous direct influence on reform activities. Referring to demographic changes has become kind of a standard phrase in reform documents and reform debates, emphasizing the need to control costs. According to the 2012 Ageing Report (European Commission, 2012) studying the budgetary implications of ageing societies, public health care expenditure – in a pure demographic scenario – would increase by 1.9 percentage points between 2010 and 2060. In a medium reference scenario combining different factors that impact on health expenditure, the increase would be 1.6 percentage points. While the demographic changes have become a major driver in long-term care reform (Österle, 2013), there is more limited emphasis of the demographic challenge in health care reform debates, apart from a standard reference to national and international studies and the broader budgetary implications arising from an ageing society.

While opponents of cost-containment approaches have repeatedly referred to the risks for accessibility and affordability, improving access has not been a major argument in the broader public debate driving health care reforms in the past decade in this country. But, public health reports have addressed specific needs of disadvantaged groups and the issue of health inequalities in Austria (Ladurner et al., 2010). In the political process, it is mostly representatives of social service providers and an anti-poverty network that have repeatedly pointed to inequalities in health and inequalities in access to health care, in particular for most vulnerable groups in society.

Also, Austria did not see any broad debate in the health care sector explicitly using the terms 'privatization' or 'managerialization'. While privatization of previously public companies as in the telecommunication or the energy industry became a major concern in Austria in the 1990s and in the first half of the 2000 decade, this debate did not expand to the health care sector. The fact that such debates did not evolve into the health care sector in Austria, as it did in other European countries, is largely due to a very high level of satisfaction with the health care system among the Austrian population (see below). While the aforementioned structural deficits are recognized, the outcome of the system is highly valued. As a consequence, there is support for reforms within the system, but very little support for the establishment of a fundamentally new institutional setting.

The mechanisms of health care reform

The actor constellation of Bismarckian health care systems tends to be more complex than that of national health systems. This is even more the case for the Austrian situation, as social health insurance only covers about two-thirds of total public health expenditure. Hence, steering of the system involves social health insurance funds, the federal level and the provincial levels, as well as other actors representing specific interests. While this section will only briefly depict the overall structure, a detailed overview to the organization of the health care system can be found in Hofmarcher and Rack (2006). Social health insurance in Austria is based on 19 self-administered insurance funds and their umbrella organization, the Main Association of Austrian Social Security Institutions. They are the main funder of health care in this country, covering about 45 per cent of total health care expenditure. While social insurance plays some role as provider in rehabilitation, there is only one acute care hospital owned by the Viennese social health insurance fund. In an important role as self-administered body, social health insurance funds negotiate reimbursement for the outpatient sector, which – apart from private payments – is almost exclusively covered by social health insurance. Funding of hospital care is different. It is based on a mix of taxes and social insurance contributions pooled in the Provincial Health Funds. In pooling these funds, different modes apply in the nine provinces. What is not covered from the regional funds is to be covered by the owner of the respective hospital, which is – for the quasi public hospitals – mostly the respective province. Hence, provinces have a very strong role in the provision and in the funding of health care. This side by side of social health insurance funds and provinces in steering the inpatient sector is seen as a major source of the structural problems in the Austrian health care system.

Besides the social insurance funds and the provinces, the federal level still has an important role in legislation and in supervision. Work on the federal level is supported by various commissions and bodies. Important responsibilities include health care planning (currently in the context of the Austrian Structural Plan for Health), developing performance-oriented reimbursement systems, developing and implementing quality specifications (in the context of the Federal Health Agency and the Federal Health Commission) and standards in the education of health professionals as well as activities in health promotion and prevention. Further major actors in health care policies are providers and their representatives and the users, current or potential future patients. Here, the Chamber of Physicians stands out because representation with this Chamber is mandatory. Also, midwives and pharmacists have a statutory representation, while other professionals, such as nurses, are only organized in voluntary membership associations. Hospitals are increasingly organized in holding organizations, both in the public and in the private sector. Finally, patient ombudsmen/-women represent patient interests.

While health care reforms did not lead to any transformative change over the past decade, the year 2000 marks an important turning point in the mechanisms of reforms. The new centre-right government started to shift power away from social partners, in particular the unions, reducing their traditional strong role in the decision-making process. The institutional reform agenda attempted to change power positions and to increase government influence in the self-administration of social insurance funds. Changes were driven by a stronger supply side orientation in economic policy, a strict orientation at reducing public debts and liberalization. Social policies were aimed at improving the targeting and reducing the misuse of benefits. The consensus orientation came to an end in that period (Obinger and Tálos, 2010; Obinger, 2005). While the reform agenda had an important impact on various social policies in that period, actual changes remained more limited in the health sector. Many of the reform measures outlined above were in line with longer term projects (such as the development of infrastructure planning and of the hospital financing system). The increase in co-payments was linked to a strong emphasis on balancing the budget, while the increase in insurance contributions was also part of a longer term project to harmonize contribution rates.

The fact that changes to the health sector remained more limited than in other welfare sectors is a consistently high level of satisfaction with the health system (see below), limiting the opportunity to denounce the system for its failures. From an institutional perspective, the particular distribution of power is the major explanatory factor. While social partners play a role in the self-administration of the social health insurance funds, and while doctors have a strong say in specific health system issues, the provinces are strong players in the development of the inpatient sector in particular. Their power is determined by their role as providers (via provincial holding organizations) and their role as financier in the inpatient sector. While the role of social health insurance funds, including their financial contribution to health care funding, is clearly defined, provinces act both as provider and as financier. Hence, the attempt to exclude social partners from the decision-making process did not have such a strong impact on the health care sector compared to other sectors. For long, provinces have been the major counterpart of the federal government. In health reform debates, different ideas about the reform direction often followed the division between federal and provincial levels rather than the lines between political parties.

Given the split of competences, state-provinces treaties became a major mechanism for developing common principles for the direction in health care reform. These treaties have the character of an agreement, which however is not binding. The accord is usually made for a period of four to six years and is linked to the fiscal equalization act. Whether and to what extent agreements are then implemented depends on the specific actor constellations and their interests. Such an agreement was made under the federal centre-right government for the 2005–2008 period and later – under a federal grand coalition – for the 2008–2013 period. While the agreements were regularly praised as the starting point of a major reform, implementing the measures has often been slow and more limited than envisaged.

A continuous issue in the state-provinces treaty was the improvement of the integration between the inpatient and the outpatient sector, and more specifically a reduction of a relatively large bed density in this country. Key actors in these attempts are the provinces. On the one hand, they have a strong budgetary interest, given that they bear a very substantial part of increasing health care costs in the inpatient sector. On the other hand, they also have a strong interest in their role as quasi owner of the majority of hospitals, both in ensuring health provision for their electorate and in maintaining an important employment sector. As a consequence, provinces have always been very reluctant in reducing the number of hospital beds or even closing down hospitals. Only few provinces made some more significant steps in this direction. As the budgetary pressure is also increasing on provincial levels, new efforts were made with the 2012 austerity programme.

The Chamber of Physicians is another important actor in the health arena. It represents doctors, for example, in the negotiation of reimbursement in the outpatient sector. But it can also have a strong say in allowing (or not allowing) for health system changes. An important recent example is the introduction of an electronic patient documentation. In the 2005 state-provinces treaty, federal and provincial levels agreed on a steering group to plan the introduction of an electronic patient documentation. In the 2008 state-provinces treaty, this was further specified. In 2011, the system was ready for legal and practical implementation. While there was broad support for this programme, the Chamber of Physicians, and in particular the Viennese section of the Chamber of Physicians, attempted to impede the implementation of the system. Their veto referred to security concerns, but also to the argument that it would limit patients' opportunities to get a second opinion. Only in December 2012, the respective law finally passed the parliament.

Taken together, the actor constellation in the health care sector is highly complex. Stewardship requires consensus among the major actors. Different from the situation in many national health systems, the state has a much weaker say. And, the federal level has a weaker say than in other Bismarckian health care systems such as Germany. The reason is that provinces play a strong role as providers of hospital care and as financier of inpatient care, while the steering role of the federal level is not adequately equipped with regulatory options. There have been many attempts to develop an institutional structure that allows for more clearly defined steering competences, but respective reform efforts often remained weak. This is because reform plans were only partly implemented (as the use of reform pool funds strengthening the role of the outpatient sector). Or, the implementation of reforms was often not sufficiently backed up by the incentive structure. Regarding the way forward, there is consensus on key issues to be addressed and even the major measures that are required: reducing hospital beds and hospital use, improving the integration of inpatient and outpatient sector and strengthening the outpatient sector. The differentiation in funding outpatient and inpatient services is seen as one of the key sources of the problems. 'Funding from one pool' has therefore become a catchword for a necessary reform. The 2012 reform agreement does lead to such a single pool for funding health care, and it attempts to develop stronger common responsibility, backed up by a sanction mechanism.

The impact of (non-)reform on performance

In this section, the above exploration of health care reform in Austria will be discussed with a view to potential impacts on performance. Indicators of health system performance surveyed include efficiency, organizational performance, citizens' satisfaction, access to health care, workforce developments and health status. This section will outline the major trends since the year 2000 and discuss these in the context of the aforementioned changes to the health care system. For an overview of selected indicators, see Table 7.1.

Economic performance

Total health expenditure as per cent of GDP was 10.0 per cent in 2000 and reached 11.2 per cent in 2009 and 11.0 per cent in 2010. The sharp increase from 2008 (10.4 per cent) to 2009 is due to the recession rather than any exceptional increase in health expenditure. In the 2000–2009 time span, on average, total health expenditure has increased by 2.2 per cent annually. This is significantly lower than in the OECD average (4.0 per cent) and similar to a group of mostly Western European countries with more moderate growth rates between 1 per cent and 3 per cent (OECD, 2011a). In a longer term perspective, health care expenditure in Austria has seen a substantial growth from 8.4 per cent in 1990 to 9.6 per cent of GDP in 1995, which was mainly due to extensions in material coverage and the introduction of a new long-term care policy. After that, increases remained more moderate but on average beyond GDP growth. In the past decade (2000–09), GDP growth on average was 1.6 per cent in the OECD and 1.0 per cent in Austria (OECD, 2011a). Differentiating health expenditure by health care sectors reveals that curative and rehabilitative care, in particular in the inpatient sector, has seen the sharpest increase. While this accounted for 5.8 per cent of GDP in 2000, it is 6.2 per cent of GDP in 2010. The two other sectors representing an important share of total expenditure and a significant expenditure increase from the 1990s are medical goods and long-term nursing care. Expenditure as a proportion of GDP on medical goods increased from 1.0 per cent in 1990, to 1.6 per cent in 2000 and 1.8 per cent in 2010. In long-term care, the increase is from 0.9 per cent in 1990, to 1.3 per cent in 2000 and 1.5 per cent in 2010 (see Table 7.1). It is these three sectors that have also been at the core of health care (and long-term care) reform debates over the past two decades.

Besides the overall expenditure picture, deficits in social health insurance funds have become a major issue in health debates in the year 2007 and 2008. For 2007, an accumulated deficit of more than €300 million was forecasted. But, social health insurance funds then became quite successful in reducing these deficits. According to 2012 estimates, deficits will be erased by 2013. There are, however, limitations to the meaning of deficit in the social health insurance system. In the 2012 health reform agenda, for example, the state plans to use a substantial reserve fund of the social health insurance fund for public employees to reduce the public deficit. This change is not related to any performance indicator but a simple transfer of money. Secondly, the economic situation of social health insurance funds only depicts part of the entire public funding picture as tax-funding accounts for about 30 per cent of total health funding in this country, most importantly in the inpatient sector and in the long-term care sector.

Since the 1990s, the hospital sector has been seen as a most critical element in terms of economic efficiency. Beyond indicators of organizational performance (see below), a few studies applying data envelopment analysis have indicated a potential to increase efficiency. Considering the limitations of the approach, the picture provided by earlier studies (undertaken after the introduction of the new hospital funding system) is not very coherent but with some tendency towards better performance among private non-profit hospitals and hospitals owned by local authorities (Sommersguter-Reichmann, 2000; Hofmarcher et al., 2002; Hofmarcher et al., 2005; Stepan and Sommersguter-Reichmann, 2005). A recent study covering all acute care hospitals confirms this by indicating that private non-profit hospitals perform better than public hospitals, but with substantial variation by region and occupancy of the hospitals (Czypionka et al., 2011). The market for medical goods is a second major target for cost-containment. Figures on total expenditure for medical goods dispensed to outpatients indicate some success of cost-containment measures in this area. While total expenditure in this sector (as per cent of GDP) has increased from 1.1 per cent in 1990 to 1.7 per cent in 2002, increases remained more moderate after that. Long-term nursing care, the third sector characterized by substantial increases in health expenditure, is a sector where extensions in material coverage have been an explicit policy objective from the 1990s. Additionally, many of the cost-containment measures in the acute care sectors imply a shift of health care costs from acute care to long-term nursing care. Significant increases in long-term care expenditure became a major concern in long-term care policies, but the need to further expand services, most importantly in the community care sector, is widely recognized (Österle, 2013; Österle and Bauer, 2012).

Organizational performance

The reduction in hospital use has been one of the key objectives of health care policies over the past two decades. Measures towards this objective include the introduction of a DRG-oriented hospital funding system, the extension of long-term care services to allow earlier discharge of those with long-term nursing care needs, stricter hospital and major infrastructure planning and – repeatedly addressed, but not yet implemented – a reorganization of the funding system furthering the integration of inpatient and outpatient care. Similar to other OECD countries, Austria has seen a substantial reduction in the average length of stay in acute care hospitals, being 6.6 days in 2010 (compared to 7.6 in 2000, 9.7 in 1995 and 11.0 in 1990). This is due to various measures attempting to reduce length of stay in hospitals, not least the DRG-oriented hospital financing scheme introduced in 1997 (Theurl and Winner, 2007) and extensions in the availability of long-term care services in nursing homes and in community care (Österle, 2013). While this could indicate some significant efficiency growth, the picture becomes more ambivalent when considering other indicators. Compared with many OECD and most other European countries, Austria is characterized by a relatively large hospital bed density (7.6 beds per 1,000 population as compared to 4.9 in the OECD average in 2010) and a relatively smaller reduction in hospital beds. At the same time, the occupancy rate has slightly increased over the past decade (almost 80 per cent in 2009). While this indicates some improvement in resource use, occupancy rate and relatively large bed density taken together confirm a relatively large level of hospital infrastructure use in this country. The most significant reduction in the 2000–10 period has taken place in the acute care sector (5.5 beds in 2010 per 1,000 population compared to 6.2 beds in 2000). Both public and private non-profit hospitals have seen a reduction in hospital beds, while the respective number has grown in the private for-profit sector.

One explanation for more intense hospital use is a larger level of health care activities. And in fact, among OECD countries, with regard to the number of surgeries per 100,000 population, Austria is fourth for hip replacement and for knee replacement, or fifth for coronary angioplasty. Also, hospital admission rates for chronic respiratory diseases are above OECD average. In other areas, hospital use does not significantly vary from OECD average. Another explanation for a larger level of hospital use in this country is a comparatively lower level of surgeries carried out as day cases.

In terms of doctor consultations, Austria is close to the OECD average with only a very moderate increase over the past decade (6.9 consultations per citizen in Austria compared to an OECD average of 6.4 in 2010). Similarly, the availability and the use of computed tomography scanners and magnetic resonance imaging units is above OECD average. Related to a strong outpatient sector for specialist health care, an important proportion of these units is in the outpatient sector. A specific issue is outpatient wards in hospitals. The introduction of a significant fee for visits in these outpatient wards in 2001 (which was abolished again in 2003) was an attempt to redirect patients to doctors in the outpatient sector. So far, this and other attempts have not been successful. Accessibility to specialist care in terms of opening hours is seen as one of the reasons that patients tend to use outpatient wards in hospitals rather than services provided by doctors in private practices. This, in turn, is also because practises tend to be single practices, while group practices allowing extended opening hours are still an exception.

The potential of de-hospitalization is to a considerable extent determined by the development of an adequate infrastructure in home care and in the long-term care sector more generally. And this is in fact one of the few sectors that have seen substantial material extensions in welfare state responsibilities over the past two decades (Österle, 2013). These extensions include cash benefits (a cash-for-care programme introduced in 1993) and services. In the home care sector, availability and use of services has consistently grown since the 1990s, also allowing earlier discharges from hospitals. In the residential care sector, the overall number of beds has remained relatively stable, but the patterns of use have changed, facilitating access for patients with severe limitations.

Citizens' satisfaction

While the health care system has often been denounced for its inefficiencies in the media, by some experts or politicians over the past decade, the general population seems highly content with the performance of the system. According to a Eurobarometer survey in 2007 (2007), the Austrian population is highly satisfied with accessibility, affordability and quality. 92 per cent of the population assess their health care system as very good or fairly good, 92 per cent of the population find access to health care easy, 89 per cent argue that health care is affordable, 93 per cent as good, accessible and affordable quality and 87 per cent regard specialist care as very good or fairly good. In all these categories, Austria is among the top four countries among the 27 EU member states surveyed.

While longitudinal data is widely missing, existing information indicates a persistently high level of satisfaction with the health care system. In a more recent Eurobarometer survey in the EU 27 member states (2010), it is again 95 per cent of the population for whom the quality of the health care system is good ('very good' and 'fairly good'), a level only exceeded by Belgium in that survey. The EU average is 70 per cent. In no other country, the same proportion assesses its health care system as very good. In Austria, it is 45 per cent of respondents, followed by 37 per cent in Belgium and 34 per cent in Sweden. The EU average for the assessment 'very good' is 12 per cent. In comparison with other countries, 64 per cent and 32 per cent of the Austrian population regard their health care system as better or as the same, respectively, than that of other EU27 countries.

While the measurement and the explanatory power of individual satisfaction with the health care system have their limitations, the very positive response to the Austrian health care system is quite consistent. The Eurobarometer results are also confirmed by various national opinion surveys and they are confirmed by the EuroHealth Consumer Index, annually published by Health Consumer Powerhouse (Health Consumer Powerhouse, 2009). This ranking is based on an analysis of health system characteristics that are identified as key issues for consumers rather than on a survey among patients or citizens. Indicators include, for example, variables describing patient rights and information, the role of e-health, waiting time or outcome measures. From 2007 till 2009, Austria was ranked 1st, 3rd and 4th among a group of between 29 and 33 European countries.

Access to public health care

The history of European health systems is also a history of broadening personal coverage to (almost) universal systems. While Austria generally sticks to basic principles of the Bismarck model, the extension of coverage is a major development taken from the national health system model. Over the 20th century this was achieved by including coverage for family members, by including the self-employed and the farmers in the 1960s, by extending coverage to recipients of social benefits or to new forms of atypical employment. This led to an estimated coverage of about 98 per cent of the population. The subgroups that are not covered under social health insurance are rather heterogeneous (Fuchs et al., 2003). Firstly, there are particular groups with other coverage arrangements, including a small group of self-employed having the opportunity to opt out of the social insurance system (about 0.5 per cent of the population) and groups with tax-funded coverage by the state (in particular those in the military). Secondly, until 2010, recipients of social assistance, if not covered otherwise, have been covered by the provincial, tax-funded social assistance scheme. With the introduction of a needs-based minimum income scheme (*Bedarfsorientierte Mindestsicherung*), those previously not covered under social health insurance are now included with contributions made by the provinces. Thirdly, there is a group whose social health insurance coverage is lacking for a transition period. Groups at risk include students, if they do not move into regular employment after their studies or spouses out of employment after a divorce if they have been co-insured with their partner before the divorce.

Additional limitations to access may derive from differences in the health care package and from private co-payments. Out-of-pocket health expenditure accounts for about 3 per cent of final household consumption in Austria (compared to 3.2 per cent in the OECD average). As most low income earners are excluded from major co-payments and given upper limits for co-payments, unmet need for financial reasons is a relatively smaller phenomenon if compared to other countries. According to EU-SILC data, among the lowest income quintile less than 2 per cent of the population indicate that need for a medical examination has not been met (OECD, 2011a). In this group, the main reason is affordability, while among upper income groups travel distance becomes a relatively more important limiting factor. Waiting time, according to EU-SILC data, is not a major factor limiting access in Austria. Unmet need becomes a more significant problem for services that are excluded from social insurance coverage or services where more substantial co-payments apply. This includes aids or dental care. According to EU-SILC data, about 8 per cent of the population in the lower income quintile reports unmet need in dental care, while the respective proportion is just about 3 per cent for the high and middle income population (OECD, 2011a).

In health reform debates addressing the closing-down of hospitals or hospital units, accessibility has repeatedly been a major argument put forward by politicians and the people in the region to maintain hospital infrastructure on the local level. In a European perspective, travel distance does in fact cause quite some limitations in access to health care. In Austria, as in other countries, physician density is largest in the capital city. At the same time, when comparing regions in terms of physician density, the Austrian regions with the lowest level of physician density still perform considerably better than regions with low physician density in most other countries (OECD, 2011a). This might explain the above-mentioned relatively smaller level of accessibility problems expressed for territorial reasons. However, local communities in very rural districts seem increasingly concerned with difficulties in attracting physicians.

While women are more frequent users of inpatient and outpatient provisions than men, Eurostat data shows relatively smaller differences for men and women in Austria. Still, unmet need – even though on relatively low levels in Austria – is slightly more pronounced for women. This applies because of limitations in affordability and travel, but also for other reasons, including lack of information, lack of time or fear (European Commission, 2010a). This might also explain some of the income inequalities in the use of health care. Respective data is very limited for Austria, but existing studies indicate that GP consultations largely correlate with need, while there is some pro-rich inequality in outpatient specialist consultations, in dental care and in hospital use (Devaux and de Looper, 2012; OECD, 2011a; van Doorslaer et al., 2006).

The healthcare workforce

The number of doctors licensed to practise is 4.8 per 1,000 population in Austria in 2010, a ratio above all other OECD countries except Greece. In 2000, the ratio was 3.9 per total population which makes an average annual growth rate of 2.1 per cent, a rate also above the OECD average. The number of nurses practising in hospitals is 7.7 in 2010 in Austria, compared to 7.2 in 2000 (OECD, 2012; see Table 7.1). For nurses, comparative figures have to be used with some caution because definitions of qualifications and professional groups differ between countries.

One factor explaining a large level of doctors licensed to practise is to be found in the educational system. Until 2005, Austria followed the principle of open admission to medical studies. Everyone successfully finishing secondary school education was entitled to be admitted to medical university. Access for foreign students, at that time, however, was limited to those who would have been admitted to the study programme in their country of origin. In 2005, the European Court of Justice then ruled that this violates the free mobility principle. Fearing even larger numbers of medical students that would further aggravate already existing huge capacity problems, medical universities started to introduce admission tests as an immediate response. With this control over medical university intake it is also expected that currently a very large level of medical graduates per 100,000 population (more than twice the OECD average) might shrink. While the number of graduates per year has still increased by 68 per cent between 2000 and 2010, the total number of students decreased by 36 per cent, while that of first year students decreased by 54 per cent in the same period (Statistik Austria, 2011).

Stress and burden related to work in the health care sector is a recurring topic in the media, not least in debates about staff shortages caused in health and social care. Pressures and burdens are also confirmed in the few existing studies. In a recent study (Brunner et al., 2010), three quarters of respondents indicate a high level of job satisfaction. At the same, about half of respondents refer to staff shortages and bureaucratic burdens as the main pressures and sources of stress. In a report by the Chamber of Physicians, 80 per cent of respondents refer to pressures arising from staff shortages, about half to pressures arising from administrative burdens (Ärztekammer, 2011). It is not least processes of managerialization and cost-containment efforts that are seen as the roots of these pressures. In early 2012, workload and work organization became key issues in protests by doctors in the medical university clinic in Vienna. After a budget cut, the management of the clinic was planning to reduce staff attendance over night and during weekends by about 14 per cent. In addition, it was planned to not fill vacancies to balance the budget cut. Doctors argued that these cuts would put quality at risk, that adequate emergency services would not be secured over night and during weekends and that training for young doctors would suffer. These concerns were put forward in employees meetings. Media reports and doctors considering strike finally led to an abolition of the plan to reduce staff attendance.

Health conditions

Taking major indicators of health status into consideration, the health situation has significantly improved over the past 10 years. Life expectancy at birth has increased from 79.0 years in 1990 for women to 81.2 years in 2000 and to 83.5 years in 2010. While male life expectancy was 6.7 years less in 1990, this gap has decreased to 5.6 years in 2010. Infant mortality has decreased, from 7.8 in 1990 to 4.8 in 2000 and to 3.9 in 2010 (OECD, 2012). With regard to age-standardized death rates, in 2009, Austria is placed eighth for women and tenth for men in the European Union (Statistik Austria, 2011). Age-standardized mortality rate for ischemic heart disease is slightly above OECD average, while the mortality rates for stroke and for cancer are below OECD average (OECD, 2011a). In a comparison of age-standardized death rates from amenable mortality in 16 high-income countries, Austria is placed average in 2006/07, but with above average improvement since 1997/98 (Nolte and McKee, 2011). With regard to health-oriented behaviour, the proportion of preventive services has increased by 30.7 per cent between 2000 and 2010. Other figures are alarming. Smoking and alcohol consumption among the 15-year-olds is more common in Austria than in most other OECD countries. Obesity has increased from 9 per cent in 1999 to 13 per cent in 2006/7, both for men and for women (Statistik Austria, 2011). Given the incremental character of health care reform in Austria, however, it is difficult to directly link overall health system changes to trends in health conditions, even more so in a relatively short-term period of one decade.

Conclusions

The development of the Austrian health care system in a long-term perspective is characterized by considerable stability in the basic principles underlying the system and an evolutionary implementation of reform steps. More critically, this has also been interpreted as rigidity and a lack of organizational innovation. This characterization is not very different for the period since the year 2000, with incremental rather than transformative changes. Hassenteufel and Palier's (2007) conclusion that structural changes occur without revolution in Bismarckian health care systems applies to the Austrian system even more than to other Bismarckian systems. The health care system in this country has upheld key principles of the traditional social insurance model up to date. Historically, the realization of almost universal coverage (similar to other Bismarckian health care systems) and a relatively strong role of tax funding as proportion of overall public health funding (different from other Bismarckian health care systems) have been major developments moderating the Bismarckian character of the health system. However, what has intensified in the past two decades, and even more so in the past decade, is the pressure arising from budgetary constraints and the calls for cost-containment.

In the recent OECD economic survey of Austria, Austria's health care system was described as highly regarded but costly (OECD, 2011b). The upper analysis of major performance measures confirms not only a high level of satisfaction with the health care system but also above average or average performance with regard to major outcome indicators. At the same time, in a comparative perspective, the availability of health care resources and the use of these resources are also above average or average. Over the past decade, health care debates have therefore increasingly addressed the question to what price the outcome is achieved. Some of the measures that have been used to increase efficiency could partly be summarized under the heading of managerialization, but this term was not actively used in the debates. Respective policies have been incremental, without fundamentally transforming the system. What has dominated health reform debates with regard to steering and cost considerations is the question of rescaling, the role of the federal level, provincial levels and social insurance funds, and most importantly the division of responsibilities between central and local levels. The past decade has seen some reform efforts and some incremental changes in this respect, which might lead to more important structural reforms if further changes are developed in a coherent way.

8
Poland: Decentralization, Privatization and Managerialization of the Health Care System

Monika Ewa Kaminska

Introduction

In Poland, as in other countries of East-Central Europe (ECE), the post-1989 transition from a communist regime to democracy and market economy brought sweeping political and economic changes which required an overhaul of welfare arrangements, including health care. In the post-war decades, the health care system in Poland with its universal entitlement to free care was an integral part of the command economy. Following the 1947 nationalization the state operated as a 'comprehensive, general insurance institution' (Kornai and Eggleston, 2001: 139). Similar to other ECE countries, all activity within the sector was centrally controlled, with a 'long ineffective chain of command down to work units' (Healy and McKee, 1997: 287). The level of investment in health care was much lower in ECE than in Western Europe because the focus in the communist economy was on 'productive' sectors of heavy industry (Estrin, 1994). Health care provision was mainly concentrated in hospitals, and primary health services were neglected (Healy and McKee, 1997). Private practice was very limited. The professional self-government bodies were dismantled, though doctors maintained control over clinical issues, unchallenged by the state administration (Wlodarczyk, 1986). After a phase of 'non-economic approach' which lasted into the 1970s, the underlying assumption that economic incentives do not matter in the organization of the national health care system began to falter (Wlodarczyk, 1986). Attempts of critical diagnosis of the Polish health care system were made and followed by a phase of 'economic approach' that started in the 1980 (Wlodarczyk, 1986). Its implementation was interrupted by the collapse of the communist regime in 1989.

The national health care system 'established grounds for the organization of massive preventive actions, badly needed in the post-war period' (Wlodarczyk and Karkowska, 2005: 380) and in the first three post-war decades produced positive results in terms of improvement of the health status of the population thanks to a 'relatively comprehensive and effective system of basic public health services such as immunizations' (Kornai and Eggleston, 2001: 139). It provided 'security, solidarity and equality, albeit at an extremely low level' (Kornai and Eggleston, 2001: 139). Polish outcomes were comparable to other ECE countries, but the progress in the region was slower than in Western Europe. Poland entered the 1990s with lower life expectancy and higher infant mortality (in 1989: 71.5 years for total population at birth and 19.1 per 1000 live births) than, for instance, Germany (respectively, 75.4 and 7.6), France (76.5 and 7.8) or UK (75.3 and 9) (OECD, 2012a).

Given that a number of major post-1989 health care reforms so far introduced in Poland date back to the 1990s, in this national portrait it is necessary to cover that decade in detail. It must be stressed that health care reforms in Poland were designed and implemented at a time of profound transformation in which 'the entire social, political and economic system had to be rebuilt' (Wlodarczyk and Karkowska, 2005: 414). Health care sector constituted an element of the system under transition and 'it could not be simply adjusted to the mechanisms of a democratic society', because these very mechanisms had to be built almost from scratch after 1989 (Wlodarczyk and Karkowska, 2005: 414).

The trajectories of the health care reforms and their rationale

The changes of the health care organization in Poland have to be considered in the context of different aspects of the post-communist transition. One of them was the liberalization of the country's economy through a 'shock therapy' (see Balcerowicz, 1994), including its labour market, and the development of the private sector that was accompanied by growing differences in income levels leading to an increase in the share of population able and willing to cover costs of health care from private resources (Tymowska, 2001: 85–6). Another aspect of the transition that formed the background for health care reforms was the decentralization of the territorial administration and a gradual introduction of territorial self-government in Poland. The first step in this direction regarded the local-level self-governed *gminas* (communes) which in 1990 ceased to depend directly on central administration, acquired democratic legitimization through general elections and were granted legal liability together with financial means and new tasks. The second step, in 1999, defined a three-tier self-government elected in direct and proportional voting (with *gmina* at the local level, *poviat* at the province level and *voivodship* at the regional level), which complemented two levels of central administration (at the regional level, parallel to the regional self-government, and at the state level) (Wlodarczyk and Karkowska, 2005).

The paragraphs below analyse the processes of decentralization, privatization and managerialization that have affected financing and provision of health care in Poland in the last twenty years.

Decentralization

During the past two decades, both financing and provision of health care have undergone decentralization but in a rather erratic manner, with bouts of re-centralization mostly due to political reasons. As for health care financing, throughout the 1990s health care services were funded from the central budget. Access was universal and based on citizenship. In 1997, a law – prepared by a left-of-centre government – was passed instituting a health insurance system financed from premiums (Wlodarczyk and Karkowska, 2005: 386). It envisaged an establishment of a number of regional sickness funds with boards elected by all the insured members. The funds were supposed to collect contributions from the insured individuals and pay for services to contracted providers. The level of contributions was defined by the parliament at 10 per cent of the income subjected to taxes (Wlodarczyk and Karkowska, 2005: 386). A centre-right coalition which came to power following the elections later that year significantly changed the bill: instead of being elected in a general ballot, the boards of the funds were to be appointed by regional self-governments; contributions were to be collected by a state agency responsible for social insurance and transferred to sickness funds; and the contribution rate was reduced to 7.5 per cent of taxable income based on a political decision imposed by the Finance Minister (Wlodarczyk and Karkowska, 2005).

This reform, enacted in the Universal Health Insurance Act and implemented in January 1999, decentralized the financing of public health care by transferring the financial responsibility away from the government to a network of sickness funds which financed the contracts with providers from compulsory employer contributions. The newly created funds arose as a new institutional tier (Filinson et al., 2003) and formally enjoyed the status of autonomous legal entities, regulated by civil law (Den Exter, 2001). However, they soon became politicized, their boards being elected appointed by regional self-governments. The contribution rate proved to provide by far too limited resources and had to be raised by 0.25 percentage points annually until reaching the current rate of 9 per cent.

In 2001, the centre-left coalition returned to power. It criticized the 1999 reform for its unclear rules regarding institutional design for sickness funds, terms of contracting, recording health services and rules of payment for services. Encouraged by the dissatisfaction of the population with the implementation of the reform which indeed had caused organizational problems in the Polish health care, in 2003 the centre-left government replaced the network of sickness funds by a single National Health Fund, NFZ (*Narodowy Fundusz Zdrowia*) with units in each region, which allegedly was supposed to address the reform's weaknesses but was as a matter of fact a political decision (see discussion below). The new institutional framework meant a re-centralization of payer functions: the NFZ gained 'huge discretionary power' and its decisions have since been difficult to control by external actors especially in terms of the distribution of resources (Wlodarczyk and Karkowska, 2005: 411, 413).

When it comes to health care provision, while some responsibilities were devolved to regional representatives of the central government already in the 1980s, after 1989 the first major change followed from the 1991 Health Care Institutions Act. Apart from formally introducing a purchaser–provider split, the Act initiated the process of decentralization by transferring the administration of most health services from the Ministry of Health and Social Welfare to the regional units of central administration (*voivodships*) and local self-governing units (*gminas*). The regional health budgets were financed by the Ministry of Finance. The regions' task was 'to plan health services, organize the structure of health institutions and allocate funds, run regional secondary and some tertiary care hospitals' (Karski et al., 1999: 9). The regions also administered integrated health care and *social services management groups* which constituted the basis for primary and secondary health for their catchment population of an average of 100,000 individuals (Karski et al., 1999: 10–11).

The new entrants in the health care systems were the *gminas*. The reform endowed them with all responsibilities not reserved for other public bodies. This included 'the responsibility of meeting the collective health needs of the community, including all public issues with local impact that had not been delegated to another agency' (Wlodarczyk and Karkowska, 2005: 389). More specifically, their tasks included mandates delegated by the central government and financed from the state budget, as well as *gminas'* own duties. However, despite the reform's decentralizing premises, which in principle delegated a lot of power to the *gminas*, their ability to act was limited by the lack of detailed legislation and scarce financial resources. Consequently, the *gminas*, rather than their own duties, were interested in performing mandates delegated by the central government and coming with financial guarantees. Thus, the reform did not radically change the *gminas'* health care activities (Wlodarczyk and Karkowska, 2005: 391).

In conformity with the 1991 Act, health care units were supposed to sign contracts with payers. Yet, only in the mid-1990s did the Minister of Health issue a regulation on the conditions of transfer of budgetary resources to self-managing institutions, which finally allowed them to sign contracts for health services and become responsible for managing their budgets (Karski et al., 1999: 11). At the same time, the position of urban *gminas* in organizing health care was strengthened: they were granted more competencies and more funding (from an increased share in personal income tax revenues) and acquired ownership of a number of health care institutions previously ran by the regional representatives of the central government (*voivods*) (Wlodarczyk and Karkowska, 2005: 393).

The 1999 reform of territorial administration (mentioned above) brought further decentralization: self-governments at the local, provincial and regional level were expected 'to develop a health policy for respective areas of jurisdiction that would involve both the structure of local health care and the sphere of public health' (Wlodarczyk and Karkowska, 2005: 396). 'The division of responsibilities (...) was based on the idea of referral level': while *gminas* were in charge of primary care, *poviats* were responsible for secondary care, and regions for tertiary care (Wlodarczyk and Karkowska, 2005: 396). As a result, many hospitals passed from *gminas* to *poviats* and by 2002 around 46 per cent of public hospital beds were owned by the *poviats* and 38 per cent by the regions (Watson, 2009). Self-governments formally retained the responsibility for maintaining health facilities but in practice their capacities remained limited, because the essential part of financial management was now transferred to sickness funds while financing from the central budget was discontinued. The mutual obligations between the sickness funds and territorial self-governments were not clearly defined, which generated conflicts. Moreover, self-governments were supposed to prepare, together with sickness funds and in consultation with the medical community, plans for outpatient health care as a basis for contracts between funds and providers. Yet, 'this obligation turned out to be a dead letter': no ministerial decree followed to specify the contents of such plans (Wlodarczyk and Karkowska, 2005: 397). A later amendment to the Health Insurance Act provided that plans for outpatient care were to be developed by *voivods* (regional representatives of the government), which meant a re-centralization of this task (Wlodarczyk and Karkowska, 2005: 398). As assessed by Sagan et al. '[t] he shift towards three levels of territorial self-government (decentralization) proceeded in parallel with the disintegration of the health care system. Each level of territorial self-government is independent – it has its own organizational units and responsibilities. This makes coordination of activities in the health sector difficult' (Sagan et al., 2011: 24). Evidence suggests poor definition, inconsistent allocation and a resulting overlap of responsibilities across different (self-)government levels (OECD, 2012b: 71). The implementation of reforms without defining the relations between actors within the new system generated what can be called a 'dispersed responsibility' (Wlodarczyk and Karkowska, 2005: 411).

Privatization

The *financing* of Polish health care has undergone a spontaneous 'privatization' of health care spending or a shift in the distribution of health care costs between the state and the citizens, which is reflected in the growing share of private spending on health services. On the one hand, following the 1997/99 reform, the insurance funds and later the centralized NFZ have financed the direct costs of health services to patients through contracts with service providers, while government budgets (state, regional and local) have continued to finance public health services, the capital costs of all health services, specialist tertiary care services and very expensive drugs

(Kuszewski and Gericke, 2005: 24). On the other hand, private expenditure has grown considerably over the last two decades. From 8.3 per cent in 1990, private expenditure on health as percentage of the total health expenditure rose to 25.4 per cent in 2009, 88.4 per cent of which was constituted by out-of-pocket (OOP) payments (WHO, 2012). Private insurance and private pre-paid plans amounted to, respectively, only 0.56 per cent and 2.2 per cent of the total expenditure on health (WHO, 2012). The growth of OOP payments has been due mostly to growing co-payments for pharmaceuticals (the reimbursement of which is much lower in Poland than in most EU countries) as well as for certain services obtained under general insurance (for example dental care, ophthalmology, accommodation in spas and long-term care institutions), but it has increasingly involved expenditure on health services offered in the parallel 'private' sector, not covered by insurance but with easy access and available without waiting lists. Many individuals prefer to purchase services in the private market to jump the queue and gain access to specialists without referral (OECD, 2012b: 51, 60). The share of various informal payments (for example gratuities paid to obtain quicker access to better quality services in public health care or as a form of appreciation for health care provision) was high at the beginning of the transition, but over the past two decades has been consistently decreasing, also thanks to the availability of private provision outside of the public insurance scheme. In 2006, different informal payments constituted about 2 per cent of the total amount of OOP expenses borne by patients (Golinowska, 2010: 20).

The privatization of health care *provision* was formally initiated by the 1991 Act. The main rationale was economic efficiency. Under the old regime, public health care units operated as 'budgetary units' owned by and dependent upon the central administration (Kozierkiewicz, 2009). 'This form of operation was considered ineffective with burgeoning bureaucracy and debts, whilst delivering poor patient services' (Kozierkiewicz, 2009: 17). The 1991 reform 'abandoned the strictly unified system' and authorized two groups of actors to establish health care institutions: 'public bodies (governmental administration and *gminas*) and private bodies such as individuals, companies, cooperatives and others' (Wlodarczyk and Karkowska, 2005: 384). As a result, health care institutions were separated into two groups: public autonomous health care units (SPZOZs) and non-public health care units (NZOZs) (Kozierkiewicz, 2009).

Throughout the 1990s, the privatization of health care provision and the establishment of non-public health care units occurred mainly in the outpatient care and was only partly a result of intentional policy design. Indeed, it mostly followed on from the liberalization of the labour market as many doctors started private practices, combining this activity with employment in the public sector (Kaminska, 2013; see Sitek, 2010). The number of private providers in the outpatient care, both with and without a public contract, was growing rather rapidly due to a bottom-up process of setting up new facilities. Since 1993, private health care facilities have been able to sign contracts for the provision of services to persons entitled to care financed from public resources. By mid-2000s the privatization of ambulatory care (primary care and specialist ambulatory services) was almost complete; it 'has not limited access to public services, as private providers have been fully integrated into the public health care system and largely operate on the same principles' (Kozierkiewicz, 2009: 17).

As the privatization of ambulatory care progressed, public health care was increasingly constituted by hospitals. Although the indebtedness of the public hospital sector was growing, the privatization of hospitals was very unpopular with the public and thus politically difficult to implement.

Incentives for self-governments provided by the 1999 Health Care Insurance Act, aimed at accelerating hospital sector privatization, and a restructuring programme implemented by the Ministry of Health proved to be rather ineffective. Although between 1999 and 2002 public hospitals capacity decreased by more than 92,000 health care staff and 35,900 hospital beds (Watson, 2009), at the beginning of the new millennium less than 50 private hospitals existed, operating only in selected specialties (Wlodarczyk and Karkowska, 2005: 403). The problem of hospital indebtedness persisted. Still, the idea of hospital privatization continued to be rejected by the public opinion and some political forces (most notably, the right-wing Law and Justice party). Thus, instead of privatization, the centre-right ruling coalition proposed a 'restructuring of hospitals', which was an attempt to change hospitals' legal structure by 'closing down' public facilities (SPZOZs) and creating NZOZs 'established by a company and owned partially or fully by local government' (Kozierkiewicz, 2009: 17).

In 2008 the same centre-right government prepared draft legislation which required all SPZOZs to transform, by the end of 2010, into limited liability or joint stock companies owned by the local community. In case of failure to do so the SPZOZs would have to be liquidated. The transformation would give the self-governments the right to close hospitals generating debts (Kowalska, 2009: 2). The proposal triggered strong political opposition and was eventually vetoed by the President of the Republic (Kozierkiewicz, 2009: 18). In response, in early 2009, the government presented new regulation (through extra-legislative route), the so-called Plan B or 'Support for Local Government aiming at Stabilization of the Health Care System', which envisaged 'commercialization' of hospitals. It encouraged hospitals to restructure by using 'financial incentives, including bailouts and special credit lines for investment' (Kozierkiewicz, 2009: 18). Provincial and regional self-governments could apply for funding to cover the debts of public hospitals providing that they prepare restructuring plans, which in effect meant the transformation of hospitals into Commercial Code companies (limited liability or joint-stock companies) (Mrozowicki, 2011; Kowalska, 2009).

Following the death of the Polish president in the early 2010, the com-mercialization of public hospitals was back on the agenda. In 2011, the re-elected centre-right coalition prepared an Act on Therapeutic Activities (effective as of 1 July 2011) which focuses on health services delivery in hospitals and similarly to Plan B offers self-governments a choice between i) covering the debts of inefficient health care units or ii) applying for extra funding from the central budget to either transform inefficient health care units into joint stock companies or close them down. The funding line will be available until the end of 2014. Any newly established health care units have to have the status of Commercial Code companies. The self-govern-ments 'will still be responsible for the availability of health services for their citizens, independently of the issue of the facilities ownership' (Kowalska, 2010: 3).

In 2011, while only 13 per cent of the 18.5 thousand medical service providers registered in Poland were public (National Register of Health Care Units, *Krajowy Rejestr Zakladow Opieki Zdrowotnej*, 2011), this still included a majority of hospitals. According to the most recent available data, in 2009 there were 754 general hospitals in Poland offering over 180,000 beds (see Table 8.1). Although the number of non-public hospitals increased from 38 in 2000 to 228 in 2009, still 90 per cent of the beds were in public hospitals. According to the Supreme Chamber of Control (*Najwyzsza Izba Kontroli*, NIK) which monitored the results of ownership transformations of

Table 8.1   Hospital resources in Poland (2000, 2004, 2009)

	Public/non-public	**2000**	**2004**	**2009**
Number of hospitals	Public	714	643	526
	Non-public	38	147	228
	Total	752	790	754
Number of beds	Public	189,707	175,631	165,012 [a]
	Non-public	1,583	7,649	18,028 [a]
	Total	191,290	183,280	183,040 [a]
Beds per 10,000 population	Total	49.5	48.0	48.0 [a]
Occupancy rate (in per cent)	Total	76.1	71.8	69.7 [a]
Average stay (in days)	Total	8.5	6.9	5.8 [a]
Hospitalized persons per year	Public	6,207,379	6,705,060	7,249,283
	Non-public	70,686	295,923	781,669
	Total	6,278,065	7,000,983	8,030,952

[a] Compared to previous years, figures for 2009 differ slightly in their underlying definition due to a change in the methodology of counting beds in general hospitals. Beds and incubators for newborns are now included.
Source: OECD (2012b).

hospitals carried out between 2006 and 2010, in a number of the controlled hospitals the change of the organizational and legal form of these units has not stopped the accumulation of debts; the quality of services has not improved; self-governments have failed to properly monitor the financial situation and the range of services of the newly transformed health care units (NIK, 2011).

Managerialization

The pursuit of economic efficiency in the Polish public health care has been attempted in a number of ways which include i) introducing management systems in health care units, ii) changing employment relations in the health care sector, iii) limiting access to care on the side of both supply (limits for providers) and demand (benefit package) and iv) implementing management systems (like clinical guidelines, protocols and standards) to govern professional practices (cf. Numerato et al., 2012). Similar to the processes of decentralization and privatization, managerialization has been characterized by frequent shifts of direction and lack of consistency.

i)   The 1991 Act and related regulations were supposed to enable the process of managerialization of public health care units: they were expected to turn into 'public self-governing institutions, equipped with managerial and financial autonomy' (Sitek, 2008: 43). This meant 'more freedom regarding financial management': they were 'exempted from strict regulation of budgetary requirements and control but became accountable [for their] actual balance of payments' (Wlodarczyk and Karkowska, 2005: 384). However, market instruments and good management practices have been applied to a limited extent, for a number of reasons. For instance, although based on the 1991 Act health care units were granted autonomy this was mostly 'a kind of political declaration not involving any freedom in practice'. As a matter of fact, hospital directors were not given management competencies. Instead, 'they were politically responsible in front of the regional and local administration (all the decisions that were made had a political nature and were not based on rational economics)' (Mokrzycka and Kowalska, 2008: 4). Moreover, the reforms endowed regional (and later – provincial) authorities with a doubtful role: they were supposed to focus mainly on the problem of the execution of ownership duties 'without any financial resources needed in this respect'; as a result their authority position was not clear (Mokrzycka and Kowalska, 2008: 5). Finally, the relevant legislation specified that liability for financial difficulties of SPZOZs rested with the public authorities, to ensure continuity of care (Kozierkiewicz, 2009: 17). This protective mechanism made it virtually impossible for SPZOZs to go bankrupt, which dramatically influenced management practices in public health care and produced growing debts of public hospitals.

While tight financial constraints by the NFZ and owners of health care units (self-governments, central government) were posing limits on the supply of care, '[m]anagers of a number of the SPZOZs, aware of their special position, often spent more than their units' revenues permitted for, increasing the level of debts' (Kozierkiewicz, 2009: 17). As a result, many public hospitals continued to build up liabilities which had to be taken over by the central government in 1994–95, 1997 and 1998. To structurally address the problems of rising hospital debts, the 1999 Health Insurance Act specified that within less than one year all health care institutions had to become independent, start contracting with sickness funds and apply general rules of accountancy binding for economic entities. To enable the start of their operations in the new system, their debts had to be cleared by the state budget for the fourth time (Kuszewski and Gericke, 2005). However, hospital debts started to grow again because the contractual rates of payments for the provision of health services were below the actual cost of services. Yet again the hospital debts had to be relieved through government intervention in 2005.

As observed by OECD,

> [r]ecurrent public interventions to clear liabilities have provided practitioners with confusing incentives and might have induced some resource misallocations, since well-managed hospitals have not been rewarded. Financial difficulties have been generated by a paradoxical combination of tight supply limitations by the NFZ and ex post reimbursement of providers who exceeded their contracted provision of services, inevitably generating moral hazard.
>
> (OECD, 2012b: 31)

ii) Recent legislation has shifted some non-wage labour costs to health care workers by extending, through the 2011 Act on Therapeutic Activities, the possibility of subcontracting services to nurses and midwives, an option that until now was mainly used by doctors. In conformity with the Act, instead of a regular employment contract hospitals can now offer service contracts to these two professional groups. To be subcontracted, the professionals must establish their individual practice as independent economic units. They are allowed to establish a contractual relationship with only one hospital. The legislation relieves the hospitals from paying social and health insurance contributions on behalf of the subcontractors, and shifts half of the burden for liabilities onto the subcontractor.

iii) Concerning limitations in the access to care, the 1997 Universal Health Insurance Act included general provisions on the entitlements to public health care services. The benefit package as well as medical standards and procedures remained underspecified until 2009 when the Minister of Health produced 13 executive regulations comprising a catalogue of publicly financed health care services (Wendt et al., 2013). Also, the already mentioned high share of OOP payments in the expenditure of pharmaceuticals poses limitations on the use of medicines.

Moreover, access to specialists is limited by a gate-keeping system: patients are required to obtain a referral from their primary-care provider (family doctor) to see (most) specialists and receive non-emergency hospital care (OECD, 2012b: 51). However, the family doctors are a scarce resource in Poland: they only constitute approximately one third of the medical personnel and – given the financing system where family doctors are paid following a modest capitation fee (a flat fee per patient) differentiated according to four age groups: 0–6 years, 7–19 years, 20–65 years and above 65 years – they are not motivated to offer extended services to their patients. Consequently, family doctors tend to frequently refer patients to specialist care.

iv) Until recently, precise definitions of different hospital services were missing. In the early 2000s, in an attempt to improve the contracting of hospital services three sickness funds introduced their own systems of diagnosis-related groups (DRGs) (Kuszewski and Gericke, 2005: 88–9). Following the re-centralization of the sickness funds into a single NFZ in 2003, a uniform classification of hospital services based on diagnostic cases was introduced containing some 1400 items, but it was basically unrelated to the actual costs of services. About 300 items from the classification allowed to account for 80 per cent of costs while many of the items remained a dead letter (Bączek, 2008). Points per case were underpriced and there was no sufficient financial coverage for costs incurred outside classified procedures. Changes had to be introduced already in 2004 in the context of a major conflict between the NFZ and the hospital staff which remained underpaid. A national DRG system based on the British Health Care Resources Groups was finally introduced by the NFZ in hospitals in 2008 and parts of ambulatory care in 2010 and 2011. The pricing system is updated every six months but providers denounce its inconsistencies and NFZ's arbitrary pricing decisions.

The modalities of change

For an analysis of how the health care reform process in Poland has developed historical institutionalist approaches seem to be suitable (Sitek, 2010). From this perspective 'understanding the context of the health care arena is fundamental' (Sitek, 2010: 587; see Giaimo, 2002).

Unlike in the political economies of advanced capitalist societies where change has unfolded 'by and large incrementally without dramatic disruptions' (Streeck and Thelen, 2005: 4), the 1989 collapse of the communist regime in Poland (and other ECE countries) constitutes a clearly disruptive event leading to institutional breakdown in the political and economic context of the health care system.

The last two decades of health care reforms in Poland have to be considered in the context of, on the one hand, a set of communist legacies and, on the other hand, the agenda of post-communist transition, both present not only in the health care sector but in the political and economic system as a whole. In the words of Stark and Bruszt (1998) the pre-1989 institutional settings did not disappear with the collapse of the communist regime, rather they lingered on and provided the base on which new institutions were built. Such a process of institution building can be called a recombinant innovation: 'when new institutional elements are introduced, their functioning is accompanied by adapting and reconfiguring existing institutions, resulting in mixed or recombined systems', shaped by both historical continuities and 'emergency' or crisis-driven discontinuities (Sitek, 2010: 577; see Bruszt and Stark, 1998: 80–4; Inglot, 2008). The former constitute a path-dependent element while the latter are identified with the rejection of the past. Together they produce a mix of continuity and change visible in the emerging health care system in Poland (see Sitek, 2010).

On the one hand, the legacies of communism include the role of the state as a provider and regulator of health care. On the other hand, the post-1989 transition, in reaction to the previous regime, has promoted the ideas of decentralization and liberalization. The mix of these (often conflicting) elements has strongly influenced both the content of health care reforms and the mode of policy-making in the sector.

As for the content of the reforms, the process of privatization of hospitals is an example of the simultaneous influence of post-communist and neoliberal constraints. Under the previous regime the public became so used to the relative security provided by the universal health care system and to the dominant role of the state in the sector that it considered this situation natural. The expectation that the state should continue to play a major role in the provision of health care remains 'one of the underlying legacies of the socialist system, with which every later policy has to reckon as a political reality' (Kornai and Eggleston, 2001: 139). Indeed, public opinion in Poland and in other ECE countries is still strongly supportive of state's responsibility for health care: 80 per cent in Slovenia, 71 per cent in the Czech Republic, 70 per cent in Hungary and 69 per cent in Poland, as compared to 52 per cent in France and 50 per cent in Germany (Kikuzawa et al., 2008). While privatization of primary care has not caused major opposition, a strong preference for a publicly owned hospital sector is expressed not only by the public opinion but also by different political forces, representatives of territorial self-government (Kowalska, 2010) and trade unions (Watson, 2011). Given the lack of consensus on the issue, and its political sensitivity, the privatization of hospital care has taken long to address and is still very much in the making. Indeed, the official discourse avoids the term 'privatization' of hospitals and instead refers to 'commercialization' (Kowalska, 2010) or 'the process of making health care units proprietary functions non-public' (Mokrzycka and Kowalska, 2008: 1). Nevertheless, during the past one and a half decade the privatization of hospitals 'has been taking place despite the absence of specific legislation' and has been very much in line with liberalization and pursuit of economic efficiency prescribed by the neoliberal reforms introduced in the Polish economy at large. The process has been based on a number of executive regulation provisions concerning the local authorities as well as health care institutions (Kowalska, 2010: 1), which is a mechanism similar to what Streeck and Thelen define as 'layering' (2005: 22–4).

The impact of the broader neoliberal reform agenda is visible also in the spontaneous privatization of financing and increased purchasing of services in the 'private' (outside the insurance system) health care market, which has taken place despite a legacy of universalism and provisions in the Polish constitution (art. 68 stresses the right of everyone to health care based on equal access regardless of the financial status of the person, Mokrzycka and Kowalska, 2008). Imposing limits on access to care both on the supply and demand side, in a context where 'equity and solidarity' are not at the core of the value system underlying health care, and where there is a growing supply of non-reimbursable but readily available services, has resulted in a privatization of risk. This process has followed a different route than the changes in the ownership of hospitals and can be described as policy drift (see Streeck and Thelen, 2005: 24–6; Hacker, 2005).

When it comes to the mode of policy-making in the health care arena, what has to be analysed is what Sitek calls 'the structure of policy actors and organizational landscape of the sector' (2010: 587–8). In Poland, this is an interesting case where the legacy of communism has been reinforced by the neoliberal paradigm underlying the economic transition. Governance and regulation of the Polish health care system is characterized by the reassertion of the role of the state accompanied by the weakness of corporate partners (Kaminska, 2013). On the one hand, the already discussed legacies regarding the expected role of the state have been matched by the state's strong institutional position, inherited from the earlier regime, at the starting point of the reforms. On the other hand, the situation of corporate partners in the health care sector in the post-1989 reality in Poland (and other ECE countries) has differed significantly from that encountered in 'health care states' of Western Europe (see Sitek, 2008; Sitek, 2010; Kaminska, 2013). While in Western Europe health care system change is usually introduced within established governance structures which can accommodate the processes of drafting and implementation of reforms (Moran, 1999; Sitek, 2010), these structures were missing at the outset of the Polish post-communist transformation. Professional self-government bodies were re-established soon after the change of regime, but they have struggled to overcome internal divisions and reconcile divergent interest of different specialisms (Sitek, 2008). Trade unions served as a political base for successive governments and their opposition and were 'captured' in an inverse dependency relationship (Avdagic, 2005), which considerably weakened their voice. Moreover, trade unions representing different professions within the sector have proved unable to present a common stance on policy issues (Kaminska and Kahancova, 2011). Consistent with the ideas about public policy inherent in the neoliberal agenda, the weakness of professional associations and sectoral unions has been matched by the policy experts' and government's unwillingness to involve them in the policy-making processes (Kaminska and Kahancova, 2011).

As a result of the historical legacies and the contingencies of the transition discussed above, the state has been able to design and implement health care reforms single-handedly (Kaminska, 2013). Indeed, almost all health care reforms have so far been initiated by the subsequent governments or the Ministry of Health (Sagan et al., 2011: 153), promoting the ideas of the respective political parties, with no or very little participation of other stakeholders. Professional associations, sectoral trade unions, but also academics with experience in the field, were mostly excluded from the process of designing reforms and 'there was never a comprehensive debate on the direction of the changes in the health sector' (Wlodarczyk and Karkowska, 2005: 413). A rare case where the government did organize consultations with stakeholders (representatives of trade unions, territorial self-governments and patient groups) to discuss further reforms was the 'White Summit' that took place in 2007. However, 'the final list of [reform] priorities was not approved by the largest trade union and the initiative failed' and the government proceeded unilaterally with reform activities (Sagan et al., 2011: 154).

Further explanations of the reform trajectories and their timing are offered by the post-1989 politics. As already mentioned, the institutional context in which the health care system was embedded was in flux in the early years of political transformation. Wlodarczyk and Karkowska summarize the situation as follows:

> The first term [of the post-1989 Polish Parliament] was concentrated on basic structural transformation in politics and economics. The second was greatly dispersed: the coalition made up of six parties struggled to devise any kind of homogenous programme, not only in health care. The third term drew up the insurance act, but as it was not supported by the opposition or medical circles, its implementation was postponed. It was only during the fourth term that enough momentum could be gathered to introduce insurance and proceed with decentralization.
>
> (Wlodarczyk and Karkowska, 2005: 414)

The institutional instability at the central level has continued well into the second millennium and contributed to the erratic reform trajectories.

The dominant position of the government (and political parties) in the reform process, the lack of involvement of other stakeholders and institutional instability have resulted in a politicization of the policy-making in the sector. First of all, frequent elections (eight since 1989 with no cases of re-election until 2011) have produced a continuous alternation of ruling coalitions with strongly conflicting ideologies due to the pre-1989 affiliations of currently existing parties (communist regime vs. its opposition); moreover, unstable ruling coalitions have witnessed many government reshuffles. Second, '[t]he process of refining the [health care] system was characterized by the need for political parties to establish their efficacy, which led to drastic but poorly thought out changes. (...) [S]trategies were modified overnight, previous achievements were rejected' (Wlodarczyk and Karkowska, 2005: 413; see also Krajewski-Siuda and Romaniuk, 2008). An undesirable result has been a lack of continuity within the Ministry of Health (for example, in the period 2001–2005 there were as many as six different Health Ministers; top bureaucrats have also been exchanged for political reasons).

These phenomena have led to a lack of continuity of the reform process. Indeed, 'a strategy for development of the health sector has never been properly defined' (Wlodarczyk and Karkowska, 2005: 375). For instance, in the 1990s the process of decentralization of provision 'was not accompanied by a coherent concept of health care reform and system structure'. In the early 1990s the delegation of health care-related tasks to *gminas* reflected the 'legislators' acknowledgement that this sphere was a public duty of local governments' (Wlodarczyk and Karkowska, 2005: 394). Within a few years the interest of the central government in local initiatives decreased following financial difficulties of the local self-government. Another example is provided by the establishment of a single health fund in 2003: a change of government and Minister of Health in 2001, and not technical arguments, was the main reason for the re-centralization of the regional sickness funds into a single NFZ (Kuszewski and Gericke, 2005: 99).

To conclude, this mode of policy-making in the Polish health care sector – politicized and excluding stakeholders – has led to inconsistencies in the reform process and policy reversals over the span of two decades.

Impact of the reforms on the health care system performance

As for the impact of reforms on the performance of the health care system, the state of the art literature does not allow to discern between the effects of privatization, managerialization and decentralization on the systems' outcomes. The picture is even more blurred given very high growth rates registered in the past two decades by the Polish economy, which is particularly remarkable if compared to other EU countries, both in Western Europe and ECE. Thus when interpreting the outcomes one has to take into account the catch-up effect from a low level of economic development in 1989. This has had an obvious impact on both financing and consumption of health care (cf. OECD, 2012b: 27).

Economic performance

In the period 1991–2001 the total health expenditure was stable as a proportion of GDP and remained between 5.5 per cent and 6.0 per cent. From 2002 it has steadily grew from 6.4 per cent to 7.4 per cent of GDP in 2009. What has to be taken into account, however, is a high rate of GDP growth in Poland, whose economy has been one of the fastest developing in the EU. This is reflected in the growth of total health expenditure measured in million US$ at 2000 PPP rates, which tripled between 1990 and 2009 (from 13,445 in 1990 to 42,015 in 2009) (OECD, 2012a).

Public spending on health as a proportion of total health expenditure fell between 1996 and 1998 (from 73.4 per cent to 69.8 per cent), rose in 1999 and 2001, and fell again in subsequent years (WHO, 2012). However, the 1999–2001 increase was connected to setting up the infrastructure for sickness funds following the 1999 reform (Kuszewski and Gericke, 2005: 36). Strikingly, the public expenditure for primary care has been stable: in 2009, 2010 and 2011 the budgets amounted to 7.3 billion zloty, although the number of consultations was increasing from year to year.

The financing of Polish health care has been facing serious problems. One of them is the low contribution rate which generates scarce resources. The 1999 reform, despite original plans supported by the professionals to establish the rate at 10 per cent of taxable income, set the rate at 7.5 per cent following a political decision of a neoliberal-minded Minister of Finance, with the central budget covering the contributions of certain social groups, including the unemployed and farmers (who do not pay income tax). It soon became clear that this contribution rate, combined with unemployment levels of around 20 per cent (currently 13 per cent) and with farmers constituting almost 19 per cent of the labour force at that time (currently – around 15 per cent), did not provide enough funds. Between 2003 and 2007 the contribution rate was raised annually by 0.25 percentage points every year until it reached the current rate of 9 per cent, which has only marginally eased the funding problems. Another major issue is the permanent indebtedness of public hospitals (as discussed above, mainly due to poor management and pricing policies of NFZ) which continues to require interventions from the central budget. Between 1998 and 2009, central government spent more than 3 billion euro on debt bailouts. 'In 2008 alone cumulative debt of public hospitals amounted to 1.5 billion euro, compared to a total health budget of approximately 14 billion euro' (Kozierkiewicz, 2009: 17).

The Polish economy has not been seriously affected by the first wave of the financial crisis in 2008–2010 and continued to grow. While in 2009 the NFZ revenue fell below the expected level for the first time in five years (which translated into less funding in 2009 than in 2008 for NFZ-contracted hospitals, depleted the resources for costs of services exceeding the limits defined in contracts and generated further debts, Watson, 2009: 31), the Polish health care system was not hit by the crisis. It is still too early to say whether the second wave of the financial turbulences related to the sovereign debt crisis which started in mid-2011 will impact the Polish economy, and thus the health care sector (Sagan et al., 2011: 163).

Organizational performance

The total number of hospital beds decreased by less than 10,000 between 2000 and 2009 (from 191,290 to 183,040). The number of beds per 100,000 inhabitants (441 in 2008) is higher than the EU average of 383, although it has decreased sharply from 632 registered in 1990 (OECD, 2012b: 69). The number of acute beds has been steadily decreasing since 1989, from 6.07 per 1000 in 1989 to 4.39 in 2009, but there is still a surplus of acute beds. Moreover, long-term beds are in short supply (Sagan et al., 2011: XXIV). Bed occupancy rate rose from 68 per cent in 1990 to 77 per cent in 2002 and dropped again to 70 per cent in 2009. These indicators might suggest persistent overcapacity (OECD, 2012b: 31). As discussed above, the gatekeeping system does not seem to function properly: 'cases tend to be pushed to the more expensive outpatient specialist or hospital segments' (OECD, 2012b: 33). Moreover, 'admission rates are high for diseases for which costly hospitalization could be avoided, judging by practices elsewhere' (OECD, 2012b: 31).

Still, signs of increasing efficiency are visible in the greater number of hospitalized people and the decrease in the average length of stay which has been halved over the past two decades (Poland now has a shorter average length of stay than the OECD average, OECD, 2012b: 31).

Citizens' satisfaction and perceived quality

According to a survey conducted in March 2012 by the Polish public opinion research agency CBOS, 78 per cent of the adult population of Poland is not satisfied with the functioning of health care. People who actually have had a direct experience with the public health care and used its medical services are more satisfied than people who have not. Nineteen per cent of Poles have a good opinion of the Polish health care system (out of those who actually have used it, 27 per cent have a good opinion) (CBOS, 2012). The percentage of those stating that the quality of health care services is not changing has been steadily growing, from 57 per cent in 2000 to 72 per cent in 2011. However, the percentage of those believing that the quality of health services is worsening has dropped from 41 per cent in 2000 to 26 per cent in 2011 (Diagnoza Społeczna, 2011).

The level of social inequalities in the access to public health care

Inequalities in access to health care are partially related to the privatization of risk discussed above. The private sector is developing fast and offering excellent diagnosis and treatment without waiting lists, financed by OOP payments. Moreover, long waiting times in the public sector have generated unregulated mechanisms of queue-jumping. Services are purchased in the private market from specialists combining private and public practice who can refer a patient to a public hospital without delay. However, access to the private sector is mostly limited to individuals with high income and able to cover the extra financial costs or working in profitable corporations which pay for their care through a so-called employee subscription system. These options are usually available only in large cities (Tymowska, 2001: 96). In 2000, 39 per cent of households made use of private health care services, a rate that has grown to 49 per cent in 2011 (Diagnoza Spoleczna, 2011). Obviously, such duplicative schemes lead to an inappropriate utilization of public resources (OECD, 2012b: 29). Moreover, the structure of drug financing discussed above, with a high rate of OOP payments, limits access to pharmaceuticals for the individuals with low income, the chronically ill and the elderly (OECD, 2012b: 62).

Inequalities between groups with different levels of income and type of employment, as well as territorial inequalities (urban vs. rural, and between different regions) are visible in the rates of renouncing on the use of health care services and pharmaceuticals. For instance, in 2011, 15.4 per cent of households in large cities (above 500 000 inhabitants) renounced on buying pharmaceuticals and 15.3 per cent on consulting a doctor, while those from rural areas did this more often (respectively, 22.6 per cent and 18.7 per cent). Those without employment renounced much more frequently on buying pharmaceuticals (44.8 per cent) and consulting a doctor (39.7 per cent) than those that were self-employed (respectively, 5.3 per cent and 6 per cent). Income inequalities are large, too: less than 4 per cent of households with income above the third quartile renounced on pharmaceuticals and consultations, while this share was as high as 41.6 per cent and 36.2 per cent, respectively, for households with income below the first quartile. Regional variation on these two indicators is also important and amounts to around 50 per cent difference in renouncement rates (Diagnoza Spoleczna, 2011: 122–4). The uneven territorial distribution of health personnel also reflects the inequalities in the geographical distribution of health care infrastructure, concentrated in large cities (Wlodarczyk and Karkowska, 2005: 381), which generates spatial inequities in access to care (OECD, 2012b: 31).

The impact of reforms on the workforce in the sector

A general scarcity of funding in the public health care sector has translated, inter alia, into low wage levels for different professional groups and has triggered different responses. On the one hand, the privatization of the health care sector, which – as discussed above – has been mostly an outcome of the liberalization of the labour market, allowed many physicians to combine work in publicly and privately funded institutions, in order to ensure higher earnings (Kaminska, 2013; see Sitek, 2010). Already at the end of the 1990s, nearly 90 per cent of dentists and almost 70 per cent of doctors in ambulatory care 'worked only as private practitioners or in addition to their public sector jobs' (Karski et al., 1999: 13). On the other hand, until recently, all professional groups in health care denounced low wages and demanded wage increases. These demands have been channelled through industrial action (protests and strikes) rather than through political action given that formal negotiation and bargaining channels are not effectively used in practice (see Kaminska and Kahancova, 2011). For instance, in 2006 and 2007, respectively, doctors in 100 and 180 out of some 600 public hospitals struck for up to 100 days. In response to the strikes, the government granted wage increases to physicians in a series of ad hoc decisions. Nurses, midwives and other health care professionals have been less successful in securing wage increases (Watson, 2011).

Yet another response to low wages and poor working conditions in the public health care has been considerable emigration of health care professionals, mainly young doctors with specialization. While exact figures are not available, an estimated 6 per cent to 7 per cent of physicians left the country between 2004 and 2008 (Kaminska and Kahancova, 2011). The outflow of health care staff, both abroad and into other sectors of the economy, has produced labour shortages in the sector, especially in rural areas. Nonetheless Poland lacks strategic planning of the supply of human resources and 'government interventions (...) are limited to general declarations and ad hoc policy interventions' (Sagan et al., 2011: 161).

The 2011 Act on Therapeutic Activities, in addition to changes in the ownership structure of health care units, introduced modifications in the employment relations with health care staff. Health care units can from now on not only employ salaried staff but also contract them as external providers, which will reduce the cost of labour for the employer. This solution has been welcomed by some individual professionals in the sector because it allows for achieving higher income, for example by ignoring the EU's Working Time Directive (2003/88/EC) and accepting longer working hours. However, the issue is highly controversial and raises several problems, including rendering the employment relation between the staff and the hospital much more precarious and generating serious risk for the patients as the service-contracted nurses work for up to 300 hours per month instead of 150–170 hours envisaged by the EU and national legislation for employment contracts (Klimek, 2010; National Labour Inspectorate, *Panstwowa Inspekcja Pracy* 2012). Trade unions, in particular those representing nurses and midwives, have (unsuccessfully) protested against this development.

The capacity of the system to directly improve health

Since 1989 Poland has registered significant improvements in health outcomes, comparable to those of the most developed countries. However, given the low starting point it has not yet caught up the ground previously lost (OECD, 2012b: 27). Still, after controlling for per capita GDP 'health outcomes are only slightly below the OECD average' (OECD, 2012b: 27).

Most countries in ECE suffered a mortality crisis after the fall of communism (Nolte et al., 2005). In Poland, a deterioration of mortality rates at the beginning of transition was followed by rapid improvements in health (Mladovsky et al., 2009: 13), although improvement for women halted in the mid-2000s (Wlodarczyk and Karkowska, 2005: 383). Adult male mortality has been declining since the early 1990s: death rates have since fallen to approximately 30 per cent lower than they were in 1991 (Mladowsky et al., 2009: 14). The standardized death rate for ischemic heart disease (the most common CVD) has halved since the fall of communism due to improvements in nutrition and health services (Mladowsky et al., 2009: 29). Poland has one of the lowest rates of cancer incidence in Europe with less than 350 per 100,000 inhabitants, against more than 800 per 100,000 inhabitants in Hungary and over 600 per 100,000 in the Czech Republic, Ireland and Denmark (Mladowsky et al., 2009: 31). Infant mortality rates have been in continuous decline. From an extremely high level of 19.1 per 1000 live births in 1989 they dropped to 5.6 in 2009. It is not possible, however, to attribute any of these – quite important – improvements specifically to privatization, decentralization or managerialization of the Polish health care system. On the negative side, we find important inequalities in mortality risk, with the largest risk incurred by people with the lowest education (OECD, 2012b: 56).

Conclusions

The reforms of the Polish health care system, including its decentralization, privatization and managerialization, have to be considered within the context of the post-communist transition, which has influenced the content and dynamics of the changes through, on the one hand, legacies of the communist past and, on the other hand, new ideas inherent in the neoliberal agenda of the economic transformation. A continuous strong role of the state in health care regulation and governance matched by a weak role of corporate actors reflects the former, while liberalization and (mostly spontaneous) privatization of ambulatory care, as well as privatization of risk for individuals provide evidence of the latter.

The reforms have proceeded at a varying pace. Different elements of the system have been reformed at different points in time and have often required further adjustments due to inconsistencies of the proposed solutions and incompatibilities between different dimensions of the system. Reform trajectories have been marked by policy reversals due to a highly politicized policy-making process, expectations of the public and protests of the professionals.

In the Polish case the reforms' trajectories represent neither 'an incremental change supporting institutional continuity through reproductive adaptation', nor 'disruptive change causing institutional breakdown and innovation and thereby resulting in discontinuity' (Streeck and Thelen, 2005: 8). Rather, what can be observed is a mix of change and continuity, with elements of layering and policy drift. Together they have produced a recombined system still under construction which despite two decades of continuous transformation has not reached a new institutional equilibrium.

While there have been clear improvements in the health status of the Polish population, it is not possible to attribute these outcomes directly to any of the three processes discussed above (privatization, managerialization and decentralization), or even to their combined effect. The amelioration of outcomes cannot be disconnected from other processes providing context for health care reforms: the economic transition from a command to a market economy and integration with the European Union which together have triggered very high GDP growth rates in the past two decades. The economic growth has produced improved living standards and health outcomes. Yet, the past two decades have also witnessed growing health inequalities.

Part II
Comparative Analysis

9
The Health Care Policy Quadrilemma and Comparative Institutional Reforms

Emmanuele Pavolini, Bruno Palier and Ana M. Guillén

Introduction

Over the last two decades, health care systems have been put under various types of pressure. The most visible one has, of course, been economic pressure, with health care spending continuing to grow much faster than GDP. But health care systems have also been challenged from a social point of view, since, in many countries, the debate about inequalities in health conditions has become increasingly relevant. Finally they were also confronted with the necessity to adapt to changes in the pathologies. The last decades have seen a shifting from acute diseases to chronic ones, while medical technologies changed radically.

Given the complexity health care systems have, the reform attempts in this policy field have been theoretically caught in a 'quadrilemma' (Palier, 2011). They should combine together an *economic objective* (to control costs and the increase in health expenditure), a *social objective* (to guarantee equality of access to health care for all), a *medical objective* (to guarantee the highest quality of care and the optimum condition of health for the population) and a *political objective* (to guarantee the responsiveness of the health care system, the satisfaction of the professionals and the users, based on freedom and comfort of the patients and professionals) (Figure 9.1).

It is often quite complicated to design a reform capable of improving all these dimensions at once, especially because trade-offs are at stake (e.g. between patients' freedom of choice and equality or between quality and cost control).

Moreover, policy reforms are not only entrapped within this quadrilemma specific to the policy field, but also by the *politics* typical of this sector. Reforming health care means quite often intervening on more general dimensions, one of which is quite relevant, that is, the Centre–Periphery relationship.

Therefore, health care systems are particularly difficult to change, for institutional and political reasons.

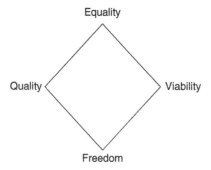

Figure 9.1   The four dimensions of health care reforms
Source: Palier (2011).

As already stated in the introduction, health care systems in Europe are very complex policy fields also in comparison with other institutions of the Welfare State. They have three peculiarities that, taken all together, make them unique: they are mostly based on services and not on transfers (as pensions for instance); they are at the same time a capital- and human-intensive sector, which requires a huge amount of investments in technology, infrastructures, but also in highly skilled professionals; they tend to offer, through various mechanisms, an universalistic-like coverage, with possible limited differentiation among users, even in SHI systems. These three characteristics have important political consequences. If welfare states are very difficult to reform in general (Pierson, 2001), it may be defended that the health care sector is even more difficult to reform, precisely because of the aforementioned characteristics.

First, reformers, whatever their aims are, have to take into consideration that the 'reforms through the path of least resistance' strategy (Bonoli and Natali, 2012) is quite difficult in this policy field. It is hard for governments to frame 'least resistance' groups and to concentrate on them the burden of reforms. Whereas it might prove relatively less complicated to promote direct retrenchment policies when it is possible to concentrate the consequences of these reforms on groups of people less likely to become veto players like younger people, as it happens in the field of pensions or unemployment benefits (Palier, 2010), it might be quite harder trying the same type of reform strategy with universalistic programmes based on services, where it is more difficult to find specific 'weak' groups, as in health care.

Second, the three characteristics of health care systems make them a valuable asset for governments (in terms of legitimation and power) and, therefore, the decisions taken inside this policy field have an impact on more general political dynamics than many other welfare fields. It is not by chance that health care is often one of the main pillars of local governments, where there has been a decentralization process, and one of the arenas where centre–periphery relationships are more complex and potentially conflictive.

What is interesting though is that despite these institutional and political hindrances to changes, many reforms have been implemented within the various European health care systems. It is thus salient to first know better what the content of the reforms were, to see which amongst the various factors (economic, social and medical) leading to change have prevailed, and second how the reform trajectories (Palier, 2011) have been shaped by both health care institutions and political actors.

The chapter is divided in the following way. The next section is dedicated to illustrate the main reforms since 1990s in a comparative and synthetic way,[1] framing them in a longer time span and taking into consideration the evolution of public expenditure in the field. The following one shows what have been the main drivers for change behind the reforms. Then it is illustrated who have been the main actors involved in the policy arena. The last section focuses on the mechanisms of change and the main consequences of the reforms in terms of governance models.

The contents of the reforms

Reforms and public resources: before discussing reforms let's have a look at money!

Before analysing reforms, it is important to look at trends and characteristics of public expenditure on health (PEH). Three indicators are used (Table 9.1): the incidence of PEH in terms of GDP; the PEH per-capita at parity purchasing power (in euros) and the average annual growth rate of PEH in real terms.[2]

In terms of GDP, the last two decades have seen an increase of the share of PEH in a good part of the countries studied. It is important to distinguish the situation before the recent economic crisis (2007) and the more recent years (2010). From 1990 to 2007 the incidence of PEH on GDP increased by 1.7–2.3 per cent in Austria, France and the UK, by 1 per cent in Spain, by 0.5 per cent in Italy and it did not practically change in Germany, Poland and Sweden. The crisis, with its negative impact on the GDP levels in many countries studied here, pushed up the indicator: apart from Poland and Sweden (the two contexts where the economic crisis hit less dramatically) and France (where expenditure was already relatively high), in all other states the incidence of PEH on the GDP increased. One should notice however that between 2009 and 2010, the share of PEH on GDP stabilised or decreased in most OECD countries. This trend seems to be confirmed for 2011. One possible explanation for this very recent trend is that there is no more hiring of personnel in the health care sector.

Taking into account the average annual growth rate of PEH, we can notice that every country increased over the last twenty years its expenditure in

Table 9.1   The public expenditure in health care (PEH) (different years)

	PEH, per cent GDP				Average annual growth rate of PHE, in real terms						PHE, capita, euro PPP
	1990	2000	2007	2010	1990–1999	2000–2007	2008–2010	1990–2007	2000–2010	1990–2010	2010
Sweden	7.4	7.0	7.2	7.8	3.1	3.7	2.3	3.4	3.2	3.2	4051 (100.0)*
UK	4.9	5.5	6.9	8.0	3.9	6.2	4.0	4.9	5.5	4.7	3800 (93.8)*
Italy	6.1	5.8	6.6	7.4	1.2	3.2	2.1	2.1	2.8	2.0	3137 (77.4)*
Spain	5.1	5.2	6.1	7.1	3.0	6.0	4.2	4.3	5.4	4.2	3015 (74.4)*
France	6.4	8.0	8.7	8.9	4.4	3.0	0.7	3.8	2.3	3.4	4071 (100.5)*
Austria	6.1	7.6	7.8	8.4	5.0	2.6	2.4	3.9	2.6	3.8	4454 (109.9)*
Germany[a]	7.8	8.3	8.0	8.9	2.3	1.0	3.5	1.7	1.7	2.0	4430 (109.4)*
Poland[a]	4.4	3.9	4.4	5.0	3.5	6.2	7.8	4.7	6.6	5.1	1323 (32.7)*

[a] Data on Germany starting from 1992; data on Poland starting from 1991.
* In parenthesis the distance from each country PEH from Sweden, having assigned to the latter a value equal to 100.
Source: OECD Health Data (2012).

real terms: from Germany and Italy, which were the ones that grew less (an average 2 per cent per year during the last two decades) to around 5 per cent in Poland and the UK. Anyhow, there are important differences between the 1990s and the 2000s. In the SHI countries, apart from Poland, the growth was quite stronger in the 1990s, whereas it worked the other way around in NHS countries, with the exception of Sweden, where the growth rates remained relatively stable. The Polish case can be explained by the fact that the 1990s were a time of still deep institutional transformation and the expenditure level was quite low: still in 2010 the Polish PHE per capita was about one third (32.7 per cent) of the Swedish one.

All the other countries present a level of per capita PHE relatively similar, with the exception of the Southern European countries, which spent a quarter less than most of the others in 2010. Anyway, Italy and Spain expenditure levels are the result of different trends: the latter came from a relatively low level of per capita expenditure and invested many resources in order to start filling the gap with the other countries; the former started in the 1990s with levels similar to Sweden and then has constantly grown at lower rates.

The background: the contents of the reforms in the 1990s

In order to better frame what happened in the 2000s, it is important to set reforms in a longer time span. The 1990s were years rich of innovation for all European health care systems (see Table 9.2). We summarize them by presenting first what happened in the NHS and then looking at SHI.

The *Swedish* health care sector underwent several important reforms in the 1990s. The general focus of reforms was on efficiency in the early 1990s, and in the latter part of the decade on structural changes in the delivery and

Table 9.2   Health care reforms since the beginning of the 1990s: a general overview

	The 1990s	The 2000s (until the economic crisis)	The years of the crisis
Sweden	Competition with private providers Patient choice and guarantees for waiting times Recentralization of regulatory powers Managerialization tools (DRGs)	Privatization in the primary care sector Competition with private providers Patient choice and guarantees for waiting times Recentralization of regulatory powers Strengthening comparisons using indicators reflecting quality and efficiency across the country	
England	Internal market in the early 1990s Substitution of the internal market with an approach based on partnership and driven by performance in the late 1990s Recentralization of the system Focus on regulation in the late 1990s	Strong increase in public expenditure Strengthening of central regulatory powers More autonomy to local commissioners of care More autonomy to Hospital Foundation Trusts (FTs) Patients' choice and rights Fostering private provision	Transformations of main hospitals in FTs Fostering private provision More patients' choice and rights Integration of health, social care and public health commissioning Severe freeze in NHS spending
Spain	Decentralization continued Managerialization tools (DRGs) Universal coverage Experimentation at the local level with new governance models Primary care teams as 'gatekeepers'	Decentralization completed Strong increase in public expenditure	Stronger control of regional deficits Higher co-payments for drugs Severe freeze in NHS spending
Italy	Internal market in the early 1990s Substitution of the internal market with an approach based on partnership in the late 1990s Decentralization of the system Managerialization tools (DRGs; managers)	Decentralization first, potential recentralization later Support to the development of the second pillar in HC	Recentralization Higher co-payments Severe freeze in NHS spending

(continued)

Table 9.2 Continued

	The 1990s	The 2000s (until the economic crisis)	The years of the crisis
France	General Social Contribution to strengthen social security funding Recentralization of regulatory, financing and planning functions Annual parliamentary vote on the Sécurité Sociale budget Managerialization tools Referring (gatekeeping) general practitioners	Recentralization of functions Strengthening of regulatory agencies Managerialization tools (DRGs; managers) Referring (gatekeeping) general practitioners Increase in co-payments	
Germany	Competition among SHI funds Increase in federal powers Partial prospective payment system for hospitals Introduction and increase of co-payments	Recentralization Competition among SHI funds Introduction and increase of co-payments	
Austria	Strengthening cooperation among the main system's actors Rationalization of supply and increase in co-payments Managerialization of hospitals' administration (including DRGs)	Strengthening cooperation among the main system's actors Introduction and increase of co-payments Development of regulatory tools Integration of outpatient and inpatient care	Freeze in SHI spending
Poland	Decentralization in provision and funding Purchaser–provider split Public health care units with managerial and financial autonomy Authorization of private health care institutions Partial privatization of ambulatory care	Recentralization of payer function Managerialization of hospitals' administration (including DRGs) Partial privatization of ambulatory care and attempts in the hospital sector	

organization of health care (WHO, 2001). In general, on one side, the NHS was gradually opened up to more competition from private providers and to an increased level of patient choice; on the other, the central state started to take back some of the regulatory powers after decades of decentralization. The bottom-up managerialist changes introduced in many county councils during the 1990s did not concern only patient choice and purchaser–provider splits but also various forms of performance-related payments systems (DRGs) (HOPE, 2006; Busse et al., 2012).

The 1990s were years of deep change for the *English* NHS. They started with the radical reforms made by the Conservative Government through the 'NHS and Community Care Act' in 1991, introducing internal markets, increased power for NHS managers and GP fundholding. After the 1997 election the Labour Government focused initially on regulation, with the establishment of a series of Agencies, rather than major structural change. With the 'Health Act 1999' the notion of a market in the NHS was rejected and substituted by 'integrated care, based on partnership and driven by performance'.

For the *Spanish* NHS, the 1990s were the years when major reforms introduced in the previous decade were implemented. The decentralization process went on. An extension of health coverage to almost all the Spanish population took place, reaching quasi universal coverage: the percentage of the Spanish population covered by public insurance shifted from around 82 per cent in 1978 to 99.4 per cent in 2000 (WHO, 2000). Experimentation took place at the regional level in terms of managerialization and privatization. Nonetheless, such experiences were minor and the bulk of the NHS remained unaltered during this period (Martin, 2003).

The 1990s started in *Italy* with reforms in 1992–93 promoting an internal market and managerialization processes similar to the British model. The reforms delegated significant managerial autonomy to hospitals and local health units (transformed into 'agencies'), introducing a partial split between purchasing and providing, promoting competition and creating 'strategic boards of directors' as the main managing institution of 'hospital and local health care agencies'. The other main innovation was the process of devolving even more health care policy making powers to regions. If internal market and 'competition' were some of key concepts in the policy changes in the first part of the decade, in the second part of the 1990s the new Center-Left Government chose to reinforce the role of the state in regulating the NHS and proposed a model of 'cooperation' among providers.

We now turn to SHI. The first measures adopted in the 1990s in *France* went in the direction of containing costs and were similar to the ones applied already in the previous decade: imposition of low prices on health care services and pharmaceuticals, new resources devoted to sickness insurances (e.g. the flat social ear-marked tax created in 1990), higher co-payments. Given the limited success of these measures, starting in the mid-1990s the government reinforced the control and regulatory capabilities of the state over the financing and the planning of the health care system. A managerialization process started in the early 1990s in hospital care. In the ambulatory sector reforms were more complicated: regulations trying to introduce potential financial sanctions against practitioners who would disregard the spending objectives set by the Parliament were ineffective, also due to the rising (juridical) protest of health professionals.

The *German* health care governance reform trend started in the early 1990s with the introduction and intensification of competition between sickness funds by giving statutory insured individuals a free choice among them. A relevant effect of the reform was the erosion of the traditional self-administration of German health care by sickness funds and doctors' unions, while strengthening state control: the latter exerted stronger control over negotiations among sickness funds and unions, as well as over the functioning of these institutions. The other main reform took place in the second part of the decade, and it focused mainly on cost-containment measures.

Also in *Austria* the 1990s represented a time of relevant policy change in health care, which took place at the beginning (1990) and in the second part of the decade (1997). The Austrian health plan (1990) was introduced to improve cooperation among the main actors of the system, focusing specifically on hospitals' planning and high-technology investments. From the mid-1990s, health care reforms increasingly emphasized budgetary control, cost-containment and efficiency orientation, with the introduction of a DRG-oriented hospital financing scheme.

Among all the countries considered in the present book, the *Polish* health care system was the one which underwent the deepest institutional transformations in the 1990s, due to the post-1989 transition from a communist regime to democracy and market economy. The first major reform was the 1991 Health Care Institutions Act. This legislation contained a transformation of the national health care system into a health insurance public system, a development of the private sector, a decentralization of the system, the introduction of the principle of purchaser–provider split and the managerialization of public health care. In 1997, a new reform established regional insurance funds, elected by regional self-governments, with contributions collected by a state agency responsible for social insurance and then transferred to funds. The reform decentralized the financing of public health care by transferring the financial responsibility away from the government to a network of independent health insurance funds.

The main reforms since the turn of the century

In most of the countries studied, the 2000s represented more a decade of continuity and implementation of reforms and ideas introduced in the previous decade than dramatic transformations, at least until the crisis did set in.

Three main reform trends were identifiable in *Sweden* during the 2000s: the strengthening of patient rights; some privatization in the primary care sector and the re-centralization of regulatory power within the system. All these reforms had roots back to the 1990s, but the 2000s seem the time where concepts introduced in the previous decade did finally find a strong (and more in-depth) implementation.

Since the beginning of last decade, there have been two main phases of reforms in the *English* NHS: changes introduced by the Labour government until 2010 and then the new and vast innovation passed by the new government with the 'Health and Social Care Act 2012'. During the Labour government a very relevant economic investment in the NHS was done, within a framework of strong central direction alongside the administrative (not political) devolution of decision-making away from the centre. Overall a new framework emerged, composed by four elements: the strengthening of local commissioners of care and of users' choice and rights; the reduction in controls on providers and the introduction of new providers; the adoption of new payment and contracting systems; and an expansion of the role of independent regulators. With the new government since 2010, a new relevant change is taking place and it should affect regulation, privatization of provision, patients' choice and role in the NHS. The new government focused also on expenditure cuts.

The evolution of the *Spanish* NHS since the beginning of last decade can also be divided in two sub-periods: the years up to 2009; the changes since 2010. In 2002, the system was decentralized to the ten remaining Autonomous Communities (ACs). There was a strong increase in public expenditure during these years, especially in terms of personnel and salaries. From 2010 on and in response to the effects of the economic crisis, several measures to cut expenditure were implemented in Spain.

In *Italy* after the 2001 Constitutional change that recognised formally a regionalization of the Italian State, also in relation to health care issues, a good part of governments' attention to the NHS has been devoted to strategies for containing costs and promoting a more effective use of financial resources. In the second part of the 2000s new legislation was also passed in order to secure extra-private funding to health care: by defining previous legislation from the 1990s in a more precise way, 'Integrative Health Care Funds' were introduced, aiming at strengthening the 'second pillar' of the Italian health care system. With the economic crisis the NHS has been strongly hit by cuts.

Turning now to SHI systems, the 2000s represented in *France* a period of continuation of policies from the previous decade. Regional health agencies were created in 2010 in order to strengthen the Ministry of Health steering capabilities on the supply of health care within and across the regions. In relation to inpatient care, a DRG system was introduced. National reforms also directly altered hospital governance by promoting a business-like entrepreneurial model of hospital management. Another important aspect of managerialism was the introduction of quality standards and evaluation of health care services. In ambulatory care the processes of rationalization were slower. Continuing along a policy approach developed since the 1980s, legislation was introduced giving more and more room to co-payments and to the rise of facultative private health insurances (*mutuelles*) as substitutes for *Sécurité Sociale* schemes.

Strengthening competition was a keyword in the *German* SHI in the 1990s and it continued to play a role in the 2000s. The 2004 'Health Insurance Modernization Act' enabled sickness funds to differentiate the range of services available to their enrollees by selective contracting with networks of local providers and by developing prevention or disease management programs. The 2007 'Competition Strengthening Act' reinforced the possibilities given to sickness funds to conclude special agreements with individual doctors or groups of doctors. As in France, increases in co-payments also did take place during the decade, as well as tendencies fostering recentralization. The 'Health Fund' was created in 2007, directly linked to the federal government: payroll contribution rates became to be set in a centralized way, with a unified payroll contribution rate for every sickness fund. Thus, sickness funds lost one of their main rights to the federal state.

Changes in the *Austrian* SHI from the beginning of 2000s can be divided into adjustments of specific parameters with an immediate effect, including changes in contribution rates or co-payments, and more structurally oriented reforms with expected mid- and longer term effects. Structural reforms tried to foster a better integration between the inpatient and outpatient sector, and a shift of services from the former to the latter. Also improving coordination and cooperation among the main actors of SHI system was put forward through the creation of new institutions at the federal and provincial levels. Moreover a more coherent strategy for quality and regulation was fostered, also through the establishment of the Federal Institute for Quality in the Health Sector. The recent economic crisis and the related increase in public debt have fuelled attempts to intensify more substantial structural reforms in the health care sector.

Since the beginning of last decade, *Poland* has witnessed a mix of policy change and continuity. In particular the main element of policy change was represented by the recentralization of payer functions: in 2003 the network of regional sickness funds was replaced by a single 'National Health Fund'. Following this recentralization, also a uniform classification of hospital services based on DRGs was introduced first in hospitals and then, later on, in parts of ambulatory care in 2010, which can be considered the most important innovation in terms of managerialization of the SHI. The main line of continuity was represented instead by the process of privatization. By mid-2000s the privatization of ambulatory care (primary care and specialist ambulatory services) was almost complete, and there are increasing attempts to propose the commercialization of public hospitals.

Drivers of change: the health care quadrilemma

If we look at the reforms introduced in the last decades in the eight countries of our study and we compare them, we notice two main logics shaping the reform trajectories. On the one hand, the logic and the drivers of change behind reforms are different in NHS and SHI systems (Table 9.3). In other words, the quadrilemma described in the introduction of this chapter takes different shapes depending on the institutional design of the health care system. On the other hand, the political factors play a central role in influencing the politics of health care reforms, whether it is a matter of centre–periphery relations, or a matter of relations between the health professionals (especially doctors) and the State.

First of all, medical objectives do not seem central in any of the reform trajectories. Of course to guarantee the highest quality of care for the population is the main aim declared for these reforms. But adjusting health care systems to new types of pathologies and health needs to new types of technologies did not seem to prevail. Looking more closely on what governments have concentrated themselves, we see that the economic (the budgetary to be more specific), political and, partially, social objectives were the real issues at stake, while the politics of healthcare was the main determinant.

In particular the NHS–SHI distinction seems quite useful to make sense of the recent changes. Already in the 1980s and the 1990s national health systems generally ensured a large degree of equality of access to health care

Table 9.3 Factors pushing for policy change until the economic crisis of the late 2000s: the form of the quadrilemma in NHS and SHI systems

	Economic and budgetary objectives	Political objectives	Social objectives	Medical objectives	Political factors
Sweden		++ (Waiting lists)	+		++ (Ideological shift)
England	++ (increase exp.)	++ (Waiting lists)	+		+ (Devolution; Ideol. shift)
Spain		+	+		++ (Aut. Parties)
Italy	++ (cost containment)	+	+		++ (Aut. Parties)
France Germany Austria	++ (cost containment and structural shortcomings)				
Poland	+ (cost containment)				++ (Institutional and Ideological shift)

and relatively low levels of health care spending, but they were known especially for their extremely long waiting lists before access to specialist care. On the contrary, the social health insurance systems, in which the supply of health care was often plentiful, allowing for patient choice, comfort and often the quality of care to be guaranteed, had often high spending levels, and occasionally inequality of access to health care.

As a result, reforms in national health care systems tried to get closer to health insurance system by providing more choice and leeway to patients and doctors (at the risk of increasing health care expenditure), whereas those introduced in health insurance systems focused on control mechanisms, mimicking NHS (such as limited access to specialists through gate keepers, or controlled budgets).

In particular, in the SHI systems of France, Germany and Austria, budgetary objectives were the most important goal of the reforms. In *France* the strong increase in health care expenditure and sickness funds deficits became a very relevant problem since the 1980s and since then an ongoing debate flourished. The French sickness insurance funds have been in deficit from 1969 to 1979, in 1981, 1986 and ever since 1990: short-term measures failed to tackle the growing deficit of the *Sécurité Sociale* funds, despite no less than 18 saving plans between 1975 and 1995.

Since the end of the 1970s cost-containment has also been the main issue in *German* health care policies because health care expenditure increased much faster than the economy grew. Technical development and demographic change led to an increasing demand for inpatient care. The first main response to this trend was the rise of social contributions paid to health insurance funds (Palier, 2010), but, as for other policies, this solution appeared already in the late 1980s as an economic dead end because it threatened the competitiveness of the German economy. In this specific case, the costs of the German reunification process accelerated in the last two decades the pressure on reforms.

In the *Austrian* case the main issues in health care reform debates have been budgetary pressures and cost-containment considerations and the increasing recognition of structural shortcomings. From the 1990s, increasing costs have regularly been called 'cost explosion'. Moreover budgetary pressures arose also from inside the health care system, given the deficits accumulated over time by the health insurance funds: the deficit issue became so relevant in the public debate about health care financing, that there was fear of a 'system collapse'.

In all these three countries a second major driver for reforms, connected to economic objectives, were structural shortcomings, related to the nature that often SHI systems took: the duplication of hospital infrastructure, fostering a large bed density; the lack of coordination and integration between the inpatient sector and the outpatient sector; incentives to over-spend and to over-use services, given the lack of strong controls.

The drivers of reforms in NHS countries are more complex. In England, Spain and Sweden, all reforms focused, first of all on the political objectives of reducing waiting times and opening choices for patients and, in the first two countries, also on economic objectives, but with a totally different orientation than the one seen in SHI countries.

In *England*, when the new Labour Government came into power in 1997, it was confronted with an NHS where the quality of care remained poor (especially if looking at waiting lists times), there were problems of lack of modern facilities and equipment and there were wide disparities in access to care and its quality across the country. It became clear that the improvement of social and political objectives required higher levels of public expenditure.

In *Spain* the problem was to develop and to strengthen a relatively 'young' NHS, meeting a series of political and social objectives. Starting from the 1980s and in the two following decades the Spanish health care system underwent a deep modernization and Europeanization process, where the main drivers for reforms were extending the coverage to all the Spanish population and improving the access to public care.

It is no surprise that in these two countries economic objectives meant increasing expenditure and not containing it.

In *Sweden* the main problem, seen also as a legitimacy issue, was the one of waiting lists. The reduction of waiting times has been a general political goal since the 1980s, but until the 2000s, without success. Moreover concerns arose in relation to the varieties (and inequalities) in care quality and access to care on a geographical base.

If the reform paths followed in the six countries analyzed so far fit well in a SHI–NHS distinction, Poland and Italy represent a partially different and more complex picture.

Poland is probably the country, among the ones studied here, where a mix of economic objectives and, above all, political factors has played a dominant role. In relation to economic objectives, given the fact that a SHI model was newly re-introduced in the 1990s, the aim was to make the health care system not too expensive in order not to hinder economic growth. But the main issue was related to the fact that health care reforms in Poland had to be framed in the context of the post-communist transition and this sector constituted a relevant element of the system under transformation: liberalization and the development of the private sector, also in the health care sector, were considered by policy makers two important tools for boosting the country's economy (through a 'shock therapy').

Italy has been a peculiar NHS. Drivers for change came from political objectives, as in Spain, Sweden and England, but economic objectives were more prominent. This situation was due not only to health care deficits and increases in expenditure, but also (and mainly) to the huge Italian public debt (on average equal to 111 per cent of the national GDP in the last two decades), which has set almost all welfare state policies in a permanent austerity situation.

Apart from drivers coming from within the policy field, as already stated, more general political factors have influenced the shape and the trajectories taken by reforms, especially in national health care systems. In Spain, Italy and the UK reforms in health care matched broader reforms concerning *the role institutionally assigned to local governments*: in all these three contexts, reforms aimed at transferring powers to local authorities (regional ones in the case of Spain and Italy, 'counties' in the case of the UK) were implemented. The reasons behind this decentralization were political as well as strictly policy related, and they were connected to the rise and the increased strength of territorial movements and parties advocating for more autonomy at the local level (Melucci and Diani, 1992). The Catalan and the Basque parties in Spain, the 'Northern League' in Italy and the 'Scottish National Party' have been quite active to ask for more decentralization: healthcare has been one of the fields where it was relevant to shift powers from the Central State.

In England and Sweden, as well as in Poland, other political factors played a role: in particular when conservative and liberal parties governed, health care reforms aimed also at proposing an ideological shift towards a more market-oriented society.

If these factors and objectives can help us to understand the drivers for change in European HC systems until the 2008 crisis, after the crisis started, economic objectives became the main concern in all the countries studied but in Sweden and Poland. In SHI systems the cost-containment goal and the fight against structural shortcomings were even more prominent than before. The same happened in Southern European countries and, especially after the 2010 election, in England. Sweden and Poland are different from this point of view: cost-containment concerns have not been an important motive behind reforms even after the crisis, given the relatively quick recovery of the Swedish and Polish economies and their comparatively sound budgetary situations.

A summary of the situation of each country in terms of economic growth and public debt over the last two decades, sustaining the interpretations just offered, is presented in Table 9.4.

The actors involved in policy change

The politics of health care reforms is of course very much dependent on the various types of actors that one finds in the various health care systems. Again, the type of health care systems as well as the type of political system matter a lot. The health care policy arena in NHS systems seems less crowded than the one often found in many SHI countries (Table 9.5). In SHI, social partners may play a role that they do not have in NHS. Trade unions are only partially relevant, especially when they do not participate in the running of health care funds. In general, bureaucratic experts do not seem

Table 9.4 The economic situation and the public debt in the last two decades in the countries studied

Country	Average annual GDP per capita growth				Total general government debt % of GDP			
	1990–99	2000–07	2008–12	1990–2012	1995–99	2000–07	2008–11	1995–2011
Austria	2.7	2.4	0.6	2.2	66.3	64.5	69.4	66.2
France	1.9	2.1	0.0	1.5	58.2	61.9	78.9	64.8
Germany[a]	1.1	1.7	0.8	1.3	59.1	64.0	76.1	65.4
Italy	1.4	1.6	–1.3	0.9	117.1	105.6	115.6	111.3
Poland[a]	3.4	4.1	3.5	3.8	42.8	43.7	52.3	45.4
Spain	2.7	3.6	–0.8	2.2	64.7	47.7	56.2	54.7
Sweden	1.8	3.2	1.1	2.1	70.3	49.9	39.8	53.5
United Kingdom	2.5	3.2	–0.5	2.1	48.5	40.8	71.1	50.2

[a] Data on Germany starting from 1992; data on Poland starting from 1991.
Source: OECD statistical database (2013) for GDP statistics; Eurostat database (2013) for debt statistics.

to play a relevant role, with some exceptions in some SHI countries. The last actor which has traditionally played a role in these systems are doctors, but doctors do not enjoy the same power depending on the type of systems and, as it will be shown, their capacity to intervene has been weakening in most of the countries studied here, and, at the most, it takes the 'veto player' form. National political actors are usually the key players. Depending also on the more general institutional structure of the State (unitary or federalist-like), regional and local governments can play a relevant or a minor role.

Over the last 60 years or so, the impetus for the introduction of major structural change in the *English* NHS has been largely political. Other stakeholders, doctors included, were never the key driver. Moreover it has tended to be central, and not local government, that has brought about the major shifts observed. This very brief description of the main policy actors holds true independently from the type of ruling coalition. However, change in majority often meant some change in directions in the health care policies. The majority system, the stability over time of governments (Tories in the 1980s and a good part of the 1990s, Labour from the end of the 1990s until 2010) and the nature of the health care system (an NHS) created the premises for in-depth changes that have been eventually reversed when different ruling coalitions came into power.

The *Swedish* situation is in part similar to the English one, although with an important element of differentiation. The first is the strong role of local government in healthcare, which makes reforms more complicated and not easily suitable to top-down decision-making approaches. The stability of governments in power, the presence of strong local authorities and the

Table 9.5 Actors in different European health care systems: a comparative view

	National govt	Local govt	Top bureaucrats	Trade Unions	Enterprises (providers)	Health care funds	Professionals (doctors)	Citizens/Patients Associations
Sweden	++	++						
England	++							
Spain	+	++		+			+	
Italy	++	++					+ (V)	
France	++		++	+		+ (V)	++ (V)	
Germany	++	+	+			+ (V)		
Austria	+	++ (V)		+		+ (V)	++ (V)	
Poland	++							

Note: V= mainly veto player; ++: very relevant role; +: relevant role.

overall cultural values have shaped the trajectories of reforms: national politics has played a relevant role and changes in the ruling parties had consequences on the types of reforms put forward, but the wills of national governments had to come partially to terms with local governments.

Spain is a country where, at least until 2010, regional governments played a strong role in reforms, with doctors supporting a good part of reforms. The reason for such a broad coalition and the scarcity of veto players have to do with the fact that healthcare in Spain was for more than two decades (from the 1980s until 2010) a 'win-all game', thanks to an increasing public expenditure, used also (and often) to rise professionals' salaries and wages. In such a situation there was also a general consensus by Centre-Right and Socialists on how to develop the system, knowing that Regions would have been anyway increasingly autonomous in deciding what and how much to implement of national reforms. This general consensus did not mean that frictions did not rise between Central governments with a political orientation and regional ones with a different one on the day-to-day managing of Centre–Regional relationship decisions in the NHS. These frictions became even more relevant after the economic crisis when the central government started to introduce very strong cost-containment policies in a policy area, such as healthcare, where Regions have powers. Recentralization attempts and blame avoidance strategies adopted by both sides (mainly the Centre–Right national government vs. the Socialist-led or the Nationalist-led Autonomous Communities) are increasing the tensions in the last years in the Spanish NHS, and more in general in State-Regional Authorities relationship.

In comparison with other NHS countries, one cannot detect in *Italy* a clear reforming coalition that has pushed through innovation (of any kind) over the last two decades, but different and often fragmented alliances that were not able to push through an overarching reform. National level top-bureaucrats were almost powerless in the policy arena, as it happened instead in a country like France. They were absent from the debate, following a traditional Italian weakness of the bureaucracy in terms of independence and capacity to influence the shape of policies (Capano and Gualmini, 2010). Political parties and regional governments played the central role. In the 1990s, there were clear cut divisions between the Centre-Left parties and governments (keen on maintaining the NHS, also reinforcing its public status) and the Centre-Right ones (aiming at privatizing the NHS or, at least, to reduce the public role in health care). The last decade was a time of more convergence in the Parliament toward a model that did not deny the importance of the NHS, but was less focused on a general discussion of its public status and more interested in effective cost-containment strategies. This convergence took an implicit form, without any explicit agreement between the two party coalitions on the development of the NHS. Regional actors came to play, especially in the last decade, an increasing role, given their powers in managing the NHS. The only other relevant actor were doctors, but their traditional fragmentation in terms of professional groups (between GPs and hospital doctors, among different trade unions) has made them relatively 'weak veto players', scarcely able to influence the managerialization and privatization process (perceived by them as a 'loss' of autonomy and power in the NHS), and only able to defend particularistic and individualistic interests (for example, the possibility for NHS doctors to maintain also a high degree of freedom in private practice). In comparison with the other countries, a relative important role has been played also by the Catholic Church, given the fact that it runs a good part of private facilities, accredited in the NHS.

In SHIs there were more actors at work. The presence of Sickness Insurance funds in itself made more complex the structure of the policy arena.

In *France* and *Germany* we find similar 'programmatic coalitions' at work (Hassenteufel et al., 2010), advocating for structural reforms since the 1980s. These programmatic coalitions were composed by two main categories of actors: political actors (the Ministry of Health, the health policy spokespersons of the leading political parties, etc.) and high-level civil servants specialised in social protection. The core beliefs of these coalitions were promoting an approach distanced both from the purely financial approach of the Treasury and from the liberal-corporatist positions of medical doctors (Pierru, 2011). Their approach was seeking a greater State autonomy from corporatist interests (especially doctors but also the social partners managing the sickness funds), since these groups were seen as the main obstacle to structural reforms. Increased sickness insurance funds deficits in the 1990s and lessons from past policy failures created a favourable political context for those 'change agents' (Mahoney and Thelen, 2010) to advocate for structural reforms.

If these are the common elements for both countries, then some differences arise. In France, one hardly sees political differences between political parties, even though the right-wing parties were keener on trying to find compromises with doctors. After a decade of fierce confrontation between doctors and the State, reforms had to come to terms with the medical power, the main effective veto player, especially in ambulatory care. In Germany the reforms concentred more on competition among sickness funds, they were negotiated by the two main political parties (SPD and CDU-CSU) and they were able to strongly limit doctors' influence. Another element differentiating France and Germany was the relevance of regional and local authorities. For obvious reasons related to the more general institutional design of the two countries, these levels of governments were almost not influent in France, whereas in Germany they were part of the programmatic coalition.

The actors' arena in *Austria* was quite different. Here key actors were also the provinces, which had a strong budgetary interest, given their direct role in the hospital sector, but at the same time they were very reluctant in reducing the number of hospital beds or even closing down hospitals. Doctors, especially through the Chamber of Physicians, were another important veto player. Moreover, different from the situation in other SHI systems, the central state had a much weaker say: provinces played a strong role as providers of hospital care and as financers of inpatient care, while the steering role of the federal level was not adequately equipped with regulatory options. The presence of many strong veto players (from Provinces to doctors) explains why Austria was probably the country where less transformation took place in the last two decades.

The *Polish* situation differed significantly from that encountered in Western Europe (Kaminska, 2013). While in Western Europe health care policy change was usually introduced within established governance structures, accommodating the processes of drafting and implementation of reforms, these structures were missing at the outset of the Polish post-communist transformation. Professional self-government bodies were re-established soon after the change of regime, but they have struggled to overcome internal divisions and reconcile divergent interest (Sitek, 2008). Trade unions were 'captured' in an inverse dependency relationship with politics (Avdagic, 2005), which considerably weakened their voice. The weakness of professional associations and unions was matched by the policy experts' and government's unwillingness to involve them in the policy-making processes. As a result, national governments were the key players leading reforms, promoting the ideas of the respective political parties, with none or very little participation of other stakeholders. However these governments were in the last two decades often weak (for example, in terms of frequent national elections, many government reshuffles and the fragmentation of the party members of ruling coalitions), and no consensus was attained on the main health care reforms between centre-right and centre-left parties. The sudden and frequent changes explain also why no top-level bureaucracy was able to influence the policy process, as in France and Germany: apart from the obvious difficulty of consolidating such a bureaucracy in few years after the 1989 change, the lack of continuity within the Ministry of Health (for example, in the period 2001–2005 there were as many as six different Health Ministers) brought with itself also a high turnover among top bureaucrats. The result has been an institutional instability at the central level that can explain the lack of continuity in the Polish health care system.

How transformations have taken place and what have been the results of policy change

The literature on institutional and policy change from the last two decades offers us a vast array of analytical tools in order to interpret how change takes place. We have used and mixed two possible frameworks for explanations: a) the Hall (1993) model of three orders of policy change and b) Streeck and Thelen's (2005) typology of institutional change.

In his essay of 1993, Peter Hall described three types of policy change. 'Third-order' policy changes take place when there is a shift in the over-arching goals that guide policy in a particular field; 'second-order' ones are related to changes in the techniques or policy instruments used to attain those goals and the easier changes are the 'first-order' ones related to changes in the precise settings of these instruments. On their part, Streeck and Thelen (2005) proposed a typology of institutional 'cumulative but transformative changes'. They underline that, beside traditional explanations of institutional stability and path dependency (which they defined as 'Reproduction by adaptation') or abrupt/disruptive institutional change ('Breakdown and replacement'), often due to external shocks, there exist incremental but disruptive institutional changes through 'gradual transformation' or situations of 'survival and return'. 'Gradual transformation' refers to institutional change that is incremental as a process but transformative in terms of results: far-reaching change can be accomplished through the accumulation of small, often seemingly insignificant adjustments. Gradual transformation means institutional discontinuity caused by incremental, 'creeping' change, often endogenous and in some cases produced by the very behaviors an institution itself generates. Therefore, significant change can often emanate from inherent ambiguities and 'gaps' that exist by design or emerge over time between formal institutions and their actual implementation or enforcement. 'Survival and return' refers, instead, to a situation where institutional reforms do appear as disruptive in terms of the process of change, but the results are far much less discontinuous from the original path than expected.

With a perspective integrating the previous ones, Palier (2010) has explained the unfreezing process that has characterized the Bismarckian welfare systems on the basis of the accumulation of small, incremental changes: 'because of the "stickiness" of welfare state institutions (Pierson, 2001), and because of their huge popularity, governments were not able to change the whole system even when they claimed that these systems were failing to deal with economic and social issues. Rather, changes were initially incremental, passing through an intermediary phase based on a relatively "silent" evolutionary institutional transformation (changes in financing, changes in power relations), that ... facilitated structural reforms based on a new social policy paradigm. Even these new social policies have not entirely replaced the former ones, but merely contributed to a conversion of the old system to the new goals' (pp. 365–6). The idea is that the accumulation and sedimentation of institutional transformations over many years has constituted a sort of 'critical mass' causing, without an explicit political decision, a radical discontinuity with the old welfare system. Only a long-time perspective on change is able to catch the real impact of a sequence of institutional relatively minor events, not individually significant if not considered within a more general sequence.

The above approach to policy reforms in healthcare can be applied using a series of cautions for various reasons: institutional changes over the last two decades have not always followed a linear unidirectional path (for instance, some decisions have been reversed over time); these changes, even inside the same country, have not followed similar paths in respect of different dimensions of the policy field. In particular, rescaling, managerialization and privatization (meant both in terms of provision and expenditure) in a given country have not been always pursued in a similar way.

Therefore we develop our analysis at two different stages: a general overview of the trajectories of change since the beginning of the 1990s, for which we adopt Hall's terminology, and a more in-depth analysis of institutional change at the level of single dimensions (managerialization, etc.), using toolkits relatively similar to Streeck and Thelen's ones.

Looking at overall trajectories over time, what appears quite clear in Table 9.6 is that in most countries the 1990s and, eventually, the most recent years after the 2008 crisis were the ones where second- (if not third) order policy changes have taken place, whereas the 2000s were a time of modification in the precise settings of instruments or implementation of second-order changes passed in the previous decade.

Practically every country in the 1990s had at least a second-order policy change. England and Poland, especially the latter, can be considered the two contexts where third-order policy change took place: Poland due to the shift from a political system to another; England for the far-reaching consequences of its internal market reforms. All the countries studied here introduced market and managerial mechanisms in the 1990s, but the difference with England is the fact that in this country quasi-markets were seen not as an amelioration in the functioning of the NHS (for instance, as in Sweden, where the aim was to reduce waiting lists and to introduce more

Table 9.6 Trajectories of change since the beginning of the 1990s: a general overview adopting Hall's typology

	Type of changes in the 1990s in comparison with the 1980s	Type of changes in the 2000s in comparison with the 1990s	Type of changes since the crisis in comparison with the rest of 2000s
Sweden	II order	I order	II order
England	III order	II order	II order
Spain	I and partially II order	I order	II order
Italy	II order	I order	II order
France	II order	II order	I order
Germany	II order	I order	I order
Austria	II order	I order	I order
Poland	III order	II order	I order

patient choice) but as a radical transformation of the system. Spain stands at the other end of the policy change spectrum: the 1990s were a time of implementation of relevant third-order reforms introduced in the 1980s. In the middle we find all the other countries, which introduced new policy instruments (competition, introduction of private provision where it did not exist before, new forms of decision-making, rescaling).

The 2000s, at least until the advent of the economic crisis, were years witnessing less important reforms in almost all countries, the two most relevant exceptions being England and Poland. In both these cases governments elected after years of different (conservative) majorities' ruling introduced and tried to implement far-reaching changes, though without undoing of what was previously done (Labour in England transformed internal markets, but it did not go back to the prior 1980s setting; the Polish government when reforming the regional funds did not shift to a different institutional model, but centralized the SHI funding mechanism at the national level). In all other countries relevant pieces of legislation were passed, but they mostly appeared as a continuation and an implementation of policy innovation introduced in the previous decade, sometimes by introducing further important steps in the same direction, as in France with the 2004 reform.

Why were the 2000s not so innovative, even in terms of second-order policy change, as the 1990s were? The main reasons seem related to the fact that, if there were (even partial) policy paradigm shifts (in relation to the role of the State in welfare and health care issues), these were often culturally elaborated in the 1980s, then transformed into legislation in the 1990s, so that the 2000s were years when these reforms and their cultural vision were implemented, also adopting a fine-tuning and policy-learning approach. Quite often some of the reforms introduced in the 1990s did not use the appropriate instrument in order to reach the goal set by reformers. In this way the 2000s was a time for refining and improving these tools. This appears quite clearly in cases like Sweden, where reforms during the two decades concentrated quite often over similar issues and goals but were developed through different mechanisms in order to reach success.

The most recent years show a new sudden wave of second and, potentially, third-order changes in NHS countries, meanwhile SHI systems have developed more limited transformations until 2012. In Spain and Italy, the magnitude of programmed health care cuts and the attempts to potentially recentralize the NHS are signs of at least second-order changes, stronger than the ones registered in the first part of the 2000s. In Sweden, and even more in England, the last years, especially after the return to power of conservative governments, have seen the renewal of strong attempts to reshape deeply the NHS. In particular the implementation of the 2012 reforms in England will tell us in the coming years if this new wave of reforms will have an impact similar to what happened two decades ago.

Given this general overview of policy and institutional change in the health care systems, we can focus more narrowly on what happened in specific dimensions: rescaling, managerialization and privatization, both in terms of provision and expenditure.

The comparative analysis of rescaling issues offers some of the most interesting insights (Table 9.7). If the 1970s and 1980s were decades when the 'decentralization' belief was at the center stage, the 1990s, and especially the more recent decade, have shown a quite important change towards recentralization. *The shapes taken by decentralization reforms have not been the same as the ones fostering recentralization.* 'Breakdown' of centralist institutional powers and 'replacement' with delegation of responsibilities to local authorities were both tools used in the previous decades in order to decentralize the system. This type of institutional change was the one adopted also in countries like Spain, Italy and Poland in the 1990s. What has taken shape in more recent years is a reversal of this trend: increasing recentralization, especially through regulatory tools. Quite often this recentralization has not been declared as an explicit policy goal, but it has been put forward often through second-order changes, able to foster a 'gradual transformation'. This has happened in NHS countries, as already Saltman (2008) indicated, but also in SHI countries. The French and German cases are good example of hidden recentralization/ *'étatisation'* through the redistribution of competencies among public actors (between the state and sickness insurance funds and between the state and hospitals). A similar situation is taking place in countries like Spain and Italy where national governments are introducing

Table 9.7 Rescaling processes in health care systems over time

	The 1990s	The 2000s The years since the crisis
Sweden	Reproduction by adaptation	Gradual transformation: hidden re-centralization
England	Breakdown and replacement: recentralization	Gradual transformation: hidden re-centralization of regulation matched by new decentralization
Spain	Breakdown and replacement: decentralization	Gradual transformation: Hidden re-centralization
Italy	Breakdown and replacement: decentralization	Gradual transformation: Hidden re-centralization
France	Gradual transformation: 'étatisation'	
Germany	Gradual transformation: hidden re-centralization	
Austria	Reproduction by adaptation	
Poland	Breakdown and replacement: decentralization	Partial new Breakdown and replacement: recentralization of financing

tools (like the Italian '*Piani di rientro*') that objectively put regional governments under a stricter national supervision and steering.

If in the NHS systems recentralization has meant shifting powers from local to central governments, in the SHI countries this process has also meant a shift from funds to central governments. Recentralization has been pursued mainly for economic reasons: contrary to what was expected, decentralization has brought with itself more difficulties for central governments to contain costs. Especially in the more recent years of economic austerity, controlling health care expenditure has become an important issue for national governments and the delegation of power to local ones has made savings and the implementation of cuts more difficult. At the same time the reason why this recentralization process took a more 'hidden' form than the previous decentralization one has to do with politics: recentralizing could have meant an open conflict with large part of societies, from trade unions to local governments and, where present, to autonomist parties. Such an open conflict could have seen central governments in a difficult situation in front of public opinion, that could have considered local governments as the actors who wanted to maintain open health care facilities and central government as the institution seeking to rationalize the supply.

In comparison with rescaling, managerialization has followed a quite similar and unidirectional trend in Europe (Table 9.8). In SHI countries and in England, managerialization was introduced through a strategy of 'breakdown and replacement' of more traditional bureaucratic administration models, and it has been an ongoing process in the last two decades, with reform waves one after the other (in terms of the tools created and health

Table 9.8   Managerialization processes in health care systems over time

	The 1990s	The 2000s	The years since the crisis
Sweden	Breakdown and replacement: managerialization	Reproduction by adaptation with territorial differences	
England	Breakdown and replacement: managerialization		
Spain	Breakdown and replacement: managerialization	Reproduction by adaptation with relevant territorial differences	
Italy	Breakdown and replacement: managerialization	Reproduction by adaptation and gradual transformation: hidden return of politics over management and relevant territorial differences	
France	Breakdown and replacement: managerialization		
Germany	Breakdown and replacement: managerialization		
Austria	Breakdown and replacement: managerialization		
Poland	Breakdown and replacement: managerialization		

care sectors' application). In France, for instance, managerial methods were first applied to hospitals (with the introduction of a DRGs-like system and new powers given to top managers), and then they have recently been introduced in the ambulatory sector, with the new performance-related funding of private practitioners. In Germany managerialization is reshaping hospital governance with professionals increasingly under pressure for fulfilling new administrative tasks and spending more and more time on documentation and controlling duties at the expense of the time dedicated to treatment.

In the remaining NHS countries managerialization was also introduced in the 1990s. In their cases the application at the local level has been somewhat less homogenous, given the autonomy of local authorities: in Sweden, Spain and Italy the implementation and the adaptation of these types of reforms depended also on the political orientation of local governments. Among the countries considered, Italy has a peculiarity: political parties are 'invading' again the realm of managers (as they used to do before the managerial reforms of the 1990s), imposing their choices.

In most of the countries studied here the introduction or the strengthening of private provision, internal markets and patient choice (where it was not already present or very limited) in healthcare has been obtained through breakdown and replacement strategies, especially in the 1990s. Apart from Austria and France, where changes were more limited but where private provision already existed, in all other countries legislation in the last two decades increased the role of private provision. In Sweden a privatization in the primary care sector is taking place and since 2007 it has been possible to sell acute care hospitals to private providers. In England, Italy and Spain, even if with territorial differences in the latter two countries, private provision has been fostered through new legislation. In the German outpatient care sector price competition has led funds to close down offices, to slim down their administrative staff or to merge with competitors in order to reduce their costs (between 1993 and 2012, the number of sickness insurance funds has diminished from more than 1200 to 146). Moreover, in Germany, the hospital sector is increasingly privatized through three strategies: the managing of public hospitals under private law (in 2010, 58.4 per cent of all public hospitals operated under private law); new forms of public–private partnerships have evolved to the level of allowing the dismiss of entire public hospitals to private owners; the closing down of public facilities and the more diffuse recourse to private provision. Also in Poland reforms fostered the privatization of ambulatory care and hospitals (Table 9.9).

Data on the incidence of hospital beds in privately owned hospitals can give us a more precise picture of trends (Table 9.10). In Austria and Italy the changes between 1990 and 2010 were quite significant with a robust rise of private provision. In Germany and Poland, the transformations were even

Table 9.9 Privatization of provision

	The 1990s	The 2000s The years since the crisis
Sweden	Partial breakdown and replacement: introduction of private provision and patient choice	Reproduction by adaptation: strengthening of private provision, competition and patient choice (perhaps leading to gradual transformation)
England	Breakdown and replacement: the introduction of quasi-markets	Partial breakdown and replacement: substitution of quasi-markets with partnership but strengthening of private provision and patient choice
Spain	Partial breakdown and replacement: introduction of quasi-markets leaving freedom of implementation to ACs	Gradual transformation: a polarization and diversification process with Autonomous Communities going different ways
Italy	Breakdown and replacement: the introduction of quasi-markets leaving freedom of implementation to Regions	Gradual transformation: a polarization and diversification process with Regional HCS going different ways
France	Reproduction by adaptation	
Germany	Breakdown and replacement: competition among health care funds Gradual transformation: privatization of provision	Gradual transformation: privatization of provision
Austria	Gradual transformation in hospital care: increasing privatization of provision	
Poland	Breakdown and replacement: opening up to private provision in ambulatory care Breakdown and replacement together with more gradual transformation in hospital care	

more pronounced. Poland shifted from practically no private provision in 1990 to around 25 per cent in 2010. The vast majority of German hospital beds (69.2 per cent) were in private facilities in 2010, while two decades before this percentage was around 49 per cent. France and Spain have seen minor changes over time in terms of private share of hospital provision, but if we focus on private for-profit providers, changes are also detectable here. In general in all European countries for-profit providers have been the ones who have gained the most from pro-market reforms, increasing substantially their share of hospital provision.

A progressive privatization of expenditure has been ongoing in some countries but not in others. Naturally these data cannot take into account the more recent transformations due to austerity, which should foster a new

Table 9.10 Private provision in hospital care

	% of beds in privately owned hospitals			% of beds in for-profit privately owned hospitals		
	1990	2000	2010	1990	2000	2010
Sweden	7.6	n.a.	5.3%		n.a.	
United Kingdom	3.1	4.0	5.8		n.a.	
Spain	32.1	33.3	32.6		n.a.	
Italy	23.5	30.4	31.6	n.a.	24.2	28.0
France	35.2	34.4	37.5	20.5	19.8	23.4
Germany[a]	49.1	59.7	69.2	14.6	21.9	32.7
Austria	23.5	25.3	29.1	6.1	7.2	11.1
Poland	n.a.	n.a.	24.4		n.a.	

[a] Data for Germany refers to 1991.
Source: OECD Health database and WHO Health for All databases (2013); for Germany Statistisches Bundesamt (2010); for the UK Boyle (2011); for France 1990 DREES (2006); for Sweden 2010 SCB (2013).

Table 9.11 Private expenditure as a percentage of total expenditure on health

	Out-of-pocket payments			Other private expenditure		
	1990	2000	2010	1990	2000	2010
Sweden	13.3*	16.6	16.8	0.1	0.1	2.2
United Kingdom	10.6	11.4	8.9	5.8	9.8	7.9
Spain	18.7	23.6	19.7	2.6	4.8	6.1
Italy	17.1	24.5	17.8	3.4	3.0	2.6
France	11.4	7.1	7.3	12.0	13.5	15.7
Germany	11.1	11.4	13.2	12.7	9.1	10.0
Austria	15.2*	15.3	15.9	10.9	7.9	7.9
Poland	8.3	30.0	22.1	0.0	0.0	6.2

* Data referred to 1995.
Source: OECD Health database (2013).

rise in private expenditure. In Poland there was a strong increase in private expenditure. In Sweden there was an important increase in out-of-pocket (OOP) payments, matched by a light increase in other types of private expenditure (insurances, voluntary funds, etc.). Spain and Italy have followed a bell curve in private OOP expenditure: there was a strong increase in the 1990s until the mid-2000s and then a decrease. In the UK and France there was a light reduction over the last two decades in OOP expenditure, while other private expenditures increased. In Austria the situation seems to have remained relatively stable, whereas in Germany an increase in OOP has taken place (Table 9.11).

Conclusions

During recent years, the health care systems in Europe have all been subjected to reforms, more or less far-reaching. These reforms have been guided by the concern for reducing or at least controlling public expenditure. The reforms tried to develop regulation mechanisms based on private provision, managerialization and competition between the agents (insurers and providers of health care), thereby hoping to enhance their efficiency. In reforms carried out since the 1990s, the formulas employed increasingly have focused on competition: competition between health care providers in national health systems and competition between insurers in health insurance systems (where the health care providers are already in competition at least in the field of ambulatory health care).

However, the development of competition is a source of inequality and of increased total health care expenditure. It might appear strange that formulas are chosen in the knowledge that they will increase the inequalities and risk a growth in total health spending. The reason is that these reforms are influenced by other constraints: firstly, the desire to adapt the health care systems to the new economic environment which demands a limitation of public expenditure (which thus justifies the increasing proportion of health spending paid for by the users and/or by private insurers), and a growing insistence on the mechanisms of competition as universal regulators. The idea seems to be less to control the total expenditure on health care than to limit the public share of health care spending by transferring a proportion of the expenses to the private sector.

Moreover, the introduction of more freedom and competition within the health care systems also seems to respond to a strong demand from the users, who have grown impatient faced with waiting lists problems of national health systems and who wish to be able to benefit immediately from all the advances in medicine (at least those who have the means to pay for them).

As we have seen, the reforms in the health care systems are as if torn between four often (potentially) contradictory. Each reform makes a choice between these objectives: social (guaranteeing the same health services for all), medical (obtaining better health results), economic (ensuring the financial viability and the competitiveness of the systems) and political (obtaining the satisfaction of users and providers, their freedom of choice and of action, the absence of waiting lists ...). Even if it is no doubt impossible to design a reform capable of improving all these dimensions at the same time, it is nevertheless important to define these challenges explicitly so that the consequences of the choices made are clear to all citizens, especially the choice of freedom and comfort at the cost of equity.

Notes

1. Of course more detailed and in-depth information and considerations are contained in the country chapters.
2. Both GDP-based and per-capita measures were used to avoid to connect PHE only to indicators, on one side, strongly influenced by the economic circle, on the other, not taking into account the general economic characteristics of a given country.

10
The Performance of European Health Care Systems

Emmanuele Pavolini and August Österle

Introduction

The previous chapter has discussed the main reforms in the last two decades in European Health Care Systems (HCS) and the logics behind them. This chapter will analyse how well these HCS have functioned and how the performance is linked to the main policy changes that occurred in terms of rescaling, privatization and managerialization. In order to clearly link this exploration with the analysis in the previous chapter, the functioning of the HCS is studied in relation to the policy quadrilemma proposed by Palier (2011): how to find a balance among potentially contrasting economic, medical, social and political objectives. In the following sections, international statistical data is combined with the results of the previous country chapters. For each of the dimensions (medical, political, social and economic), several indicators are used. The selection is in part similar to the selection adopted in earlier studies (for example Mackenbach and McKee, 2013; OECD, 2010; Or et al., 2010) and attempts to capture the diversity of aspects that make up the four dimensions. The major source of the statistical data is the OECD, but – depending on the indicators chosen – also other sources such as WHO and Eurostat are used. The methodological limitations and the difficulties with regard to the comparability of health care data on a highly aggregated level have been widely discussed in the literature. This chapter does not intend to identify an overall ranking or grouping of countries that have been more or less successful in health care reform. Rather, it attempts to identify common or single country trends in achieving medical, political, social and economic objectives and to discuss these with a view to the role of rescaling, privatization and managerialization in health care reform. The next four sections are dedicated to analyse each objective, whereas the last section tries to synthesize the overall results, placing the eight countries in a broader comparative perspective.

The medical objectives

To guarantee the highest quality of care and the optimum condition of health for the population is, of course, a primary goal of a HCS. In order to understand what has been happening over time in terms of medical objectives, the present analysis focuses on three dimensions: the functioning of the hospital system, using the lens of appropriateness of care; the functioning of out-patient care, focusing on chronic-long term care illnesses and prevention activities; and health final outcomes.

How appropriate (meaning to what extent a certain type of care is in line with evidence-based or consensus-based guidelines) hospital treatments are, is a very relevant issue. In Table 10.1 we use four typical indicators employed in the literature: for the first three of them (hospitalization rate, caesarean births rate and asthma hospital admission rates) we can argue that in general the lower the value the more appropriate is the type of care provided,[1] whereas for the percentage of cataract surgery performed as day cases the opposite is valid (the higher the percentage the more appropriate the treatment).

On average NHS countries function better than SHI (social health insurance) systems. Sweden has the best or very close to the best result in three out of four indicators (only the level of hospitalization rate is quite higher than in the other NHS countries). The UK could have performed quite better if it was not for the high levels of the asthma admissions rate in hospitals. Italy and Spain perform relatively well: their situation could have been better if caesarean births rates (in the case of Italy) and asthma admission rates

Table 10.1 Appropriateness in hospital care

	Hospitalization rate (every 1000 individuals)			Caesarean births rate (per 1000 live births)			Asthma hospital admission rates (age-sex-stand. rate per 100000 pop.)			Cataract surgery % performed as day cases		
	1990	2000	2010	1990	2000	2010	1990	2005	2010	1990	2000	2010
Sweden	n.a	161	163	104	145	168	n.a	24.6	19.3	n.a	92.8	97.4
UK	126	133	136	113	200	240	n.a	75.5	73.7	n.a	n.a	98.1
Spain	95	112	102	142	214	255	n.a	n.a	43.9	n.a	85.9	95.9
Italy	n.a	157	128	208	333	384	n.a	16.7	19.2	n.a	37.6	85.4
France	n.a	190	169	139	172	203	n.a	n.a	43.4	n.a	31.6	80.1
Germany	178	199	240	157	209	314	n.a	21.1	20.8	n.a	n.a	5.2
Austria	212	247	261	n.a	168	282	n.a	54.0	52.8	n.a	1.2	32.8
Poland	n.a	146	203	138	n.a.	260	n.a	62.1	68.8	n.a	3.8	17.4

Source: OECD Health database (2013).

in hospitals (in the case of Spain) would have been lower. The French SHI presents mixed results: it seems to work in a relatively appropriate way in terms of cataracts surgery and caesarean births rate, whereas it has problems of hospitalization rates and hospital admissions for asthma. Austria, Germany and Poland usually present lower levels of appropriateness, with only few exceptions indicating better functioning, as in the case of asthma admission rates in Germany.

Looking at changes over time, in relation to the data available, we can divide our countries in three subgroups: NHS where the situation remains stable or slightly improved (Sweden, UK, Spain), given the fact that already at the beginning of the 2000s or even at the beginning of 1990s they showed relatively good results; SHI systems (Germany, Austria and Poland) where the situation remains stable at an unsatisfactory level (e.g. day cases of cataract surgery) or it has worsened (in particular in reference to hospitalization rates that have increased); and France and Italy, where indicators show an improvement in the appropriateness of their hospital functioning. The only major exception to these trends is represented by caesarean births rate that have increased in all the countries studied.

Focusing on different indicators (ranging from the level of inpatient expenditure to home and residential care for the elderly, to mammography screening and children immunization), Sweden, again, is the country that seems to have the best system fostering out-patient care, de-hospitalization and prevention. For this set of issues the comparison between NHS and SHI systems proves to be less relevant (Table 10.2).

Table 10.2   Out-patient care and prevention

	Total inpatient expenditure as % of total health expenditure			Home and residential care LTC coverage (% of 65+ beneficiaries)		% of women 50–69 screened for mammography			Immunization: D.T.P. – % of children immunized		
	1990	2000	2010	1995	2005	1987[a]	2005	2010	1990	2000	2010
Sweden	55.2	51.7	29.4	20.4	15.7	n.g.	83.6	n.g.	99.0	98.0	98.0
UK	n.g.	n.g.	n.g.	18.1	16.1	15.5	75.1	73.4	81.0	91.0	96.0
Spain	44.1	28.2	28.4	3.9	8.3	11.2	n.g.	73.3	93.0	95.0	97.0
Italy	42.9	43.2	45.8	4.0	4.8	16.2	60.9	70.0	83.0	87.0	96.0
France	44.3	38.3	37.5	4.8	8.1	23.1	72.8	75.4	95.0	97.0	99.0
Germany	34.7	35.4	34.3	10.6	10.5	26.9	n.g.	54.3	94.1	90.0	93.0
Austria	39.8	39.5	42.0	16	17.8	n.g.	80.2	n.g.	90.0	81.0	83.0
Poland	n.g.	29.1	34.0	n.g.	0.7	n.g.	24.8	58.1	96.0	98.0	99.0

[a] Eurobarometer data from 1987.
Source: OECD Health database (2013); Ranci and Pavolini (2012) for LTC coverage.

Sweden and the UK function very well practically for all indicators used. Austria and Spain show relatively high scores on all indicators but one, namely, the high level of inpatient expenditure in the Austrian case and the relatively low level of LTC (long-term care) coverage in the Spanish case. Germany and France find themselves in a relative good situation but they have problems in terms of LTC coverage (France) and screening (Germany). LTC service provision is probably the weakest point for both Italy and Poland.

Looking at trends for the data available over the last two decades, again three NHS (Sweden, Spain and the UK), together with France, improved the coverage level of prevention and shifted expenditure from hospital to out-patient care, although in these countries there was either a diminution of LTC services coverage (but they had already some of the highest coverage rates in the middle of the 1990s, as in the UK or Sweden) or a robust increase (but starting from very low levels, as in Spain). The four remaining countries share growing prevention coverage rates over time, but a stable level in the relative weight of inpatient expenditure as well as in terms of LTC needs coverage (although it should be added that in the case of Austria and Germany reforms in the early 1990s had increased very substantially public intervention in this area).

It is complicated to identify health outcomes which are related to the functioning of the HCS and not too much to other factors (e.g. life styles, level of economic development, etc.). We have decided to avoid one typical outcome indicator used in many studies (for instance WHO, 2000), which is life expectancy, because it is difficult to understand to what extent variations over time and across countries of this indicator are related to the effectiveness of the HCS or, instead, to other factors (Navarro, 2002). Therefore we have focused on six indicators. The first two measure the survival rates to severe diseases (breast cancer[2] and acute myocardial infarction); two others are dedicated to the area of pregnancy (neonatal and maternal mortality). The fifth is dedicated to amenable mortality to health care,[3] as measured by Nolte and McKee (2011). The last one is related to life expectancy at 65 years old and, given the fact that old age is the time of life when more diseases and need for chronic care tend to concentrate, it is probably the type of life expectancy indicator that better catches the role of the HCS.

As Table 10.3 shows, looking at all the indicators Sweden remains the best performing country, followed, in this case, by Austria. The UK, Spain, France, Germany and Poland show in general lower performance levels than the Swedish and Austrian ones. In an intermediate situation we find Italy.

Overall indicators show improvements over the last two decades practically for all countries: life expectancy at 65 y.o., breast cancer and infarction survival rates increased, while neonatal and maternal mortality rate decreased. In some countries, the improvements have been quite relevant. For instance in Poland the neonatal and maternal mortality rates decreased quite dramatically.

Table 10.3 Health final outcomes

	Breast cancer five year relative survival rate (age-stand. rate - %)			Admission-based AMI 30 day in-hospital mortality rate (age-sex stand. rate - %)			Neonatal mortality rate (Deaths per 1000 live births)			Maternal mortality rate (Deaths per 100000 live births)			Life expectancy at age 65 (years)			Amenable mortality to health care		Average Score (1-100)
	1995	2000	2005	2000	2005	2010	1990	2000	2010	1990	2000	2010	1990	2000	2010	1997–07*	2007**	2007–10
Sweden	81.8	85.3	86.0 / 16.7[a]	6.2	3.9	3.6	3.5	2.3	1.6	3.2	4.4	2.6	17.5	18.7	20.0	-3.3	68.1	88.4
UK	72.2	78.4	81.3 / 22.1[a]	n.a.	6.3	5.2	4.5	3.9	2.9	8.0	6.8	5.0	16.3	17.6	19.8	-5.2	86.1	67.7
Spain	n.a.	n.a.	20.3[a]	9.4	6.6	5.6	5.0	2.8	2.1	5.5	3.5	4.1	17.5	19.0	20.9	-2.7	70.4	70.8
Italy	n.a.	n.a.	22.8[a]	n.a.	4.0	3.7	6.3	3.2	2.3	8.6	3.0	3.4	17.3	18.8	20.5	-4.7	65.1	78.3
France	n.a.	82.8	.. / 20.4[a]	n.a.	n.a.	n.a.	3.6	2.9	2.5	10.4	6.5	7.7	18.7	19.5	21.3	-2.8	58.8	70.2
Germany	74.0	77.4	83.3 / 21.5[a]	n.a.	7.3	6.8	3.7	2.7	2.3	9.1	5.6	5.5	16.4	18.1	19.6	-3.7	81.2	67.9
Austria	76.1	80.6	81.2 / 26.9[a]	11.1	6.8	5.7	4.4	3.3	2.7	6.6	2.6	1.3	16.8	18.4	20.0	-4.8	69.4	82.6
Poland	n.a.	70.2	70.2 / 28.3[a]	n.a.	5.7	3.9	11.5	5.6	3.5	12.8	7.9	2.2	14.6	15.9	17.7	-2.9	137.8	67.4

[a] Ratio between (age standardized) breast cancer deaths/incidence of breast cancer.
* Age-standardized rates per 100,000 population.
** Annual change in amenable mortality between 1997 and 2007.
Source: OECD (2013); data on amenable mortality are taken from Nolte and McKee (2011).

If we look at reforms introduced in the last two decades and possible connections to the medical objectives, the information and analyses contained in the country chapters offer us a clear answer in most cases: in general there was no direct and relevant effect of rescaling and privatization, whereas the effect of managerialization deserves more detailed considerations. The reasons why this is the case are manifold.

First, certain countries (as Sweden) have chosen to follow the path of incremental reforms in a system already working relatively well over time: the result is that reforms helped the 'maintenance' of health care, fostering a gradual improvement on most health outcome indicators, without any relevant medical breakthrough.

Second, as shown in the previous chapter, usually the drivers for reforms were different from medical ones (e.g. cost containment, etc.) and they were not directly connected to medial objectives, if not as a general overarching goal.

Third, among the four objectives studied here, the medical ones are those most influenced by developments in medical technology (Blank and Burau, 2010), which means that attention in this area has to be paid to investment and, again, as shown already in the previous chapter, there have been constant increases of expenditure over time in the last two decades.

Country chapters show that, if privatization and rescaling did not affect directly medical objectives, managerialization has meant, in many countries, a closer look and attention to hospital appropriateness as well as the diffusion of guidelines and regulatory authorities, controlling, observing and proposing more effective practices. In this sense also the common trend of (at least regulatory) recentralization, taking place in many countries, has had a positive effect on medical objectives, given the possibility for national agencies and observatories to promote better organizational and professional practices.

The political objectives

Each HCS has to deal with the guarantee of its responsiveness and the satisfaction, based on freedom, comfort and decent working conditions, for patients and professionals.

Starting from the users' point of view, we have used a series of indicators that show, on one side, how citizens are satisfied with their HCS and for which aspects; on the other side, how the issue of waiting lists is affecting users.

Table 10.4 is based on Eurobarometer data. The first important element that arises from the table is the fact that most countries have very high levels of citizens' satisfaction with their HCS. Apart from Italy (54 per cent) and, most of all, Poland (30 per cent), in all other countries at least four individuals out of five declare their satisfaction, with Austria ranking on top (95 per cent). Moreover, the last fifteen years saw an increase in individual satisfaction everywhere, which was particularly intense in three of

Table 10.4 Quality of the health care system perceived by citizens

	% of individuals who declare								
	Good quality of hospital care	Easy access to hospital care	Hospital care not (very) affordable	Good medical and surgical specialists	Specialists not (very) affordable	Good family doctors or GPs	Easy access to family doctors or GPs	Satisfaction with their health care system	
	2007							1994	2010
Sweden	90.0	68.0	8.0	71.0	7.0	68.0	63.0	67.3	90.0
UK	77.0	80.0	7.0	71.0	13.0	88.0	86.0	48.1	86.0
Spain	82.0	84.0	10.0	81.0	22.0	89.0	94.0	35.6	81.0
Italy	63.0	69.0	23.0	75.0	49.0	77.0	83.0	16.3	54.0
France	83.0	80.0	17.0	87.0	48.0	93.0	93.0	65.1	91.0
Germany	79.0	87.0	24.0	77.0	28.0	88.0	94.0	66.0	86.0
Austria	92.0	92.0	11.0	87.0	39.0	93.0	94.0	63.3	95.0
Poland	42.0	69.0	21.0	57.0	31.0	73.0	90.0	n.g.	30.0

Source: Data from European Commission (1998); Eurobarometer (2007; 2010).

the NHS: the UK, Spain and Italy. National statistics, presented in various country chapters of the book, confirm this trend of increasing satisfaction. In England national data show that satisfaction with the NHS increased from 35 per cent in 1997 to 70 per cent in 2010 and, in 2009, 92 per cent of people that were inpatients in NHS hospitals rated the quality of care positively, with the share of people giving an excellent rating increasing from 38 per cent to 44 per cent (2002–2009) (see Chapter 2). The same took place in Spain: the percentage of individuals satisfied with their NHS increased since 1995, especially in the more recent years. The individuals stating that the entire system needed to be reformed dropped from 10 per cent in the 1990s to 3 per cent in 2010 (see Chapter 3).

The only main exception to this trend is Poland (see Chapter 8): on one side, data on the early 1990s are not available; on the other side, still in 2011 a large majority of individuals (72 per cent) believed that the quality of healthcare services was not changing and it was relatively poor.

A Eurobarometer survey of 2007 helps us to better understand what are the functions and aspects of HCS that seem more problematic or positively judged by citizens. Three types of services were considered: hospital, specialist and primary care ones. In relation to these services the quality, the accessibility and the affordability were considered. Practically each country shows a peculiar position in respect to the others. Poland is the most problematic case, presenting levels of relative satisfaction only in terms of quality and accessibility to family doctors and, to a minor extent, the accessibility to hospitals. Spain, the UK and Austria are on the opposite side of the continuum with high levels of satisfaction for all the services and dimensions, with the sole exception of the affordability of specialist care in the latter country. The issue of affordability of services (first of all specialist care) is very relevant also in Germany and, especially, in France and Italy. This seems to be the price that German and French citizens have to pay to enjoy a HCS evaluated as good and easily accessible. The Italian situation seems slightly different, given the fact that affordability problems are not always matched by a hospital system judged as good and easily accessible. Sweden seems a context where good hospital quality and low affordability problems, go along with relatively still positive but less satisfactory evaluation of accessibility (see below on the issue of waiting lists) and quality of specialists and family doctors.

A second main issue related to users, already partially discussed in Table 10.4, is the ways and times of access to health care services: waiting lists have been a major concern for many HCS in Europe, in particular for NHS ones. It is difficult to investigate waiting lists length and trends over time due to the lack of comparative data and the difficulty to collect them. Two publications can help us to shed some light on the issue. The Health Consumer Powerhouse (HCP) produces a report named 'Euro Health Consumer Index' since the middle of the 2000s, that measures both the level of patient rights and information[4] and the waiting times treatment[5] in many European countries. The OECD published a comparative report in 2013 on waiting lists policies that is helpful also in providing some quantitative data (Siciliani et al., 2013).

Looking at Table 10.5, it results clear that, if differences among countries are relevant both in terms of patients' rights and information, the situation is even more polarized in terms of waiting lists treatment. In terms of patients' rights the UK is the country that ensures them best. In the opposite situation stands Spain. Austria, France, Sweden and Italy find themselves in a relatively similar intermediate position, whereas Germany and Poland have a slightly lower rank. In terms of waiting times there is a clear cut differentiation between the German SHI countries (Austria and Germany) and most NHS (Sweden, the UK and Spain), together with Poland, with the former having quite limited problems compared to the latter. Italy and France stand in the middle. Apart from Poland (where 4.1 per cent of adults reported unmet medical needs due to waiting lists in 2011), accessibility problems do not seem to reach the point of not allowing individuals to be cared for: EU-SILC data estimate that 1 per cent or less of the population might find itself in such a harsh situation.

The data presented by OECD (Table 10.6) confirm (with all the caution possible, given the heterogeneity in the sources and information) that waiting lists are mainly a problem for NHS countries. For instance, when comparing Sweden and the UK with France and Germany, there are quite strong differences in terms of waiting times for elective surgery.

If HCP indexes and OECD information tend to converge in terms of mapping how different European health care systems score in relation to

Table 10.5 Waiting lists and patient rights

	Health consumer power house index: patient rights and information (max. positive score: 175)[a]			Health consumer power house index: waiting times for treatment[6] (max. positive score: 200)[a]			Self reported unmet medical needs due to waiting lists[b] (EU-SILC)		
	2005	2009	2012	2005	2009	2012	1990	2005	2011
Sweden	100	117	141	83	100	83	n.a.	2.0	0.8
UK	83	123	160	83	83	117	n.a.	2.2	1.1
Spain	75	84	102	150	100	83	n.a.	0.6	0.2
Italy	67	110	131	117	117	133	n.a.	1.4	0.8
France	100	143	136	200	183	133	n.a.	0.3	0.4
Germany	100	123	117	200	183	167	n.a.	1.6	0.7
Austria	n.a.	149	141	n.a.	167	167	n.a.	0.1	0.1
Poland	58	117	126	67	100	83	n.a.	2.4	4.1

Source: [a] Health Consumer Powerhouse (2005; 2009; 2012); [b] Eurostat – EU-SILC (2005; 2011).

Table 10.6 Information on waiting lists problems in different European health care systems

Waiting time of 4 months or more for elective surgery (% of individuals):	
Sweden	22% (2010)
United Kingdom	41% (2005); 21% (2010)
France	7% (2010)
Germany	6% (2005); 0% (2010)
Waiting time of more than 3 months in Sweden in specialist care and 42 procedures (%):	25.2% (2008); 10.1% (2011)
Waiting time of more than 3 months in England (% of individuals):	49.6% (1995); 49.5% (2000); 9.0% (2010)
Median waiting time for elective admissions in England (weeks):	15.9 (1993); 12.9 (2000); 8.5 (2010)
Average waiting times for visits to specialists in Spain (days):	81 (2003); 59 (2009)
Average waiting times for surgical procedures in Spain (days):	77 (2003); 67 (2009)
Waiting time of more than 2 months for a specialist visit in Spain (% of individuals):	29% (2006); 37% (2009)
Waiting time of 1–3 months for a diagnostic test in Italy (% of individuals):	21.1% (2009)
Waiting time of more than 3 months for a diagnostic test in Italy (% of individuals):	13.6% (2009)

Source: OECD (2013).

accessibility, there are differences in the interpretation of trends over time. The picture coming out of HCP analysis is quite less straightforward (in terms of reduction of waiting times), than the one offered by the OECD report. In the HCP study improvement from 2005 to 2012 took place only in Italy and the UK, whereas in the other countries the situation either remained stable or it even deteriorated. The OECD research shows improvements for all the countries where data on trends over time are available. This is the case for the United Kingdom and, more specifically, England, but also Germany and Sweden, with Spain showing a more complex situation (some indicators improved, while other ones did not).

The data and information included in the country chapters of this volume tend to support more the view and interpretations of trends over time offered by the OECD.

The general increase in citizens' satisfaction and the lowering of accessibility problems (waiting lists) in many countries seem to be related to reforms introduced in the last years even if precise evaluations are often quite difficult for obvious methodological issues. Apart from specific reforms, as reported in country chapters, increases in public expenditure, for instance in England and Spain, were positively and strongly associated with satisfaction. In Sweden, a light increase in the general level of satisfaction with the health care system between 2008 and 2011 can be traceable, as a plausible, albeit not certain, result of the primary care choice and waiting-time guarantee reforms. The increase in satisfaction of Swedish citizens is probably connected also to further improvements thereafter: waiting times for appointments with GPs improved significantly after these reforms. In England waiting times went down after a decade of investments and new regulation aiming at solving the accessibility problem. The chapter on Spain helps us to shed light on the more mixed results in terms of waiting lists: if until 2009 the changes in the NHS improved the quality and the accessibility, budget cuts since the onset of the crisis have increased again waiting list problems. In Poland, and to a minor extent in Italy, reforms have not been able to tackle the long waiting lists problems in the public sector: they have mainly tried to solve accessibility issues by fostering the 'exit' of patients to the private sector, especially for specialist and diagnostic care. In both countries specific legislation gave more room to private specialists and providers also in order to cut down waiting lists (see also on this point Siciliani et al., 2013). Also in France the reforms related to gatekeeping functions and the attempts to better regulate specialists' activity saw, as a by-product, a possible deterioration in terms of waiting times in the outpatient sector. Another result, particularly dramatic in Italy and France, has been the high economic costs associated to the access to specialist care, as already discussed in Table 10.3.

As already stated, health care systems are not only complex institutions dealing with patients and citizens, but they are also powerful organizations providing work opportunities for a vast and diversified array of occupations and professions. Especially in post-industrial societies, as European ones are becoming, the employment in this field is increasingly relevant (Table 10.7). In Sweden almost one worker out of six is employed in health or social care. In the UK and Germany between 12 and 13 per cent of workers find employment in this sector, whereas in Italy (7.4 per cent), Spain (6.3 per cent) and Poland (5.7 per cent) the figures are quite lower. In the middle we find France and Austria with around 10 per cent of employment in health and social care.

Moreover, trends over the last two decades show, for almost all countries, (with the exceptions of the ones at both ends of the ranking, Sweden and Poland) a robust increase in the relative incidence of health and social care on total employment.

Studying workers' conditions in health care is very relevant not only for reasons related to the more general structure of the labour market, but also for the functioning of the HCS in terms of quality, effectiveness and efficiency of provision. Given the fact that health care is a labour-intensive

Table 10.7 Total health and social employment (as a percentage of total civilian employment)

	1990	2000	2010
Sweden	n.a.	18.5	15.7
United Kingdom	8.8	11.0	13.3
Spain	4.4	5.4	6.3
Italy	5.8	6.2	7.4
France	8.2	8.9	9.5
Germany	7.9	10.0	11.9
Austria	n.a.	8.0	9.7
Poland	n.a.	6.5	5.7

Source: OECD database (2012).

sector, as well as a capital-intensive one, employment plays a fundamental role.

Focusing on the main professionals in the sector, doctors, nurses and midwives, we notice quite relevant differences among the various countries. Austria is by far the case with the highest diffusion of physicians in the population (4.7), whereas the UK (2.7) and, above all, Poland have the lowest, with all the other countries finding themselves in the middle (from 3.4 in France to 3.8 in Sweden). One factor explaining a large diffusion of doctors licensed to practice in Austria is to be found in the educational system: until 2005, Austria followed the principle of open admission to medical studies.

In general, the relative diffusion of doctors does not seem associated to the type of HCS (NHS vs. SHI). The same consideration applies to the density of nurses and midwives in the population. Germany (11.1) and Sweden (11.9) score the highest values, followed by the UK (10.3). In the Southern European countries (Italy 6.6 and Spain 5.1) and Poland (5.8) the relative diffusion is quite lower. In the middle we find Austria and France.

Given the fact that there are often relevant differences among countries in terms of density of physicians and nurses/midwifes, the ratio between these two professional groups changes quite strongly. Sweden, the UK and Germany are countries where there are relatively more nurses and midwives per doctor, whereas Spain, Italy and Austria show quite lower ratios (in Spain there are 1.4 nurses and midwives for each doctor). Poland and France stick in the middle.

In all the countries but Sweden and the UK, this ratio has grown over time and there seems to be a shift in the HCS to less doctor-centred and increased presence of other health professions-based care models, at least from a strictly quantitative point of view. This conclusion can be deduced by looking at the variations in the last decade in the number of physicians, nurses and midwives. In all countries, apart from the two just quoted, there were more pronounced increases of nurses and midwives than doctors.

More in general the professional occupation in the sector grew strongly in the last decade, especially for nurses and midwives, at paces often much stronger than those of the general employment level (see the last three columns on the right of Table 10.8). For example in the UK the overall employment grew by 4.7 per cent between 2000 and 2009; meanwhile physicians increased by around 26 per cent and midwives by 16 per cent. The only two main outlier countries in this picture that failed to witness a robust health care labour market growth were Italy and Poland. In Italy if there was a robust increase in the number of nurses and midwives (also related to the low level of density in 2000), there was practically no change in the absolute number of physicians. Even more pronounced is the Polish specificity: the 2000s witnessed a decrease in the number of doctors (–2.6 per cent) and only a relatively limited growth of nurses and midwives (if compared to what happened in other countries or to the overall Polish labour market).

If health care professionals' employment grew in the 2000s, it is important also to understand what happened to professionals' working conditions.

If we start by looking at salaries and income, with all the cautions due to missing data, the trend for doctors seems to be often a quite robust increase in income, with the partial exception of the UK and Austria, where income grew for certain types of doctors (for example self-employed GPs in the UK) but not for others (for example self-employed GPs in Austria).

The data on nurses are unfortunately more limited and it is difficult to identify overall trends: for the few countries where data are available over time what can be noticed is also an increase in salaries.

In general it can be noticed how differentiated incomes are among different countries and professionals' profiles (self-employed vs. employees; GPs vs. specialists; doctors vs. nurses). In general NHS systems (apart from the UK) tend to remunerate doctors less than SHI systems, but this situation

Table 10.8   Doctors, nurses and midwives in European health care systems

	Density per 1000 population (2009)		Nurses/ Physicians	Relative variation in the number of (2000–09)		
	Physicians	Nurses and Midwives	ratio (2009)	Physicians	Nurses and Midwives	Overall employment
Sweden	3.8	11.9	3.1	+26.1%	+16.4%	+5.4%
UK	2.7	10.3	3.8	+43.9%	+13.7%	+4.7%
Spain	3.7	5.1	1.4	+37.0%	+52.4%	+21.7%
Italy	3.5	6.6	1.9	–0.1%	+23.9%	+9.1%
France	3.4	8.9	2.6	+8.2%	+38.0%	+9.8%
Germany	3.6	11.1	3.1	+11.1%	+14.9%	+4.7%
Austria	4.7	7.9	1.7	+29.9%	+33.0%	+8.8%
Poland	2.2	5.8	2.6	–2.6%	+5.2%	+10.4%

Source: WHO database (2013).

might also depend on the broader diffusion of self-employed physicians in the latter.

If we concentrate on salaried specialist doctors, where present, their income is relatively more similar (for instance between Italy, Germany, Spain and, partially, France) with the exception of Poland on the one side (with the lowest salaries) and the UK on the other (with the highest ones).

Nurses' incomes tend to be more similar across countries: only the polish case is different from the others, but the salary gap is less pronounced than the one among doctors (Table 10.9).

Other information on changes in working conditions can be detected by using Eurostat Labour Force Surveys (EU-LFS) data over time. EU-LFS microdata allow for focusing on two specific occupational groups: 'health professionals' (mainly composed by doctors) and 'health nurses and midwives'. Tables 10.10 and 10.11 show which are and how some relevant aspects of the professionals' work have changed over time.[7]

In relation to health professionals, the SHI share common features: a relatively high use of atypical contracts (part-time and temporary contracts), self-employment (between 40 and 49 per cent), unpaid overtime and very long hours of work (between 43 and 46 per week). These characteristics explain also why on average SHI physicians are paid more than many of their counterparts in other countries. On the contrary, health professionals in NHS countries tend to be less exposed to atypical contracts, even if these contracts are quite present. In the vast majority of cases they are employees (with the exception of Italy); only in a minority of situations they work unpaid overtime; and the average number of hours worked is

Table 10.9 Health care professionals remuneration (income, US$ PPP)

	General Practitioners		Specialist Physicians		Nurses [b]
	2000	2010	2000	2010	2010
Austria	106202[a]	106987[a]	156864[a]	171077[a]	n.a.
France	56767[a]	81689[a]	89251[a]	137829[a]	36292
				84372[b]	
Germany	113310[a]	139724[a]	154711[a]	189109[a]	43048
				90449[b]	
Italy	75142[a]	84321[a]	79231[b]	94019[b]	36111
Poland [b]	n.a.	45593	18259	33582	23219
Spain [b]	n.a.	92566	n.a.	99604	43957
Sweden [b]	62556	74512	71110	80423	n.a.
UK	127230[a]	161585[a]	n.a.	123402[b]	51673
		88665[b]			

[a] Self-employed; [b] Salaried.
Source: OECD database (2012).

Table 10.10 Working conditions of 'health professionals'

	Part-time workers (%)		Workers with temporary contracts (%)		Self-employed workers (%)		Workers working unpaid overtime (%)		Average N° working hours	
	2000	2010	2000	2010	2000	2010	2000	2010	2000	2010
Sweden	9.3	17.9	18.4	16.5	9.8	9.2	n.a.	7.8	38.4	38.6
UK	20.1	19.9	17.2	7.8	34.1	26.9	n.a.	n.a.	44.7	40.7
Spain	6.2	11.2	19.5	20.5	21.5	18.6	n.a.	3.1	39.5	37.2
Italy	6.6	12.4	5.1	6.4	39.7	44.1	n.a.	5.1	38.1	38.1
Germany	13.2	11.5	16.5	17.7	48.1	45.3	n.a.	12.7	45.2	45.1
France	17.1	21.9	10.7	14.7	56.5	48.8	n.a.	6.7	41.9	45.5
Austria	17.7	18.6	9.5	13.5	48.8	39.8	n.a.	18.8	43.0	43.7

Source: own re-elaboration of EU-LFS microdata (2000; 2009).

Table 10.11 Working conditions of health nurses and midwives

	Part-time workers (%)		Workers with temporary contracts (%)		Workers working unpaid overtime (%)		Average N° working hours	
	2000	2010	2000	2010	2000	2010	2000	2010
Sweden	39.8	42.1	6.9	9.2	n.a.	2.4	34.0	35.1
UK	39.4	31.4	6.4	2.2	n.a.	n.a.	33.9	34.7
Spain	3.7	8.0	21.2	29.3	n.a.	0.3	37.9	35.2
Italy	5.5	11.6	5.0	12.6	n.a.	3.7	36.3	35.0
Germany	28.3	32.0	14.1	11.4	n.a.	4.7	33.9	34.7
France	22.9	27.4	8.8	8.5	n.a.	16.1	31.3	35.6
Austria	31.6	38.9	3.3	6.4	n.a.	2.4	34.8	34.0

Source: own re-elaboration of EU-LFS microdata (2000; 2010).

around or below 40 per week. The last decade witnessed some changes: an overall increase in atypical contracts in many countries (with the exception of Germany, where the situation remained still, and the UK, where there was a sharp decrease in temporary contract holders); a decrease of self-employment (with Italy as the main exception); and a substantial stability in the weekly hours workload.

The nurses and midwives world is quite more homogeneous in terms of average number of hours worked per week (around 35), the limited presence of unpaid overtime situations (with the partial exception of France), the consistent presence of atypical working conditions (with some countries fostering more part-time work and others temporary contracts). The only main change over time has been the diffusion of atypical work.

The information contained in the country chapters mainly support the picture described so far through the data and provide richer information about the role played by different types of reforms on the labour force working in the sector.

There is already a quite broad literature studying the effects of managerialization on health care professionals, focusing mainly on doctors (Numerato et al., 2012). Even if this literature seems to propose possible different interpretations of the impact of managerialization on professions, ranging from 'colonization' to 'hybridization' (Kuhlmann, 2011), there seems to be a common element to most empirical analysis: the labour conditions are changing, not only in terms of work contracts (as discussed just above), but also in terms of less professional autonomy and new demands in terms of documentation and administrative work due to higher pressures for transparency, leading to heavier work load and increased stress. As shown in Chapter 1 dedicated to Sweden, stress levels of doctors increased significantly between 1992 and 2010: doctors complained about lack of support from their supervisors, lost responsibilities, too little time to take part of new scientific evidence. In France there was a decline in overall satisfaction among health professionals with many of them not having enough time to accomplish their work (surveys show increases of not satisfied professionals from 32 per cent in 1998 to 41 per cent in 2003). In Germany managerialization had a great impact on the power distribution, with working conditions of hospital staff deteriorating and professionals becoming more and more engaged in management activities: in 2006 doctors formally protested in relation to the financial constraints in the health care system and the growth of bureaucratic activity (see Chapter 6). Pressures and burdens on health care professionals are also confirmed in the few existing studies on the Austrian case. Brunner et al. (2010) report that about half of respondents to a specific survey on the issue of satisfaction referred to staff shortages and bureaucratic burdens, connected to managerialization, as the main pressures and sources of stress. In a report by the Chamber of Doctors, 80 per cent of respondents referred to pressures arising from staff shortages, about half to pressures arising from administrative burdens (Ärztekammer, 2011). The mix between low wages and increasing managerial control is fostering in Poland, on one side, protests and strikes, on the other, emigration of healthcare professionals.

Matching the information on managerialization with the ones on professionals' income tells us that most health care systems have probably tried to mitigate the negative effects of managerialization on professionals' satisfaction with increases in salaries and earnings. In Spain working conditions and salaries improved due to this reason and also as a result of the 'race' between the ACs for better labour conditions and political legitimacy (see Chapter 3).

The country studies also tell us that in many HCS the recent economic crisis and the following austerity plans mean pay freezes and cost-cutting which are likely to deteriorate the working conditions of health staff. Budget cuts have led or might soon lead to tensions between professional staff, health care consumers and the public bodies governing the system (as in Spain or England).

The social objectives

While European health care systems are quite distinct with regard to the relative importance of Bismarckian, Beveridgian or market orientations, they all attempt to guarantee equal access to health care for the entire population. More specifically, health care systems aim at equal access for equal need, irrespective of other characteristics such as income, gender, residence or ethnicity. Generally, the objective refers to a broadly defined package of acute health care services, while explicit or implicit limitations are more common for services such as rehabilitation, aids or dental care. Comparative studies on access to health care indicate that most countries are more successful in achieving equal access to GP care in the outpatient sector, whereas considerable pro-rich inequalities have been identified for access to specialists.

A recent study of 19 OECD countries (Devaux and de Looper, 2012) and an earlier study covering 21 OECD countries (van Doorslaer and Masseria, 2004) identify relatively little inequities for GP consultations (after standardization for need). Only a few countries show either a slight pro-poor (Denmark in the 2012 study) or pro-rich inequities (Poland or France in the 2012 study). The picture is different for specialist care in the outpatient sector. After standardization for need, those in higher income groups have better access to specialist care across most countries. Italy (in the 2004 study) and France and Spain have been identified as countries where the inequity is particularly strong. One of the few exceptions is the UK with relatively little inequity, a result, however, that stands in contrast to some UK studies. Even sharper pro-rich inequalities in health care use are identified for dental care, a result that also applies for the UK. With regard to hospital care, the picture is less clear, not least for methodological reasons. Overall, while the two studies differ in methodology and data sources, the conclusions in terms of equity in access to health care are quite consistent and also indicate – with a few exceptions – considerable stability over the past decade.

One reason for inequalities is non-take-up of health services when in need. According to self-reports, across the eight countries, between less than 1 per cent and almost 10 per cent of the population did not have a medical examination because of financial reasons, because it is too far to travel or because of waiting times (Table 10.12). The incidence is below 2 per cent in 2005 and also in 2010 in Austria, France and Spain. It is above 3 per cent in Italy and Poland in 2010, but also in Germany in 2005. Self-reported unmet need is far more common in the lowest income quintile. Most pronounced are respective differences for France, Germany and Italy. Most outstanding reductions in unmet need between 2005 and 2010 occurred for Germany

Table 10.12   Inequalities in self-reported unmet need

	Self-reported unmet needs for medical examination: too expensive, too far to travel or waiting list		Self-reported unmet needs for medical examination: I income quintile (per cent)		Self-reported unmet needs for medical examination: V income quintile (per cent)		Self-reported unmet needs for medical examination: ratio I – V income quintile	
	2005	2010	2005	2010	2005	2010	2005	2010
Austria	0.5	0.6	DNS	DNS	DNS	DNS	DNS	DNS
France	1.7	2.0	4.0***	5.2***	0.4***	0.6***	10.0***	8.7***
Germany	9.4	1.9	18.2***	4.1***	4.6***	0.7***	4.0***	5.9***
Italy	4.9	5.0	10.0***	9.1***	2.0***	1.6***	5.0***	5.7***
Poland	9.9	8.5	14.1***	13.1***	6.2***	4.9***	2.3***	2.7***
Spain	1.2	0.3	DNS	DNS	DNS	DNS	DNS	DNS
Sweden	2.6	1.8	3.1**	3.1**	1.4**	1.0**	2.2**	3.1**
United Kingdom	2.3	1.1	DNS	DNS	DNS	DNS	DNS	DNS

DNS: difference between income quintile I and income quintile V are not significant.
* Sign. <0.05; ** Sign. <0.01; *** Sign. <0.001.
Source: Eurostat (based on EU SILC).

and for Poland (but are still on relatively large levels in the latter country), while unmet needs have slightly increased in Austria and in France. As a general trend, the differences in unmet need between the lowest and the highest income quintile have increased between 2005 and 2010. The exception here is France. In this country, however, differences are still largest compared to the other countries.

Costs involved are reported as the main reason for self-reported unmet needs for medical examinations (see Table 10.13). Most importantly, it is in Germany, Italy and Poland that respondents refer to the expenses involved as a reason for unmet need. Respective levels are considerably lower in Austria, Spain, Sweden and the UK, even though Austria and Sweden have seen an increasing number of people in the lowest income quintile that report unmet need because of the expenses involved. Waiting time is relatively more important for unmet need in Sweden and the UK as well as Italy and Poland. For most countries, the data indicate a reduction in unmet need because of waiting time between 2005 and 2010, not least as a consequence of explicit policies to reduce waiting time. Poland instead has seen some growth in waiting time as a limiting factor in using medical examinations, both in lower and in upper income groups.

Private expenditure on health care, in 2010, ranges between less than 20 per cent of total health expenditure in Sweden and in the UK, and

Table 10.13 Unmet needs by reason

	too expensive				waiting list			
	2005		2010		2005		2010	
	Quintile I	Quintile V	Quintile I	Quintile V	Quintile I	Quintile V	Quintile I	Quintile V
Austria	0.7	0.1	1.6	:	0.1	0.2	0.1	0.2
France	3.6	0.2	4.8	0.3	0.3	0.2	0.3	0.2
Germany	16.4	3.0	3.1	0.2	1.3	1.5	0.6	0.5
Italy	8.0	0.7	7.2	0.7	1.9	1.2	1.8	0.9
Poland	12.2	2.5	7.1	0.8	1.6	3.6	4.8	4.0
Spain	0.9	0.1	0.3	0.1	0.8	0.5	0.1	0.0
Sweden	0.9	0.2	1.2	:	2.1	1.1	1.6	1.0
UK	0.2	0.1	0.0	:	2.2	2.1	1.5	0.8

Source: Eurostat (based on EU SILC).

between 20 per cent (Italy) and 29 per cent (Poland) in the other countries of this country sample (see Table 10.14). This is a result of a traditionally much stronger role of the state in the Beveridgian countries as compared to Bismarckian countries. These differences, however, have become less marked, not least because the largely varying emphasis on private provision of health care and the different forms of private (co)-funding of health care not so much linked to the tradition of Beveridge vs. Bismarck. With regard to out-of-pocket payments as a percentage of total health expenditure, in many countries the respective proportion was larger in 2000 compared to 1990, but smaller in 2010 compared to 2000. Most importantly, this is the case in Italy, Poland and Spain. But even in other countries, levels in 2010 are only slightly larger than in 2000. Most importantly, this development is due to the implications of the fiscal and financial crisis that have led to lower individual consumption of health care goods and services that are not covered by the public health care system.

The incidence of health expenditure on total household expenditure ranges between 1.2 per cent in the UK and 4.6 per cent in Poland (in 2005). For most countries, the range of change is relatively little between the mid 1990s and 2005 and does not allow for the identification of a clear common trend. Also in most countries, the respective incidence is larger for the highest income quintile, in particular in three Bismarckian countries, Austria, France and Germany. In Poland, another social insurance country, instead, the incidence of health expenditure is larger for the lowest income quintile.

As discussed in the introductory chapter, health care reform with a focus on rescaling, privatization or managerialization is usually aimed at a multitude of objectives. Even if, in the past two decades, the primary goal has often been cost containment and/or increasing efficiency, particular importance is repeatedly ascribed to the objective of 'equal access to health care'. Given the importance of the objective, even when specific reform agendas entail a substantial risk for access, policy makers tend to insist – explicitly or implicitly – that reform efforts will not endanger or deteriorate access to health care.

In the country analyses in this volume, territorial inequalities are the most common and most widespread concern with regard to social objectives. Variations in the density of health care provision occur across all the countries. Most importantly, many countries report a lack of GP and partly specialist practices in the more rural and remote areas, a trend that might become more pressing in many countries. As a consequence, together with the regional concentration of hospital services and specialist services, variations in travel time to access health care could grow, even if travel distance – according to EU-SILC data – currently is a smaller barrier in terms of unmet need if compared to costs involved and waiting time. Apart from the issue of deprived areas in terms of health care provision, some countries also point at huge regional variations beyond the urban rural divide.

Table 10.14 Health equity

	Out-of-pocket payments, % TEH			Public expenditure on health, % TEH			Private expenditure on health not OOP, % TEH			Incidence of health expenditure on total household exp. (%)			Incidence of health care on total household exp: I quintile			Incidence of health care on total household exp: V quintile			Incidence of health care on total household exp: ratio I – V quintile		
	'90	'00	'10	'90	'00	'10	'90	'00	'10	'94	'99	'05	'94	'99	'05	'94	'99	'05	'94	'99	'05
Austria	..	..	15.9	72.9	75.6	76.2	..	..	7.9	2.1	2.4	3.1	2.0	2.1	2.6	2.4	2.6	3.4	0.8	0.8	0.8
France	11.4	7.1	7.3	76.6	79.4	77.0	12.0	13.5	15.7	5.2	3.9	4.2	4.8	3.5	3.4	4.8	3.8	4.6	1.0	0.9	0.7
Germany	11.1	11.4	13.2	76.2	79.5	76.8	12.7	9.1	10.0	3.1	3.6	3.6	1.6	2.3	2.2	4.7	5.3	5.2	0.3	0.4	0.4
Italy	17.1	24.5	17.8	79.5	72.5	79.6	3.4	3.0	2.6	3.0	4.4	3.9	2.6	4.7	..	3.4	3.9	..	0.7	1.2	..
Poland	8.3	30.0	22.1	91.7	70.0	71.7	0.0	0.0	6.2	..	4.5	4.6	..	..	5.5	..	..	4.0	..	..	1.4
Spain	18.7	23.6	19.7	78.7	71.6	74.2	2.6	4.8	6.1	2.8	2.5	2.2	2.2	2.6	2.1	2.8	2.3	2.2	0.8	1.1	1.0
Sweden	..	16.6	16.8	89.9	84.9	81.0	..	0.0	2.2	2.0	3.0	2.3	2.4	2.2	1.9	1.8	2.4	2.0	1.4	0.9	1.0
UK	10.6	11.4	8.9	83.6	78.8	83.2	5.8	9.8	7.9	1.2	1.1	1.2	0.8	0.8	0.7	1.2	1.3	1.6	0.7	0.6	0.4

Source: Eurostat database (2013).

In Italy, regionalization has worsened a territorial divide in health care performance between the North and the South, even more so in the past decade. Similarly, Spain reports territorial inequalities not only in terms of the urban rural divide, but also related to the regionalization of health care. But also Germany reports growing territorial differentiation as a result of rescaling, in particular in outpatient care.

The importance of privatization in health care reform, and the actual characteristics of privatization vary quite considerably across the eight countries. The privatization of health care risks is most pronounced in Poland. An increasing share of the population uses private health care – if affordable – to prevent having to wait or to have access to presumably better quality health care. For others in Poland, a relatively large share of out-of-pocket payments limits access to health care, most importantly for the older low income population. The analysis for Sweden articulates concern on health care use – even though there is no evidence yet – with negative effects of the privatization of providers. As profit oriented primary care centres are mostly established in affluent areas, this might lead to further territorial inequalities.

So far, the discussion referred to reforms that had an indirect effect on issues of access to health care. Other reforms are more specifically aimed at access to health care. In Germany, in the early 2000s, a growing number of uninsured citizens have become a major equity concern. This was resolved in 2007 by implementing mandatory health insurance coverage which has almost immediately led to a substantial reduction in the number of those uninsured. This change might also explain a substantial reduction in unmet need for financial reasons between 2005 and 2010 in EU-SILC data. An example of policies specifically addressing issues of access is waiting time policies. Waiting time has become a serious concern in England and in Sweden in particular. Both these countries have implemented policies to successfully reduce waiting time. Sweden, however, reports indications that the waiting time guarantee might favour the better-off as they are more likely to exercise this new right.

In the 2000s (at least before the economic crisis started to affect health care policies and health care utilization), there is no unidirectional trend in terms of improving or worsening access to health care in the eight countries. Private expenditure on health care (as a proportion of total health expenditure) shows considerable variability, with quite significant increases in the 1990s, and more stability or even a reverse trend in the 2000s, a trend that is not least determined by the economic crisis and its impact on individual health consumption. According to EU SILC data, unmet need has not changed dramatically in any of the countries between 2005 and 2010, except for unmet need for cost reasons in Germany. But this also means that unmet need has not seen any substantial improvement. Similarly, even if comparisons across time are limited, studies on health care use do not identify any systematic change in terms inequalities in doctor consultations or health care treatment. When comparing the different reasons for unmet need, in the past decade, costs involved had more significant negative effects vis à vis waiting time and travel distance. Many country reports, however, point at increasing territorial variation and inequalities which might increase the relative importance of travel distance as a limiting factor in accessing health care.

Finally, it remains to be seen how the economic crisis and austerity policies implemented to reduce public debt and deficits will affect access to health care. There is already evidence that the crisis (and the responses to the crisis) did not only negatively affect health care services and health professionals but also patients' access to health care across Europe (e.g. HOPE, 2011; Karanikolos et al., 2013). A reduction in services and increasing out-of-pocket payments have considerably decreased access to care and the affordability of care, most importantly in countries with the most dramatic cuts in health care. Given the character of many of the austerity programmes, it is to expect that this will lead to growing inequalities in access to health care in many European countries.

The economic objectives

While social, medical and political objectives remain high on the health policy agenda, considerations of controlling costs and increasing efficiency have become key concerns in health policy development across Europe since the 1990s. (e.g. OECD, 2010; Stabile et al., 2013). In 1990, total health expenditure as a percentage of GDP was between 4.8 per cent in Poland and 8.4 per cent in Austria and in France, as compared to an OECD average of 6.9 per cent (see Table 10.15). Until 2010, all countries have seen significant increases, ranging between 2.2 percentage points in Poland and 3.7 percentage points in the UK. While recent increases in total health expenditure as a percentage of GDP are largely due to decreasing GDP, some countries

Table 10.15   Health expenditure (1990–2010)

	1990		1995		2000		2005		2010	
	PHE % TEH	TEH % GDP	PHE % TEH	TEH % GDP	PHE % TEH	TEH % GDP	PHE % TEH	TEH % GDP	PHE % TEH	TEH % GDP
Austria	72.9	8.4	73.5	9.6	75.6	10.0	75.3	10.4	76.2	11.0
France	76.6	8.4	79.7	10.4	79.4	10.1	78.8	11.2	77.0	11.6
Germany	76.2	8.3	81.4	10.1	79.5	10.4	76.6	10.8	76.8	11.6
Italy	79.5	7.7	70.8	7.2	72.5	8.0	76.2	8.9	79.6	9.3
Poland	91.7	4.8	72.9	5.5	70.0	5.5	69.3	6.2	71.7	7.0
Spain	78.7	6.5	72.2	7.4	71.6	7.2	71.0	8.3	74.2	9.6
Sweden	89.9	8.2	86.6	8.0	84.9	8.2	81.2	9.1	81.0	9.6
UK	83.6	5.9	83.9	6.8	78.8	7.0	81.7	8.2	83.2	9.6

Source: OECD database (2013).

have experienced the most significant increases in the early 1990s (such as Austria, France, Germany), others in the past decade (in Italy, Poland, Spain and Sweden) or across the past two decades (in the UK).

Public health expenditure as a share of total health expenditure is larger in Beveridgian systems than in Bismarckian systems, accounting for between 72 per cent in Poland and 83 per cent in the UK in 2010. While there have been some ups and downs in the relative shares over the past two decades, data for single countries reveal a significant trend in one direction. There was a constant, but very moderate increase in the public expenditure share in Austria, while the public share has been decreasing in Sweden. Similarly, in Spain, public shares have been decreasing. The recent increase might be largely due to the economic crisis limiting the private consumption of health care. In Poland, the public expenditure share has seen a dramatic change with the transformation, but remained relatively stable since then. And, while Italy reached the lowest level in public expenditure share in the 1990s with increasing shares since then, it is almost the reverse case in Germany.

While the relative share of public expenditure did not change dramatically, the increase in public expenditure over the past two decades is very significant in terms of per capita public health expenditure (see Table 10.16). Using US$ purchasing power parities, public expenditure on health per capita has doubled in Italy and in Sweden between 1990 and 2010, almost tripled in Austria, France and to a lesser extent in Germany, and more than tripled in Poland, Spain and the UK.

Despite advances in identifying the determinants of healthcare expenditure, the relative importance of these determinants and measuring overall efficiency of a health care system remains rather controversial, both for methodological reasons and because of data limitations (e.g. Martín et al., 2011; OECD, 2010; Smith, 2012). In the literature, various indicators have been used to assess efficiency or the potential for improving efficiency. In this analysis, given the relative importance of the inpatient sector, the

Table 10.16 Public expenditure on health/capita, US$ purchasing power parity (1990–2010)

	1990	1995	2000	2005	2010
Austria	1195	1659	2192	2639	3349
France	1106	1673	2020	2597	3061
Germany	1370	1853	2130	2577	3331
Italy	1079	1085	1497	1917	2359
Poland	264	297	407	594	995
Spain	686	860	1101	1614	2267
Sweden	1432	1510	1941	2405	3046
United Kingdom	802	1131	1446	2206	2857

Source: OECD database (2013).

number of acute care beds, occupancy rates and average length of stay in hospitals are used as major indicators for efficiency (see Table 10.17). With regard to our country sample, OECD (2012) data reveals considerable variations in these indicators. In 2010, the number of acute care hospital beds per 1,000 population ranges between 2.0 in Sweden; between 2.0 and 3.0 in Italy, Spain and the UK; 3.6 in France; 4.3 in Poland; 5.5 in Austria; and 5.7 in Germany. Across all countries, however, the number of beds has been reduced significantly, to the largest extent in Italy, Poland and Sweden, the latter country already having a relatively low number of acute care beds in 1990. Similarly, large differences but also pronounced reductions in the past two decades occur in terms of average length of stay (in acute care, for all causes of inpatient care). While average length of stay was between 6.5 days (in Sweden) and 12.8 days (in Germany) in 1990, it is between 4.6 days (in Sweden) and 7.3 days (in Germany) in 2010. Reductions have been sharper in countries with larger length of stay in 1990 (40 per cent and more in Poland, Germany and Austria), but still amounted to 25 per cent and 30 per cent in France and Sweden, respectively. While reducing average length of stay is a continuous – and in many countries on-going – process, reductions have been more pronounced in the 1990s. An exception is Poland, where reductions have been more marked in the 2000s. A third indicator of efficiency in hospital use is occupancy rates. Variations in acute care bed occupancy rates in 2010 are much smaller than for the other indicators and also compared to 1990. In 2010, occupancy rates range between 74 per cent in Poland and 79 per cent in Italy, with a substantial deviation only in the UK (almost 85 per cent occupancy rate).

An OECD (2010) study on health system efficiency concludes that efficiency estimates vary more within country groups sharing similar institutional

Table 10.17   Efficiency in hospital bed use

	Acute care beds occupancy rate			Average length of stay (acute care), all causes, days			Acute care hospital beds, per 1000		
	1990	2000	2010	1990	2000	2010	1990	2000	2010
Austria	79.1	76.8	78.4	11.0	7.6	6.6	6.8	6.1	5.5
France	77.7	75.0	75.0	7.0	5.6	5.2	n.a.	4.2	3.6
Germany	84.0	81.5	76.1	12.8	9.2	7.3	7.5	6.4	5.7
Italy	68.8	75.6	78.8	9.5	7.0	6.7	5.8	4.1	2.8
Poland	68.0	74.0	74.0	12.5	8.9	5.0	6.3	5.1	4.3
Spain	74.2	77.1	77.1	9.6	7.1	6.3	3.3	2.8	2.5
Sweden	72.3	77.5	77.5	6.5	5.3	4.6	3.9	2.5	2.0
UK	n.a.	82.3	84.3	n.a.	8.0	6.6	n.a.	3.1	2.4

Source: OECD database (2012).

characteristics than between these groups. The in-depth country analyses in this book supports this statement, at least in terms of trends. Groups of countries differ in their relative positioning, e.g. in terms of larger bed density and larger length-of-stay in Bismarckian countries. But, across groups, countries share some major trends in health expenditure development and in efficiency indicators.

Health expenditure has increased across all the eight countries, more pronounced in the 1990s except for Poland with more significant increases in the 2000s. In Europe, in 2010, growth in health spending (in real terms) is considerably lower than the 2000–2009 average (Morgan and Astolfi, 2013). Many countries have even realized an annual growth rate that came close to zero (including the UK, Austria and Poland). In France and Italy, 2010 growth rates are at around 1.5 per cent, but still moderate compared to earlier years. Some European countries, mostly those with harsh austerity programmes also affecting health care such as Estonia and Greece, have even seen a reduction in total health spending as a proportion of GDP by more than 5 per cent. In Spain, preliminary figures point at a continuation of this trend, at least for 2011. In some countries, major cuts will only become visible in the 2011 data. Very moderate growth rates in health care spending or even a reduction in health care spending in the most recent years is in some countries partly due and in other countries above all due to austerity programmes because of the economic crisis. Among the eight country group in this study this is currently most importantly the case in Spain. Apart from measures that attempt to reduce publicly funded health care or to increase the private burden in funding health care, the crisis also has an impact on the demand for health care, in particular where considerable co-payments apply or where out-of-pocket payments dominate.

But apart from these very recent developments in terms of cuts in health expenditure, there is also an overall trend of more moderate growth rates in the 2000s as compared to the 1990s (except for Poland). Apart from specific reforms, it is difficult to attribute this to single reforms emphasizing rescaling, managerialization or privatization. In reality, it is not the overall reform direction that counts, but the details of the ways in which new policies are implemented in the overall health care system. For example, the case of Sweden indicates that privatization did not lead as yet to any significant change in costs, most importantly because the particular remuneration system did not change. Italy, instead, reports quite significant increases in private health expenditure as a consequence of privatization in the 1990s. In Spain, increases in health expenditure have been mainly attributed to rescaling. Poland is an exception. It has seen a sharp increase in private health expenditure in the early 1990s after the transformation. Overall, however, the increase in health expenditure has been stronger in the 2000s as compared to the 1990s.

With regard to efficiency, country analyses have been even more cautious in drawing very general conclusions of health reforms emphasizing either rescaling, managerialization or privatization. This is partly because there usually is no simple causal relationship between a specific reform activity and one outcome parameter. At the same time, efficiency studies often use variables that are only rather vague indicators for the outcome of a health care system. For example, WHO (2001) ranks countries by using life expectancy (which is not primarily and definitely not only due to the provisions of health care systems) and salaries paid in the health care sector.

While there is a general trend in health care policies characterized as managerialization, the emphasis the eight countries put on privatization and rescaling, and the direction of respective policies, varies largely across the country group. At the same time, there is a very clear and strong common trend towards reduced bed density and reduced length-of-stay in acute care, a trend even stronger in countries with larger respective levels in 1990. This indicates that these changes are not directly linked to a specific approach in terms of privatization or rescaling, but specific efforts to reduce respective levels, attempts that are often described as part of the managerialization approach. Italy, for example, shows that there is no direct link between regionalization and efficiency, but rather it is effective managerialization that allows for providing health care more efficiently. Across the eight country group, policies that are often seen as part of managerialization, include, e.g., changes of the hospital funding regimes (with major reforms dating back to the 1990s in many cases), a strengthening of treatments on a day case basis rather than hospitalization, an improvement of the coordination between inpatient and outpatient care or an increase in occupancy rates. Respective policies are still on the agenda in most countries, in particular those where benchmarking indicates that there still is considerable room for improving efficiency.

Conclusions

This final section attempts to synthesize the results of the analysis. In doing so, it proposes three steps. In a first step, it summarizes the previous sections on how each of the eight countries performs in respect to the quadrilemma of medical, political, social and economic objectives. Then, in a second step, the situation in the eight countries will be framed in a broader European and OECD country context. In a third step, this final section considers how the various dimensions of performance have changed over time and how this development was shaped by reforms emphasizing rescaling, privatization and managerialization.

Table 10.18 reports the standardized scores[8] each HCS has on the base of the quadrilemma. In relation to political objectives, following the discussion above, users and workers have been separated. The last column on the right reports the public per capita expenditure on health care, expressed in terms of PPP. Deriving standardized scores allows us to summarize rather

Table 10.18 A general overview of the performance of the eight countries

	Medical objectives	Political objectives: users	Political objectives: workers	Economic objectives	Social objectives	Economic resources: public HCE P-C PPP
Sweden	0.90	0.16	0.35	0.85	0.51	0.50
UK	0.00	0.59	-0.15	0.79	1.19	0.25
Spain	0.38	-0.40	0.00	0.11	0.44	-0.50
Italy	0.10	-0.42	-0.56	0.08	-0.42	-0.38
France	0.20	0.46	0.38	0.01	-0.62	0.51
Germany	-0.24	0.32	0.60	-1.09	-0.28	0.86
Austria	-0.10	0.86	0.29	-0.56	0.36	0.88
Poland	-0.80	-1.38	-0.67	-0.19	-1.19	-2.12

Source: own calculation based on the previous tables from the present chapter.

complex issues. However, there are important limitations that have to be considered in any interpretation. The results produced largely depend on the variables chosen, the extent to which variables in one group might compensate for each other, and the way in which they are standardized. Hence, such scores can provide a preliminary picture of how well countries are performing with regard to different policy objectives, and over time. But deriving policy conclusions just from these scores would be too simplistic and often misguiding. Therefore, the discussion in this section combines quantitative information with the richness of information provided in the country chapters.

When using the standardized scores for studying the quadrilemma of objectives, the limited correlation between health expenditure and major objectives comes at first sight. Traditional SHI countries (Germany Austria and, partially, France) spend more than the other ones, but they do not necessarily obtain better results. Germany and Austria, both beyond average spending, score relatively well in terms of political objectives and – in the case of Austria – in terms of social objectives, while they are not perform-ing particularly well in terms of medical objectives and efficiency, given the amount of resources spent. Larger levels of spending correlate with relatively positive results in all objectives, but the social objectives. But if we com-pare France and Sweden, two countries which practically spend the same in per capita terms, the latter performs the same or quite better in almost all objectives, except political objectives referring to the user. In the fourth SHI country, Poland, performance is below average for almost all indicators. However, the country is in a different situation compared to all the others, in terms of the transformation in the 1990s and because of a comparatively low level of funding that has an impact on the functioning of the system.

Among NHS countries the amount of public resources appears more relevant in determining how well the HCS functions: at least it helps to differentiate between the UK and Sweden, on the one side, and the two Mediterranean countries on the other. Italy seems the worst off among the four countries, showing problems in terms of political and social objectives, whereas Spain, even if spending less than Italy, has mainly problems in terms of users' political objectives. Sweden seems the best performing country, followed by the UK, which has some problems in terms of political objectives.

In a second step, the eight countries are compared with a series of other OECD countries (Table 10.20): practically most of the EU countries (excluding the three Baltic States, Luxemburg, Cyprus, Malta, Greece, Slovakia and Slovenia), plus Norway, Canada, the USA and Australia. It was not always possible to find exactly the same data for countries outside Europe. What helped the comparison, which should be taken with caution, is an 'International Health Policy Survey' run by the Commonwealth Fund in 2010 in 11 countries (Schoen and Osborn, 2011), which included some of the European countries we studied in this book (France, Germany, Sweden and the UK), together with Norway, the USA, Canada and Australia, which made some (careful) comparison possible. The main conclusions that can be drawn from the comparison are the following. First, Sweden and the UK rank among the

Table 10.19 The quadrilemma and policy changes in the 2000s

	Public expenditure (P–C)	Economic objectives	Medical objectives		
		Efficiency in hospital beds use	Appropriateness in hospital care	Out-patient care and prevention	Health final outcomes
Sweden	Increase	Light improvements	Stability / Improvements	Stability / Improvements	Improvements
UK	Strong increase	Improvements	Stability / Improvements	Stability	Improvements
Spain	Increase	Light improvements	Stability / Improvements	Improvements	Improvements
Italy	Increase	Light improvements	Stability / Improvements	Stability / Improvements	Improvements
France	Increase	Light improvements	Improvements	Stability	Improvements
Germany	(Weak) increase	Light improvements	Stability / Worsening	Stability	Improvements
Austria	Increase	Improvements	Stability	Stability	Improvements
Poland	Strong increase	Improvements	Stability / Worsening	Stability / Improvements	Improvements

[a] Comparison with 1994.
[b] Comparison with 2005.

first group of countries in terms of the objectives of the quadrilemma. Then the other countries, but Poland, join a medium group that is characterized by different trade-offs between the different objectives of the quadrilemma. For example Italy functions better in terms of medical and economic objectives and worse in terms of political and social ones, whereas Austria performs better in terms of political and social objectives. In Poland, together with other Central-Eastern European countries, but also Australia and the USA, there is considerable potential for improvement for most of the objectives.

If we study the development in the eight country group over time (see Table 10.19), we notice that most countries were able to push forward to many of the 'angles' of the quadrilemma, often softening the trade-offs between different objectives. Efficiency in hospital care is detectable in practically all countries, especially in the UK, Austria and Poland. The same can be said for medical health final outcomes, whereas the other medical objectives indicators (related to appropriateness of hospital care, outpatient care and prevention) show more a mix between stability and some improvements, with Germany and Poland registering also some worsening. Social objectives are the ones where the situation has remained more stable or there have been some light improvements. The political objectives have been tackled as well and there have been improvements on the users' side

Social objectives		Political objectives			
		Patients/Citizens		Workers	
Health inequalities[a]	Health equity	Satisfaction[b]	Waiting lists and access	Density and composition	Working conditions
Stability	Stability	Improvements	Light improvements	Improvements	Stability
Stability – Light improv.	Light improvements	Improvements	Improvements	Improvements	Improvements
Stability – Light improv.	Improvements	Improvements	Light improvements	Improvements	Improvements
Stability	Improvements	Improvements	Stability	Light improvements	Stability
Stability – Light wors.	Stability	Improvements	Stability	Improvements	Improvements
Improvements	Stability – Light wors.	Improvements	Stability	Improvements	Improvements
Stability	Stability	Improvements	Stability	Improvements	Stability
Stability – Light improv.	Stability – Light improv.	n.a.	Stability	Stability / Worsening	Stability

Table. 10.20 A general overview of the performance of several HCS in Europe and other OECD countries

	Medical Objectives	Political objectives: users		Political objectives: workers		Economic objectives	Social objectives		Economic resources: public HCE P-C PPP
		All indicators	Common-wealth Fund	All indicators	Only density and ratio		All indicators	Common-wealth Fund	
Norway	0.54	0.20	-0.51	0.59	0.80	1.24	1.01	-0.14	1.88
Sweden	0.68	0.10	-0.05	0.20	0.21	0.76	0.56	0.14	0.27
UK	0.09	0.47	1.41	0.02	0.11	0.59	0.78	0.56	0.07
Finland	0.77	0.32		0.00	1.02	0.53	-0.15		-0.38
Denmark	-0.14	0.78		0.68	0.94	0.95	0.58		1.05
Netherlands	0.72	1.14	0.87	0.73	1.09	-0.69	-0.28	0.53	1.31
Belgium	0.48	0.67		0.89	0.47	-0.72	0.14		0.22
France	0.38	0.41	0.05	0.36	0.45	0.08	-0.13	0.37	0.28
Austria	-0.01	0.79		0.29	0.06	-0.60	0.32		0.58
Canada	-0.15		-0.66		0.60	0.43		-0.24	0.38
Ireland	0.12	-0.72		-0.15	1.36	0.71	-0.32		-0.21
Spain	0.52	-0.53		-0.58	-0.59	0.10	0.34		-0.54
Italy	0.38	-0.42		0.16	-0.94	-0.01	-0.16		-0.45
Germany	-0.20	0.33	0.39	0.08	0.07	-1.15	0.05	0.02	0.56
Czech Rep.	-0.29	-0.12			-0.51	-0.91	0.77		-1.26
Australia	0.03		-0.78		-0.18	0.30		-0.31	-0.28
Poland	-0.69	-1.33			-1.04	-0.15	-0.52		-1.86
USA	-0.89		-0.41		0.07	-0.10		-1.65	1.22
Portugal	0.00	-0.96		-1.17	-1.34	-0.28	-0.94		-1.03
Hungary	-1.48	-1.11		0.04	-1.04	-0.41	-1.21		-1.82

both in terms of general satisfaction with the HCS and waiting time (with the exception of Italy, Poland and the other SHI countries, where this was a minor problem). The last decade has also witnessed an increase in the density of the main health professional profiles (with the partial exception, again, of Italy and Poland), although not always matched by improved working conditions: in the UK, Spain, France and Germany this was the case (at least in terms of incomes and contract stability). In the other countries the situation has remained relatively stable. Finally, in terms of economic resources, the UK and Poland witnessed relevant increases, whereas the other countries underwent more moderate ones, especially in the German case. In the most recent past, the economic crisis has created an enormous shock for public policies. Countries are responding with often dramatic austerity programs, not least in the health care sector. The mid- and long-term effects cannot yet be assessed in detail. But existing data not only show that health expenditure growth came to a halt in many countries in 2010 and 2011 (and even to very substantial cutbacks in many countries), but that this will also lead to a deterioration in terms of medical, political and social objectives.

The underlying question of this chapter is whether reforms implemented in the past decade have an influence on these trends. Focusing on the 2000–2009 period (before major cutbacks in health care as a response to the economic crisis came into force), the answer is complex and cannot be given in relation to all types of objectives. In particular, it seems that economic objectives and some of the medical objectives (appropriateness) are the ones more positively affected by managerialization as well as recentralization (thanks to the increasing use of monitoring devices on hospital resource allocation). Health final outcomes were the least affected by reforms due to the fact that this type of objective is the one more incremental and technology-related. Health inequalities and equity have not been affected too much by reforms (not even in negative terms by the ones aiming at privatizing expenditure). This is also because there were mostly economic or political objectives at the core of health reforms in the 2000s. And these policies were often accompanied by regulations or re-regulations aiming at preventing deterioration in terms of social objectives.

The different mixes of reforms (mainly increasing consumer choices, also through privatization of provision, and fostering more regulations on waiting lists from steering national bodies and governments) have had often a positive effect in terms of political objectives related to patients (satisfaction and waiting lists). The relationship between political objectives related to workers and reforms is more complex: on the one side, an increasing number of workers has been put under pressure by managerialization and by (attempts) to privatize health care facilities (and therefore changing labour contracts); on the other, there are clear signs of an increasing number of professional jobs being created in the last decade and also some signs of increased salaries in some countries. An exchange between more manage-rialization and higher salaries or job opportunities might have taken place. Apart from policy reforms, the study also indicates that for some of the countries more money put into the system has led to the improvements described above. This seems definitely the case for the UK and Spain.

Taking the information together, all eight countries have obviously suc-ceeded to improve on many of the 'angles' of the quadrilemma in the 2000s decade, even if specific deficiencies in single dimensions have persisted in many countries. At the same time, health expenditure was still increasing in the 2000s, but at more moderate growth rates than in the 1990s. Also considering demographic changes, this is a strong indication that health policies have significantly improved cost-effectiveness. At the same time, this book has shown that the role of decentralization or recentralization and the role of privatization vary largely across the eight countries and even within groups of countries representing the same HCS type. This allows for concluding that it is not so much the overall dimension of health care reform that counts, but the very specific details in which policies are imple-mented in an existing system, the relative weight given to medical, political, social and economic objectives, and the ways in which reforms attempt to accomplish such objectives.

Notes

1. For instance, asthma problems should not be treated in general through hospital care but outpatient care: high asthma hospital admission rates indicate that the health care system is not able to avoid this type of inappropriate use of hospital care. The same holds for cesarean births. Natural births should be the rule and cesareans should be the exception: if a country has a quite higher cesarean births rate than other countries, it means that probably its health care system functions in an inap-propriate way, treating natural phenomena (such as birth) as a 'medical' issue.
2. The main measure used to study breast cancer survival rates is the one provided by OECD: breast cancer five year relative survival rate (age-stand. rate). Given the fact some countries do not have available data at all on this indicator, we have also used a more simple measure, also proposed by Health Consumer Powerhouse (2012): the ratio between the number of (age standardized) breast cancer deaths and the number of women with a diagnosis of breast cancer.
3. Amenable mortality is generally defined as premature deaths that should not occur in the presence of effective and timely care.
4. The patient rights and information index refers to dimensions such as, for instance, access to own medical record; right to second opinion; patients' right in health care laws. These data are collected through qualitative questionnaires sent to key informants in each country and analyses on the national legislation.
5. The Accessibility (waiting time for treatment) Index is based on dimensions such as, for instance, the access to the family doctor in the same day of request; the access to a major elective surgery within three months; starting a cancer therapy within three weeks since the decision. These data are collected through qualitative questionnaires sent to key informants in each country.

6. The waiting time for treatment index was slightly changed in comparison with the one directly proposed by Health Consumer Powerhouse: on the one side a homogenization criteria was used to make data comparable over time; on the other side, in order to build the index, the item related to the direct access to specialists was not considered, given the fact that it is highly contestable if the presence or absence of a gatekeeping system can be seen as a positive or negative element in a health care system.
7. Unfortunately data on Poland are not available.
8. The standardization procedure adopted is the usual one: each country value has been confronted with the mean value of the eight countries and then divided by the standard deviation.

11
Health Care Provision: An Exploratory Analysis of Increase, Decline, Converging Trends and Driving Forces in Comparative Perspective

Ingalill Montanari and Kenneth Nelson

Introduction

The stagnation and decline of welfare states are prominent issues in comparative research, where structural pressures are assumed to limit the possibility to develop or even maintain social citizenship rights. The role of national politics for institutional change is negligible in this theoretical framework, and ultimately welfare states are believed to converge to some common international standard.

Most research on welfare state conformity and decline is based on changes in social benefit programmes. However, public services have not been immune against expectations on welfare state austerity. In an influential study on the reorganization of European welfare states, Clayton and Pontusson (1998) have argued that public services, including health care, would be more subject to decline than cash benefits, due to less visibility of unpopular reforms and a presumed risk of social tourism in a unifying Europe. Developments at European level have also spilled over into a discussion about possible convergence of health care (Wendt et al., 2005).

In this chapter we will broaden large scale comparative analysis on social citizenship rights beyond social benefit programmes and focus on developments in one of the core public services, namely health care. We devote attention to levels of provision, which is a central dimension of health care citizenship rights, including health employment, hospital beds and medical technology. Our purpose is twofold: to subject hypotheses of decline and convergence in health care provision to empirical tests and to examine the role of partisan politics for health care reform in affluent OECD countries. Thus, besides a large number of European countries, we analyse developments in several non-European English speaking welfare states, where liberal political doctrines have had strong influence on social policy. The analysis covers the years 1980–2005 and includes Austria, Belgium, Canada, the Czech Republic, Denmark, Estonia, Finland, France, Germany, Greece, Hungary, Ireland, Italy, Japan, the Netherlands, New Zealand, Norway, Poland, Portugal, the Slovak Republic, Slovenia, Spain, Sweden, Switzerland, the United Kingdom and the United States. We begin by discussing the most common reform pressures on welfare states, where after we bring partisan politics into the theoretical framework. Data and measurement issues are subsequently discussed, followed by a presentation of the results that precedes the concluding discussion.

Social citizenship under pressure

During the first three decades after the Second World War most affluent countries had established elaborate systems of income replacement programmes, and in several countries also public services became an additional component of social citizenship. The slowdown of economic growth at the end of the 1970s largely put a halt to this expansion of welfare states, and in some programmes cutbacks were introduced. The stagnation and subsequent decline of social citizenship have to a large extent been linked to the financial burden of too generous welfare states operating on increasingly trans-national production markets.

The alleged need to reorganize welfare states has been recognized both in politics and academia. Several scholars have argued that maintenance, let alone expansion, of social citizenship needs to be characterized by more social investment friendly policies, or transformed in a market-enhancing direction (e.g. Bonoli et al., 2000; Esping-Andersen, 1996, 2002; Ferrera and Hemerijck, 2003; Rieger and Leibfried, 2003; Scharpf and Schmidt, 2000; Swank, 2002). Parallel ideas have surfaced in politics, perhaps most explicitly by proponents of the Third Way in Britain and the Active Welfare State in Belgium, but also in the EU social inclusion discourse (Frazer et al., 2010). Supply-side strategies, in the form of a functioning technical and logistic infrastructure, and social investment in human capital have thus become central objectives of governments in facilitating a sound investment climate (Scharpf, 2002). The de-regulation of financial capital thus seems to have tilted power in favour of letting market forces and not politics decide where in society resources should be allocated, in order to maximize returns on investments (Strange, 1997). In this process competitiveness has no longer become an exclusive hallmark of firms operating on the market, but has been extended to cover also collective responsibilities (Cox, 1998). According to this welfare state efficiency thesis social policy development is heavily constrained. It should be emphasized, however, that a sound investment climate also includes social stability and a well functioning labour market, where social policy and possibly also health care may challenge and potentially counteract the allocating power of the market economy (Arrow,

1963; Barr, 2001; Freeman, 2002). The discursive blueprints of a European social model provide some evidence of this political need (Palme et al., 2009).

The European countries are subject to additional structural pressures for welfare state institutional change emanating from EU economic and financial policy, EU competition frameworks, and the Open Method of Coordination (OMC) (Greve, 1996; Leidl, 2001; Mossialos and McKee, 2002; McKee and Mossialos, 2006; Taylor-Gooby, 1996). The Broad Economic Policy Guidelines of the EU include low inflation, balancing of national budgets and exposure to competition in every field, under conditions of harmonized social regulations. Not only are procedures of governance subject to regulation, but also the very content of economic policy (Gustavsson, 2010). In this way the space for national variation in economic and financial policy is heavily circumscribed. Since social policy, including health care, formally still is a national prerogative according to the principle of subsidiarity, any effects on national social policies are presumably caused by indirect convergence (Montanari et al., 2008).[1]

Competition policy is the very baseline for European integration, along its development from the European Community, over to the Single Market and the European Union, in order to promote growth and productivity. This may have important consequences for the possibilities to collectively organize production of public services. The European Court of Justice has in fact increasingly become the guardian of strict application of competition policy in all production fields including public services. The legal environment in which health care systems contract employees, purchase goods, finance services and organize themselves is thereby transformed (Greer, 2008).

The OMC was constituted in order to promote development in various fields, such as education, employment, poverty, and health care, with the explicit objective of cross-country convergence, by continuous benchmarking exercises (Falkner, 2005; O'Connor, 2005). It may at first sight appear that 'soft' governance of this kind is mostly relevant for convergence of standards in an upward direction; however, commonly defined benchmarks may also be used as a scapegoat to decrease levels of provision.

Besides these external structural pressures on welfare states there are domestic factors that sometimes are held to create obstacles for growth and productivity, thus enforcing austerity and welfare state decline. Demographic shifts and particularly the ageing of societies is one example, where the increase of non-economically active citizens and strengthened demand for care services work in tandem, entailing financial pressure on welfare states (Lindh et al., 2005). The growth of the service sector is another example (Iversen and Cusack, 2000). The transition to an economy dominated by service sector employment is certainly a common development for all welfare states, despite sometimes substantial cross-country differences. It is here relevant to differentiate between the advanced and lower echelons of the service sector. With regard to the former, banks and insurance companies have recently been joined by a series of independent consultants, fiscal and financial experts, who earlier performed their tasks within firms. In contrast to these advanced services there are the less complicated services within trade, restaurants and transport, as well as the various community and social care services. Particularly the professional caring of children and the elderly places limits to efficiency and productivity. Some countries have tried to solve this problem by adopting New Public Management techniques, or simply outsourced provision to private firms (Clarke and Newman, 1997; Lindqvist, 2008).

In this new era of post-industrialism, globalization, Europeanization and ageing societies it is often assumed that the solutions entailing austerity and welfare state decline are similar across countries and unrelated to ideological orientations (Pierson, 1996). Ultimately, welfare states are expected to converge, although the speed and nature of these processes of cross-country institutional conformity are subject to discussion (Schmitt and Starke, 2011). To the extent that national responses with regard to welfare state sustainability are at all believed to differ across countries, the role of partisan politics is mostly dismissed in this largely structural theoretical framework. Sometimes reference is made to the organization of interest among economic actors more generally (Soskice, 1999), where main architects of welfare state reform are linked to employer organizations and not party-political actors (Hall and Soskice, 2001). In health care specifically, effects of partisan politics on policy are supposed to have weakened considerably (Jordan, 2010).

National politics and health care

Structural factors of the type discussed above are obviously important for the development of social citizenship. Nonetheless, building on the tradition of social scientists recognizing fundamental differences in the institutional organization of welfare states more generally (Esping-Andersen, 1990; Huber et al., 1993; Korpi and Palme, 1998; Scharpf and Schmidt, 2000) and health care specifically (Bambra, 2005; Moran, 2000; Olafsdottir and Beckfield, 2006; Schieber and Poullier, 1987; Wendt, 2009; Wendt et al., 2009), we do not believe that there is enough empirical evidence to simply rule out the role of partisan politics for institutional change. Considering social benefit programmes, for example, there is some evidence that the stagnation and decline of entitlement levels since the 1980s is linked to the main political orientation of governments (Korpi and Palme, 2003).

The emphasis on partisan politics in explaining institutional development does not imply that welfare states are easy to change. While it certainly is true that welfare states are resilient for major systemic change, due in part to risks of electoral backlash (Esping-Andersen, 1996; Pierson, 1996), it has also to be remembered that welfare state institutions are path-dependent only as long as political support for redistribution remains strong (Korpi, 2001). However, so far the basic principles governing social policy seem largely intact in their core dimensions (Palme et al., 2009), although programmatic changes have been frequent and often in the downward direction. Income replacement due to sickness, unemployment, work-accident and old age has suffered from retrenchment in recent decades, albeit to differing extent cross-nationally (Montanari et al., 2007; 2008). Similar downward long-term trends have appeared also in social assistance, something that has increased cross-national variation (Nelson, 2008). Thus, countries have responded differently to seemingly common structural reform pressures.

We see no general reason why determinants for health care services should be substantially different from those of social benefit programmes noted above. We therefore remain sceptical to apolitical theories on welfare state institutional change, as well as the common presumption in comparative research to portray welfare state development in terms of convergence. One likely reason for continued variation in health care provision might be its position as an important social investment, which may have created an effective barrier against austerity and decline. Health care typically enjoys strong popular support (Blekesaune and Quadagno, 2003), and even political opponents to other forms of social citizenship are reluctant to deny health care to citizens in need. One reason for this positive opinion on health care is probably the limited degree of moral hazard; its usefulness in procuring a healthy workforce another one. Health care may in fact be considered an eminent supply-side strategy of social investment in human capital, thus removing obstacles that may hamper economic participation (Midgley, 1999).

The popular support of health care and its prime position as a social investment are likely to reduce the risk of welfare state decline. The development of health care may in fact show more similarity with that of paid parental leave and child care than more traditional forms of cash benefits, such as unemployment and social assistance benefits noted above. In the Nordic countries particularly, but also elsewhere in Europe, paid parental leave and child care have continued to be expanded, also during the era of welfare state stagnation and decline beginning in the 1980s (Ferrarini, 2006). However, we do not expect any clear signs of upward convergence in health care. Although single reforms in specific countries may be linked to reform pressures of the type discussed above, such as EU influence on market based principles in Danish health care (Sindbjerg Martinsen and Vrangbaek, 2008) and health care coverage in Spain (Guillén and Álvarez, 2004), health care systems still show strong national traits. In their review of comparative health care research Marmor et al. (2005: 338) concludes 'there is as much evidence of continued difference (or divergence) in national arrangements for the finance, delivery and regulation of health care as there is of increasing similarity'.

Despite that countries seem to be subject to similar structural pressures for welfare state reorganization, ideological orientations have previously been used to explain continued cross-national diversity of health care, likewise the path dependent nature of policy reforms (Jacobs, 1998; Hacker, 2004). Observations such as these naturally draw attention to partisan politics as a major driver for institutional change, something that has been shown to be important for developments in cash benefits (Korpi, 1989) and public services at the aggregate level (Huber and Stephens, 2000). We presume that partisan politics is of relevance also for the development of health care provision, where political solutions may vary according to parliamentary incumbency. Based on power resource theory we expect left governments to be positively linked to health care and thus associated with increased levels of provision.

Data and measurement issues

A social citizenship rights perspective on health care should focus on the content of services that are being offered, rather than expenditure levels as such, the latter dimension being a primary focus in health economics (Barros, 1998; Blomqvist and Carter, 1997; Gerdtham, 1992; Hansen and King, 1996; Hitiris and Posnett, 1992; McCoskey and Selden, 1998; Roberts, 1998). In comparative welfare state research on social citizenship three core analytical dimensions of social benefit programs have been identified; namely eligibility (coverage), financing and entitlement or benefit level (Esping-Andersen, 1990; Ferrarini, 2006; Korpi, 1989; Montanari, 2001; Palme, 1990).

Analyses of public services lack an elaborated social citizenship rights perspective. One analytical challenge in comparative health care research is thus to identify relevant policy dimensions and to develop policy indicators that are comparative both cross-nationally and over time. Coverage and financing remain core dimensions in analyses of public services, although not analysed in this chapter. However, there is no parable to entitlement levels in health care research and we will here instead use the concept of provision. Both service coverage and financing have occasionally been of some interest in the ongoing discussion of health care typologies, whereas kinds and levels of service provision have more recently come into focus (Wendt et al., 2009). Conceptualization and measurement of health care provision is therefore still in its infancy and in need of empirical sophistication. The approach developed in this chapter borrows extensively from the conceptual and empirical framework of health care provision elaborated by Montanari and Nelson (2013), where we distinguished between three subindices: health employment, hospital beds and medical technology.

The empirical analysis of health care is based on OECD Health Data (2011). Health employment is an index of the number of practicing physicians and nurses per 1000 inhabitants. The index of hospital beds includes total and acute care beds per 1000 inhabitants. The index of medical technology includes five separate items; the number of computed tomography scanners, magnetic resonance imaging units, radiation therapy technology, lithotripters and mammographs per 1000 inhabitants. Health care provision is an additive index including the sub-indices of health employment, hospital beds and medical technology.[2]

OECD health data has been transformed to facilitate index construction. For methodological reasons we have used different techniques to transform original data. In the analyses of levels of health care provision, OECD health data has been indexed according to 1980 variable scores for each country. In the analyses of cross-country variation, OECD health data has been normalized according to the maximum variable score in our sample of countries. In the regression analyses on determinants for health care provision, OECD health data has been transformed into standard scores, which are normally distributed with a mean of zero and a standard deviation of one. The number of observations differs between sub-indices due to missing values in OECD health data. Substantial breaks in trends due to the inclusion of additional countries in the analysis have been smoothened empirically.

Results

Health care provision differs extensively across countries and substantial changes have occurred over time. This section begins with a temporal examination of levels where after patterns of cross-country variation in health care provision are assessed. Drivers for health care provision are analysed at the end.

Trends in levels of health care provision

To what extent has health care provision suffered from welfare state decline in recent decades? In order to provide a preliminary answer to this question, Figure 11.1a–d shows the index of health care provision and the composite sub-indices of health employment, hospital beds and medical technology for 27 countries between 1980 and 2009. Averages for three non-mutually exclusive groups of countries are shown: Europe, OECD, and Central and Eastern Europe (CEE).[3] Due to a large amount of missing data, medical technology is shown from 1990 onwards.

Whereas health employment and medical technology have increased almost continuously over the period, the number of hospital beds has declined. Thus, we do not find any uniform pattern of decline in the various dimensions of health care provision. If any overall tendency can be observed, it is mainly described in terms of improvements and continued expansion of health care provision, although we do not know whether access to services is equally distributed in society.

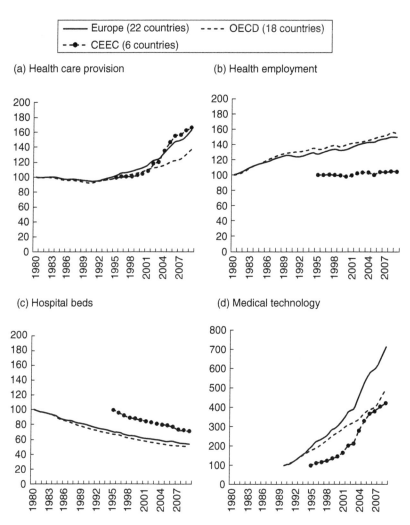

Figure 11.1a–d Levels of health care provision in 27 countries (1980–2009) (index 1980=100)

Note: The European category includes Austria, Belgium, the Czech Republic, Denmark, Estonia, Finland, France, Germany, Greece, Hungary, Ireland, Italy, the Netherlands, Norway, Poland, Portugal, the Slovak Republic, Slovenia, Spain, Sweden, Switzerland, and the United Kingdom. Besides the European countries, the OECD category includes Australia, Canada, Japan, New Zealand and the United States. The CEE category includes the Czech Republic, Estonia, Hungary, Poland, the Slovak Republic and Slovenia.

Source: OECD Health Data (2011).

The index of health care provision was fairly stable up to the mid-1990s, where after there has been a substantial increase due to the expansion of health employment and medical technology described above. The number of physicians has increased faster than the number of nurses, although both professional categories add to the expansion of health employment (not shown).[4] The most notable exceptions to this pattern are among the CEE countries, where health employment has been fairly stable for the years where we have data. The substantial increase of medical technology since 1990 reflects the fast and consistent growth of the biomedical and pharmaceutical sectors (Clemente et al., 2008; Saltman et al., 2002), considered to be important drivers for increasing per capita health expenditure (Newhouse, 1992; Okunade and Murthy, 2002).

The development of hospital beds should be interpreted with caution. Although the number of hospital beds provides some indication of the availability of hospital care, one should recognize that as part of a major restructuring of health care services several countries have shifted from hospital to specialized nursing care, community-based health or social care services. Parts of this re-organization of health care are due to new treatment and care options, but another plausible explanation is cost-cutting pressures (Healy and McKee, 2002). In the United Kingdom, for example, worries have been raised that the number of beds no longer reaches demands (idem). Others have claimed that financial resources not necessarily are reallocated and used for appropriate non-institutionalized care (Mechanic and Rochefort, 1990). The re-organization of Swedish psychiatric care in the mid-1990s is one illustrative example, where many municipalities lacked alternative caring facilities necessary to comply with decentralization of health care from county to local levels (SoS, 1999).

Dispersion of health care provision

The expansion of health care provision noted above largely rules out the possibility of downward convergence. Instead the question addressed here concerns more the extent to which increases in health care provision has invoked upward convergence, where countries with comparatively low levels of health care provision have been catching up. Figure 11.2a–d shows the amount of dispersion in the index of health care provision and the composite sub-indices of health employment, hospital beds and medical technology for 27 countries 1980–2009. Cross-national dispersion is measured by the coefficient of variation, corresponding to the standard deviation divided by the mean. We use the same grouping of countries as in the analyses of trends in levels above.

Medical technology varies most extensively across countries and it is the only dimension where we actually can observe any clear evidence of convergence. The coefficient of variation has decreased substantially on this dimension, particularly in the European category and at a more moderate

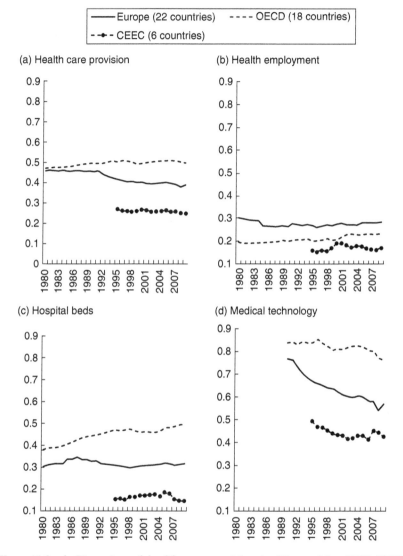

Figure 11.2a–d Dispersion of health care provision in 27 countries (1980–2009) (coefficient of variation)

Note: The European category includes Austria, Belgium, the Czech Republic, Denmark, Estonia, Finland, France, Germany, Greece, Hungary, Ireland, Italy, the Netherlands, Norway, Poland, Portugal, the Slovak Republic, Slovenia, Spain, Sweden, Switzerland, and the United Kingdom. Besides the European countries, the OECD category includes Australia, Canada, Japan, New Zealand and the United States. The CEE category includes the Czech Republic, Estonia, Hungary, Poland, the Slovak Republic and Slovenia.

Source: OECD Health Data (2011).

pace among the OECD countries. In terms of levels of medical technology, the CEE countries have come closer to the long-standing EU democracies. In the mid-1990s the average level of medical technology in the CEE countries was about half of that of the longstanding EU democracies, something that can be compared to a fraction of two thirds at the end of the period (not shown).[5] Among the European countries we can therefore observe processes of upward convergence in medical technology, where countries having lower levels to start with are moving closer to countries having higher levels of provision. Although it is not possible here to determine the extent to which this convergence is related to European integration, institutional conformity in health care has been expected in connection with the OMC framework particularly (McKee et al., 2004; Hervey, 2007). Health care service is in fact an important component of the OMC programme.

Countries vary much less on the other two dimensions of health care provision, and here it is not possible to observe any clear trend towards convergence. In fact, the coefficient of variation for both health employment and hospital beds has been quite stable over the period, both in the European and OECD categories. Thus, convergence in health care provision seems to be restricted to levels of medical technology, foremost in European countries. There is even a slight tendency of divergence in the number of hospital beds across the OECD countries, something that is due to more pronounced downsizing of hospitals and growth of outpatient care options in the non-European countries.

The descriptive analyses of health care provision above show that the hypotheses of welfare state decline and convergence are not fully supported by empirical data. Considering the three dimensions of health care provision analyzed in this chapter, only the number of hospital beds has declined due to relative shifts in inpatient and outpatient care, and clear signs of convergence can only be observed for levels of medical technology, especially in the European countries. The increase and continued cross-national variation in health care provision make it interesting to analyse drivers for social change and the role of partisan politics for health care, something that is addressed next.

Drivers for health care provision

Welfare state development has been linked to often competing driving forces, including both structural factors and actor-oriented theories. In order to explore the role of partisan politics for health care, in this section we report results from a series of unbalanced OLS regressions of health care provision. In addition to parliamentary incumbency we have added controls for the most commonly alternative explanatory factors, including GDP, service sector employment, elderly population, trade openness, constitutional veto points and voting rights.[6] We have also recognized that there might be interdependencies in the components of health care systems and have thus included controls for health care coverage, as well as total and private health expenditure.[7] Since service sector employment partly is included in health employment, we have in all regression models excluded this measure on deindustrialization without any substantial changes in results.

Table 11.1 shows results from fixed effects regression models of health care provision.[8] For reasons of data availability the analysis covers developments 1980–2005 in 18 OECD countries.[9] Left government strength is positively related to the index of health care provision, which to large extent is the result of developments in health employment.[10] Confessional political incumbency is negatively related to hospital beds, whereas there is no statistically significant effect of left government strength. The significant negative coefficient for confessional cabinet shares is congruent with Wendt's (2009) classification of health care institutional types, where one distinct hallmark of the Continental European countries (having strong tradition of confessional Christian democratic parties in government) was the high level of provision in outpatient sectors, notably in Germany.

Similar to the descriptive analyses of levels and dispersion of health care provision above, medical technology is analysed from 1990 and onwards. Both left and confessional government strength is positively related to medical technology, although coefficients are far from being statistically significant. Political incumbency may lack effect on medical technology for various reasons. To some extent the insignificance of partisan politics may be data driven and due to the shorter time period and large amount of missing values on this dimension of health care provision.

Table 11.1 Fixed effects OLS regressions of health care provision on various independent variables in 18 OECD countries (1980–2005)

	Health care provision	Health employment	Hospital beds	Medical technology**
Left gov.	0.220*	0.293*	0.019	0.020
Conf. gov.	0.516	0.500	−0.194*	0.702
GDP	0.010	0.121*	0.040*	−0.017
Health cov.	1.059	5.889*	−0.157	1.666*
Health exp.	0.004	−0.075	0.119*	0.400
Public health exp.	0.071	0.000	−0.024*	0.007
Const. struct.	0.877	−0.057	−0.734*	−0.465
Service ind.	2.598*	4.392*	0.807	0.725
Pop. > 64 years	0.199	−0.008	−0.076	0.093*
Trade openness	−0.003	0.004	−0.001	−0.001
No. Obs.	367	274	312	145

Note: *p<0.05. Country and year dummies are not shown. Constant is not shown. All regression models use cluster robust standard errors.
**1990–2005.

Discussion

Predictions of welfare state decline and convergence of social citizenship are almost legion in comparative research, where structural pressures are assumed to be main drivers for institutional change, outscoring the importance of national politics. Most evidence in support of such expectations is based on changes in social benefit programmes. In this chapter we have broadened the scope of analysis to cover public services, with an explicit focus on health care provision, including health employment, hospital beds and medical technology. Based on developments in 27 OECD countries 1980–2009 we have analyzed the extent to which health care provision has been subject to decline, signs of convergence in levels of health care provision, and the role of partisan politics for the most recent development of health care provision.

Health care provision is shown to be characterized rather by increase than decline, with limited signs of convergence. Of the three dimensions of health care provision analysed in this chapter, only the number of hospital beds have been scaled down, partly as a response to increased emphasis on outpatient care. Convergence is mainly observed for medical technology in European countries, where developments particularly in the CEE countries are characterized by major improvements. Partisan politics seem to explain parts of development in health care provision, where left governments tend to increase levels of health care provision more extensively than governments dominated by secular centrist and right political parties. This finding on the role of partisan politics is largely driven by developments in health employment.

Although health care provision is an important component of health care citizenship rights there are further issues that call for systematic comparative investigation. The regulation of the medical profession is one example that concerns qualifications of medical personnel and conditions of professional performance (Moran, 2000). In historical perspective the independence of the medical profession has gradually been restricted with regard to the range and forms of exercise (Scott, 2000). This long-term trend is being partly reversed through privatization of services also in countries with tax-financed health care (Ameringer, 2008). Greater independence of the medical profession may restrict the political setting of priorities, thus limiting the role of political incumbency for health care reform.

Another possible extension of this study is to focus more explicitly on the introduction of purchaser–provider splits, or quasi-markets, in countries with mainly tax-financed health care. This relatively new innovation in health care governance has resulted in the appearance of private for-profit firms and non-profit organizations as actual providers of services, alongside the public sector. These quasi-markets have been at focus in studies of single countries (see Herr, 2008; Shafrin, 2010). Comparative research may here provide additional insights, for example, in relation to the consequences of different types of contractual regulation and reimbursement methods on the distribution of health care provision. Are all citizens, or holders of social insurance, eligible for every kind of treatment, or are especially costly services reserved for those with an additional private insurance? Comparative research may also provide new evidence concerning the means available for policy makers to prevent escalating health care expenditure and cream-skimming on part of private providers.

Another interesting topic is patient mobility particularly in the context of European integration. EU citizens are free to demand health care services in the Member States, something that has been actively promoted by the European Commission. One issue of debate is whether permissions should be granted beforehand by domestic authorities, which are responsible for payments. We do not consider this issue to be a prominent cause of future convergence in any of the dimensions of health care provision analysed in this chapter. The possibility to demand health care in foreign countries will probably also in the future be an option mostly for well educated and situated persons, not least because language, cultural values and epistemic identity tend to be of paramount importance in the relationship between patient and medical professionals.

Although several questions remain concerning the comparative analysis of health care, the explorative empirical framework for studying health care provision sketched above shows promising areas for further cross-national research. One challenge is to improve the conceptual framework and empirical assessment of central health care dimensions, facilitating large-scale comparative analysis of health care citizenship rights. The results presented here show that developments in public services and cash benefits share common traits and possess unique tendencies, which deserve closer inspection in a methodologically coherent and theoretically sound cross-national perspective.

Notes

1. EU social regulations, which mainly regard health and safety at the workplace, aim at establishing a level playing field for firms operating in the EU area, and should not be confounded with traditional social policies (Majone, 1993; Montanari, 1995).
2. With OECD Health Data it is only possible to analyse health provision at the country level. Since eligibility to collectively organized health care services is next to universal in all countries except the United States, we may assume that the distribution of health care provision among citizens follows need.
3. The European category includes Austria, Belgium, the Czech Republic, Denmark, Estonia, Finland, France, Germany, Greece, Hungary, Ireland, Italy, the Netherlands, Norway, Poland, Portugal, the Slovak Republic, Slovenia, Spain, Sweden, Switzerland, and the United Kingdom. The OECD category includes the

European countries plus Australia, Canada, Japan, New Zealand and the United States. The CEE category includes the Czech Republic, Estonia, Hungary, Poland, the Slovak Republic and Slovenia.

4. OECD statistics do not distinguish between full-time and part-time employment, which would be highly relevant for nurses (Montanari, 2009). Health employment may thus have increased less than here indicated in terms of hours of service.

5. The long-standing European democracies include Austria, Belgium, Denmark, Finland, France, Germany, Ireland, Italy, the Netherlands, Norway, Sweden, Switzerland, and the United Kingdom.

6. Independent variables are from various sources. The political variables of government composition are from Korpi and Palme (2003) and updated to 2005. Left parties include social democrats and parties to their left. The confessional category includes European Christian democratic parties, whereas the remaining parties belong to the secular centrist/right category. The measure on constitutional veto points and voting rights is an additive index comprising four items from the Comparative Welfare State Dataset (Huber et al., 2004): federalism, bicameralism, popular referenda and presidentialism. Economic development is measured by GDP per capita in constant purchasing power adjusted US dollars from the OECD. The degree of deindustrialization is based on data from OECD Labour Force Statistics covering the proportion of the population 15–64 years that are employed in the service sector. From the same data source we use the percentage share of the population above 64 years as a measure of the demographic burden of elderly populations. For trade openness we use data from OECD National Accounts and it is measured as exports and imports of goods and services as percentage of GDP. Trade openness is often used to measure the degree to which countries are exposed to globalization.

7. Health care coverage and expenditure are based on OECD Health Data 2011. Health care coverage refers to the share of citizens in total population that are eligible for publicly financed health care services. Total health expenditure includes both public and private health care spending as percentage of GDP. Private health expenditure is measured as percentage of total health expenditure.

8. We cannot use a conventional fixed effects model and include a full set of country dummies since the constitutional veto point variable hardly changes over time. In correspondence with Swank and Martin (2001) we include country dummies only when the associated t statistic exceeds 1.00.

9. Included in the regression analysis are Australia, Austria, Belgium, Canada, Denmark, Finland, France, Germany, Ireland, Italy, Japan, the Netherlands, New Zealand, Norway, Sweden, Switzerland, United Kingdom and the United States.

10. Regression models with lagged (one year) independent variables show similar results.

12
Conclusions

Emmanuele Pavolini and Ana M. Guillén

European Health Care Systems (HCS) have undergone deep changes in the last two decades and their central role in the overall functioning of the Welfare States and in European economies should be kept in mind.

The present book has tried to introduce a broader framework of analysis in the study of European HCS than the one often found in the literature. In particular the attempt was to match an analysis of policy reforms (focusing on the contents of these reforms, the role of different types of actors, the forms of policy and institutional change and the trajectories of change) with an evaluation of how well these HCS perform (taking into consideration four possible broad objectives: medical, political, economic and social ones).

The results of the research are quite rich and complex. Before briefly summarizing some of the main findings, it is important to be aware that the data and information available nowadays, especially the statistical ones, are not always the ones we would desire to frame with more precision what happens. Therefore some caveats with interpretation have to be taken into account.

However the book presents enough evidence to push the research on this policy field decidedly further. The first result is that the distinction between NHS (National Health Services) and SHI (Social Health Insurances) still holds, even if there are clear lines blurring the edges among the two ideal types (Or et al., 2010; Wendt, 2009). Table 12.1 synthesizes the results obtained in Chapter 10. On average NHS tend to perform better in terms of medical, social and economic efficiency objectives than the SHI ones. These latter tend to be stronger only in terms of political objectives, both in relation to users and workers of the system. More specifically Nordic and Anglo-Saxon NHS seem to present the best combination in achieving all the quadrilemma objectives.

The second result is that we should never forget that the amount of economic resources provided to a HCS matters quite a lot when facing the quadrilemma. However, the relationship between economic resources and the quadrilemma is a complex one and it is related also to the type of HCS (Table 12.2).

Table 12.1   Type of health care system and the quadrilemma

	Medical objectives	Users	Workers	Economic efficiency	Social Objectives
NHS	++	–	–	++	+
SHI	–	+	+	– –	=

Table 12.2   Type of health care system, the quadrilemma and economic resources

	Strength of the relationship between per-capita public health expenditure and				
	Medical objectives	Users objectives	Workers objectives	Economic efficiency	Social objectives
Total	++	+++	++	+	++
Only NHS	=	+++	+++	+++	++
Only SHI	+++	+++	++	– –	+

A good part of the political and scientific discussion about health care reforms and HCS functioning in Europe has focused more on the relevance of governance and regulation than on the amount of resources provided to the system. The data on this book say something that perhaps it is too often taken for granted: in order to improve HCS functioning it is necessary to provide adequate resources. The analysis of the trajectories of reforms in the country chapters, as well as the data provided in Chapters 10 and 11, tell us that there is a strong positive relation between, on one side, medical, political and social objectives, and, on the other, per-capita public expenditure. There seems to be only a less strong relation between economic efficiency and public expenditure. The Spanish and the English NHS are cases where major improvements in respect to many objectives of the quadrilemma were achieved thanks to increased resources in the last decades.

If this holds true in general, when we focus on the HCS types, we notice some interesting differences. NHS countries tend to obtain similar medical results partially independently from the amount of economic resources provided: the cases of Spain and Italy are clear examples of relatively acceptable medical results, even if public expenditure is quite lower than in Scandinavian or Anglosaxon countries (or, especially, the main Western European SHI systems). In SHI countries there is a stronger relation between medical objectives and public expenditure, but this is in part explainable due to the broader differentiation among these countries (with the presence of Central-Eastern European HCS). In general the relationship between the other objectives and public expenditure holds true in a similar way for SHI and NHS countries, with only a relevant and interesting exception: whereas economy efficiency goes hand in hand with economic resources in NHS countries, in SHI ones the opposite applies: the richer the HCS is, the less efficient it risks to be. The reasons for the paradox seem to be related to the way the two types of health care system work: the problems of coordination among different actors and types of care (inpatient and outpatient) become even more economically relevant (creating inefficiencies) in those SHI systems where traditionally quite a vast amount of resources has been available.

The third result, strictly connected to the previous one, is the fact that the main trade-offs among different objectives of the quadrilemma deal with economic resources. If we consider the relation among the other goals (Table 12.3), we notice that quite often they are positively connected to each other: social objectives tend to be positively related to all the other objectives; the same holds true for medical objectives. The only two relations where there seems not to be a relevant connection among goals are between economic efficiency and users' satisfaction and between social objectives and workers' conditions.

How do these performances relate to the main reforms introduced in the last decades, in particular privatization, decentralization and managerialization?

The fourth result is that, looking first at privatization, after two decades of reforms the situation is only partially blurred. The blurring effect is due to the difference between reforms' aims and results. Many reforms tried to increase users' choice through two tools: opening up to more private provision and more competition among providers (i.e., allowing patients to move from a facility to the other). The latter tool was more often effectively used and it turned out to be able to deliver more successful results (for example decreases in waiting times, more users' satisfaction, etc.). The opening up to increased private provision was less relevant, even if a good part of the scientific and political debate focuses on it. Privatization in provision has not followed a straightforward path. Between 1990 and 2010 hospital care in private hospitals grew only in some SHI countries (but not in France) and Italy (where it took mainly place in the 1990s). Germany, Poland and,

Table 12.3 The trade-offs in the quadrilemma apart from the issue of economic resources

	Medical objectives	Users	Workers	Economic efficiency
Total				
Users	++			
Workers	+	+++		
Economic efficiency	+	=	+	
Social objectives	++	++	=	+

partially, Italy are the countries where privatization was stronger. What has happened is often a substitution of more traditional non-profit providers with profit-oriented ones. Looking at Table 12.4 it results clear that Germany and Poland are the most relevant cases, at least among the ones where data are available, where privatization of hospital care has taken place. Especially the German hospital system is becoming more and more similar to the USA one.

If we look at privatization of expenditure the interpretation becomes clearer: at least in the last decade most of the countries in our study have witnessed a substantial stability of the incidence of out-of-pocket (OOP) expenditure (France, Austria and Sweden) or a strong diminution (Spain, Italy, Poland and the UK), with the only exception of Germany. The stability or diminution trend in OOP expenditure, indicating that no substantial privatization of expenditure has taken place, is quite common also with many other OECD countries: in this sense, Germany, together with the Czech Republic and Portugal, represent the outliers.

Summing up, policy reforms with potential effects related to privatization did not have, in the 2000s, neither a substantial negative impact in terms of privatization of expenditure (social objective), but, on the contrary, the incidence of citizens' expenditure decreased, nor a substantial impact on the level of private hospital care provision in the HCS. Germany is one of the few

Table 12.4 Privatization in different HCS

	% of hospital beds in private facilities			Out-of-pocket payments (% of total exp.)		
	2000	2010	Variation	2000	2010	Variation
United States	73.7	75.1	=	14.9	11.8	–
Germany	56.1	69.2	+++	11.4	13.2	+
France	34.4	37.5	=/+	7.1	7.3	=
Spain	33.3	32.6	=	23.6	19.7	– –
Italy	30.4	31.6	=	24.5	17.8	– –
Australia	31.8	30.5	=/–	19.8	18.6	–
Austria	25.3	29.1	+	15.3	15.9	=
Portugal	22.2	27.0	++	24.3	26.0	+
Poland	n.a.	24.4		30.0	22.1	– –
Czech Republic	n.a.	13.2		9.7	14.9	++
United Kingdom	4.0	5.8	=/+	11.4	8.9	–
Sweden	7.6*	5.3	–/=	16.6	16.8	=
Finland	3.5	4.5	=	22.3	19.2	–
Denmark	0.8	4.5	+/=	14.7	13.2	–
Hungary	8.3	3.2	–	26.3	26.2	=

* Data referred to early 1990s.
Source: Chapter 9 and OECD (2013).

relevant exceptions. There were often mainly positive effects in terms of political goals related to users.

The fifth result relates to the dynamics of rescaling and managerialization. Both these processes went often hand in hand in many countries under a common ideological heading: less central state, more (managerialized) local government. These types of approaches were started before the 2000s, but the last decade was really the one when, on one side, managerialization was implemented, on the other, afterthoughts about the shortcomings of decentralization rose. This has meant that managerialization has probably started to improve economic efficiency and the more general running of HCS in many countries. At the same time many professionals, mainly doctors, in the sector have started to feel unease with these changes. It is possible that increases in salaries and incomes have been introduced in order to limit part of the professionals' dissatisfaction. This is an issue that is in need of more intense and detailed research efforts in the future.

Rescaling has followed a different path: whereas until the early 2000s HCS decentralization was one of the main goals of policy reforms, the last decade has witnessed in many countries a shift towards recentralization again, mainly as a consequence of cost containment issues (economic objectives)[1] and, in certain HCS, rising territorial inequalities in the access to services (social objectives). The politics of recentralization has not followed the same path of the politics of decentralization: the latter was implemented through reforms that stated clearly the intent to transfer powers from the Centre to local governments in order to improve legitimacy (decisions taken at a level closer to citizens) and effectiveness. The former has followed a 'gradual transformation' path of institutional change (Streeck and Thelen, 2005): a 'creeping' recentralization has taken place in many countries in order, on the one side, to put costs under tighter control, and, on the other, not to lose too much legitimacy after decades of political rhetoric about bringing democratic decisions closer to citizens. This means that many countries have introduced new regulatory bodies (for instance National Agencies) and have strengthened steering, coordination and monitoring powers of central governments and institutions in order to gain more control over the system, at least in terms of costs, without declaring it as a public goal. In many countries we have nowadays a mix of formally still decentralized HCS, where a substantial part of power has been taken back by national governments. This situation might have a complex effect on the performance of the health care systems. On one side, it could foster a decrease in territorial inequalities in the access to services (social objectives) and a more careful use of resources (economic and, perhaps, medical objectives). On the other, it could have a negative impact on users' participation and involvement in the health care system.

The final result of our analysis is that we should take into consideration even more seriously health care issues when we study the trajectories of change of the European Welfare State. Much of the literature on welfare state retrenchment, restructuring and recalibration tends to focus mainly on transfers such as pensions and unemployment benefits (see for example the seminal Esping-Andersen 1990 book). More recently the debate has been enriched, focusing also on policies coping with 'new social risks' (Taylor Gooby, 2004) and fostering "social investment" (Morel et al., 2012): care and reconciliation, active labour policies, education and social assistance. Health care has remained more at the margin of the entire debate.

The contents and the findings of this book show that health care should be brought back at the centre of the general debate about the present and the future of our welfare states. In the European Union, health care represents the second most important source of public expenditure in social policies, after pensions. Moreover, in comparison with pensions and unemployment benefits, no sign of real retrenchment can be detected in this sector, at least until the recent crisis. In the last two decades, HCS have gone through a mix of recalibration, restructuring and expansion in terms of public programs' coverage, generosity and expenditure (expansion is a word unheard lately within the other traditional welfare state fields). As stated in Chapter 11, health care provision is shown to be characterized rather by increase than decline: in comparison with two decades ago, most HCS have improved in terms of dealing with all the four quadrilemma issues.

In this respect health care shares more common elements with other types of social policies, namely the main 'social investment' ones (for example, care and reconciliation), which have witnessed an expansion in the last two decades. What health care has in common with these policies is not only the fact that some sort of expansion has taken place, but also that they share also some common elements: health care and especially some relevant trends taking place inside it (de-hospitalization, more focus on primary care and prevention, outpatient services for those chronically ill, etc.) can play a central role in keeping workers into the labour market, thanks to the promotion of their health. That is the reason why prevention and effective care become even more relevant also in terms of social investment. That is also the reason why a stronger outpatient care HCS can help to reconcile work and care for the increasing number of workers who have to deal with their own chronic diseases or with those of their relatives.

This general overview of the findings of the book would not be completed if we did not take into account what has started since 2010, namely, the austerity measures adopted by many countries as a consequence of the economic crisis started in 2008. Given the fact that the crisis is not over yet in many countries, it is not easily predictable what impact it will have on HCS and their quadrilemma. What the book elicits, by analysing reforms and changes that have been taken place until mid 2013, is that some relevant retrenchment signs are really in sight for the first time in some countries, more prominently Southern European ones. If it is in this area of Europe where austerity measures seem to have hit harder, nevertheless many other European countries seem to be willing to challenge the actual HCS institutional designs following a retrenchment path.

The relationship between the crisis, austerity and HCS retrenchment will be one of the main issues on the agenda of future research in this policy field, together with other issues taken into consideration in this book, such as, for example, the impact of managerialization on the functioning of HCS and on professionals, the consequences of the new recentralization trends, the development of de-hospitalization policies and the functions the health care system can play in terms of a new social investment welfare state.

Note

1. Decentralization has often brought increases in expenditure, as many HCS have witnessed (see Chapter 9).

References

Aballea, P., Bartoli, F. Eslous, L. and Yeni, I. (2007), 'Les dépassements d'honoraires médicaux', *IGAS*, rapport n° RM 2007-054P, avril 2007.

Ameringer, C. F. (2008), *The Health Care Revolution: From Medical Monopoly to Market Competition*, Berkeley: University of California Press.

Anell, A. (1996), 'The monopolistic integrated model and health care reform: the Swedish experience', *Health Policy*, 37(1), July, 19–33.

Anell, A. (2011), 'Choice and privatisation in Swedish primary care', *Health Economics, Policy, and Law*, 6(4): 549–69.

Anell, A., Glenngård, A. H. and Merkur, S. (2012), *Sweden: Health system review: Health Systems in Transition*, 2012, 14(5): 1–159.

Appleby, J. (2011), 'How satisfied are we with the NHS?', *BMJ*, 342:d1836.

Swedish Work Environment Authority (2012), Nationell tillsyn av överbeläggningar inom akutsjukvården. Arbetsmiljöverket Projektrapport 2012: 2.

Arrow, K. J. (1963), 'Uncertainty and the welfare economics of medical care', *The American Economic Review*, LIII(5): 941–73.

Ärztekammer (2011), *Wahrnehmungsbericht 2009 und 2010. Gesundheitswesen unter der Lupe*, Wien: Österreichische Ärztekammer.

Audit Commission (2011), *NHS financial year 2010/11 A summary of auditors' work*. http://www.audit-commission.gov.uk/sitecollectiondocuments/downloads/20110808_nhsperformance.pdf

Avdagic, S. (2005), 'State-labour relations in East Central Europe: explaining variations in union effectiveness', *Socio-Economic Review*, 3(1): 25–53.

Bączek, I. (2008), 'Amerykańska klasyfikacja ma porządkować polski system'. http://www.rynekzdrowia.pl/Finanse-i-zarzadzanie/Amerykanska-klasyfikacja-ma-porzadkowac-polski-system,92,1,drukuj.html

Balcerowicz, L. (1994), 'Economic transition in Central and Eastern Europe: comparisons and lessons', *Australian Economic Review*, 27(1): 47–59.

Bambra, C. (2005), 'Worlds of welfare and the health care discrepancy', *Social Policy and Society*, 4(1): 31–41.

Bandelow, N. (2009), 'Health governance in the aftermath of traditional corporatism: one small step for the legislator, one giant leap for the subsystem', *German Policy Studies*, 5(1): 3–20.

Barómetro Sanitario (2010), *Informe anual*, Madrid: Ministerio de Sanidad, Servicios Sociales e Igualdad.

Barr, N. (2001), *The Economics of the Welfare State*, Oxford: Oxford University Press.

Barros, P.P. (1998), 'The black box of health care expenditure growth determinants', *Health Economics*, 7: 533–44.

Behar, B. and Wichels, R. (2009), 'Einweisermanagement in Gesundheitsnetzwerken – Ein schmaler Grad zwischen Kooperation und Wettbewerb', in V.E. Amelung, J. Sydow, J. and A. Windeler (eds), *Vernetzung im Gesundheitswesen – Wettbewerb und Kooperation*, Stuttgart: Kohlhammer: 349–58.

Bejerot, E., Aronsson, G., Hasselblad, H. and Bejerot, S. (2011), 'Läkarkåren en profession med allt mindre stöd och inflytande. Enkätstudie av svenska läkares arbetsmiljö 1992 och 2010', *Läkartidningen*, 50(108): 2652–6.

References 279

Béland, D. and Gran, B. (eds) (2008), *Public and Private Social Policy: Health and Pension Policies in a New Era*, Basingstoke: Palgrave Macmillan.
Bernal, E., Campillo, A., González, B., Meneu, R., Puig-Junoy, J., Repullo, J.R. and Urbanos, R. (2011), 'La sanidad pública ante la crisis. Recomendaciones para una actuación pública sensata y responsable', Working Paper, Asociación de Economía de la Salud, AES: Barcelona.
Bestmann, B. and Verheyen, F. (2010), 'Patientenzufriedenheit, Ergebnisse einer repräsentativen Studie in der ambulanten ärztlichen Versorgung', Hamburg: Wissenschaftliches Institut der TK für Nutzen und Effizienz im Gesundheitswesen (WINEG).
Blank, R.H. and Burau, V. (2010), *Comparative Health Policy, 3rd edition*, Basingstoke: Palgrave Macmillan.
Blekesaune, M. and Quadagno, J. (2003), 'Public attitudes toward welfare state policies: a comparative analysis of 24 nations', *Sociological Review*, 19(5): 415–27.
Blendon, R. J., Kim, M., and Benson, J.M. (2001), 'The public versus the World Health Organization on health system performance', *Health Affairs*, 20(3), May–June 2001.
Blomqvist, Å. and Carter, R.A.I. (1997), 'Is health care really a luxury?', *Journal of Health Economics*, 16(2): 207–29.
Blomqvist, P. (2002), 'Ideas and policy convergence: health care reforms in the Netherlands and Sweden in the 1990s', Dissertation Columbia University.
Blomqvist, P. (2004), 'The choice revolution: privatization of Swedish welfare services in the 1990s', *Social Policy and Administration*, 38(2): 139–55.
Blomqvist, P. and Bergman, P. (2010), 'Regionalisation Nordic style: will regions in Sweden threaten local democracy?', *Local Government Studies*, 36(1): 43–74.
Blomqvist, P. (2013), 'Citizenship, choice and social equality in welfare services', in U. Mörth and S. Karin (eds.), *The Political Role of Corporate Citizens – An Interdisciplinary Approach*. London: Palgrave.
BMAS and Hauptverband (eds) (1989), *100 Jahre österreichische Sozialversicherung. Festschrift*, Wien: BMAS und Hauptverband.
Böckmann, R. (2009), 'The private health insurance: demarketisation of a welfare market?', *German Policy Studies*, 5(1): 119–40.
Bocquet, P. Y., Bonnet, J. L., Lalande, F. and Scotton, C. (2012), 'Fusions et regroupements hospitaliers: quel bilan pour les 15 dernières années?', *IGAS*, rapport n° RM2012-020P, mars 2012.
Bode, I. (2006), 'Fair funding and competitive governance: the German model of health care organization under debate', *Revue Française des Affaires Sociales*, 2(3): 183–206.
Böhm, K. (2009), 'Federalism and the new politics of hospital financing', *German Policy Studies* 5(1): 99–118.
Bojke, C., Castelli, A., Goudie, R., Street, A., and Ward, P. (2012), *Productivity of the English National Health Service 2003/4-2009/10*. CHE Research Paper 76, York: University of York.
Bonoli, G., George, V. and Taylor-Gooby, P. (2000), *European Welfare Futures. Towards a Theory of Retrenchment*, Cambridge: Polity Press.
Bonoli, G. and Natali, D. (eds.) (2012), *The Politics of the New Welfare State*, Oxford: Oxford University Press.
Boyle, S. (2011), *United Kingdom (England): Health System Review*, London: European Observatory on Health Systems and Policies.
Boyle, S., Appleby, J. and Harrison, A. (2010), *A Rapid View of Access to Care*, London: King's Fund.

Brede, F. (2006), 'Politikberatung in der Gesundheitspolitik', in S. Falk, D. Rehfeld, A. Römmele and M. Thunert (eds) *Handbuch Politikberatung*, Wiesbaden: VS: 436–448.

Bristol Royal Infirmary Inquiry (2001), *The Report of the Public Inquiry into Children's Heart Surgery at the Bristol Royal Infirmary 1984–1995: Learning from Bristol*, London: The Stationery Office.

Brunner, A., Bürg, T.M., Bobens, C., Schmid, T., Troy, C.D., Wagner, A. (2010), *Arbeitsbedingungen und Arbeitsbelastungen in den Gesundheitsberufen Niederösterreich*, Wien: Sozialökonomische Forschungsstelle.

Bundesgeschäftsstelle Qualitätssicherung (BQS) (2009), 'Gemeinsame Registrierungsstelle zur Unterstützung der Umsetzung des § 140d SGB V Bericht zur Entwicklung der integrierten Versorgung 2004–2008', Düsseldorf: BQS.

Busse, R., Geissler, A., Quentin, W. and Wiley, M. (2012), *Diagnosis-Related Groups in Europe Moving Towards Transparency, Efficiency and Quality in Hospitals*, England: Open University Press.

Cacace, M., Goetze, R. and Schmid, A., and Rothgang, H. (2008), 'Explaining Healthcare System Change', Paper presented at the 4th International ESPA-net Expert Conference, University of Aalborg.

Campbell, J. (2004), *Institutional Change and Globalization*, Princeton: Princeton University Press.

Cantarero, D. (2010), 'Financiación regional en el sistema sanitario español: análisis del sistema actual y agenda pendiente' in J. Cabasés (Dir.) *La Financiación del Gasto Sanitario en España: Valoración del Sistema de Financiación, Medida de la Necesidad Relativa y Equidad* (Informes 2010-Economía y Sociedad, Fundación BBVA).

Capano, G. and Gualmini, E. (2010), *Le pubbliche amministrazioni in Italia*, Bologna: Il Mulino.

Care Quality Commission (2010), *National NHS Patient Survey Programme – Survey of Adult Inpatients 2009*, Electronic only: Healthcare Commission.

CBOS (Centrum Badania Opinii Publicznej) (2012), *Komunikat z badan. Opinie o funkcjonowaniu systemu opieki zdrowotnej*. https://docs.google.com/viewer?url=http%3A%2F%2Fwww.cbos.pl%2FSPISKOM.POL%2F2012%2FK_034_12.PDF

CEIS (2010), *VI Report Health Research*, Rome: CEIS.

CES (2010), *Informe sobre desarrollo autonómico, competitividad y cohesión social en el sistema sanitario*, Consejo Económico y Social.

Churchill, L. R. (1999), 'The United States Health Care System under Managed Care: How the Commodification of Health Care Distorts Ethics and Threatens Equity', *Health Care Analysis*, 7(4): 393–411.

Clarke, J. and Newman, J. (1997), *The Managerial State: Power, Politics and Ideology in the Remaking of Social Welfare*, Thousand Oaks, CA: Sage.

Clarke, J. and Newman, J. (1997), *The Managerial State: Power, Politics and Ideology in the Remaking of Social Welfare*, London: Sage.

Clasen, J. and Siegel, N. (eds) (2007), *Investigating Welfare State Change: The Dependent Variable Problem in Comparative Analysis*, Cheltenham: Edward Elgar Publishing.

Clayton, R. and Pontusson, J. (1998), 'Welfare-State Retrenchment Revisited: Entitlement Cuts, Public Sector Restructuring, and Inegalitarian Trends in Advanced Capitalist Societies', *World Politics*, 51(1): 67–98.

Clemente, J., Marcuello, C. and Montañés, A. (2008), 'Pharmaceutical expenditure, total health-care expenditure and GDP', *Health Economics*, 17(10): 1187–206.

Clery, E. (2011), 'Taking the pulse: attitudes to the health service', in A. Park, E. Clery and M. Phillips (eds) *British Social Attitudes 28th Report*. http://www.natcen.ac.uk/study/british-social-attitudes-28th-report

Coldefy, M., and Lucas-Gabrielli, V. (2008), 'Les territoires de santé : des approches régionales variées de ce nouvel espace de planification', *IRDES*, working paper, DT No. 10, May 2008.

Collins, C. and Green, A. (1994), 'Decentralisation and Primary Health Care: Some Negative Implication in Developing Countries', *International Journal of Health Services*, 24(3): 459–75.

Collyer, F. M. (2003), 'Theorising Privatisation: Policy, Network Analysis, and Class', *Electronic Journal of Sociology*, 7(3).

Cour des Comptes (2008), *La Sécurité sociale*, septembre 2008, Paris: Cour des Comptes.

Cour des Comptes (2011), *La Sécurité sociale*, septembre 2011, Paris: Cour des Comptes.

Cour des Comptes (2013), *La Sécurité sociale*, septembre 2013, Paris: Cour des Comptes.

Cox, R.H. (1998), 'The Consequences of Welfare State Reform: How Conceptions of Social Rights are Changing', *Journal of Social Policy*, 27(1): 1–16.

Czapinski, J., and Panek, T. (2011), *Diagnoza spoleczna. Warunki i jakosc zycia Polakow. Raport*, Warszawa: Rada Monitoringu Spolecznego.

Czypionka, T., Kraus, M., Mayer, S., Röhrling, G. and Schnabl, A. (2011), *Hospital Ownership and Efficiency in Austria, Are Public Hospitals Better off?*, Manuscript.

De la Fuente, A. and Gundín, M. (2009), 'Sobre el reparto de la financiación sanitaria', *Investigaciones Económicas*, 33(3): 473–527.

Delas, A. (2011), 'L'hôpital public, un nouvel acteur territorial entre aménagement sanitaire et rivalités stratégiques', *Hérodote*, 2011/4, 143: 89–119.

Den Exter, A.P. (2001), 'Legal Reforms of the Polish Health Care System in View of Accessing the European Union', *European Journal of Health Law*, 8(1): 5–25.

Department for Work and Pensions (2011), *Households Below Average Income: An analysis of the income distribution 1994/95 – 2009/10*, London: Department for Work and Pensions.

Department of Health (1989), *Working for Patients, CM 555*, HMSO: London.

Department of Health (1997), *The New NHS: Modern, Dependable*, London: Department of Health.

Department of Health (2000), *The NHS Plan: A Plan for Investment, a Plan for Reform*, London: Department of Health.

Department of Health (2001), *Health Secretary announces new plans to improve health in poorest areas, Press Release 2001/0108 (28 February)*, Electronic only: Department of Health. http://webarchive.nationalarchives.gov.uk/+/www.dh.gov.uk/en/Publicationsandstatistics/Pressreleases/DH_4014292

Department of Health (2007a), *Choice Matters 2007–08: Putting Patients in Control*, London: Department of Health.

Department of Health (2007b), *Trust, Assurance and Safety – The Regulation of Health Professionals in the 21st Century*, London: The Stationery Office.

Department of Health (2008a), *Framework for Managing Choice, Cooperation and Competition*, London: Department of Health.

Department of Health (2008b), *High Quality Care For All: NHS Next Stage Review Final Report*, London: TSO.

Department of Health (2008c), *GP Extended Opening Hours Results for July 2008*. Electronic only: Department of Health. http://www.dh.gov.uk/prod_consum_dh/groups/dh_digitalassets/@dh/@en/documents/digitalasset/dh_089690.xls

Department of Health (2009), *GP Extended Opening Hours Results for July 2009*. Electronic only: Department of Health. http://www.dh.gov.uk/prod_consum_dh/groups/dh_digitalassets/@dh/@en/@ps/@sta/@perf/documents/digitalasset/dh_104001.xls

Department of Health (2010a), *NHS Referral to Treatment (RTT) Waiting Times Statistics for England 2009 Annual Report*. Electronic only: Department of Health. http://www.dh.gov.uk/prod_consum_dh/groups/dh_digitalassets/@dh/@en/@ps/@sta/@perf/documents/digitalasset/dh_112663.pdf

Department of Health (2010b), *Revision to the Operating Framework for the NHS in England 2010/11*, London: Department of Health.

Department of Health (2010c), *Equity and excellence: Liberating the NHS*, Norwich: The Stationery Office.

Department of Health (2010d), *Department of Health – Spending Review 2010*, London: Department of Health.

Department of Health (2010e), *Imaging and Radiodiagnostics*, Electronic only: Department of Health. http://www.dh.gov.uk/en/Publicationsandstatistics/Statistics/Performancedataandstatistics/HospitalActivityStatistics/DH_077487

Després, C., Dourgnon, P. Fantin, R. and Jusot, F. (2011), 'Le renoncement aux soins pour raisons financières : une approche économétrique', *IRDES*, Questions d'économie et de la santé, n°170, novembre 2011.

Destais, N. (2003), *Le système de santé, organisation et régulation*, Paris: LGDJ.

Deutscher Bundestag (2009), 'Gesetz zur Sicherung von Beschäftigung und Stabilität in Deutschland vom 2. März 2009 (StabSiG)', Bundesgesetzblatt Jahrgang 2009 Teil 1(11): 416–33.

Devaux, M. and de Looper, M. (2012), *Income-Related Inequalities in Health Service Utilisation in 19 OECD countries, 2008–2009*, OECD Health Working Papers No. 58, Paris: OECD.

Devaux, M., and de Looper, M. (2012), 'Income-Related Inequalities in Health Service Utilisation in 19 OECD countries, 2008–2009', *OECD Health Working Papers No. 58*, Paris: OECD.

DGOS (2010), *Les chiffres clés de l'offre de soins. Edition 2010*, Paris: DGOS.

Dixon, A., Le Grand, J., Henderson, J., Murray, R. and Poteliakhoff, E. (2007), 'Is the British National Health Service Equitable? The Evidence on Socioeconomic Differences in Utilization', *Journal of Health Services Research & Policy*, 12(2): 104–9.

DKG (2009), 'Deutsche Krankenhausgesellschaft – Aufgaben und Ziele', http://www.dkgev.de/dkg.php/cat/ 23/aid/2/title/Aufgaben_und_Ziele, 10 August 2009.

Dourgnon, P. and Naiditch, M. (2009), 'The preferred doctor scheme: A political reading of a French experiment of Gate-keeping', *IRDES working paper*, DT No. 22, March 2009.

DREES (2010a), *Comptes nationaux de la Santé 2010*, Paris: DREES.

DREES (2010b), *Le panorama des établissements de santé. Edition 2010*, Paris: DREES.

DREES (2012), *Le panorama des établissements de santé. Edition 2012*, Paris: DREES.

Drucker, P. (2010), *The Changing World of the Executive*, Boston: Harvard Business Press.

Edwards, D. J. (1998), 'Managerial Influences in Public Administration', *International Journal of Organization Theory and Behavior*, 1(4): 232–51.

Esping-Andersen, G. (1990), *The Three Worlds of Welfare Capitalism*, Oxford: Oxford University Press.

Esping-Andersen, G. (1996), *Social Foundations of Postindustrial Economics*, Oxford: Oxford University Press.

Esping-Andersen, G. (2002), *Why We Need a New Welfare State*, Oxford: Oxford University Press.

Estrin, S. (1994), 'The Inheritance' in N.Barr (ed.) *Labor Markets and Social Policy in Central and Eastern Europe: The Transition and Beyond*, New York: Oxford University Press.

Eurobarometer (2007), 'Health and Long-term Care in the European Union', *Special EU barometer* N° 283 , 67.3.

Eurobarometer (2010), 'Patient Safety and Quality of Health Care', *Special EU barometer* No 327, 72.2.

European Commission (1998), 'Citizens and Health care systems', Luxemburg: Office for Official Publications of the European Communities.

European Commission (2009), *The 2009 Ageing Report. Economic and Budgetary Projections for the EU-27 Member States (2008–2060)*, Joint Report Prepared by the European Commission (DG ECFIN) and the Economic Policy Committee (AWG), Brussels: European Commission.

European Commission (2009), *Joint Report on Social Protection and Social Inclusion 2009 – France*, Brussels: EC.

European Commission (2012), *The 2012 Ageing Report. Economic and Budgetary Projections for the 27 EU Member States (2010–2060)*, Joint Report Prepared by the European Commission (DG ECFIN) and the Economic Policy Committee (AWG). Brussels: European Commission.

FADSP (2012), *Informe sobre los recortes sanitarios en las comunidades autónomas*, Madrid: FADSP.

Falkner, G. (2005), *Complying with Europe: EU Harmonisation and Soft Law in the Member States*, Cambridge: Cambridge University Press.

Fattore, G., Mariotti, G. and Rebba, V. (2013), 'Italy', in L. Siciliani, M. Borowitz and V. Moran (eds), *Waiting Time Policies in the Health Sector: What Works?*, OECD Health Policy Studies, OECD Publishing.

Ferrarini, T. (2006), *Families, States and Labour Markets: Institutions, Causes and Consequences of Family Policy in Post War Welfare States*, Cheltenham: Edward Elgar Publishing.

Ferrera, M., and Hemerijck, A. (2003), 'Recalibrating Europe's Welfare Regimes', in J. Zeitlin and D.M. Trubek (eds), *Governing Work and Welfare in a New Economy*, Oxford: Oxford University Press.

Filinson, R., Chmielewski, P., and Niklas, D. (2003), 'Back to the Future: Polish Healthcare Reform', *Communist and Post-Communist Studies*, 36(4): 385–403.

France, G. (2008), 'Seeking a Better Balance: Developments in Intergovernmental Relations in the Italian Healthcare', *Eurohealth*, 133: 16–19.

France, G. and Taroni, F. (2000), 'Starting Down the Road to Targets in Health: The Case of Italy', *European Journal of Public Health* 10 (4 Supplement): 25–9.

France, G. and Taroni, F. (2005), 'The Evolution of Health-Policy Making in Italy', *Journal of Health Politics, Policy and Law*, 30 (1-2): 169–84.

Frazer, H., Marlier, E., Natali, D., Van Dam, R., and Vanhercke, B. (2010. 'Europe 2020: Towards a More Social EU?', in Marlier, E., Natali, D. and Van Dam, R. (eds), *Europe 2020: Towards a More Social EU?*, Brussels: P.I.E. Peter Lang.

Fredriksson, M. (2012), 'Between Equity and Local Autonomy: A Governance Dilemma in Swedish Healthcare', Dissertation, Uppsala universitet, Uppsala.

Fredriksson, M., Blomqvist, P. and Winblad, U. (2012), 'Conflict and Compliance in Swedish Health Care Governance: Soft Law in the "Shadow of Hierarchy"', *Scandinavian Political Studies*, 35(1): 48–70. doi:10.1111/j.1467-9477.2011.00279.x

Fredriksson, M., Blomqvist, P. and Winblad, U. (2013), 'The trade-off between choice and equity: Swedish policymakers' arguments when introducing patient choice', *Journal of European Social Policy*, 23(2): 192–209.

Freeman, R. (2000), *The Politics of Health in Europe*, Manchester: Manchester University Press.

Freeman, R. (2002), *Inequality around the World*, Basingstoke: Palgrave Macmillan.

Freire, J. and Repullo, J. (2011), 'El buen gobierno de los servicios de salud de producción pública: ideas para avanzar', *Ciência&Saúde Coletiva*, 16(6): 2733–42.

Freire, J.M. (2010), *Recomendaciones del consejo asesor sobre el buen gobierno de la sanidad pública vasca*, Departamento de Sanidad y Consumo, Gobierno Vasco.

Friedemann, J., Schubert, H.-J. and Schwappach, D. (2009), 'Zur Verständlichkeit der Qualitätsberichte deutscher Krankenhäuser: Systematische Auswertung und Handlungsbedarf', *Gesundheitswesen*, 71(1): 3–9.

Fuchs, M., Schmied, G. and Oberzaucher, N. (2003), *Quantitative und qualitative Erfassung und Analyse der nicht-krankenversicherten Personen in Österreich*, Wien: Bundesministerium für Gesundheit und Frauen.

García, A. (2011), 'Is Spanish Public Health Sinking?', *BMJ*, 343(7833): 1086–7.

García, S., Abadía, M.B., Durán, A., Hernández, C. and Bernal, E. (2010), 'Spain: Health System Review', *Health Systems in Transition*, 12(4): 1–295.

Geissler, A., Wörz, M. and Busse, R. (2010), 'Deutsche Krankenhauskapazitäten im internationalen Vergleich', in K. Jürgen, M. Geraedts, J. Friedrich (eds), *Krankenhaus-Report 2010. Schwerpunkt: Krankenhausversorgung in der Krise?* Stuttgart: Schattauer: 25–40.

Gerdtham, U.G. (1992), 'Pooling International Health Care Expenditure Data', *Health Economics*, 1(4): 217–31.

Gerlinger T. (2010), 'Health Care Reform in Germany', *German Policy Studies*, 6(1): 107–42.

Gerlinger T. and Schmucker, R. (2009), 'A Long Farewell to the Bismarck System: Incremental Change in the German Health Insurance System', *German Policy Studies* 5(1): 3–20.

Gerlinger, T. (2008), 'Wettbewerbsinduzierte Unitarisierung. Der Wandel der Bund-Länder Beziehungen in der Gesundheitspolitik', in H. Scheller, and J. Schmid (eds), *Föderale Politikgestaltung im deutschen Bundesstaat: Variable Verflechtungsmuster in Politikfeldern*, Baden-Baden: Nomos: 242–63.

Giaimo, S. (2002), *Markets and Medicine: The Politics of Health Care Reform in Britain, Germany, and the United States*, Ann Arbor: University of Michigan Press.

Golinowska, S. (2010), 'Oplaty nieformalne w ochronie zdrowia. Perspektywa i doswiadczenia polskie', *Zeszyty naukowe ochrony zdrowia. Zdrowie publiczne i Zarzadanie*, 8(1): 12–28.

González, B. and Barber, P. (1996), 'Changes in the Efficiency of Spanish Public Hospitals after the Introduction of Program-Contracts', *Investigaciones Económicas*, 20: 377–402.

González, B. and Barber, P. (2006), 'Desigualdades territoriales en el Sistema Nacional de Salud (SNS) de España', Documento de trabajo 90/2006, Laboratorio de Alternativas, Fundación Alternativas.

González, E., Cárcaba, A. and Ventura, J. (2010), 'Value Efficiency Analysis of Health Systems: Does Public Financing Play a Role?', *Journal of Public Health*, 18: 337–50.

Government Bill. Prop. 2008/09:29 Lag om valfrihetssystem.

Government Bill. Prop. 2008/09:74 Vårdval i primärvården.

Government Commission (2012), Gör det enklare! SOU 2012:33.

Greer, S.L. (2008), 'Choosing Paths in European Union Health Services Policy: A Political Analysis of a Critical Juncture', *Journal of European Social Policy*, 18(3): 219–31.

Greve, B. (1996), 'Indications of Social Policy Convergence in Europe', *Social Policy and Administration*, 30(4): 348–67.

Griffiths, R. (1983), *NHS Management Inquiry Report*, London: Department of Health and Social Security.

Guardian (2000), Blair's £12bn pledge to NHS. http://www.guardian.co.uk/society/2000/jan/17/futureofthenhs.health1

Guillén, A.M. and Álvarez, S. (2004), 'The EU's Impact on the Spanish Welfare State: The Role of Cognitive Europeanization', *Journal of European Social Policy*, 14(3): 285–99.

Gustavsson, S. (2010), 'European Transnational Constitutionalism: End of History, or a Role for Legitimate Opposition?', in E. Özdalga and S. Person (eds), *Contested Sovereignties: Forms of Government and Democracy in Eastern and European Perspectives*, London: IB Tauris.

Hacker, J.S. (1998), 'The Historical Logic of National Health Insurance', *Studies in American Political Development*, 12: 57–130.

Hacker, J.S. (2004), 'Review Article: Dismantling the Health Care State? Political Institutions, Public Policies and the Comparative Politics of Health Reform', *British Journal of Political Science*, 34(4): 693–724.

Hacker, J.S. (2005), 'Policy Drift: The Hidden Politics of US Welfare State Retrenchment', in W. Streeck and K. Thelen (eds) *Beyond Continuity: Institutional Change in Advanced Political Economies*, New York: Oxford University Press, 40–82.

Hall, P. A. (1993), 'Policy Paradigms, Social Learning, and the State The Case of Economic Policymaking in Britain', *Comparative Politics*, 25(3): 275–96.

Hall, P.A. and Soskice, D. (2001), *Varieties of Capitalism: The Institutional Foundations of Comparative Advantage*, Oxford: Oxford University Press.

Hansen, P. and King, A. (1996), 'The Determinant of Health Care Expenditure: A Cointegration Approach', *Journal of Health Economics*, 15(1): 127–37.

Harker, R. (2012), *NHS Funding and Expenditure*. Electronic only: House of Commons Library. http://www.parliament.uk/briefing-papers/SN00724

Harrison, A. and Appleby, J. (2009), 'Reducing Waiting Times for Hospital Treatment: Lessons from the English NHS', *Journal of Health Services Research & Policy*, 14(3): 168–73.

Hassenteufel, P. (2001), 'Liberalisation through the State: Why Is the French Health System becoming so British?', *Public Policy and Administration*, 16(4): 84–95.

Hassenteufel, P. (2009), 'Le rôle de l'Etat dans la régulation de l'assurance maladie' in J. L. Bras, G. de Pouvourville and D. Tabuteau (eds), *Traité d'économie et de gestion de la santé*, Paris: Editions de Santé ; Les Presses de Sciences Po.

Hassenteufel, P. and Palier, B. (2005), 'Les trompe-l'œil de la "gouvernance" de l'assurance maladie : contrastes franco-allemands', *Revue française d'administration publique*, 113: 13–27.

Hassenteufel, P. and Palier, B. (2007), 'Towards Neo-Bismarckian Health Care States? Comparing Health Insurance Reforms in Bismarckian Welfare Systems', *Social Policy and Administration*, 41(6): 574–96.

Hassenteufel, P., Smyrl, M. and Genieys, W. and Moreno, J. (2010), 'Programmatic Actors and the Transformation of European Health Care States', *Journal of Health Politics, Policy and Law* 35(4): 509–530.

Health Consumer Powerhouse (2005), *Euro Health Consumer Index 2005. Report*, Danderyd: Health Consumer Powerhouse.

Health Consumer Powerhouse (2009), *Euro Health Consumer Index 2009. Report*, Danderyd: Health Consumer Powerhouse.

Health Consumer Powerhouse (2012), *Euro Health Consumer Index 2012. Report*, Danderyd: Health Consumer Powerhouse.

Healy, J. and McKee, M. (2002), 'The Evolution of Hospital Systems', in M. McKee and J. Healy (eds), *Hospitals in a Changing Europe*, Buckingham: Open University Press.

Healy, J. and McKee, M., (1997), 'Health Sector Reform in Central and Eastern Europe: The Professional Dimension', *Health Policy and Planning*, 12(4): 286–95.

Hellgren, J., Baraldi, S., Falkenberg, H. and Sverke, M. (2006), 'Bäst arbetsklimat på sjukhus som bolagiserats eller privatiserats. Läkares upplevelser av att arbeta i olika driftsformer', *Läkartidningen* nr 26-27, 103: 2040–4.

Herr, A. (2008), 'Cost and Technical Efficiency of German Hospitals: Does Ownership Matter?', *Health Economics*, 17(9): 1057–71.

Hervey, K. (2007), 'EU Law and National Health Policies: Problem or Opportunity', *Health Economics, Policy and Law*, 2(1): 1–6.

Hinrichs, Karl (2010), 'A Social Insurance State Withers Away: Welfare State Reforms in Germany – or: Attempts to Turn Around in a Cul-de-sac', in B. Palier (ed.), *A Long Goodbye to Bismarck? The Politics of Welfare Reform in Continental Europe*, Amsterdam: Amsterdam University Press: 45–72.

Hirschman A.O. (1970), *Exit, Voice and Loyalty Responses to Decline in Firms, Organizations, and States*, Cambridge: Harvard University Press.

Hitiris, T. and Posnett, J. (1992), 'The Determinants and Effects of Health Care Expenditure in Developed Countries', *Journal of Health Economics*, 11(2): 173–81.

Hofmarcher, M.M. and Rack, H. (2001), *Health Care Systems in Transition. Austria*, Copenhagen: European Observatory of Health Care Systems.

Hofmarcher, M.M. and Rack, H. (2006), *Austria: Health Systems Review*, Copenhagen: World Health Organization.

Hofmarcher, M.M., Lietz, C. and Schnabl, A. (2005), 'Inefficiency in Austrian Inpatient Care. Identifying Ailing Providers Based on DEA Results', *Central European Journal of Operations Research*, 13(4): 341–63.

Hofmarcher, M.M., Paterson, I. and Riedel, M. (2002), 'Measuring Hospital Efficiency in Austria. A DEA Approach', *Health Care Management Science*, 5(1): 7–14.

HOPE (2011), *The Crisis, Hospitals and Health Care*, Brussels: European Hospital and Healthcare Federation.

Huber, E. and Stephens, J.D. (2000), *Development and Crisis of the Welfare State: Parties and Policies in Global Markets*, Chicago: University of Chicago Press.

Huber, E., Ragin, C. and Stephens J.D. (1993), 'Social Democracy, Christian Democracy, Constitutional Structure and the Welfare State', *American Journal of Sociology*, 99(3): 711–49.

Huber, E., Ragin, C., Stephens, J.D., Brady, D. and Beckfield, J. (2004), *Comparative Welfare States Data Set*, Northwestern University, University of North Carolina, Duke University and Indiana University.

Immergut, E. (1992), 'The Rules of the Game: The Logic of Health Policy-making in France, Switzerland, and Sweden', in S. Steinmo and K. Thelen K. (eds), *Structuring Politics. Historical Institutionalism in Comparative Analysis*, Cambridge: Cambridge University Press.

Information Centre (2010), *HESonline: Headline figures*. Electronic only: Information Centre. http://www.hesonline.nhs.uk/Ease/servlet/ContentServer?siteID=1937&categoryID=193

Inglot, T. (2008), *Welfare States in East Central Europe, 1914–2004*, Cambridge: Cambridge University Press.

Institute of Fiscal Studies (2012a), Revenue (including forecasts) since 1963/64. IFS electronic only. http://www.ifs.org.uk/fiscalFacts/fiscalAggregates

Institute of Fiscal Studies (2012b), Spending by function since 1945/46. IFS electronic only. http://www.ifs.org.uk/fiscalFacts/fiscalAggregates

IRDES (2012), *Eco-Santé France 2012*, Paris: IRDES.

Istat (2012), *Health for All Database*, Rome: Istat.

Iversen, T. and Cusack, T. (2000), 'The Causes of Welfare State Expansion: Deindustrialization or Globalization?', *World Politics*, 52(3): 313–49.

Jacobs, A. (1998), 'Seeing Difference: Market Health Reform in Europe', *Journal of Health Politics, Policy and Law*, 23(1): 1-33.

Jordan, J. (2010), 'Health Care Politics in the Age of Retrenchment', *Journal of Social Policy*, 40(1): 113–34.

Kamarudeen, S. (2010), *Amenable Mortality as an Indicator of Healthcare Quality – A Literature Review*, Newport: Office For National Statistics. http://www.ons.gov.uk

Kaminska, M. E., and Kahancova, M. (2011), 'Emigration and Labour Shortages: An Opportunity for Trade Unions in the New Member States?', *European Journal of Industrial Relations*, 17(2): 189–203.

Kaminska, M.E. (2013), 'The Missing Dimension: A Comparative Analysis of Healthcare Governance in Central and Eastern Europe', *Journal of Comparative Policy Analysis: Research and Practice*, 15(1): 68–86.

Karanikolos, M. et al. (2013), 'Financial Crisis, Austerity, and Health in Europe', *The Lancet*, 382(9874): 1323–31.

Karski, J., Koronkiewicz, A. and Healy, J. (1999), *Health Care Systems in Transition: Poland*, Copenhagen: European Observatory on Health Care Systems.

Kassenärztliche Bundesvereinigung (2011), 'Die ärztliche Versorgung in der Bundesrepublik Deutschland zum 31 Dezember 2010', *Blaue Reihe*, 63/2011.

Kastberg, G. and Berlin, J. (2011), *Styrning av hälso- och sjukvård*, Malmö: Liber.

Kikuzawa, S., Olafsdottir, S. and Pescosolido, B.A. (2008), 'Similar Pressures, Different Contexts: Public Attitudes toward Government Intervention for Health Care in 21 Nations', *Journal of Health and Social Behavior*, 49: 385–99.

Klimek, D. (2010), 'Kontraktowa forma swiadczenia pracy w ochronie zdrowia – szansa czy zagrozenie?', *Polityka Spoleczna* 7, 10–15.

Kmietowicz, K. (2003), 'Foundation trusts "will pressure regulator to allow changes to licence"', *BMJ* September 13; 327(7415): 581. http://www.ncbi.nlm.nih.gov/pmc/articles/PMC1140693/

Koch, K. and Schürmann, C. and Sawicki, P. T. (2010), 'The German Health Care System in International Comparison: A Patient Perspective', *Deutsches Ärzteblatt International*, 107(24): 427–34.

Konkurrensverket (2010), Uppföljning av vårdval i primärvården. Valfrihet, mångfald och etableringsförutsättningar. Slutrapport. Konkurrensverkets rapportserie 2010: 3.

Kornai, J. and Eggelston, K. (2001), *Welfare, Choice, and Solidarity in Transition. Reforming the Health Care Sector in Eastern Europe*, Cambridge: Cambridge University Press.

Korpi, W. (1989), 'Power, Politics and State Autonomy in the Development of Social Citizenship: Social Rights during Sickness in Eighteen OECD Countries since 1930', *American Sociological Review*, 54(3): 309–28.

Korpi, W. (2001), 'Contentious Institutions: An Augmented Rational-action Analysis of the Origins and Path Dependency of Welfare State Institutions in Western countries', *Rationality and Society*, 13(2): 235–83.

Korpi, W. and Palme, J. (1998), 'The Paradox of Redistribution and Strategies of Equality: Welfare State Institutions, Inequality, and Poverty in the Western Countries', *American Sociological Review*, 63(5): 661–87.

Korpi, W. and Palme, J. (2003), 'New Politics and Class Politics in the Context of Austerity and Globalization: Welfare State Regress in 18 Countries 1975–95', *American Political Science Review*, 97(3): 425–46.

Kowalska, I. (2009), 'Odpowiedzialność samorządu lokalnego za zdrowie. Podstawowa opieka zdrowotna – oczekiwania a rzeczywistość', *Polityka Społeczna*, 11(12): 44–9.

Kowalska, I. (2010), 'The Project Law on Healing Activities', *Health Policy Monitor*, October

Kozierkiewicz, A. (2009), 'Poland: Will Legal Restructuring Affect the (Real) Economy of Hospitals?', *Eurohealth* 15(2): 17–18.

Krajewski-Siuda K. and Romaniuk, P. (2008), 'System ordynatorski vs. system konsultancki', *Zdrowie Publiczne*, 118(2): 206–9.

Krajowy Rejestr Zakladow Opieki Zdrowotnej (National Register of Healthcare Units) (2011), http://www.rejestrzoz.gov.pl/RZOZ/. Accessed 15 November 2011.

Krause, U. (2010), *Zwischen Wunsch und Wirklichkeit – Hausarztmodelle in Deutschland Nutzerorientierung, Grundlagen und Umsetzung*, Bremen: Universität Bremen.

Kreutzer, K. and Jäger, U. (2010), 'Volunteering Versus Managerialism: Conflict Over Organizational Identity in Voluntary Associations', *Nonprofit and Voluntary Sector Quarterly online first*, published on 21 May: 1–28.

Kuhlmann, E. (2006), *Modernizing Health Care: Reinventing Professions, the State and the Public*, Bristol: The Policy Press.

Kuhlmann, E. (2011), 'Medicine and Management in European Healthcare Systems', *The International Journal of Clinical Practice*, 65(7): 722–4.

Kuhlmann, E. and Saks, M. (2008), *Rethinking Professional Governance: International Directions in Healthcare*, Bristol: The Policy Press.

Kuszewski, K., and Gericke, C. (2005) *Health Systems in Transition: Poland,* Copenhagen: WHO Regional Office for Europe on behalf of the European Observatory on Health Systems and Policies.

Labour Party (1997), New Labour because Britain deserves better. Electronic only: Labour Party. http://www.labour-party.org.uk/manifestos/1997/1997-labour-manifesto.shtml

Ladurner, J., Gerger, M., Holland, W.W., Mossialos, E., Merkur, S., Stewart, S., Irwin, R. and Soffried, J. (eds) (2010), *Public Health in Austria: An Analysis of the Status of Public Health*, European Observatory on Health Systems and Policies Studies Series No. 24, Copenhagen: World Health Organization.

Lamping, W. and Rüb, F. W. (2001), *From the Conservative Welfare State to 'Something Uncertain Else': German Pension Politics in Comparative Perspective*, University of Hannover, Centre for Social and Public Policy, Discussion Paper No. 12. Hannover.

Le Breton-Lerouvillois, G. (2011), 'Atlas de la démographie médicale en France', *Conseil de l'Ordre des Médecins*.

Le Lan, R. and Baubeau, D. (2004), 'Les conditions de travail perçues par les professionnels des établissements de santé', *DREES Etudes et Résultats*, n°335, août 2004.

Leibenstein, H. (1966), 'Allocative Efficiency vs. *X-efficiency*', *American Economic Review*, 56: 392–415.

Leidl, R. (2001), 'Konvergenz der Gesundheitssysteme in der Europäischen Union', *Gesundheitsökonomie und Qualitätsmanagement*, 6(2): 44–53.

Leisering, Lutz (ed.) (2011), *The New Regulatory State: Regulating Private Pensions in Germany and the UK*, Basingstoke: Palgrave Macmillan.

Lijphart, A. (1977), *Democracy in Plural Societies: A Comparative Exploration*, New Haven: Yale University Press.

Lindh, T., Malmberg, B., and Palme, J. (2005), 'Generations at War or Sustainable Social Policy in Aging Societies', *Journal of Political Philosophy*, 13(4): 470–89.

Lindorff, D. (1992), *Marketplace Medicine: The Rise of the For-Profit Hospital Chains*, New York: Bantam Books.

Lindqvist, E. (2008), *Will Privatization Reduce Costs?* IFN Working Paper No. 736, Stockholm: Research Institute of Industrial Economics.

López, L.A., Martinez, J.I., Fernández, A., March, J.C., Suess, A., Danet, A. and Prieto, M.A. (2012), '¿Está en peligro la cobertura universal en nuestro Sistema Nacional de Salud?', *Gaceta Sanitaria*, 4(26): 298–300.

Lüngen M., Siegel M. (2011), 'Determinanten der Patientenzufriedenheit in der ambulanten Versorgung. Eine empirische Abschätzung für Deutschland', *Studien zu Gesundheit, Medizin und Gesellschaft*, 2011(5), 16 November 2011.

Lütticke, J. and Schellschmidt, H. (2005), 'Qualitätsberichte nach § 137 SGB V – Bewertung und Vorschläge zur Erweiterung', in J. Klauber, B.P. Robra and H. Schellschmidt (eds), *Krankenhaus-Report 2004*, Stuttgart: Schattauer: 197–212.

Mackenbach, J. and McKee, M. (2013), 'A Comparative Analysis of Health Policy Performance in 43 European Countries', *European Journal of Public Health*, 23(2): 195–344.

Magnussen, J., Vrangbæk, K. and Saltman, R.B. (eds), *Nordic Health Care Systems: Recent Reforms and Current Policy Changes*, Berkshire: Open University Press.

Mahoney, J. and Thelen, K. (2010), *Explaining Institutional Change*, Cambridge: Cambridge University Press.

Maier, F., Leitner, J., Meyer, M. and Millner, R. (2009), 'Managerialismus in Nonprofit Organisationen', *Kurswechsel*, (4): 94–101.

Majone, G. (1993), 'The European Community between Social Policy and Social Regulation', *Journal of Common Market Studies*, 31(2): 153–70.

Mapelli, V. (2007), *I sistemi di governance dei servizi sanitari regionali*, Milano: Quaderni del Formez.

Marburger B. (2006), *Die Arbeitssituation Deutscher Krankenhausärzte* (www.marburger-bund.de), date accessed 20 March 2013.

Marburger B. (2010), *Die Arbeitssituation Deutscher Krankenhausärzte* (www.marburger-bund.de), date accessed 20 March 2013.

Marinacci, C., Ferracin, E., Landriscina, T., Cislaghi, C., Gargiulo, L. and Costa, G. (2010), 'Differenze geografiche o differenze sociali?' In IOHCR (ed.), *Rapporto Osservasalute 2010*: 473–84. Rome: IOHCR

Marmor, T., Freeman, R. and Okma, K. (2005), 'Comparative Perspectives and Policy Learning in the World of Health Care', *Journal of Comparative Policy Analysis: Research and Practice*, 7(4): 331–48.

Marmor, T. and Wendt, C. (2012), 'Conceptual Frameworks for Comparing Healthcare Politics and Policy', *Health Policy*, 107: 11–20.

Martin, J. (2003), 'Nuevas fórmulas de gestión en las organizaciones sanitarias', *Fundación Alternativas*, Working paper 14.

Martín, J.J.M., des Amo González, M.P.L. and García, M.D.C. (2011), 'Review of the Literature on the Determinants of Healthcare Expenditure', *Applied Economics*, 43: 19–46.

Mattei, P. (2009), *Restructuring Welfare Organizations in Europe: From Democracy to Good Management?*, Basingstoke: Palgrave Macmillan.

McCoskey, S.K. and Selden, T.M. (1998), 'Health Care Expenditure and GDP: Panel Data Unit Root Test Results', *Journal of Health Economics*, 17(3): 369–76.

McKee, M. and Mossialos, E. (2006), 'Health Policy and European Law: Closing the gaps', *Public Health*, 120(S1): 16–22.

McKee, M., MacLehose, L. and Nolte, E. (2004), *Health Policy and EU Enlargement*, Maidenhead: Open University Press.

McKinsey & Company and FEDEA (2010), *Impulsar un cambio posible en el sistema sanitario*, Madrid: FEDEA.

McLellan, A., Middleton, J. and Godlee, F. (2012), 'Lansley's NHS "Reforms" Something Like This must Never Happen Again', *BMJ*; 344:e709.

Mechanic, D. and Rochefort, D.A. (1990), 'Deinstitutionalization: An Appraisal of Reform', *Annual Review of Sociology*, 16: 301–27.

Melucci, A. and Diani, M. (1994), *Nazioni senza Stato*, Milano: Feltrinelli.

Meneu, R. and Ortún, V. (2011) 'Transparencia y buen gobierno en sanidad. También para salir de la crisis', *Gaceta Sanitaria*, 25(4): 333–8.

Midgley, J. (1999), 'Growth, Redistribution, and Welfare: Toward Social Investment', *Social Service Review*, 73(1): 3–21.

Ministero della Salute (2011), *Rapporti annuali sui ricoveri ospedalieri*, Roma: Ministero della Salute.

Mladovsky, Ph., Allin, S., Masseria, C., Hernández-Quevedo, C., McDaid, D., Mossialos, E. (2009), *Health in the European Union. Trends and analysis*. Observatory Studies Series No 19. European Observatory on Health Systems and Policies.

Mokrzycka, A. and Kowalska, I. (2008), 'Status of Health Care Units: Project of Law', *Health Policy Monitor* April (http://hpm.org/survey/pl/a11/2)

Montanari, I., Nelson, K. and Palme, J. (2008), 'Towards a European Social Model? Trends in Social Insurance among EU Countries 1980–2000', *European Societies*, 10(5): 787–810.

Montanari, I. (1995), 'Harmonization of Social Policies and Social Regulation in the European Community', *European Journal of Political Research*, 27(1): 21–45.

Montanari, I. (2001), 'Modernization, Globalization and the Welfare State: A Comparative Analysis of Old and New Convergence of Social Insurance since 1930', *British Journal of Sociology*, 52(3): 469–94.

Montanari, I. (2009), 'Europe, Women and Work: Is the "Adult Worker Ideal" Achieved?', *International Journal of Health Services*, 39(2): 245–69.

Montanari, I. and Nelson, K. (2013), 'Social Service Decline and System Convergence: How Does Health Care Fare?', *Journal of European Social Policy*, 23(1): 102–16.

Montanari, I., Nelson, K. and Palme, J. (2007), 'Convergence Pressures and Responses: Recent Social Insurance Development in Modern Welfare States', *Comparative Sociology*, 6(3): 295–323.

Moran, M. (1999), *Governing the Health Care State: A Comparative Study of the United Kingdom, the United States and Germany*, Manchester: Manchester University Press.

Moran, M. (2000), 'Understanding the Welfare State: The Case of Health Care', *British Journal of Politics and International Relations*, 2(2): 135–60.

Morel, N., Palier, B. and Palme, J. (eds.) (2012), *Towards a Social Investment Welfare State?*, Bristol: Policy Press.

Morgan, D. and Astolfi, R. (2013), *Which Countries, Which Sectors are Most Affected*, OECD Health Working Paper No. 60, Paris: OECD.

Mosca, I. (2006), 'Is Decentralization the Real Solution? A Three Country Study', *Health Policy*, 77 (1): 113–20.

Mosebach, K. (2009), 'Comercializing German Hospital Care? Effects of New Public Management and Manged Car under Neoliberal Conditions', *Germany Policy Studies*, 5(1): 65–98.

Mossialos, E, and McKee, M. (2002), *EU Law and the Social Character of Health Care*, Brussels: P.I.E.- Peter Lang S.A..

Mrozowicki, A. (2011), 'Poland: Industrial Relations in the Health Care Sector', http://www.eurofound.europa.eu/eiro/studies/tn1008022s/pl1008029q.htm

NAO (2007), *Pay Modernisation: A New Contract for NHS Consultants in England*, London: The Stationery Office.

NAO (2009), *NHS Pay Modernisation in England: Agenda for Change*, London: The Stationery Office.

Navarro, V. (2002), 'Assessment of the World Health Report 2000', *The Lancet*, 356: 1598–601.

National Board of Health and Welfare (2011), Uppföljning av den nationella vårdgarantin och 'kömiljarden', Socialstyrelsen, årsrapport 2011.

National Competition Agency (2010), Uppföljning av vårdval i primärvården. Valfrihet, mångfald och etableringsförutsättningar. Slutrapport. Konkurrensverkets rapportserie 2010: 3

Nelson, K. (2008), 'Minimum Income Protection and European Integration: Trends and Levels of Minimum Benefits in Comparative Perspective 1990–2005', *International Journal of Health Services*, 38(1): 103–24.

Newhouse, J.P. (1992), 'Medical Care Costs: How much Welfare Loss?', *Journal of Economic Perspectives*, 6(3): 3–21.

NICE (2010), *Technology Appraisal Recommendation Summary*. Electronic only: NICE. http://www.nice.org.uk/newsroom/nicestatistics/TADecisionsRecommendation Summary.jsp

Nicholson, D. (2012), *The Year: NHS Chief Executive's annual report 2011/12, including The Quarter, Quarter 4 2011/12*, London: Department of Health.

NIK (Najwyzsza Izba Kontroli, Supreme Chamber of Control) (2011), *Informacja o wynikach kontroli przeksztalcen wlasnosciowych wybranych szpitali w latach 2006–2010*. Warszawa: Najwyzsza Izba Kontroli.

Nolte, E. and McKee, M. (2011), 'Variations in Amenable Mortality. Trends in 16 High-income Nations', *Health Policy*, 103(1): 47–52.

Nolte, E., McKee, M. and Gilmore, A.B. (2005), 'Morbidity and Mortality in Transition Countries of Europe' in *The New Demographic Regime: Population Challenges and Policy Responses*. New York and Geneva: United Nations, 153–76.

Numerato, D., Salvatore, D., and Fattore, G. (2012), 'The Impact of Management on Medical Professionalism: A Review', *Sociology of Health & Illness*, 33(4): 626–44.

O'Connor, J. S. (2005), 'Policy Coordination, Social Indicators and the Social-policy Agenda in the European Union', *Journal of European Social Policy*, 15(4): 345–61.

Obinger, H. (2005), 'Austria. Strong Parties in a Weak Federal System', in H. Obinger, S. Leibfried and F.G. Castles (eds), *Federalism and the Welfare State: New World and European Experiences*, Cambridge: Cambridge University Press.

Obinger, H., Tálos, E. (2010), 'Janus-Faced Developments in a Prototypical Bismarckian Welfare State: Welfare Reforms in Austria since the 1970s', in B. Palier (ed.), *A Long Goodbye to Bismarck? The Politics of Welfare Reforms in Continental Europe*, Amsterdam: Amsterdam University Press.

OECD (2003), *Privatising State-owned Enterprises: An Overview of Policies and Practices in OECD Countries*, Paris: OECD.

OECD (2009), *Health at a Glance 2009*, Paris: OECD.

OECD (2010), *Health Care Systems. Efficiency and Policy Settings*, Paris: OECD.

OECD (2011), *Health at a Glance 2011*, Paris: OECD.

OECD (2012), *Health at Glance 2012*, Paris: OECD.

OECD (2013), *Health at Glance*, Paris: OECD.

Okunade, A.A. and Murthy, V.N.R. (2001), 'Technology as a "Major Driver" of Health Care Costs: A Cointegration Analysis of the Newhouse Conjecture', *Journal of Health Economics*, 21: 147–59.

Olafsdottir, S. and Beckfield, J. (2011), 'Health and the Social Rights of Citizenship: Integrating Welfare-State Theory and Medical Sociology', in B.A. Pescolido (ed.), *Handbook of the Sociology of Health, Illness and Healing: A Blueprint for the 21st Century*, New York: Springer.

Oliver, A. (2005), 'The English National Health Service: 1979–2005', *Health Economics*, 14(S1): S75–S99.

ONS (2009), *Population Trends Winter 2009*, Newport: Office for National Statistics.

Or, Z. (2008), 'New Regional Health Governance', *Health Policy Monitor*, 12 October 2008.

Or, Z. (2010), 'Activity Based Payment in Hospitals: Evaluation', *Health Policy Monitor*, 15 April 2010.

Or, Z., Cases, C., Lisac, M., Vrangbaek, K., Winblad, U. and Bevan, G. (2009), 'Are Health Problems Systemic? Politics of Access and Choice under Beveridge and Bismarck Systems', Working Papers DT27, IRDES Institute for Research and Information in Health Economics, revised Sep 2009.

Or, Z., Cases, C., Lisac, M., Vrangbæk, K., Winblad, U. and Bevan, G. (2010), 'Are Health Problems Systemic? Politics of Access and Choice under Beveridge and Bismarck Systems', *Health Economics, Policy, and Law*, July 5(3): 269–93.

Ortún, V. (ed.) (2009), *El buen gobierno sanitario*, Madrid: Springer.

Ortún, V. and López, G. (2002), 'Financiación capitativa; articulación entre niveles asistenciales y descentralización de las organizaciones sanitarias', Fundación BBVA, Working paper 3.

Österle, A. (2006), *The Austrian Health Care System 1970–2003. Gradual Changes or Paradigm Shift?*, Unpublished Manuscript.

Österle, A. (2012), 'Long-term Care Reform in Austria, Emergence and Development of a New Welfare State Pillar', in C. Ranci and E. Pavolini (eds), *Reform in Long-term Care Policies in European Countries*, New York: Springer.

Österle, A. and Bauer, G. (2012), 'Home Care in Austria: The Interplay of Family Orientation, Cash-for-care and Migrant Care', *Health and Social Care in the Community*, 20(3): 265–73.

Österle, A. and Heitzmann, K. (2009), 'Welfare State Development in Austria: Strong Traditions Meet New Challenges', in K. Schubert, S. Hegelich and U. Bazant (eds), *The Handbook of European Welfare Systems*, London: Routledge.

Palència, L., Espelt, A., Rodríguez-Sanz, M.B., Rocha, K., Isabel Pasarín, M. and Borrell, C. (2013), 'Trends in Social Class Inequalities in the Use of Health Care Services within the Spanish National Health System, 1993–2006', *European Journal of Health Economics*, 14(2): 211–19.

Palier, B. (2005), *Gouverner la Sécurité sociale : les réformes du système français de protection sociale depuis 1945*, 2d Edition, Paris: Presses universitaires de France, Le lien social.

Palier, B. (2011), *The Health Care Policy Quadrilemma*, Unpublished Manuscript.

Palier, B. (2012), *La réforme des systèmes de santé*, 6th Edition, Paris: PUF, Que sais-je ?.

Palier, B. (ed.) (2010), *A Long Goodbye to Bismarck? The Politics of Welfare Reforms in Continental Europe*, Amsterdam: Amsterdam University Press.

Palme, J. (1990), *Pension Rights in Welfare Capitalism*, Dissertation Series No. 14, Stockholm: Swedish Institute for Social Research.

Palme, J., Nelson, K., Sjöberg, O. and Minas, R. (2009), *European Social Models, Protection and Inclusion*, Research Report 2009/1, Stockholm: Institute for Futures Studies.

Panstwowa Inspekcja Pracy (National Labour Inspectorate) (2012), *Sprawozdanie Głównego Inspektora Pracy z działalności Państwowej Inspekcji Pracy w 2011 roku*. Warszawa: Panstwowa Inspekcja Pracy.

Parmsund, M., Aldering, M., Målqvist, I. and Åborg, C. (2009), *Arbetsförhållanden, levnadsvanor och hälsa inom vård och omsorg – En jämförelse mellan anställda inom landsting, kommun och privat sektor i Stockholms län*. Rapport (2009:24). Karolinska institutets folkhälsoakademi, Stockholm.

Pavolini, E. (ed.) (2011), *Il cambiamento possibile*. *La sanità in Sicilia fra Nord e Sud*, Roma: Donzelli.

Pavolini, E. and Vicarelli, G. (2009), 'Il ruolo degli attori privati nel sistema sanitario italiano', *Mecosan*, 71: 31–38.

Pavolini, E. and Vicarelli, G. (2012), 'Is Decentralization Good for your Health? Transformations in the Italian NHS', *Current Sociology*, 60(4): 472–88.

Peiró, S., Librero, J., Ridao, M., Bernal, E. and Grupo VPM en el SNS (2010), 'Variabilidad en la utilización de los servicios de urgencias hospitalarios del Sistema Nacional de Salud', *Gaceta Sanitaria*, 24(1): 6–12.

Peñaloza, M-C., Hardie, M., Wild, R. and Mills, K. (2010), *UK Centre for the Measurement of Government Activity- Public Service Output, Inputs and Productivity: Healthcare*, Newport: Office For National Statistics.

Peterson, M.A. (1997), 'The Limits of Social Learning: Translating Analysis into Action', *Journal of Health Politics, Policy and Law*, 22(4): 1077–114.

Pfeiffer, D. (2009), 'Politische Entwicklungen im deutschen Gesundheitswesen', in H. Rebscher and S. Kaufmann (eds), *Gesundheitssysteme im Wandel*, Heidelberg: Economica: 47–58.

Phelps, M.G., Kamarudeen, S., Mills, K. and Wild, R. (2010), *UK Centre for the Measurement of Government Activity: Total Public Service Output, Inputs and Productivity*, Newport: Office for National Statistics.

Piacenza, M. and Turati, G. (2010), *Does Fiscal Discipline towards Sub-national Governments Affect Citizens' Well-being? Evidence on Health*, Department of Economics and Public Finance 'G. Prato' Working Paper Series, n° 12.

Pierru, F. (2011), 'Budgétiser l'assurance maladie – heurs et malheurs d'un instrument de maîtrise des dépenses publiques: l'enveloppe globale (1976–2010)' in Bézès, P. and Siné, A. (eds), *Gouverner (par) les finances publiques*, Paris: Presses de Sciences Po.

Pierson, P. (1996), 'The New Politics of the Welfare State', *World Politics*, 48(2): 143–79.

Pierson, P. (2001), 'The New Politics of the Welfare State', Oxford: Oxford University Press.

Pollit, C. (1993), *Managerialism and the Public Services: Cuts or Cultural Change in the 1990s?*, Oxford: Blackwell Business.

Power, M. (1997), *The Audit Society: Rituals of Verification*, Oxford: Oxford University Press.

Power, M. (2000), 'The Audit Society – Second Thoughts', *International Journal of Auditing*, 4(1): 111–19.

Puig-Junoy, J. (2011), '¿Recortar o desinvertir?', *Economía y salud: Boletín Informativo*, AES, vol. 72.

Putnam, R., Leonardi, R. and Nanetti, R. (1990), *Making Democracy Work: Civic Traditions in Modern Italy*, Princeton: Princeton University Press.

Ranci, C. and Pavolini, E. (eds) (2012), *Reforms in Long Term Care Policies in Europe*, New York: Springer.

Rehnberg, C. et al. (2009), *Uppföljning av Vårdval Stockholm år 2008*. Rapport nr 2009:6, Stockholm: Karolinska Institutets folkhälsoakademi.

Rehnberg, C. et al. (2010), *Uppföljning av husläkarsystemet inom Vårdval Stockholm – redovisning av de två första årens erfarenheter*. Rapport nr 2010:12, Stockholm: Karolinska Institutets folkhälsoakademi.

Repullo, J. (2009), 'Las debilidades estructurales del sistema nacional de salud ante la crisis', *Referent-Revista de Management per al Sector Sanitari i Social*, 8: 4–11.

Repullo, J. and Freire, J. (2008), 'Gobernabilidad del SNS: mejorando el balance entre los beneficios y los costes de la descentralización', *Gaceta Sanitaria*, 22(1): 118–25.

Rieger, E. and Leibfried, S. (2003), *Limits to Globalization: Welfare States and the World Economy*, Cambridge: Polity.

Roberts, J. (1998), *Sensititivy of elasticity estimates for OECD health care spending: analysis of a dynamic heterogeneous field*. Paper presented for the Seventh European Workshop of Econometrics and Health Economics, STAKES, Helsinki, Finland, 9-12 September.

Rodríguez, M. and Puig-Junoy, J. (2012), '¿Por qué no hay que temer al copago?', *Gaceta Sanitaria*, 26(1): 78–9.

Rodríguez, M. and Urbanos, R. (eds) (2008), *Desigualdades sociales en salud. Factores determinantes y elementos para la acción*, Elsevier España.

Rodwin, M. A. (2011), *Conflicts of Interest and the Future of Medicine: The United States, France and Japan*, Oxford: Oxford University Press.

Rondinelli, D.A. (1983), *Decentralization in Developing Countries: A Review of Recent Experience*. Staff Working Paper 581, Washington: World Bank.

Rosenbrock, R. and Gerlinger, T. (2006), *Gesundheitspolitik. Eine systematische Einführung*, Bern: Hans Huber.

Rothgang, H., Cacace, M., Frisina, L. and Schmid, A. (2008), 'The Changing Public/Private-Mix in OECD Healthcare Systems', in M. Seeleib-Kaiser (ed.), *Welfare State Transformations in Comparative Perspective: Shifting Boundaries of 'Public' and 'Private' Social Policy?*, Houndmills, Basingstoke: Palgrave Macmillan: 132–46.

Rothgang, H., Cacace, M., Frisina, L., Grimmeisen, S., Schmid, A. and Wendt, C. (2010), *The State and Healthcare: Comparing OECD Countries*, Basingstoke: Palgrave Macmillan.

Rüb, F. W. (2004), 'Vom Wohlfahrtsstaat zum, manageriellen Staat'? Zum Wandel des Verhältnisses von Markt und Staat in der deutschen Sozialpolitik', in R. Czada and R. Zintl (eds), *Politik und Markt. PVS-Sonderheft*, Wiesbaden: VS: 256–99.

Sagan, A., Panteli, D., Borkowski, W., Dmowski, M., Domański, F., Czyżewski, M., Goryński, P., Karpacka, D., Kiersztyn, E., Kowalska, I., Księżak, M., Kuszewski, K., Leśniewska, A., Lipska, I., Maciąg, R., Madowicz, J., Mądra, A., Marek, M., Mokrzycka, A., Poznański, D., Sobczak, A., Sowada, C., Świderek, M., Terka, A., Trzeciak, P., Wiktorzak, K., Włodarczyk, C., Wojtyniak, B., Wrześniewska-Wal, I., Zelwiańska, D., Busse, R. (2011) 'Poland: Health System Review', *Health Systems in Transition*, 13(8): 1–193.

Saltman, R. B. (2008), 'Decentralization, Re-centralization and Future European Health Policy', *The European Journal of Public Health*, 18(2): 104–6.

Saltman, R. B., Bankhauskaide, V. and Vrangbaek, K. (eds) (2007), *Decentralisation in Health Care. Strategies and Outcomes*, Berkshire: Open University Press.

Saltman, R., and van Otter, C. (1995), *Implementing Planned Markets in Health Care*, Buckingham: Open University Press.

Saltman, R.B., Busse, R. and Mossialos, E. (2002), *Regulating Entrepreneurial Behaviour in European Health Care Systems*. European Observatory on Health Care Systems Series, Buckingham: Open University Press.

Sawicki, P. T. (2005), 'Qualität der Gesundheitsversorgung in Deutschland. Ein randomisierter simultaner Sechs-Länder-Vergleich aus Patientensicht', *Medizinische Klinik*, 100(11): 755–68.

Scharpf, F.W. (2002), 'The European Social Model: Coping with the Challenges of Diversity', *Journal of Common Market Studies*, 40(4): 645–70.

Scharpf, F.W. and Schmidt, V.A. (eds) (2000), *Welfare and Work in the Open Economy. Vol. II. Diverse Responses to Common Challenges*, Oxford: Oxford University Press.

Schieber, G.J. and Poullier, J.P. (1987), *Financing and Delivering Health Care: A Comparative Analysis of OECD Countries*, Paris: OECD.

Schmidt, C. and Möller, J. (2007), 'Katalysatoren des Wandels im deutschen Krankenhausmarkt', in J. Klauber, B.-P. Robra, and H. Schellschmidt (eds), *Der Krankenhausreport 2006. Schwerpunkt: Krankenhausmarkt im Umbruch*, Stuttgart: Schattauer: 3–19.

Schmitt, C. and Starke, P. (2011), 'Explaining Convergence of OECD Welfare States: A Conditional Approach', *Journal of European Social Policy*, 21(2): 120–34.

Schoen, C. and Osborn, R. (2011), *The Commonwealth Fund 2010 International Health Policy Survey in Eleven Countries*, www.commonwealthfund.org.

Scott, R.W. (2000), *Institutional Change and Healthcare Organizations: From Professional Dominance to Managed Care*, Chicago: Chicago University Press.

Shafrin, J. (2010), 'Operating on Commission: Analyzing how Physician Financial Incentives Affect Surgery Rates', *Health Economics*, 19(5): 562–80.

Siciliani, L., M. Borowitz and Moran, V. (eds) (2013), *Waiting Time Policies in the Health Sector: What Works?*, OECD Health Policy Studies, OECD Publishing.

Sindbjerg Martinsen, D. and Blomqvist, P. (2009), 'The European Union: Single Market Pressures', in J. Magnussen, K. Vrangbæk and R.B. Saltman (eds), *Nordic Health Care Systems: Recent Reforms and Current Policy Changes*, Berkshire: Open University Press: 294–316.

Sindbjerg Martinsen, D. and Vrangbaek K. (2008), 'The Europeanization of Health Care Governance: Implementing the Market Imperatives of Europe', *Public Administration*, 86(1): 169–84.

Sitek, M. (2008), 'Politics and Institutions in the Reforms of Health Care in the Czech Republic, Hungary and Poland', *Polish Sociological Review*, 1(161): 39–53.

Sitek, M. (2010), 'The New Institutionalist Approaches to Health Care Reform: Lessons from Reform Experiences in Central Europe', *Journal of Health Politics, Policy and Law*, 35(4): 569–93.

SKL (2005), Ekonomirapporten november 2005. Sveriges kommuner och landsting, Stockholm.

SKL (2010a), Ekonomirapporten 2010. Om kommunernas och landstingens ekonomi, Sveriges kommuner och landsting, Stockholm.

SKL (2010b), Statistik om hälso- och sjukvård samt regional utveckling. Verksamhet och ekonomi i landsting och regioner, Sveriges kommuner och landsting, Stockholm.

SKL (2011), Socalstyrelsen (2011), Öppna jämförelser av hälso- och sjukvårdens kvalitet och effektivitet. Jämförelser mellan landsting 2011, Sveriges kommuner och landsting, Stockholm.

Smith, J. (2004), *The Shipman Inquiry Fifth Report Safeguarding Patients: Lessons from the Past – Proposals for the Future Cm 6394-1*, London: The Stationery Office.

Smith, Peter (2012), 'What Is the Scope for Health System Efficiency Gains and how can they be Achieved?', *Eurohealth*, 18(3): 3–6.

Socialstyrelsen (2011), Uppföljning av den nationella vårdgarantin och 'kömiljarden', Årsrapport 2011.

Socialstyrelsen (2012), Folkhälsan i Sverige. Årsrapport 2012.

Sommersguter-Reichmann, M. (2000), 'The Impact of the Austrian Hospital Financing System on Hospital Productivity, Empirical Evidence on Efficiency and Technology Changes Using a Non-parametric Input-based Malmquist Approach', *Health Care Management Science*, 3(4): 309–21.

SOM-rapport (2011), Swedish trends 1986–2010, SOM.

SoS. (1999), *Välfärd och valfrihet? – Slutrapport från utvärderingen av 1995 års psykiatrireform*, Stockholm: The National Board for Health and Social Welfare.

Soskice, D. (1999), 'Divergent Production Regimes: Coordinated and Uncoordinated Market Economies in the 1980s and 1990s', in Kitschelt, H., Lange, P., Marks, G. and J. D. Stephens (eds), *Change and Continuity in Contemporary Capitalism*, Cambridge: Cambridge University Press.

Stabile, M., Thomson, S., Allin, S., Boyle, S., Busse, R., Chevreul, K., Marchildon, G. and Mossialos, E. (2013), 'Health Care Cost Containment Strategies Used in Four other High-income Countries Hold Lessons for the United States', *Health Affairs*, 32/4: 643–52.

Stark, D., and Bruszt, L. (1998), *Postsocialist Pathways: Transforming Politics and Property in East-Central Europe*, Cambridge: Cambridge University Press.

Statistik Austria (2011), *Jahrbuch der Gesundheitsstatistik*, Wien: Statistik Austria.

Statistisches Bundesamt Deutschland (2010), *Gesundheit: Grunddaten der Krankenhäuser*. Fachserie 12 Reihe 6.1.1. Wiesbaden: SBD.

Steffen, M. (2010), 'The French Health Care System: Liberal Universalism', *Journal of Health Politics, Policy and Law*, 35(3), June 2010.

Stepan, A. and Sommersguter-Reichmann, M. (2005), 'Applied Performance Measurement, A Case Study Using DEA and Other Frontier Production Function-Related Indexes', in M. Steven and S. Sonntag (eds), *Quantitative Unternehmensführung*, Heidelberg: Physica-Verlag.

Strange, S. (1997), 'Territory, State, Authority and Economy: A New Realist Ontology of Global Political Economy', in R.W. Cox (ed.), *The New Realism: Perspectives on Multilateralism and World Order*, Basingstoke: Macmillan Press.

Streeck, W. and Thelen, K. (eds) (2005), *Beyond Continuity: Institutional Change in Advanced Political Economies*, Oxford: Oxford University Press.

Swank, D. (2002), *Global Capital, Political Institutions, and Policy Change in Developed Welfare States*, Cambridge: Cambridge University Press.

Swank, D. and Martin, C.J. (2001), 'Employers and the Welfare State: The Political Economic Organization of Firms and Social Policy in Contemporary Capitalist Democracies', *Comparative Political Studies*, 34(8): 889–923.

Swedish Agency for Health Care Services Analysis (2012), Patientcentrering i svensk hälso- och sjukvård. En extern utvärdering och sex rekommendationer för förbättring. Myndigheten för vårdanalys, rapport 2012:5.

Swedish Medical Association (2004), Brist på vårdplatser – kris inom svensk sjukvård. Sveriges Läkarförbund 2004.

Swedish Association of Local Authorities and Regions, National Board of Health and Welfare (2008), Quality and Efficiency in Swedish Health Care. Regional Comparisons 2008.

Swedish Association of Local Authorities and Regions (2010) (SALAR), Ekonomirapporten 2010. Om kommunernas och landstingens ekonomi.

Swedish Association of Local Authorities and Regions (SALAR), National Board of Health and Welfare (2008), Quality and Efficiency in Swedish Health Care. Regional Comparisons 2008.

Swedish Association of Local Authorities and Regions (SALAR), National Board of Health and Welfare (2011), Quality and Efficiency in Swedish Health Care. Regional Comparisons 2010.

Tabuteau, D. (2006), *Les contes de Ségur*, Paris: Ophrys santé.

Tabuteau, D. (2010), 'Du plan Seguin à la loi HPST: les évolutions de la politique de santé', *Les Tribunes de la santé*, 2010/5, HS n°1: 37–51.

Tálos, E. (1981), *Staatliche Sozialpolitik in Österreich. Rekonstruktion und Analyse*, Wien: Verlag für Gesellschaftskritik.

Tang, K., Petrie, D. e Rao, P. (2009), 'Measuring Health Inequality with Realization of Potential Life Years', *Health Economics*, 18: 55–75.

Taylor, G. and Hawley, H. (2010), *Key Debates in Healthcare*, Berkshire: Open University Press.

Taylor-Gooby, P. (1996), 'The Response of Government: Fragile Convergence?', in George, V. and Taylor-Gooby, P. (eds), *European Welfare Policy: Squaring the Welfare Circle*, London: Macmillan.

Taylor-Gooby, P. (ed.) (2004), *New Risks, New Welfare. The Transformation of the European Welfare State*, Oxford: Oxford University Press.

Tchouaket, E., Lamarche, P., Goulet, L. and Contandriopoulos, A.-P. (2012), 'Health Care System Performance of 27 OECD Countries', *International Journal of Health Planning and Management*, 27(2): 104–29.

Tediosi, F., Gabriele, S. and Longo, F. (2009) 'Governing Decentralization in Healthcare under Tough Budget Constraint', *Health Policy*, 90(2): 303–12.

The Mid Staffordshire NHS Foundation Trust Inquiry (2010), *Independent Inquiry into care provided by Mid Staffordshire NHS Foundation Trust January 2005 – March 2009 Volume I (The Francis report)*, London: The Stationery Office.

Theurl, E. and Winner, H. (2007), 'The Impact of Hospital Financing on the Length of Stay: Evidence from Austria', *Health Policy*, 82(3): 375–89.

Thorlby, R. and Maybin, J. (eds) (2010), *A High-performing NHS? A Review of Progress 1997–2010*, London: King's Fund.

Tiemann, O., Schreyögg, J., Wörz, M. and Busse, R. (2010), 'Leistungsmanagement in Krankenhäusern', in R. Busse, J. Schreyögg and O., Tiemann (eds), *Management im Gesundheitswesen*, Berlin: Springer: 47–76.

Trampusch, C. (2005), 'From Interest Groups to Parties: The Change in the Career Patterns of the Legislative Elite in German Social Policy', *German Politics*, 14(1): 14–32.

Trukeschitz, B., Schneider, U. and Czypionka, T. (2013), 'Federalism in Health and Social Care in Austria', in J. Costa-Font, J. and S.L. Greer (eds), *Federalism and Decentralisation in European Health and Social Care*, Basingstoke: Palgrave Macmillan.

TSO (2012), *Health and Social Care Act 2012 c. 7*, London: The Stationery Office.

Tymowska, K. (2001), 'Health Care under Transformation in Poland', *Health Policy*, 56: 85–98.

Umpierre, M. and Utrilla, A. (2012), 'La adecuación de la financiación sanitaria a la evolución de las necesidades y al gasto por Comunidades Autónomas. Un análisis de las repercusiones de los modelos de financiación en el periodo 1999–2009', XIX Encuentro de Economía Pública, Universidad de Santiago de Compostela.

Unison (2003), *Seven Reasons why UNISON Is Opposed to Foundation Trusts*, London: Unison.

Unison (2007), *In the Interests of Patients? The Impact of the Creation of a Commercial Market in the Provision of NHS Care*, London: Unison.

Urbanos, R. (2001), 'Explaining Inequality in the Use of Public Health Care Services: Evidence from Spain', *Health Care Management Science*, 4: 143–57.

van Doorslaer, E. and Masseria, C. (2004), *Income-Related Inequality in the Use of Medical Care in 21 OECD countries*, OECD Health Working Papers No. 14, Paris: OECD.

Van Doorslaer, E., Masseria, C., and Koolman, X. for the OECD Health Equity Research Group (2006), 'Inequalities in Access to Medical Care by Income in Developed Countries', *Canadian Medical Association Journal*, 174(2): 177–83.

Ventura, J. (1992), 'La reforma del Servicio Nacional de salud. El informe Abril', *Información Comercial española*. *Revista de Economía*: 708–9.

Ventura, J. (2004), *Organización y gestión de la atención sanitaria*, Informe anual del Sistema Nacional de Salud, Chapter V, Madrid: Sistema Nacional de Salud.

Ventura, J., González, E. and Cárcaba, A. (2004), 'Efficiency and Program Contract Bargaining in Spanish Public Hospitals', *Annals of Public and Cooperative Economics*, 75(4): 549–73.

Vicarelli, G. (1997), *Alle radici della politica sanitaria in Italia: società e salute da Crispi al fascismo*, Bologna: Il Mulino.

Vicarelli, G. (2011), *Gli eredi di Esculapio. Medici e politiche sanitarie dall'Unità d'Italia a oggi*, Roma: Carocci.

Vicarelli, G. (ed.) (2005), *Il malessere del Welfare*, Napoli: Liguori.

Vicarelli, M.G., Tousjin, W. and Speranza, L. (eds) (2009), *I medici in Italia: motivazioni, autonomia, appartenenza*, Bologna: Il Mulino.

Vincent, G. (2005), 'Les réformes hospitalières', *Revue française d'administration publique*, 113, 2005/1: 49–63.

Vrangbaek, K. (2007), 'Towards a Typology for Decentralisation in Health Care', in R.B. Saltman, et al. (eds): 45–62.

Wanless, D., Appleby, J., Harrison, A. and Patel, D. (2007), *Our Future Health Secured? A Review of NHS Funding and Performance*, London: King's Fund.

Watson, P. (2009), 'Hospital Privatisation in Poland', *Eurohealth*, 15(4): 28–31.

Watson, P. (2011), 'Fighting for Life: Health Care and Democracy in Capitalist Poland', *Critical Social Policy*, 31: 53–74.

Wendt, C., Grimmeisen, S. and Rothgang, H. (2005), 'Convergence or Divergence of OECD Health Care Systems?', in B. Cantillon and I. Marx (eds), *International Cooperation in Social Security. How to Cope with Globalization?*, Antwerpen-Oxford: Intersentia.

Wendt, C. (2009), 'Mapping European Healthcare Systems: A Comparative Analysis of Financing, Service Provision and Access to Healthcare', *Journal of European Social Policy*, 19(5): 432–445.

Wendt, C., Agartan, T. and Kaminska, M.E. (2013), 'Social Health Insurance without Corporate Actors. Patterns of Self-regulation in Germany, Poland and Turkey', *Social Science and Medicine*, 86: 88–95.

Wendt, C., Frisina, L. and Rothgang, H. (2009), 'Health Care System Types: A Conceptual Framework for Comparison', *Social Policy & Administration*, 43(1): 70–90.

Wheller, L., Baker, A., Griffiths, C. and Rooney, C. (2007), 'Trends in Avoidable Mortality in England and Wales, 1993–2005', *Health Statistics Quarterly*. 34: Summer.

WHO (2000), *The World Health Report: Year 2000. Health Systems: Improving Their Performance*, Geneva: WHO.

WHO (2001), *The World Health Report 2000. Health Systems: Improving Performance*, Geneva: WHO.

WHO (2012), WHO online database http://data.euro.who.int/hfadb/

WHO Europe (2012), *European Health for All Database*, WHO.

Winblad, U. (2008), 'Do Physicians Care about Patient Choice?', *Social Science & Medicine*, 67: 1502–11.

Winblad, U., Isaksson, D. and Bergman, P. (2012), *Effekter av valfrihet inom hälso- och sjukvård – en kartläggning av kunskapsläget*, Rapport 2012:2, Myndigheten för vårdanalys.

Winblad, U., Vrangbæk, K. and Östergren, K. (2010), 'Do the Waiting-time Guarantees in the Scandinavian Countries Empower Patients?', *International Journal of Public Sector Management*, 23(4): 353–63.

Wlodarczyk, C. (1986), 'In Search of Economic Rationality: The Experience of the Polish National Health Service', *Health Policy*, 7(2): 149–62.

Wlodarczyk, C. and Karkowska, D. (2005), 'Decentralizing the Healthcare Sector in Poland in the 1990s' in G. Shakarishvili (ed.) *Decentralization in Healthcare, Analyses and Experiences in Central and Eastern Europe in the 1990s*, Budapest: Local Government and Public Service Reform Initiative.

Wollmann, H. (1999), 'Politik- und Verwaltungsmodernisierung in den Kommunen: zwischen Managementlehre und Demokratiegebot', *Die Verwaltung*, 32(3): 345–75.

Index

Printed and bound in Great Britain by
CPI Group (UK) Ltd, Croydon, CR0 4YY